LUKE

ABINGDON NEW TESTAMENT COMMENTARIES

LUKE

ROBERT C. TANNEHILL

Abingdon Press
Nashville

ABINGDON NEW TESTAMENT COMMENTARIES:
LUKE

This book is printed on recycled, acid-free, elemental-chlorine–free paper.

Library of Congress Cataloging-in-Publication Data

Tannehill, Robert C.
    Luke / Robert C. Tannehill.
       p. cm. — (Abingdon New Testament commentaries)
    Includes bibliographical references and index.
    ISBN 0-687-06132-6 (pbk. : alk. paper)
    1. Bible. N.T. Luke—Commentaries.
  I. Title. II. Series.
  BS2595.3.T36 1996
  226.4'07–dc20
                        96-30769
                        CIP

96 97 98 99 00 01 02 03 04 05— 10 9 8 7 6 5 4 3 2 1

MANUFACTURED IN THE UNITED STATES OF AMERICA

To Alice,
my companion on the long journey
and my reminder that life is more than books,
since August 13, 1955

CONTENTS

FOREWORD

The *Abingdon New Testament Commentaries* series provides compact, critical commentaries on the writings of the New Testament. These commentaries are written with special attention to the needs and interests of theological students, but they will also be useful for students in upper-level college or university settings, as well as for pastors and other church leaders. In addition to providing basic information about the New Testament texts and insights into their meanings, these commentaries are intended to exemplify the tasks and procedures of careful, critical biblical exegesis.

The authors who have contributed to this series come from a wide range of ecclesiastical affiliations and confessional stances. All are seasoned, respected scholars and experienced classroom teachers. They take full account of the most important current scholarship and secondary literature, but do not attempt to summarize that literature or to engage in technical academic debate. Their fundamental concern is to analyze the literary, socio-historical, theological, and ethical dimensions of the biblical texts themselves. Although all of the commentaries in this series have been written on the basis of the Greek texts, the authors do not presuppose any knowledge of the biblical languages on the part of the reader. When some awareness of a grammatical, syntactical, or philological issue is necessary for an adequate understanding of a particular text, they explain the matter clearly and concisely.

The introduction of each volume ordinarily includes subdivisions dealing with the *key issues* addressed and/or raised by the New Testament writing under consideration; its *literary genre, structure, and character;* its *occasion and situational context,* including its wider social, historical, and religious contexts; and its *theological and ethical significance* within these several contexts.

In each volume, the *commentary* is organized according to literary units rather than verse by verse. Generally, each of these units is the subject of three types of analysis. First, the *literary analysis* attends to the unit's genre, most important stylistic features, and overall structure. Second, the *exegetical analysis* considers the aim and leading ideas of the unit, deals with any especially important textual variants, and discusses the meanings of important words, phrases, and images. It also takes note of the particular historical and social situations of the writer and original readers, and of the wider cultural and religious contexts of the book as a whole. Finally, the *theological and ethical analysis* discusses the theological and ethical matters with which the unit deals or to which it points, focusing on the theological and ethical significance of the text within its original setting.

Each volume also includes a *select bibliography,* thereby providing guidance to other major commentaries and important scholarly works, and a brief *subject index.* The New Revised Standard Version of the Bible is the principal translation of reference for the series, but the authors draw on all of the major modern English versions, and when necessary provide their own original translations of difficult terms or phrases.

The fundamental aim of this series will have been attained if readers are assisted, not only to understand more about the origins, character, and meaning of the New Testament writings, but also to enter into their own informed and critical engagement with the texts themselves.

Victor Paul Furnish
General Editor

PREFACE

Anyone familiar with New Testament scholarship knows that there are already many commentaries on the Gospel of Luke. Why write another one? Although it may be surprising to some, the methods and interests of biblical scholarship change, opening new insights into the ancient text. This commentary reflects some of those new methods and interests.

In my recent writing I have studied Luke and Acts as narrative literature (see *The Narrative Unity of Luke–Acts: A Literary Interpretation*, 2 vols. [Philadelphia and Minneapolis: Fortress, 1986, 1990]). Although the second volume of this work—the volume on Acts—is a specialized sort of commentary, the first volume (on Luke) is organized differently. The central chapters study how Jesus interacts with important groups within the Gospel story (for instance, the religious leaders, the oppressed and excluded people, the disciples). Each chapter passes through the Lukan story without attempting a well-rounded commentary on the passages being discussed, and there are parts of Luke that receive little attention. Thus there was still reason, I felt, for me to write a commentary on Luke.

This commentary reflects my previous work on Luke as narrative literature but also seeks to apply methods and insights recently developed by others. Studies of the ancient Mediterranean social world suggest previously unrecognized significance to words and actions in the Lukan story. Special studies on the role of women and the experience of the poor raise important issues for discussion. I have tried to apply these studies in my commentary on Luke, and therefore I am occasionally able to propose unusual readings of the familiar texts. Of course, I must also try to share, briefly, some of the collective wisdom of Gospel scholarship that may be unfamiliar to many readers.

This commentary was written during a sabbatical leave granted to me before I assumed the duties of academic dean at the Methodist Theological School in Ohio. I am grateful to the faculty, president, and trustees for granting me the sabbatical leave. Special thanks go to Dr. Ed Trimmer for assuming the role of acting dean so that I could have time to write. I also wish to thank the Association of Theological Schools in the United States and Canada for a Theological Scholarship and Research Award supporting this period of writing. Likewise, I want to thank the Institute for Ecumenical and Cultural Research in Collegeville, Minnesota, where the first part of the book was written. The Institute provides excellent facilities and gracious hospitality for visiting scholars.

Robert C. Tannehill

LIST OF ABBREVIATIONS

AB	Anchor Bible
ABD	D. N. Freedman (ed.), *Anchor Bible Dictionary*
AnBib	Analecta biblica
B. Bat.	*Baba Batra*
BETL	Bibliotheca ephemeridum theologicarum lovaniensium
Bib	*Biblica*
BTB	*Biblical Theology Bulletin*
CBQ	*Catholic Biblical Quarterly*
CurTM	*Currents in Theology and Mission*
ETL	*Ephemerides theologicae lovanienses*
FRLANT	Forschungen zur Religion und Literatur des Alten und Neuen Testaments
Git.	*Gittin*
HTKNT	Herders theologischer Kommentar zum Neuen Testament
ICC	International Critical Commentary
Int	*Interpretation*
JBL	*Journal of Biblical Literature*
Jdt	Judith
Josephus *Ant.*	Josephus, *The Antiquities of the Jews*
Josephus *J. W.*	Josephus, *The Jewish War*
JSNT	*Journal for the Study of the New Testament*
JSNTSup	Journal for the Study of the New Testament —Supplement Series
Jub.	*Jubilees*

Kil.	*Kil'ayim*
KJV	King James Version
LCL	Loeb Classical Library
LXX	Septuagint
m.	*Mishnah*
NIGTC	The New International Greek Testament Commentary
NovT	*Novum Testamentum*
NovTSup	Novum Testamentum, Supplements
NRSV	New Revised Standard Version
NTS	*New Testament Studies*
OBT	Overtures to Biblical Theology
OTP	J. H. Charlesworth (ed.), *The Old Testament Pseudepigrapha*
Pesah.	*Pesahim*
Pss. Sol.	*Psalms of Solomon*
RB	*Revue biblique*
RSV	Revised Standard Version
Sanh.	*Sanhedrin*
SBLDS	SBL Dissertation Series
SBLSP	SBL Seminar Papers
Shab.	*Shabbat*
Sir	The Wisdom of Jesus the Son of Sirach
SNTSMS	Society for New Testament Studies Monograph Series
ST	*Studia theologica*
TDNT	G. Kittel and G. Friedrich (eds.), *Theological Dictionary of the New Testament*
T. Levi	*Tesatament of Levi*
Tob	Tobit
WBC	Word Biblical Commentary
Wis	The Wisdom of Solomon
WW	*Word and World*

INTRODUCTION

APPROACHING THE GOSPEL

This commentary will focus on the significance of the Gospel of Luke in its final form for its original audience. Although modern readers may be eager to discover the Gospel's significance for themselves, there are features of Luke that will only take on significance—or deeper significance—if matched with an appropriate historical and cultural context in the first century. My hypothesis (which you can test in reading this commentary) is that a detour through the experience of a first-century audience will enrich our own hearing and reading.

Since I am focusing on Luke in its final form, I will give little attention to hypothetical earlier forms of the Jesus tradition that may have been adapted for use in Luke. I am not engaging in the quest for the historical Jesus or even seeking to trace the Gospel traditions back to earlier forms. When I refer to Jesus in this commentary, I almost always mean Jesus as portrayed in Luke. Asking to what extent Luke's Jesus reflects the historical Jesus raises a set of problems that are not addressed here. The reader should not assume that statements about Luke's Jesus in this commentary also apply to the historical Jesus. The portrait of Jesus that emerges here may also differ significantly from the composite picture of Jesus, based on the four Gospels, the rest of the New Testament, and later Christology, with which churches have operated through many centuries. The intent here is to let Luke's portrait of Jesus emerge as clearly as possible by paying careful attention to Luke's story of Jesus, with its unique features.

Recent study of Luke has been heavily influenced by redaction criticism, a method based on careful comparison of Luke with its source material. (According to most scholars, these sources include Mark and the hypothetical document Q, to which we have access by isolating the material shared by Matthew and Luke but not found in Mark.) This careful comparison highlights editorial changes made by the author of Luke, which are taken as clues to the author's special concerns and purposes. Although I have learned from redaction criticism, and will note some of the differences between Luke and the other canonical Gospels, this commentary is not primarily an application of redaction criticism.

Redaction criticism can have a narrowing effect because of its focus on editorial changes. However, any material incorporated into Luke becomes Lukan, irrespective of its origin and the degree of editorial change. That is, it becomes part of the total communication experience that we call the Gospel of Luke. The contribution of each section of Luke to the whole should be considered, regardless of whether we can trace editorial changes or not. This is a more wholistic approach, but it need not reduce the Gospel to a simple unity. Rather, this approach should make us aware that none of the Gospels presents a simple message, nor can each be summarized in a few theological themes. The Gospels are complex messages that contain variety and tension—perhaps even contradiction—within them. This rich complexity appears when we listen for the possible message(s) of each part and also consider how the part relates to other parts and the whole. Although this commentary cannot complete this task, it intends to make a contribution.

IDENTIFYING THE AUTHOR

The document that we will study has been known as the Gospel According to Luke since at least the end of the second century AD. This title is found at the end of the oldest surviving copy of Luke, Papyrus Bodmer XIV ($\mathfrak{P}^{75}$), dating from AD 175-225 (cf. Fitzmyer 1981, 35-36). The question is hotly debated whether the attribution of this Gospel to Luke is accurate information or a secondary development resulting from the early church's desire to attribute the Gospels either to apostles or followers of apostles. This question cannot be answered with certainty. However, the following factors are relevant to the issue.

In Phlm 24 Paul refers to a certain Luke who is one of his "fellow workers," and Col 4:14 refers to "Luke, the beloved physician" (cf. also 2 Tim 4:11). In documents from the end of the second century AD we find reference to Luke as the author of one of the Gospels, and this Luke is identified as the physician who worked with Paul. These documents are the Muratorian Canon, Irenaeus' writing *Adversus haereses* 3.1, 1 and 3.14, 1, and the ancient Gospel prologues commonly called the Anti-Marcionite Prologues. (These texts may be found in the original languages in Aland 1964, 533-38; see also Fitzmyer 1981, 37-39). Nevertheless, doubts can be raised about this testimony. Did the church of the second century too quickly assume that the Luke who wrote this Gospel must appear in the records of the earliest church and thus falsely identify him with Luke, Paul's fellow worker? Did the second-century church too hastily infer from the "we" passages of Acts that the author was a companion of Paul and then settle on the Luke who was known to Paul as the most likely candidate?

It is widely recognized that Luke and Acts were written by the same author (cf. Acts 1:1-2). If there is evidence in either Luke or Acts that the author was a companion of Paul, the traditional identification of the author becomes probable. Some find this evidence in the "we" passages of Acts, but these passages raise vexing questions. In Acts 16:10, in the midst of a narrative in the third person, the narrator suddenly writes, "*We* immediately tried to cross over to Macedonia" (emphasis added). Use of the first-person plural in narration continues through 16:17, then disappears. Similar "we" passages appear in 20:5-15; 21:1-18; and 27:1-28:16. The introduction of "we" is abrupt, and the narrator who uses it is never identified. This narrator is, however, a companion of Paul in some of his travels. Since there is no indication that a new narrator has taken over, the initial impression is that the narrator of the whole of Acts (and Luke) is now telling of incidents in which he was a participant.

There are, however, problems and puzzles that have led a large group of scholars to reject this conclusion. They point to conflicts between information about Paul from his authentic letters and the portrait of Paul in Acts. For instance, the number of Paul's Jerusalem journeys in Acts, up through the Jerusalem consultation in Acts 15, does not agree with Paul's account in Gal 1:11–2:10. Furthermore, the Paul of Acts seems inclined to accommodate Jewish sensibilities in a way that the Paul of the letters did not, and Paul's sermon in Acts 13:16-41 sounds more like Peter in Acts than Paul in the letters. Both speakers are probably expressing the views of the author of Acts. One would think that someone who worked with Paul and supported his mission would be better informed about him and wish to present a more accurate portrait.

I would add that some of the content of the "we" passages is puzzling, for it contains some detailed records of voyages day by day and port by port. If, as is likely, Acts is reporting voyages that took place more than twenty years earlier, it is hard to believe that the author would recall the stages of the journeys so exactly, since he is not reporting remarkable events. It is also difficult to believe that these insignificant travel details were preserved in writing for that length of time.

But can the "we" passages be explained as fiction? The travel details do not refute this possibility. It is probable that the author has exercised considerable license in dramatizing events with detail elsewhere, and the travel details lend a certain weightiness to the stories of Paul's last trip to Jerusalem and his voyage to Rome, journeys that are important in the author's portrait of Paul. The "we" narration can also have a useful effect, encouraging the Lukan audience to identify with the participant observer who is narrating and imaginatively become a companion of Paul (cf. Tannehill 1990, 246-47). Nevertheless, the theory that the "we" is a fictional technique leaves some unanswered questions. It is puzzling that the "we" appears only in the four listed passages. Why is it used there and not elsewhere? If there are literary advantages, why was the technique not used more broadly? The supposition that "we" narration is a way of gaining historical credibility, through the presence of an eyewitness, for accounts that are actually fictional does not explain the curious choice of passages. The "we" passages are not of greater importance than many other sections of the

Pauline portion of Acts. There is also a remarkable lack of interest in scoring points for historical credibility. The participant narrator is not properly introduced to the reader and is never named. The other companions who make up the "we" are never named as guarantors. Thus the theory of a fictional "we" seems to lack an explanation of why this technique is used in the particular way that it is. (Robbins 1978 attempted an explanation, but his argument has not gained acceptance; cf. Praeder 1987, 210-14.)

The traditional view that the Gospel was written by Luke, a coworker of Paul, is able to offer a plausible explanation of the presence of "we" narration in some passages but not in others: Luke and Paul were together only part of the time. The differences between the Paul of the letters and the Paul of Acts remain a major problem for this view, but critics may have assumed too quickly that the portrait of Paul in Acts could not have been written by someone who sometimes traveled and worked with Paul in his earlier days. Decades have passed, and the purposes of Luke–Acts are not the same as the purposes of Paul's letters. The author of Acts may not have been well-informed about certain parts of Paul's career. In any case, he was writing a dramatic narrative that allowed some embellishment, and he was an independent thinker who gave his own accent to the church's heritage, drawing from not only Paul but also from other church tradition, including the Jesus tradition. The difference between preaching in Acts and the themes of Paul's letters is not necessarily due to ignorance of Paul (see the hints of Pauline themes in Acts 13:38-39 and 15:11; cf. Tannehill 1990, 185-86). Perhaps Luke chose to draw from themes of Paul—or the early church of which Paul was a part—that served his purposes and neglected other themes that we regard as characteristic of Paul. This is not an impossible development.

Thus it is possible that Luke and Acts were written by the Luke who spent a portion of his life working with Paul. It is also possible that the "we" passages are based on a source that the author (not Luke) utilized at certain points, although it is somewhat strange that he neither adapts the "we" to the literary context nor names his source. It is also still possible that the "we" passages provide no trustworthy information about the author of Luke–Acts. One's decision about this matter will probably tip the scales in deciding whether to accept the traditional designation of the author as Luke, companion of Paul.

UNDERSTANDING THE AUDIENCE AND THE SETTING

Fortunately, the commentary that follows does not depend on a solution to the difficult problem of authorship just discussed. It would be helpful, however, if we had some understanding of the audience to which Luke was addressed. I speak of "audience" because I assume that most first-century people would encounter Luke through a public reading in a Christian community. There would not be multiple copies for individual use, and many people would be unable to read.

A Gospel, unlike a Pauline letter, is not a type of writing that deals clearly and effectively with the immediate and specific problems of a group. The purpose and effect of a Gospel are likely to be broader: molding the character of a community for the long haul. It is doubtful that we can use the Gospel of Luke, with its rich assortment of stories and sayings, to construct a specific picture of the Christian community to which it was addressed. We can, however, say a few things about the general situation and makeup of Luke's audience. The relevance of these remarks will become apparent as I later discuss Lukan passages.

I believe that the primary audience for which Luke was designed was a group of late first-century churches of diverse social composition. By diverse social composition I mean that these churches included people of different ethnic and religious backgrounds, social status, and wealth. There were Jews and Gentiles, women and men, poor and relatively wealthy people, common people and a few members, perhaps, of the elite or of the retainer class who had important positions with the elite. If we keep this diversity in mind and ask how these different people would react to passages in Luke, it will make a difference in our understanding of this Gospel's significance.

Questions might be raised about two of these groups. First, is there evidence that some who were relatively wealthy and belonged to a higher social class participated in these churches? Acts, even if we allow for some exaggeration, provides evidence of such persons. In Acts there are general references to the conversion of "leading" people or people of "high standing," especially women (17:4, 12), and specific converts with varying degrees of status and wealth include Cornelius the centurion, Sergius Paulus the proconsul of Cyprus, Dionysius the Areopagite, and Crispus the synagogue ruler. Lydia, too, may have had some wealth. These persons represent others of relatively high status in the Lukan communities. Theophilus, to whom the author writes in the preface (Luke 1:1-4), may have been one of these believers of high standing, for he is addressed as "most excellent." Much of the teaching about poverty and wealth in Luke makes most sense when directed to people who have some wealth. The conclusion of Halvor Moxnes is cautious but supports my basic point, "We can envisage Luke's community as a group of nonelite persons who are culturally and ethnically mixed but who also include among them some who come from the elite periphery" (Moxnes 1994, 387). Although people of a higher class might be few in numbers in the Lukan churches, their status and wealth would give them influence. Indeed, local groups probably depended on their patronage.

Second, since Luke and Acts have commonly been regarded as documents of the Gentile church, the presence of Jews in these churches may be doubted by some. However, the kind of knowledge that Luke–Acts presupposes in its audience and the kind of people who dominate the narrative in Acts provide evidence that Jews and God-fearers (Gentiles who participated in the synagogue and learned there about Jewish matters) were influential in the Lukan churches. We cannot, of course, assess their numbers. We can assess their influence, however, for Luke–Acts honors such people and is written in a way to be persuasive to them. Full appreciation of Luke–Acts requires considerable knowledge of Jewish Scripture. Luke–Acts goes beyond the explicit citing of scripture as proof-texts to a rich use of scripture by allusion (as in the infancy narrative). Those who do not know scripture well will not know what they are missing, for there is no citation to alert them. Furthermore, Acts insists that Paul remained a faithful Jew. This would be most significant to those for whom the Jewish people and way of life remained important. Those individuals presented in Acts as leaders of the early church, even at a local level, are almost all Jews (or God-fearers, if we include Cornelius, Lydia, and Titius Justus as probable patrons of house churches). One would think that if the leaders of the Lukan churches were mainly of a different background, the author of Luke–Acts would have provided more appropriate models of these future leaders.

The ending of Acts, of course, announces that, in light of Jewish resistance, the Christian message is now being sent to the Gentiles (28:28). A change is signaled here, but this change is not as big as some have supposed. Basically this announcement recognizes the fact that Christian missionaries can no longer address the Jewish community, assembled as a synagogue, as Paul did. This does not prevent contact with individual Jews who may become believers (cf. Tannehill 1990, 346-57), and it does not mean that believing Jews quickly disappeared or lost influence in the early church. Their influence is strong on the author of Luke–Acts, who, in turn, assumes that their concerns will be important to the audience. (Further argument for the importance of Jews and God-fearers in the Lukan churches may be found in Esler 1987, 30-45.)

The time of the completion and first circulation of Luke was probably a decade or two after AD 70, the date of the destruction of Jerusalem and the temple by Roman forces. Most interpreters agree that Luke was written after this event, but since a few do not, I will cite some of the evidence. In Luke 1:1 the author acknowledges that previous accounts of Jesus have already appeared. Most scholars agree that the author of Luke made use of at least two earlier documents, Mark and Q. Mark provides the narrative framework for large sections of Luke, while Q provides the large amount of teaching material that Luke shares with Matthew. Since Mark itself seems to reflect the situation of the Roman-Jewish war, Luke must have been written later. When we compare the Marcan description of the great tribulation with Lukan accounts, we see that the latter refer much more clearly to a military siege of

Jerusalem (cf. Mark 13:14-20; Luke 19:43-44; 21:20-24). The shift from Mark to Luke makes the correspondence to the actual events in AD 70 much more apparent. Luke does more than anticipate what would happen in any siege of a city, for it is not true that any siege would include the described events (cf. Esler 1987, 27-28).

Furthermore, Luke gives more emphasis than the other Gospels to the destruction of Jerusalem. A series of passages refers to this, and these passages are distributed among the journey to Jerusalem (13:32-35), the entry to the city (19:41-44), the prophecies in the temple (21:5-6, 20-24), and the Crucifixion (23:27-31). Thus there is evidence of a deliberate distribution of this material for maximum effect, showing planning by the author. (Matthew's parallel to Luke 13:34-35 is found in a Jerusalem setting.) Indeed, already in Luke's infancy narrative there is preparation for the scene of Jesus weeping over Jerusalem (see the commentary on 1:68-79). These signs of emphasis and plot construction are best explained as being due to the author's awareness that Jerusalem had been destroyed, an event of great significance. And these passages would have had their greatest impact on an audience that was also aware of Jerusalem's fate.

Even though most interpreters agree that Luke was written after AD 70, they have not given sufficient thought to the effect of Luke on a first-century audience aware of the Roman destruction of Jerusalem and the temple (but see Tiede 1980, 1-11, 65-96). This commentary will give greater attention to this matter.

READING THE NARRATIVE

A commentary is expected to give attention to each section of a document. By discussing the problems within a text and the setting of the text, a commentary should help its readers to understand the meaning of a text more clearly and the significance of the text more fully. Most modern readers of Luke will find passages that are puzzling. Insofar as possible, this commentary will try to bring clarification. It will also disclose and discuss some of the puzzles that are covered up by an English translation, for translators do their own interpretation, sometimes hiding the fact that a different understanding of the text is possible. To be sure, in a commentary of this scope, I must treat these issues selectively.

The attention to details typical of commentaries carries the danger of leaving readers only with thousands of details. Readers may never gain understanding and appreciation of the writing as a whole. They may even miss the ways in which parts of a scene fit together to make it effective. It is important to ask how the details contribute to larger functioning units. At a first level, we can think of the individual scene within the Gospel, a scene that may open with indications of time, place, and a particular set of participants and then close when these circumstances change. Generally this commentary will proceed by discussing Luke scene by scene, although it will be useful to break some of the large scenes into subunits. Illumination may come when we understand how the parts of a scene contribute to it as a functioning whole.

The individual scenes have their own integrity, yet they also contribute to the larger narrative of Luke as a whole (which is part of a still larger work that includes Acts). That individual scenes have their own integrity means that they are not completely subservient to themes and concerns that are prominent in the larger narrative. There may even be tensions among scenes in Luke. We should not ignore the individuality of the scenes, for this adds to the richness of the total work. Nevertheless, it can also be illuminating to consider Luke as a unitary narrative and ask how each scene functions within this narrative. We can ask about an overall plot in Luke, and about dominant themes and the prevailing characterization of participants. I will suggest at various points how a particular scene contributes to Luke as a developing narrative. In doing so, I will often be drawing on my previous work (see Tannehill 1986, 1990).

In this commentary I will broaden my previous literary interpretation of Luke through consideration of the social context of the Lukan stories and the Lukan audience, drawing on recent work that applies studies of the Mediterranean social world to Luke (see especially Neyrey 1991). These studies work with broad models of social behavior, which may tend to obscure the surprising diversity of individual behavior in history. Nevertheless, these studies are useful to current biblical scholarship, partly because they challenge the common assumption that biblical people thought and acted just as we do. Studies of the social world of first-century Mediterranean people help us to imagine what the impact of the Lukan narrative would be within the social context, thereby helping us to discover hidden significance.

Readers may be better able to understand the broad interests of this commentary if we place Luke within a communication model that seeks to take account of the whole communication event, involving not only the author who wishes to communicate and the written or spoken signs that are the means of communication, but also including the audience who receives the communication and must interpret it in light of a large amount of presupposed information about language and society (cf. Petersen 1978, 32-35). It is important to consider the first-century audience and reflect on the possible effects of Lukan passages on them. (Here I touch base with the "audience-oriented" criticism of John Darr; cf. Darr 1992, 11-59). In my treatment of some passages (usually at the end), I make suggestions about these effects. I am suggesting that something important was at stake for some people through the communication taking place.

To take these remarks about the effects on the audience as statements about the present significance of the passage would be a hasty, and possibly hazardous, conclusion. By pondering effects of the text in its first-century setting, we may indeed find significance for us that we would not otherwise consider. However, these effects may underline the distance between the first century and our time, requiring us to find significance, if we can, by applying the text in a different way. In any case, for those seeking modern relevance, this commentary supplies food for thought but does not seek to settle present application.

Communication does not happen without active participation of the audience. We can remind ourselves of this by distinguishing clearly between a *text* (the marks on a sheet of paper or patterns of sound waves) and a *work* (effective communication). The audience must be actively engaged if a text is to become a work. The audience must supply a great deal and must be prepared to do so. This fact is obvious at certain levels. For instance, a person who does not know a particular language will not be able to turn a text into a work. Language involves a large set of rules that the recipient of a message must use in order to understand the meaning of the message. There is much more extratextual knowledge that is presupposed by many texts, including well-known historical events, classical and canonical literature, standard literary forms, and social data about how people are expected to behave in normal society. The significance of the text appears when it is combined with the right extratextual knowledge in the recipient. Since we not only use a different language but live in a very different society, we may be missing the point if we do not try to recover some of the extratextual knowledge that people of a different culture could assume.

In responding to a narrative text, there is additional work to be done. Inevitably, a narrative text is schematic, and therefore assumes that the audience will fill out the text from extratextual knowledge. Even so, there will be gaps and ambiguities in the text, places where events and characters can be understood in more than one way. Partly this is a result of the temporal character of reading and hearing. We cannot wait until the end of the story to interpret it. We are continually forming hypotheses about the story and its characters on the basis of partial information, and then revising these hypotheses as the story continues. A story's effect results, in part, from this active involvement of the audience in making judgments and revising them. The route by which we have come to the end of a story contributes to the ending's significance.

Even when we have heard the complete story, gaps and ambiguities are likely to remain. These ambiguities may result from obscurities in key scenes, but are also likely to result from the difficulty of constructing a whole from a narrative of many parts. Constructing a whole requires not only deciding what to emphasize, but also deciding how to make connections among the parts. The narrator may seek to guide this process, but it is difficult to control it completely, and different interpretations are likely to result. This is still true today, in spite of sophisticated exegetical methods.

I cannot, in this commentary, engage in reviews of past interpretation nor extensive arguments with other interpreters. Nevertheless, when there are varying views, I try (briefly) to give reasons for the choice that I have made. If the decision is an important one, the reader should not regard the matter as settled and should consult other commentaries. In some cases I am content to point out an ambiguity in the text and note that we have the freedom to understand it in several different ways.

Members of the audience will tend to react differently to different characters in the story—identifying with them or distancing themselves from them—because of perceived similarities or dissimilarities with themselves, or their ideal images of themselves. This process will also contribute to different interpretations. In thinking of the reception of Luke by the Lukan community, we must allow for diverse responses due, in part, to this community's social diversity. It would not be surprising if Jews in the audience heard the story in terms of God's promises to Israel while the poor understood it as a promise of rescue for the poor. In the commentary, I will occasionally suggest how a Lukan scene might affect different groups differently. The actual impact of Luke on its first-century audience was probably much more diverse than I am able to suggest.

A story such as the Gospel of Luke is rhetorically crafted. It seeks to persuade its audience and uses literary means to that end. Ranged against the Gospel's rhetoric, however, is the audience's resistance, either active (suspicion, doubt) or passive (inertia). The rhetoric of persuasion anticipates this resistance, yet this rhetoric is largely indirect. Even for its first audience, the Gospel was primarily a story about the past. Presumably the story was relevant also to the time of the first audience. However, there was a large area of freedom and responsibility for the audience at this point. There were major decisions to be made about how the story about the past impinged on the present. The audience had to decide what in the story was prescriptive for themselves and what was simply descriptive of the past or applicable to others. The story offered the audience multiple opportunities for change, but it could not, and did not, take away the audience's responsibility to decide which of these calls for change was right for them. The situation is the same for a modern audience.

COMMENTARY

PROLOGUE (1:1-4)

Luke differs from the other Gospels in that it begins with a formal preface similar to other Greek writings of its time. The preface consists of a single complex sentence. The writing style contrasts sharply with the narrative style that follows, which uses simpler sentences and is influenced by the language of the LXX. In the preface the author suggests that the following writing is not the product of a reclusive sect but a work deserving the attention of a broad audience, including those with some claim to Greek culture. The preface does not by itself determine the genre of the work. Although some view the preface as an indication that the author is presenting the work as a history, other technical and professional literature of the time began with similar prefaces (cf. Alexander 1993). The contents, form, and function of Luke–Acts as a whole may nevertheless suggest that it belongs with the historical writing of the period (cf. Sterling 1992, who classifies Luke–Acts as "apologetic historiography"). In the preface, the author, who normally avoids stepping into the spotlight, openly speaks about the task of writing.

◊ ◊ ◊ ◊

In a preface it was common to refer to one's predecessors. Our author refers to "many" who have already composed narratives on the subject at hand. (The word *diēgēsis*, translated "account" in NRSV, refers to a narrative.) Modern scholars assume that the author is referring to written sources used in the composition of Luke, and most of them would identify these as the Gospel of Mark, the sayings source Q, and one or more sources used only in Luke, sometimes designated L. It is clear that Luke is not the earliest writing about Jesus. The title or content of a Greek writing was often indicated by a phrase beginning with the preposition *peri* ("concerning," but translated "of" in v. 1). However, "the events that have been fulfilled among us" seems a rather vague statement about the subject of the predecessors' work and of this new work. To announce the subject as the life of Jesus, however, would not be appropriate for Luke–Acts as a two-volume work. The one distinctive element is the emphasis on fulfillment. "Events . . . fulfilled among us" may be a loose way of speaking of events that fulfill previous prophecy, but, strictly speaking, it is the events that have been fulfilled. This phrasing may suggest that the events not only fulfill prophecy but themselves come to fulfillment through the continuing mission and faith-response to which the events give rise.

The author's qualifications to write this work are presented in verse 3. The clause in verse 2 prepares for this by referring to the availability of a tradition that goes back to the original participants in the events. The "many" made use of this tradition "handed on to us" by the original eyewitnesses, and the author of Luke will too. The author does not claim to be an eyewitness, but he claims a foundation for his work in a reliable tradition that comes from a group of eyewitnesses. The word order of the Greek suggests two stages in the life of this group: They were eyewitnesses from the beginning and (later) became servants of the word (a nuance missed in NRSV). This interpretation corresponds to a feature of the Lukan story: Jesus' first followers—among whom the apostles have central place—are transformed, through the risen Messiah and the coming of the Spirit, into bold witnesses for Jesus. The author's claim that the tradition comes from those who were both eyewitnesses to events and servants of the word indicates that the tradition is based on direct contact with Jesus but also permits us to recognize the influence of the early church's preaching on the Gospel story.

The announcement in verse 3 of the author's decision to write is accompanied by assurances of his qualifications to do so. The word translated "investigating" implies that the author has followed the events with his mind. (Since the Greek participle in question is masculine, we know that the author presents himself as male; cf.

Sterling 1992, 326.) He has done so "carefully" and with attention to the full scope of relevant material ("everything") and the full scope of the relevant time ("from the very first"). His writing will also be "orderly" *(kathexēs)*. Although this could refer to accurate chronological order, many modern scholars doubt that this was possible. The order in question may be a literary order that seeks to clearly display the overarching purpose of God being realized in these events, according to the author (cf. Tannehill 1986, 9-12). The description of Theophilus as "most excellent" probably indicates he is a person of high social standing, but it does not prove that he is a government official. He is not a Roman, for he has a Greek name.

The purpose of the writing is expressed in verse 4. Theophilus (and the wider audience that he represents) is not learning about Jesus for the first time. He has already been "instructed" (NRSV). The verb *katēcheō* could refer to formal instruction in the Christian faith, or it could refer to less formal reports about Jesus. The word translated "truth" *(asphaleia)* means firmness, security, or reliability. Thus the Lukan narrative is meant to lead Theophilus and others to full conviction that what they have heard is a trustworthy basis for life decisions. The author does not attempt to convince people to make a correct life decision through arguments about historical fact, but by presenting an appealing portrait of Jesus and the early church, and by showing how they fit valued hopes rooted in scripture.

The Infancy Narrative (1:5–2:52)

The Lukan infancy narrative raises several important questions. It will be useful to consider some of these before turning to the interpretation of individual scenes.

Structure: Many interpreters have noted that there are parallels between scenes that focus on John the Baptist and scenes that focus on Jesus. There is also considerable repetition of themes within the infancy narrative. These features help to make the infancy narrative a special section within Luke. They also raise the question of whether the infancy narrative has been constructed according to some overall literary pattern of which the more obvious parallels and repetitions are a part.

The parallels are most noticeable in the first two scenes, in which the angel Gabriel announces the birth of a son, on the one hand, to Zechariah and his wife, and on the other hand, to Mary. When we compare the core of the annunciation to Zechariah with the annunciation to Mary that follows, we note the following common elements: the angel appears; Zechariah and Mary are disturbed by the angel's appearance; the angel reassures them ("Do not be afraid"); the angel announces the birth of a son and designates his name; the future career of the special son is described (in both cases the angel says, "he will be great" and connects the promised baby with the Holy Spirit); the parent asks a question indicating the difficulty of birth in his or her circumstance; the angel replies. (We will note later that the tone of Gabriel's reply is remarkably different in the two cases.)

Later both Mary and Zechariah praise God with hymns (or "canticles"), and the birth, circumcision, and naming of John and Jesus are reported. After the annunciations to the parents, however, the parallels between John scenes and Jesus scenes are less obvious. Nevertheless, there are some significant similarities to be observed. Scholars often try to exhibit these similarities in an outline, but there is continuing debate as to how the visitation scene (1:39-56), the presentation scene (2:22-40), and the scene of the boy Jesus in the temple (2:41-52) fit. The uncertainty results from the fact that the connections among scenes are more complex than an outline can easily convey.

While recognizing this difficulty, I would suggest that the following outline is helpful in getting a sense of the infancy narrative as a whole.

I. Preparation for the Births

    A. John
        1. Luke 1:5-23. Angelic annunciation 1: Gabriel to Zechariah.

2. Luke 1:24-25. (Limited) human recognition of God's saving work, with focus only on the end of Elizabeth's barrenness.

B. Jesus
   1. Luke 1:26-38. Angelic annunciation 2: Gabriel to Mary.
   2. Luke 1:39-56. Human recognition of God's saving work; Elizabeth's praise of Mary and Mary's praise of God (= hymn 1, the Magnificat).

II. The Births

A. John
   1. Luke 1:57-66. Birth, circumcision, and naming, with response of joy and wonder.
   2. Luke 1:67-79. Human recognition of God's saving work (= hymn 2, the Benedictus).
   3. Luke 1:80. Concluding refrain of growth.

B. Jesus
   1. Luke 2:1-21. Birth, circumcision, and naming, with response of joy and wonder. Also contains angelic annunciation 3: angel to shepherds.
   2. Luke 2:22-39. Presentation in the temple, with human recognition of God's saving work (= hymn 3, the Nunc Dimittis).
   3. Luke 2:40-52. Refrain of growth (2:40, 52), with the growth in wisdom illustrated by the story of the youthful Jesus in the temple (cf. Green 1995, 53).

One might question the division of 1:57-80 into two parts in the outline above because there is no narrative transition at 1:66 indicating another scene. The division above is nevertheless useful, for it calls attention to similarities between 1:67-80 and 2:22-40, which both center on a hymn recognizing the significance of the boy recently born. There are similarities between Zechariah and Simeon in these scenes: Both are Spirit-inspired, both have waited for a child, both are associated with the temple, and both hymns are introduced as blessings of God (1:68; 2:28 [NRSV translates *eulogēsen,* "blessed," as "praised"]) but are accompanied by specific predictions about the future of the child (1:76-77; 2:34-35). Furthermore, these scenes conclude with similar refrains of growth (1:80; 2:40). On the other hand, there are similarities between Mary's Magnificat and Zechariah's Benedictus. These are more fully developed hymns of praise than the Nunc Dimittis, and they come from the parents who were addressed by the angel, recognizing that the angel's promise is being fulfilled. In the outline above, therefore, we should recognize links among all three scenes containing hymns (I.B.2; II.A.2; II.B.2). These scenes serve a similar function, for they express human response to God's saving work and provide theological interpretation of the events narrated.

Repeated elements can be expanded or contracted by the narrator. The birth of John is reported in only two verses (1:57-58). The narrative concentrates instead on the day of his circumcision and naming. The division in the case of Jesus is the opposite: the birth of Jesus is told broadly, while the circumcision and naming occupy one verse (2:21). Compare also 1:24-25 with 1:39-56. The result of Gabriel's announcement for Elizabeth is told briefly in 1:24-25. These verses certainly do not have the weight of the scene that follows the announcement to Mary (1:39-56), but there is a reason for this. The parent to whom Gabriel disclosed the special meaning of the child is not ready to respond with praise. He has been silenced. Therefore, Mary, not Zechariah, first expresses the meaning of God's new saving work for God's people. Elizabeth in 1:25 can only speak of her release from barrenness. Similarly, 1:80 is expanded in 2:40-52.

The balanced structure of the infancy narrative, discussed above, encourages a reading process of comparison, in which both similarities and differences between John and Jesus are noted. The similarities present John and Jesus as key figures in a development with consistent features, while some important differences reserve the more important role for Jesus. The balanced structure also allows the narrator to emphasize certain themes through repetition, and to deepen their significance as they reappear. Thereby the particular Lukan understanding of God's purpose in Jesus Christ is gradually developed, and the recipients of Luke's Gospel are invited to share this understanding.

Use of Scripture: The process of comparison applies not only to the balanced scenes featuring John and Jesus. Those acquainted with the Jewish Scripture are also encouraged to compare the infancy narrative with stories and prophecies in those older writings. Those well versed in Scripture will note many echoes in Luke. These are not formal quotations but hints given through description of characters and events in the story, and through the use of telling phrases. Here as elsewhere in Luke–Acts, the narrative works typologically. That is, there is an assumption that God's new action will follow scriptural patterns, by which it can be recognized and understood. The process is subtle, and Luke's narrative is not reduced to wooden repetition of old stories. But the echoes of these old stories and promises enrich the experience of the new story. The recipients of Luke's story can say to themselves: Aha! It is like this . . . only different. Thereby the old stories of faith and hope encourage new faith and hope in the Lukan audience.

The process sketched above engages the imagination of the audience in an exploration of associations. Once initiated, it is difficult to limit this exploration, and some modern interpreters advocate questionable associations with scriptural texts. These exercises of the religious imagination are of the same type as those encouraged by the author of Luke and therefore should not be quickly censured, although they may sometimes draw us away from the main message of the text. In my discussion of Lukan passages, I hope to concentrate on connections that are well supported by the Lukan text and important for understanding it. There is still much to note in the Lukan infancy narrative. To fully appreciate the first three scenes (Luke 1:5-56), the reader needs to know the story of Abraham and Sarah, the elderly childless couple to whom God promised a son (Gen 15:1–18:15); the story of Hannah, a barren woman who asks God for a son and then gives him to the Lord, with a hymn of praise celebrating God's overturn of society (1 Sam 1:1–2:11); the prophecy of the messenger who will prepare the Lord's way, who seems to be identical to the returning Elijah (Mal

3:1; 4:5-6); the promise to David that his descendant would rule on his throne and be recognized as Son of God (2 Sam 7:4-17); and other scriptural passages.

Significance: The infancy narrative in Luke is very important for understanding Luke–Acts as a whole. Literary critics speak of the "primacy effect" in narrative. What the narrator presents first, when the reader is seeking basic orientation, will stand out and affect the reading of the rest of the story. To be sure, not everything will be disclosed at the beginning, and the narrator may be setting the reader up for a later surprise, but the beginning of the story will make an impact that the skilled narrator can use to good effect. We should approach Luke–Acts like any other story, as a continuous narrative to be experienced by moving from beginning to end. The beginning of a narrative can be used to influence the reader's understanding of everything that follows.

Furthermore, in the infancy narrative we find a concentration of broad statements about the saving purpose of God that is unmatched by anything later in Luke. Thus the infancy narrative provides much of the theological context for understanding Jesus' ministry in the rest of the Gospel. The connecting thread that unifies the narrative—the saving purpose of God—can only be understood as the author wishes if we pay close attention to the infancy narrative, and especially to the three angelic announcements and the three hymns or canticles. These contain material especially suited to reveal the basic understanding of the purpose of God that underlies the Lukan narrative. I find four (overlapping) types of material especially illuminating: (1) Reviews and previews. There are statements of broad temporal scope, recalling ancient promises and anticipating future events. Authors frequently provide reviews and previews in order to remind and prepare the reader, thereby helping the reader to interpret key events. The author of Luke is doing the same in the infancy narrative. (2) Commission statements. The angelic announcements also contain broad commission statements—disclosures of what God has commissioned John and Jesus to do in their future ministries that guide readers in understanding those ministries. (3) Highlighted or repeated scripture references.

The author understands the story of Jesus as the fulfillment of scripture. It is scripture that discloses the purpose of God in its broad scope. We must note which scriptural texts are given special attention in the narrative and how they are being understood. (4) Theological statements by reliable characters. Some characters are presented as good, perceptive, and authoritative. Unless this impression is later reversed, they should be taken as spokespersons for the viewpoint of the implied author. The angel Gabriel is a messenger from God, speaking with God's authority. Zechariah and Simeon are inspired by the Spirit as they praise God in their hymns, an indication that they, too, are reliable characters at these points.

Much of the angelic announcements and human hymns falls into one or more of the categories above, which should alert us to their importance in Luke. Yet the infancy narrative arouses expectations that are not fulfilled in the following narrative. The infancy narrative, apart from 2:30-32, seems to focus entirely on salvation for the Jewish people. Furthermore, it understands that salvation to include political freedom (1:71, 74). However, Jesus will be rejected in Jerusalem, and the course of events will lead not to freedom for the Jewish people but to defeat by the Romans. The resulting tension between initial expectation and later result is a meaningful part of the Lukan story, underscoring a tragic turn in the narrative (which need not be final). I will comment on this tension at appropriate places. (For an overview, see Tannehill 1985, 69-85.)

The three announcements by angels and the three hymns of response are linked thematically. That is, themes introduced early in these scenes are repeated and developed in later scenes, while new themes are introduced along the way to enrich the scenes. Thus we will understand the full theological perspective only if we consider all six statements and compare them with one another. There is a process of gradual disclosure of God's saving purpose, and, to some extent, 2:30-32 can be understood as the climax.

Relation to Matthew's Infancy Narrative: Luke shares certain details with the only other New Testament narrative of the birth of Jesus, Matt 1:18–2:23. Both Matthew and Luke report that Jesus was born in Bethlehem and relate his birth to the reign of King

Herod. His mother was Mary, a virgin engaged to Joseph, a man from the line of David. In both cases the conception is connected with the Holy Spirit, and the name Jesus is given by an angel. Nevertheless, the two infancy narratives are quite different. In Matthew, Joseph rather than Mary has the chief role. The angel appears only after Joseph is already contemplating the divorce of Mary for her pregnancy, and the angel's appearances are concerned with specific instructions to Joseph. The birth is followed by a visit from magi rather than shepherds. Herod is a threat to Jesus, requiring an escape to Egypt. Scripture is used differently, with a number of explicit citations in Matthew. There is conflict in the two Gospels' views of Mary and Joseph's home: Luke must explain how people who live in Nazareth nevertheless have a baby in Bethlehem (Luke 2:1-7), and Matthew must explain how people who live in Bethlehem come to reside in Nazareth upon their return from Egypt (Matt 2:22-23). If we are to understand Luke's story, it is important not to allow Matthew's different story to unduly influence our understanding.

Announcement of the Birth of John (1:5-25)

The passage may be divided into (1) the introduction of Zechariah and Elizabeth, with general description of their character (1:5-7); (2) the appearance in the temple of the angel, who announces to Zechariah the coming birth of a son and describes his future role, leading to Zechariah's question, the angel's rebuke, and Zechariah's reappearance to the people, unable to speak (1:8-23); and (3) the resulting conception, with Elizabeth's response (1:24-25).

◊ ◊ ◊ ◊

The core of this passage, the angel's appearance to Zechariah (1:11-20), is similar in structure to the following story of the angel's appearance to Mary. Following the appearance of the angel, both Zechariah and Mary are "disturbed" (*etarachthē*, v. 12; *dietarachthē*, v. 29). Gabriel reassures both with the words "Do not be afraid," delivers to each his message concerning the coming birth of a son, and supplies his name. In both cases the angel indicates that the promised son "will be great" and associates the Holy Spirit with him even prior to birth. In both cases the adult role of the baby in God's saving purpose is indicated. The angel's announcement is followed by a question from the parent indicating the impossibility of conception from a human perspective (vv. 18, 34). Following this, the scenes differ, for Zechariah is rebuked for unbelief and is silenced. Mary, on the other hand, receives further explanation and reassurance, and the second scene ends with Mary's willing acceptance of her role.

Raymond Brown understands the two scenes as following a five-step scriptural pattern found in the announcements of birth in Gen 16:7-13; 17:1-3, 16-21; 18:1-2, 10-15 and Judg 13:3-23 (Brown 1993, 156-59, 296-97). Brown is right; these stories of a divine messenger announcing to a parent the coming birth of a child have contributed to the Lukan annunciation scenes. However, parts of the five-step pattern are not well represented in Brown's examples. We need to look more widely at epiphany scenes in Jewish Scripture. When a person receives a divine call or commissioning, the story may show formal similarities to Luke's annunciation scenes. Benjamin Hubbard has analyzed "commissioning stories" into the following components: the *introduction,* which sets the scene; the *confrontation,* an encounter with an authoritative commissioner (often God or an angel); the *reaction,* often expressing fear or unworthiness; the *commission*; the *protest* (the commission may seem impossible); the *reassurance,* which may occur following the reaction, the protest, or both; and the *conclusion,* which rounds off the scene. Some examples from the twenty-seven passages cited by Hubbard: Gen 15:1-6; 28:10-22; Exod 3:1–4:16; Judg 4:4-10; 6:11-24 (Hubbard 1977, 107). (Not all components are present in every passage.) This outline fits Luke 1:5-25, 26-38 (introduction: 1:5-10, 26-27; confrontation: 1:11, 28; reaction: 1:12, 29; reassurance ["Do not be afraid"]: 1:13, 30; commission: 1:13-17, 31-33; protest: 1:18, 34; reassurance [or reinforcement]: 1:19-20, 35-37; conclusion: 1:21-23, 38). In the Lukan scenes, however, the commission includes an announcement of birth, thus making the scenes similar to the stories cited by Brown, and applying the commission aspect not to the parent but primarily to the promised child, for in both cases we have significant description of the child's future role in the plan of God. It is also noteworthy that divine messages in the passages cited by Hubbard may emphasize God's promise as much as, or more than, God's commission. Indeed, in Gen 26:23-25 (a brief example of the form) the message consists entirely of reassurance and promise. Therefore, I prefer to designate this type of story as "promise and commission epiphanies" (see Tannehill 1995, 64-65). I would include Luke 1:8-23 in this category.

◊ ◊ ◊ ◊

For those acquainted with Jewish Scripture, the initial scenes of Luke recall the birth announcements of crucial figures in the story of Israel and the calls and promises addressed to patriarchs, liberators, and prophets. Luke's stories carry the memories and hopes associated with the old stories into the recent history of God's people. God is acting in familiar ways as Israel's story moves to its climax.

Temple worship, with its sacrificial rituals, is unfamiliar to us. However, it would not be unfamiliar to Luke's original audience. Even Gentiles would have some basis for understanding, since there were analogous rituals in pagan temples. There is no criticism here of temple worship nor of life according to the law, of which temple worship was a part. Zechariah and Elizabeth are presented positively (they are "righteous" and live "blamelessly according to all the commandments" [v. 6]), and the sanctuary is assumed to be an appropriate place for a priest to receive a message from God.

Priests served in the temple under a system of rotation. Zechariah's "priestly order" would serve for a week at two different times during the year, then return home. To be "chosen by lot . . . to enter the sanctuary of the Lord and offer incense" was a special event that would come rarely. It meant entering the sanctuary building (most sacrifices were offered on the altar in front of the building). At the incense altar inside, the priest would be as close to the Holy of Holies as anyone other than the high priest would ever come. There Zechariah encounters an angel.

The angel says, "your prayer has been heard." Apparently, the barren couple had prayed for a son. Yet what is about to happen is

God's response to a larger prayer also. While Zechariah was offering incense, "the whole assembly of the people was praying outside." Statements about Simeon and Anna, who are also associated with the temple, suggest the nature of this prayer. Simeon is "looking forward to the consolation of Israel," and Anna, who is continually fasting and praying, speaks to people like herself "who were looking for the redemption of Jerusalem" (2:25, 37-38). As Acts 26:6-7 also indicates, true temple worship in Luke–Acts centers in prayer for fulfillment of God's promises to the Jewish people, and the angel's message to Zechariah will answer not only the personal prayer of a childless couple, but also the prayer of the people, whom Zechariah represents before God as a priest. Therefore, not only Zechariah and Elizabeth but "many will rejoice" at their son's birth.

In 1:15-17 we find a brief preview and summary of John the Baptist's future role, using scriptural language. This preview fits closely the description of John in the rest of Luke. His role is to "turn" the people to God (v. 16) and to one another (v. 17), bringing reconciliation. John will fulfill this commission through his message and baptism of repentance (3:3, 8). This turning in repentance is essential preparation for receiving God's salvation and for the restoration of Israel. It is John's task to "go before" the Lord and, through repentance, to "make ready a people prepared for the Lord" (1:17). In calling the people to repentance, John will act as a prophet and will have the authority of the ancient prophets. He "will be filled with the Holy Spirit" and will come "with the spirit and power of Elijah" (1:15, 17). Later passages will reemphasize John's role as the prophet who will go before the Lord and prepare the people by calling them to repentance (1:76; 3:2-5; 7:26-27). In both 1:76-77 and 3:2-6 this preparation through repentance is closely linked to salvation.

Renunciation of "wine or strong drink" is an act of special consecration. It is part of the vow of the nazirite, one "separated" to the Lord (see Num 6:2-3). The influence of scriptural birth stories may continue in this detail. Hannah, the mother of Samuel, promises that her son will be consecrated as a nazirite (1 Sam 1:11), and abstinence from intoxicants is imposed on the mother of Samson in the story of his birth (Judg 13:4).

The promises of a son to Abraham and Sarah in Gen 15–18 and to Hannah, the mother of Samuel, in 1 Sam 1 provide part of the scriptural background for this scene. In addition, the description of John's future role recalls the words of Mal 3:1; 4:5-6, where the messenger who will prepare the way before the day of the Lord and restore the temple cult is identified with Elijah. It is noteworthy that Malachi, in the Hebrew text (and NRSV), speaks of a mutual turning of the parents to the children and the children to the parents, while Luke 1:17, like the LXX, speaks only of the turning of the parents (literally, the "fathers") to their children. This places primary responsibility for reconciliation on those who had power and authority in ancient society.

Zechariah responds as Abraham did in Gen 15:8, yet he is strongly rebuked for his doubt and then made mute. Mary asks a similar question about the possibility of what was promised (1:34) but is treated much more gently. She is not punished, and she receives additional explanation and reassurance. Luke's audience is left to puzzle over this discrepancy. Several considerations might be relevant: Birth to an aged, childless couple has biblical precedent; virgin birth does not. Zechariah, who uses Abraham's words, might be expected to remember the outcome of Abraham's story and not doubt the angel's message (see Coleridge 1993, 39). Furthermore, Mary is probably a young girl (girls were usually engaged at age twelve or thirteen), while Zechariah is a man, an elder, and a priest. He could be expected to know the traditions of Israel. The silencing of Zechariah is punishment, but it is not rejection. He must learn in silence about the fulfillment of the promise. Then he will speak, praising God with one of the major hymns of the Lukan infancy narrative.

Gabriel rebukes Zechariah "because you did not believe my words" (1:20). Later Mary will be praised because she did believe (1:45). The narrative not only emphasizes the commission statements in the annunciations, allowing the audience to anticipate the future roles of John and Jesus, but also highlights the issue of faith. Faith in the promises is the right response, but it is not easy, as Zechariah demonstrates.

Because Elizabeth "remained in seclusion" after conception, her pregnancy does not become public knowledge. News of it will later be disclosed by Gabriel to Mary as a sign of God's power (1:36), leading Mary to visit Elizabeth to confirm this news. Elizabeth's response to her pregnancy in verse 25 is similar to Mary's Magnificat (cf. vv. 48*a*, 49*a*), but is limited to praise of God for a personal benefit. Since Zechariah doubts and has been silenced, we cannot assume that he has shared with his wife the angel's message about the special role of their son in God's saving work.

◊ ◊ ◊ ◊

If we imagine the Gospel of Luke being read to a community of Christians of mixed background some time after AD 70, can we make some educated guesses as to the effect of these words? The Jews in the group—or at least persons well-versed in Jewish Scripture—would be best prepared to appreciate the words of the Gospel. For such hearers, however, the reminder of John's mission of "turning" Israel to the Lord might produce pain as well as hope. Israel had not turned to the Lord nor received the promised salvation, but had become involved in a war in which they were defeated by the Romans. Even worse, Jew had slaughtered Jew in the holy city (cf. Josephus *J.W.* 5 §1-20). Is there hope now that Israel will turn to the Lord? Those with the strongest emotional ties to the Jewish people might have even more difficulty than Zechariah in believing the angel's words.

Announcement of the Birth of Jesus (1:26-38)

On the literary form of this passage, and its relation to birth announcements and promise-commission epiphanies in Jewish Scripture, see pp. 42-44.

1:26-33: Mary is introduced as "a virgin engaged to a man" named Joseph. Engagement was the first step in a two-stage marriage process in ancient Jewish society. It was a binding legal agreement between two families concerning a daughter and a son. It gave the young man marital rights over the young woman in the sense that any sexual involvement of the woman with other men could be punished as adultery. After engagement, the girl would continue to live with her parents for about a year, followed by a formal transfer of the bride to the husband's family home, where she would live from that point on. This was essentially a transfer of the girl from the control of her father to the control of her husband. Romantic love was not recognized as a significant factor in these family arrangements. In any case, the girl was too young to exercise much independent judgment. (Girls were usually engaged at age twelve or thirteen.)

Before Mary goes to live with her husband, she encounters an angel with a divine message, after the pattern of the promise and commission epiphanies of scripture. Her first reaction (v. 29) focuses on the angel's greeting, for it is extraordinary. The angel's first word, to be sure, is the ordinary Greek greeting (*chaire*, "greetings"). Its root meaning, however, is "rejoice," and that seems appropriate to the context. Gabriel's following words are remarkable, for he says, "The Lord is with you" (as the angel said to Gideon [Judg 6:12]), and describes Mary as "favored one" (*kecharitōmenē*, one who has received grace or favor). In verse 30 Gabriel explains by saying "you have found favor [*charis* = favor or grace] with God." The favor Mary is receiving is not for her alone; it is a great benefit for her people. Yet to be chosen for a special role in fulfilling God's saving purpose is a great honor.

It is assumed in ancient Mediterranean culture that a person of power and status will become a patron through bestowing favors on clients, who, in return, will support and honor their patron (on patron-client relations, see Moxnes in Neyrey 1991, 241-68; Malina and Rohrbaugh 1992, 326-29). Thus, in Acts, both Pharaoh and the Roman governors Felix and Festus are mentioned as sources of *charis,* or favor (Acts 7:10; 24:27; 25:9). God was also understood as a patron who bestowed favors on clients. Unlike human patrons, however, God does not bestow favor primarily on people who can supply something in return. God bestows favor on Mary, who is female and young in a society that honors males and elders, a girl who will later speak of her "lowliness" (1:48) and identify herself with the poor (1:52-53). As 1:48-53 will indicate, the divine patronage can upset the class system and redress the injustices of human patronage. In her perplexed reaction to the angel's greeting, Mary shows her surprise at being addressed as "favored one," since in human affairs she is not favored. But the angel announces a radical change in her status, for she has "found favor with God." Notice that the narrator focuses on Mary and pays no attention to the possible meaning of these events for Joseph (contrast Matthew's birth narrative).

Mary is informed that her son will be the Messiah. The Messiah is understood here as a king from the line of David who will rule over the Jewish people. God will give him "the throne of his ancestor David," and "he will reign over the house of Jacob." The phrase "house of Jacob" makes clear that the Jewish people, not the Christian church, is meant. The title "Son of the Most High" or "Son of God" also belongs to such messianic expectation. When, through the prophet Nathan, God promised David that God would "establish the throne of his kingdom forever," God also said of David's offspring, "I will be a father to him, and he shall be a son to me" (2 Sam 7:13-14; cf. Ps 2:7). The statement in Luke that "he will reign . . . forever" is probably a transformation of the promise to David of an everlasting dynasty, now understood eschatologically as the endless reign of the Messiah. (For a similar messianic interpretation of 2 Sam 7 in Qumran, see Brown 1993, 310-11.)

1:34-38: Mary's response "How can this be?" ignores the fact that she will soon be living with her husband. For some reason she assumes that this child will not be conceived in the normal way. On the striking difference between Gabriel's rebuke of Zechariah and gentle treatment of Mary, although both ask how the angel's promise is possible, see p. 46.

The "Holy Spirit" and "the power of the Most High" are two ways of describing the divine power that will enable Mary to conceive as a virgin. Unlike Matt 1:23, there is no citation of Isa 7:14 in its LXX form, which reads, "The virgin *(parthenos)* will conceive" (differing from the Hebrew). Nevertheless, it is likely that this Greek translation of Isa 7:14 has influenced Luke's, as well as Matthew's, infancy narrative. From conception through the Holy Spirit, Gabriel draws a conclusion about the nature of the child:

"Therefore the child . . . will be holy" and "Son of God." (There is a grammatical ambiguity in the Greek at this point, as revealed in the difference between the RSV and NRSV translations, but in any case the logic of verse 35 moves from conception through the Holy Spirit to the special nature of the child.) In discussing verse 32 we noted that there are scriptural passages in which the Jewish king is called God's son. A virgin birth is not implied. In verse 35 we have a different understanding of what it means to be Son of God, tracing it to divine intervention at conception and a resulting special nature. Nevertheless, Gabriel defines the task and destiny of this Son of God in terms of the ancient promise to David of a son who would assume his throne (vv. 32-33).

Elizabeth's conception was also beyond normal human power. Gabriel discloses Elizabeth's pregnancy as a reassuring sign to Mary of what God's creative power can do. This information will provide the motivation for Mary's visit to Elizabeth in verses 39-40. Gabriel's concluding statement, "for nothing will be impossible with God," reinforces the parallel between Elizabeth and Sarah, for it is very similar to Gen 18:14 of the LXX. The reassuring sign, then, is not only Elizabeth but also Sarah.

Although Gabriel's message occupies most of the passage, the narrator concludes the scene with a statement by Mary, accepting the role to which she is being called. This conclusion shows an interest in Mary and in the way that humans respond to divine promises and commissions. Mary's willing response contrasts with Zechariah's failure to believe (v. 20) and provides the basis for the praise of Mary's faith in verse 45. Mary speaks of herself as the Lord's *doulē* (slave girl). This is an acknowledgment of God's sovereignty. It is not degrading to Mary, for the honor of a servant is based on the greatness of the Lord one serves.

◊ ◊ ◊ ◊

Apart from the endless reign, verses 32-33 do not break through earthly and political hopes. They refer to the restoration of a Davidic king to rule over the Jewish people. Modern readers may assume that this has a symbolic rather than a literal meaning, for the author of Luke could not have really hoped for a political restoration of the Jewish nation. As a caution against this assumption, I would point out that the proclamation of Jesus as royal Messiah, fulfilling the promise to David, is not only found in the infancy narrative but is emphasized in the message to Jews in Acts (2:29-31, 36; 13:22-23, 32-37; 15:16) and is accompanied by hope for the restoration of Israel (3:20-21). To be sure, the hope for a restored Jewish nation under its messianic king is not fulfilled in the course of Luke–Acts, forcing us to ask whether it is later dropped, spiritualized, or only postponed. Further comments about this difficult issue will be made at appropriate points.

Although the main concern of our passage is Mary's son and his future role, the narrator shows an interest in Mary and in what it means for her to be one of God's "favored" ones. Without denying Mary's special honor, participants in the early church, upon hearing this story, might recapture some of the thrill of hearing the word of God's "favor *(charis)*" for each of them, calling them to share the inheritance of those who are holy or "sanctified" (Acts 20:32) and to be part of God's "people *(laos),*" chosen from all nations (Acts 15:14). The women, particularly, in Luke's audience might find the favor that Mary received and the faith with which she responded to be incentives for recalling the fundamentals of their own religious life.

Virginal conception is assumed, but not emphasized, in Luke 1:26-38. In itself it is a negative concept: conception without participation by a male. The positive side, expressed in verse 35, is conception through the creative power of the Spirit. This, in turn, serves the affirmation that Jesus is the Son of God, fully prepared by God's initiative for a unique role. Although Gabriel's message is full of scriptural language, it would be easy for some in the Lukan audience to relate verse 35 to pagan stories of the birth of heroes through impregnation of a woman by a god (cf. Plutarch, 227-29; Suetonius, 265-67).

Meeting of the Two Mothers (1:39-56)

Luke's audience has heard that the angel Gabriel appeared to two persons and announced to each the birth of a son who will have a special role in God's redemption of Israel. So far these are two unconnected events, but now the narrative threads are drawn together. The two mothers meet and share their responses to what is happening. Presumably Mary visits Elizabeth in order to confirm the news given by the angel in verse 36 and to share Elizabeth's joy.

The two annunciation scenes in 1:5-23 and 1:26-38 are parallel in structure, but the second wonder announced by the angel exceeds the first. John will be born to an aged childless couple, but Jesus will be born to a virgin. "Even before his birth" John "will be filled with the Holy Spirit" (1:15), but Jesus is conceived through the Holy Spirit (1:35). John will be a prophet who will lead many to repentance, but Jesus will be God's Son, the Messiah. The visitation scene makes the greater importance of Mary's son quite clear. Elizabeth praises Mary, speaking of her as "the mother of my Lord." Mary does not praise Elizabeth in return but praises God for the salvation that she and her people are receiving through these events. The visitation scene basically consists of Elizabeth's and Mary's statements of praise.

1:39-46: The angel's message to Mary is confirmed not merely by Elizabeth's pregnancy but by the child leaping in her womb, which is taken as a prophetic sign of recognition of Mary and her child. The future role of John as proclaimer of a "more powerful" one than himself (3:16) is here anticipated. Elizabeth is "filled with the Holy Spirit" (1:41), allowing her to interpret this sign. She is the first of a series of prophetic figures in the infancy narrative. This role is shared by women and men. (Anna is specifically called a prophet in 2:36.) The function of these prophets is to supply divinely inspired interpretation of the saving purpose of God that is coming to fulfillment through these births. Or, to use the language of narrative criticism, these prophetic statements provide previews to the reader of the significance of John and Jesus in the work's narrative world and encourage the reader to hope for, and expect, the salvation for Israel celebrated in these statements. Within the cultural context, angels and persons filled with the Holy Spirit speak with divine authority. They are "reliable characters"; that is, they reliably convey the perspective of the implied author, who has presented them with this divine authority. That makes the angelic annunciations and the prophetic hymns very important for understanding the theological perspective of Luke (see Tannehill 1986, 20-22).

Elizabeth's inspired exclamation honors Mary. She is declared to be blessed, first, because she has been chosen to be the mother of the Messiah (vv. 42-43). A woman could gain honor by being the mother of a great son. Mary deserves great honor for this reason, yet later in Luke this view will be qualified. More important than the blood relation of mother and son is hearing the word of God and obeying it as a disciple (11:27-28). Mary is honored for a second reason: she is "blessed" (here the word is *makaria,* which can also mean "fortunate" or "happy") because she believed. Through Elizabeth the narrator makes clear that Mary's statement of acceptance in verse 38 was a great act of faith. It was important that Mary believe the promise that God would bring the Messiah to Israel through her and that she be willing to offer herself for this purpose. The contrast with Zechariah, who initially did not believe (v. 20), also highlights the significance of her response. For the Lukan audience, the issue of faith in response to the promises would also be important—and difficult—because the experiences of the Jewish war and of repeated rejection of the gospel by many Jews (as reported in Acts) seem to challenge the claim that Jesus will reign over the house of Jacob, bringing freedom and peace to the Jewish people (1:33, 71, 79).

1:46-56: The special honor that the narrator gives to Mary—and to Mary's faith—is also clear from a further feature of the story's plot. Zechariah, a priest, and therefore a person of status, is the first to receive Gabriel's happy news, but Mary, a lowly girl, is the first to praise God with a hymn. Zechariah will join in belatedly with his own hymn (1:68-79). Here the plot turns on the issue of faith. Zechariah did not believe and Mary did. Therefore she was able to respond with praise while Zechariah was tongue-tied.

Although Elizabeth praises Mary, Mary praises God. She accepts Elizabeth's statements about herself, as verse 48*b* indicates, but she recognizes God as the source of her unexpected honor. Furthermore, she does not separate herself from others because of God's favor. She continues to think of herself in solidarity with the poor. What God has done for her is a sign of what God has done and will do for them, according to the Magnificat (so called because of the first word of the Latin version of Mary's hymn).

The Magnificat is a hymn of praise, similar to a number of the psalms that begin with a statement of praise, followed by the reasons for praise, introduced by "for" (see vv. 48a, 49a). However, another pattern is also noticeable. In the Greek text many of the lines begin with a strong action verb (sometimes preceded by a conjunction). This pattern emphasizes the action of God (to whom many of these verbs refer) and also helps to mark off the lines. The return of a verb marks the beginning of a new line, encouraging the reader to read these lines in a rhythmic parallelism. There are some exceptions to this pattern: in verse 48b there is a parenthetical personal reference, and in verse 53 a different poetic pattern, involving rhyme and alliteration, takes over. Different also are verses 49b-50 and 54b-55, but these two sections resemble each other. They create a sense of pause by lengthening the final sentence, and these two sections place God's "mercy *(eleos)*" in the perspective of the ages ("from generation to generation"; "forever"). (On the poetic structure of the Magnificat, see further Tannehill 1974, 263-75; Tannehill 1986, 26-29.)

Because the Magnificat twice moves from short, rhythmic sentences with initial strong verbs to a longer sentence that puts God's mercy in the perspective of the ages, I think it is appropriate to speak of two strophes, consisting of verses 47-50 and 51-55. This pattern of strophes encourages the comparison of strophe one, which is largely Mary's statement of what God has done for her, with strophe two, which is concerned with God's action in society as a whole. Poetic patterns encourage a complex process of interaction of words and phrases within the poem. The strophic pattern is accompanied by patterns of synonymous and antithetical parallelism. The Magnificat begins with two statements of praise in synonymous parallelism (v. 47). Later it will use antithetical parallelism (vv. 52-53). Synonymous parallelism emphasizes and enriches the thought, while antithetical parallelism heightens the sense of contrast and in verses 52-53 proclaims a dramatic reversal in society. In verses

51-53 Mary is declaring that God has overturned society in favor of the oppressed.

There are significant links between strophe one (the personal part) and strophe two (the social part), indicated by the repeated use of key concepts. Mary speaks of her own "lowliness" in v. 48 and later speaks of what God has done for "the lowly" in general (v. 52). She speaks of God as "the Mighty One *(ho dynatos)*" in verse 49 and later speaks of "the powerful *(dynastas)*" whom God has brought down (v. 52). In both parts God acts as "the Mighty One" who shows "strength" (vv. 49, 51), but that strength is demonstrated as "mercy" (vv. 50, 54). In stating her reason for praising God, Mary first contrasts her own "lowliness" (v. 48) with God, who is "the Mighty One" (v. 49). This contrast emphasizes the wonder not only of God's power but of God's concern, which stretches across this great gap. Beginning with verse 51 the contrasts become more complex, for a third party is introduced: the "proud," "powerful," and "rich." This group has power that might seem to rival God's. It has demonstrated it by oppressing "the lowly" (who are also "the hungry" and therefore economically deprived). But God's superior strength appears in scattering the proud and bringing down the powerful in order to rescue the lowly. The most powerful language of the poem is used in verses 52-53 in order to stress this rescue. Strong contrast in a chiastic pattern ($a'b'b'a'$ = powerful/lowly; hungry/rich) is here combined, in the Greek, with rhyme to proclaim that God has overturned society.

When we consider the two parts of the Magnificat together, we see that a parallel is suggested between God's powerful mercy for one lowly girl and the way that God acts throughout time and society. Mary's story is presented as the emblem of a much larger experience and expectation. The Magnificat encourages faith that God can and will intervene for the rest of the poor and not merely for Mary.

The statements about God's action are in the past tense. This is striking, for the power structures of society have not been disturbed so far. At most one can say that Gabriel, in favoring Mary over Zechariah, has ignored social status in Jewish society. But it makes sense for Mary to speak in the past tense if she is both recognizing that God has already done something very significant for her and that what God has done for her and will do through her son fits the mold of God's action throughout the history of Israel. The reference to God's powerful "arm" in verse 51 recalls descriptions in the LXX of God's power demonstrated in the Exodus (Exod 6:1, 6; 15:16; Deut 3:24; Jer 39:21 [= 32:21 NRSV]; cf. Nolland 1989, 71). Thus the Magnificat summarizes what God did in rescuing a slave people while anticipating what God is beginning now.

God is intervening to help "Israel" (v. 54). One can, then, understand "the powerful" who oppress "the lowly" as foreign powers who oppress the Jewish people. But when read within the context of Luke as a whole, the Magnificat will rightly be understood to apply also to classes of people within Israel (who will fall and rise, according to 2:34). The Magnificat is closely related to Jesus' later beatitudes for the poor and woes for the rich (6:20-26). Sarah and Abraham were in the background as the story of Zechariah and Elizabeth unfolded. Now Abraham is mentioned explicitly (v. 55) in connection with the promise given to him. This promise is important in Luke–Acts. It will be cited and interpreted in 1:73-75 and again in Peter's temple speech, where we learn that the promise to Abraham involved a covenant with Israel but also included a promise to "all the families of the earth" (Acts 3:25).

◊ ◊ ◊ ◊

The Magnificat is a joyful hymn of praise, but not everyone in the Lukan audience would find it easy to rejoice with Mary. Since the Gospel of Luke addresses both rich and poor, we should assume that there were some of relative wealth and status in the audience. Mary's words are good news for the lowly and hungry, but they do not sound like good news for the powerful and rich. A person like Cornelius, for instance (Acts 10), might find Mary's words disturbing, for he was a person of power, gained through serving people still more powerful, and, at least by the end of his active service, he would be a person of some wealth. He might wonder if he is being condemned and excluded. Later he will learn that he is not being excluded, but the price of inclusion is considerable.

The Magnificat is a remarkably *theological* statement. In Zechariah's hymn, Christology begins to appear, but the Magnificat is entirely a description and celebration of God. It has a key role in the narrative because it is the initial characterization of that hidden character who is most powerfully shaping the whole series of events. The Lukan audience is to understand these events as the work of this kind of God, one who is mighty, but who uses that might in mercy toward the weak, one who is revolutionary in upsetting human ranks but conservative in keeping ancient promises. This God is not the placid ruler who maintains social order but the *overruler* of human power and plans. This understanding of God will have a deep effect on the Lukan interpretation of the death and resurrection of Jesus (cf., e.g., Acts 2:23-24, 36).

The Birth and Growth of John (1:57-80)

1:57-66: This narrative reports the birth of John briefly and focuses on the eighth day of his life, when John was circumcised and named. The narrative of Jesus' birth makes the opposite choice: events surrounding the birth are extensively told, while the circumcision and naming take one verse (2:21). In the case of John, the narrator has something unusual to tell about his naming. Against the will of the crowd, Elizabeth insists that her son should be named John. It is not clear how she came to this conviction. Has there been communication between Elizabeth and Zechariah, even though he cannot speak? How would this take place? (We cannot assume that Elizabeth could read.) Or has Elizabeth received instructions from an angel, as Zechariah did in 1:13? There is a "gap" in the narrative at this point.

The assembled group appeals to Zechariah, the father, even though they must make their request known by motioning or making signs. This procedure seems to imply that Zechariah is deaf as well as mute. Zechariah chooses the same name as his wife, which amazes the crowd. This scene suggests that the naming of the baby John was a significant act. Perhaps the name itself is significant, even though the narrator does not translate it for us. It means "Yahweh has shown favor" (cf. Fitzmyer 1981, 325). In any case, Zechariah's choice of this name, contrary to family tradition, is significant because it shows his obedience to the angel's command (1:13). Thereby Zechariah is also acknowledging that Gabriel's message was true and that the child would have the special role ascribed to him by the angel. With this act of acknowledgment, Zechariah's power of speech returns, and he immediately uses it to express his newfound faith by praising God (v. 64). The Benedictus (a name derived from the Latin version of 1:68-79) will also express that praise, but it is long, and the narrator chooses to report reactions to these events (vv. 65-66) before presenting it.

The effect of these events on neighbors, relatives, and more distant folk is carefully noted. First the neighbors and relatives rejoice with Elizabeth (v. 58). At this point they do not anticipate that the baby has any importance beyond the family and village. The sudden return of Zechariah's speech after naming the baby, however, convinces these people that a divine power and purpose is at work, and the news of these events spreads to a wider region (v. 65), for such an amazing event at the beginning of a child's life suggests a special destiny (v. 66). In verse 66 those who heard these things "pondered" them, according to NRSV. Literally, they "placed" these things "in their heart." Similar statements will be made about Mary in 2:19, 51. The observers know that these events have special importance, but their full significance will only be disclosed later. In the meantime the people ask, "What then will this child become?"

1:67-80: Although the Benedictus will, in part, answer the question of what John will become in verses 76-77, this hymn focuses primarily on the Messiah rather than on John. Zechariah's hymn is not restricted to what he learned from Gabriel but presupposes all that we have been told in the infancy narrative so far. It picks up previous themes and expands them. Not only does Zechariah summarize Gabriel's message by describing John as a prophet who will "go before" the Lord and "prepare" (1:17, 76), but he also combines the reference to an heir to David's throne, found in the annunciation to Mary (cf. 1:32, 69), with the fulfillment of the promise to Abraham, mentioned in the Magnificat (cf. 1:55, 73).

Thus Zechariah celebrates the fulfillment of divine promises associated with two central figures of scripture, David and Abraham. He also expands Mary's reference to God as "savior" (1:47) by repeated references to God's "salvation" (1:69, 71, 77) and also repeats her references to God's "mercy" (1:50, 54, 72, 78). Other phrases used at the end of the Magnificat (1:54-55) reappear in 1:69-70, 72-73. The Benedictus, in turn, introduces the themes of light (1:78-79) and peace (1:79) that will reappear in the words of angels and the prophet Simeon (2:14, 29, 32). These are indications that the angelic announcements and prophetic hymns fit together as a gradually unfolding revelation of the significance of John and Jesus. Only by considering these statements together do we get the full picture of God's purpose in sending the forerunner and the Messiah.

The NRSV has broken up the Greek into smaller sentences, for the whole hymn consists of two complex sentences in the Greek (1:68-75, 76-79). Zechariah begins with a traditional expression of praise, followed by "for" and the reason for this praise. This reason is first stated as follows: God "has looked favorably on his people" (1:68). Although this translation accurately conveys the meaning, readers need to know that a special term, derived from Scripture and employed at key points in Luke, is being used. The verb (*episkeptomai*) was translated "visit" in the RSV, and the noun (*episkopē*) is still translated "visitation" in 19:44 of the NRSV. The basic meaning of the verb is to "examine" or "inspect," but it can also be used when one "visits" someone to find out how the person is doing. Although God's inspection could result in judgment on a guilty people, the word often means that God is taking careful note of their need and responding to it, as in Exod 4:31 of the LXX. The verb recurs in Luke 1:78, where the NRSV translates it as "break upon," a translation that fits the context but is a doubtful rendering of the word itself.

In verse 69 "a mighty savior" is not a literal translation; the Greek says, "a horn of salvation." In scripture a "horn," as of a wild buffalo or a bull, is a symbol of strength. Since this "horn of salvation" is "in the house of David," it clearly refers to the powerful king who will ascend David's throne, that is, the Messiah.

The word "salvation" in verse 69 is repeated at the beginning of verse 71, indicating that verse 71 is defining the kind of salvation that was previously mentioned. The NRSV paraphrases at the beginning of verse 71, as well as in verse 69, making this connection less clear.

The statement in verse 71, together with verse 74, raises one of the main exegetical questions in interpreting the Benedictus. In spite of the reference to "our enemies" and "all who hate us," most interpreters believe that these verses cannot refer to rescue of the Jewish people from nations that conquer and oppress them (which at the time of Jesus would mean the Romans). To be sure, those who believe that the Benedictus originated either among followers of John the Baptist or in early Jewish Christianity may see a political sense to these words at that stage, but would not attribute that meaning to the author of Luke, who does not depict Jesus as a political revolutionary and would not view rescue of the Jewish people from the Romans as an appropriate task of the Messiah. This interpretation, I believe, falsely removes these words from their political and social context. Zechariah is speaking of what God, through the Messiah, will do for the people and, in this context, speaks of "our enemies." These are not the enemies of various individuals but of the people as a whole. (Therefore, the phrase "my enemies," which occurs in 1 Sam 2:1 and frequently in the Psalms, is not comparable.) Although the enemies might include more than the Romans (Herod Antipas and his officials; rich landowners), it is hard to imagine that the Romans would be excluded. The contrary view rests on the following false assumptions: (1) It is sometimes assumed that opposition to Roman rule necessarily meant a willingness to take up arms. E. P. Sanders notes, however, that there were four kinds of Jewish resistance to the Romans, and the fourth group "quietly prayed for God to liberate his people" (E. P. Sanders 1992, 288). Zechariah does not necessarily believe that the Romans will be conquered by a human army. (2) It is also assumed that the earthly ministry of Jesus completes his task, as far as Luke is concerned. Since Jesus is not a political and military leader during his ministry, political freedom for the Jewish people is not part of his agenda. Indeed, it could not be, because it clearly didn't happen. In my opinion, the narrator is well aware that it didn't happen and regards that as a tragedy. The narrator has not depoliticized the scriptural promises concerning a messianic king, but believes that the hope of the people for a life of peace in freedom was lost, for the foreseeable future, when Jerusalem rejected Jesus.

To make this point, the entry into Jerusalem is reworked in Luke, introducing terms from the infancy narrative (especially the Benedictus), but with a tone of pathos as Jesus indicates that the hope previously expressed by these terms is being lost. Thus, as Jesus weeps over the city, he, like Zechariah, speaks of "peace," of God's "visitation," and of Israel's "enemies" (19:41-44; note also the connection between 2:14 and 19:38). Here the enemies are clearly the Roman army. Jerusalem, not recognizing the time of visitation, is missing its opportunity for peace, and will be conquered by those enemies from whom it might have been saved. Between the infancy narrative and Jesus' death, there is a tragic turn. Zechariah's hymn reveals what could have been and would have been, apart from the rejection of the Messiah. The narrative invites us to rejoice with Zechariah as he anticipates the redemption of Israel through its Messiah, but this joyful anticipation will cause us, later, to feel more sharply the tragic loss. Then the audience should share Jesus' pain as he weeps for Jerusalem.

The oath sworn to Abraham is understood in a similar way. It, too, requires rescue "from the hands of our enemies" (vv. 73-74), but the thought expands here to include the situation that will follow. Rescue from enemies will permit Israel to "serve" God "without fear, in holiness and righteousness." The word translated "serve" *(latreuō)* refers especially to cultic service, such as the duties that priests may perform at the temple, but by extension may include all the activities of the religious life understood collectively as worship of God. The promise to Abraham is interpreted in a similar way in Acts 7:5-7. God promises the land as a possession for Abraham and his descendants. However, his descendants will be enslaved in a foreign land. Nevertheless, "after that they shall come out and worship [or "serve," again using *latreuō*] me in this place" (Acts 7:7). Freedom from slavery will enable Israel to worship God without hindrance in its own land. Zechariah's interpretation of the promise to Abraham is not a narrow nationalism but a hope for religious freedom so that Israel can shape its own identity as the worshiping people of God.

There is a shift at verse 76 as Zechariah turns to his own child and describes his future role, first in terms that paraphrase Gabriel's message in 1:17, and then by relating John's work to the forgiveness of sins (v. 77). (For John's "baptism of repentance for the forgiveness of sins," see 3:3.) What is the relation of "salvation . . . by the forgiveness of their sins" in verse 77 to salvation "from our enemies" (v. 71)? The two understandings of salvation may seem to conflict, the one being "religious" and the other "political." This conflict is a mirage caused by modern assumptions. In the ancient Jewish context, many would admit that Israel's sins were responsible for its captivity. Therefore, forgiveness is necessary for the renewal of its national life.

The complex statement in verses 78-79 repeats previous key words ("mercy," "visit" [translated "break upon"], "way of peace" [cf. the Lord's "ways" in v. 76]) and mingles them with the new image of dawning light. "Tender mercy" is a translation of a difficult phrase that includes reference to God's *splanchna*, the "inward parts," corresponding more or less to "heart" in our usage. The visitation of the "*anatolē* from on high" probably carries a double meaning. Basically *anatolē* means "rising." It can refer to the rising of the sun, that is, the dawn, and this meaning fits the light and darkness imagery of verse 79. However, *anatolē* is also used three times in the LXX (Jer 23:5; Zech 3:8; 6:12; cf. Fitzmyer 1981, 387) to refer to the Davidic heir as the "shoot" (that is, a new shoot growing from the stump of a felled tree; see Isa 11:1). Thus it seems to be a designation for the Davidic Messiah, which means that verses 78-79 are no longer referring primarily to John the Baptist. "Peace," in the biblical context, is a broad term that refers to a social condition of harmony, prosperity, and happiness. This final word of the Benedictus should be understood to include the "salvation from our enemies" (v. 71), freedom of religion (vv. 74-75), and "forgiveness of sins" (v. 77) mentioned earlier.

The childhood of John is completed in verse 80 with a refrain that will reappear, with variations, in 2:40, 52. The summary in verse 80 prepares for the narrative of John's ministry in 3:1-20.

◊ ◊ ◊ ◊

The Benedictus might produce conflicting feelings in the Lukan audience. Zechariah, now that his tongue is loosed, speaks under the inspiration of the Holy Spirit (v. 67). Thus the narrator clearly wants the audience to accept the Benedictus as an authoritative statement of God's plan for Israel. The Christian Jews in the audience, perhaps others also, would be sympathetic to this hope. At the same time, they would have the disturbing knowledge that the coming of John and Jesus did not save Israel from its enemies, for many Jews perished in the Roman war, and the temple now lies in ruins. Thus a tension appears in the narrative already at this early point. There would be added difficulty for someone like Cornelius, who served in the army of Israel's "enemies." It would be difficult, especially after the Roman-Jewish war, to serve the Roman government while maintaining sympathy for Jews, sharing their prayer life (cf. Acts 10:2), and participating in a sect with Jewish roots. The Benedictus aggravates the problem caused by these conflicting social ties.

There is a long history of using the Magnificat and Benedictus in Christian prayer. This practice encourages Christians to apply the fulfilled promises, celebrated in these hymns, immediately to themselves. We should pause and ask whether it is right to do so. An alternative would be to say that it is only by considering the significance of these words for Israel, and placing these words back into the story of Israel in Luke–Acts (and the rest of the Bible), that we can understand, by analogy, their relevance for Christians. Clearly Luke–Acts proclaims that Gentiles share in the promises to Israel, but there are many indications, including the Benedictus, that the author of Luke–Acts continues to be theologically concerned with the ancient people to whom the promises were originally given.

The Birth and Growth of Jesus (2:1-52)

The births of both John and Jesus are followed by hymns (1:68-79; 2:29-32). The latter hymn is comparatively short, but it has great importance for understanding the Lukan perspective on the divine purpose that underlies these events. Furthermore, it is supplemented by a third angelic annunciation, this time to shepherds (2:8-14), and by an oracle (2:34-35). The actual birth of John is reported in two verses (1:57-58), while the birth of Jesus becomes a comparatively lengthy episode (2:1-20).

Jesus' Birth (2:1-21)

2:1-7: The registration decree of Augustus would have been for the purpose of taxation. (There are serious reasons for historical doubt concerning Luke's report of this registration; cf. Brown 1993, 394-95, 412-13, 547-56, 666-68.) The narrator uses the registration as a way of explaining how Mary's baby came to be born in Bethlehem, but it may also have further significance. Beginning the episode with the decree of Emperor Augustus throws the shadow of his rule over subsequent events. We will note later that the announcement of the angel in verses 10-11 applies to Jesus language that parallels the politically motivated praise of Augustus that we find in inscriptions. To be sure, Luke–Acts does not encourage open conflict with the Roman Empire. Furthermore, Acts 5:37 shows awareness that the census under Quirinius provoked a rebellion. The fact that Joseph and Mary peacefully submitted to the decree could be taken as rejection of rebellion. Nevertheless, there may still be a subtle suggestion that another better deserves the title of savior and the acclamation of peace bringer that were given by many to Augustus.

The birth itself is reported very briefly in verse 7. Mary "wrapped" her baby "in bands of cloth." This refers to the practice of swaddling, that is, wrapping a baby tightly over the whole body. She also "laid him in a manger." This is a more surprising comment, and the narrator feels a need to explain: "because there was no place for them in the inn." The traditional translation "inn" is probably not appropriate. The Greek simply means a lodging, and it could refer either to the main room of a simple home or an attached room used for guests. If Joseph had relatives in Bethlehem, the original audience would probably assume that he would stay with them.

With the birth of the baby, however, there was no longer room in the cramped quarters.

The manger was a feeding trough for animals. Moving to the manger might take only a few steps, if we assume a one-room farmhouse where the family quarters might be separated from the animal quarters only by being on a raised platform (cf. Hengel in Kittel and Friedrich 1974, 9.52). Since the manger is mentioned three times (vv. 7, 12, 16), it must be important in the story. A baby in a manger is sufficiently unusual to serve as a "sign" to the shepherds. When the shepherds find such a baby, they recognize that the angel spoke the truth. Finding the one who is Messiah and Lord in such impoverished circumstances is additional cause for amazement (v. 18).

2:8-21: The shepherds fit the setting of Jesus' birth. They are ordinary folk who work with animals. Although some interpreters appeal to later rabbinic writings to argue that shepherds were viewed as sinners, it is doubtful that this view is assumed in this scene (agreeing with Fitzmyer 1981, 396; Brown 1993, 673). Probably there is a connection between the shepherds and the repeated reference to Bethlehem as the "city of David" (vv. 4, 11). David was a shepherd before being anointed king (1 Sam 16:11), and later he is told, "It is you who shall be shepherd of my people Israel" (2 Sam 5:2). Ezekiel speaks of a future David who will be shepherd over Israel (34:23), and Micah, in speaking of the ruler who will come from Bethlehem, says that he will "feed his flock in the strength of the LORD" (5:4). The figure of the shepherd has the same ambiguous quality as a royal baby in a manger. A shepherd is an ordinary fellow who would not feel out of place in a stable. A shepherd is also a symbol of kingship.

The angel's appearance to the shepherds in the field is the third angelic appearance in the infancy narrative. This appearance, like the two previous, has standard features of a biblical epiphany scene (see pp. 43-44), but this time the appearance is not to a parent. It is appropriate for others to hear about this baby from an angel, for the Messiah will mean joy "for all the people" (v. 10). Although the appearance to the shepherds differs from the previous annunciations in that there is no protest against the angel's message, the shepherds still receive a reassuring sign (v. 12). The description of brilliant "glory" shining in the night around the shepherds employs dramatically the darkness and light imagery in 1:79 and Isa 9:1 LXX (9:2 NRSV; cf. Coleridge 1993, 153).

Although the angelic appearances in Luke 1–2 follow biblical patterns, reports of prophecies, omens, and prodigies in connection with the birth of someone great also appear in Greco-Roman literature. Suetonius, for instance, reports a series of omens of future greatness in connection with the birth of Augustus, including a dream of his father that "his son appeared to him in a guise more majestic than that of mortal man, with the thunderbolt, sceptre, and insignia of Jupiter Optimus Maximus" (Suetonius, 267; cf. Talbert 1980, 129-41). Furthermore, the angels' words in verses 10-11, 14 employ concepts that were important in the ruler ideology of the ancient Mediterranean world, concepts that were applied to Augustus. I am referring to the "good news" of the ruler's birth, the title "savior," and the proclamation of "peace." In Rome there stood an altar to Augustan peace; the Greek cities of Asia Minor had adopted a new calendar with Augustus's birthday as the first day of the year, calling him "savior"; and the Priene inscription lauds Augustus in these terms: "The birthday of the god has marked the beginning of the good news for the world" (Brown 1993, 416). Those aware of the extravagant language being used to curry the Roman emperor's favor would recognize that the angels' words are a counterclaim for another ruler.

The central announcement in verse 11 fits the expectations aroused in 1:32-33, 69. Jesus is the Messiah, that is, the promised king of David's line who will rule over Israel and bring it salvation. The reference to birth "in the city of David" underscores the Davidic connection, and the title "savior" picks up the reference to salvation in 1:69, 71, 77. Jesus is twice called "savior" in Acts (5:31; 13:23), and in Acts 13:22-23, as in Luke 2:11, the title "savior" refers to Jesus' role as messianic king, heir to David's throne. Acts 13:22-23 is evidence of the continuing importance in Acts of the theme of Jesus as Davidic Messiah. This theme is strong in the infancy narrative. Jesus is savior because he will save his people from their enemies, as Luke 1:71, 74 indicate. He is savior also because, as ruler, he can grant amnesty, the forgiveness of sins (Acts 5:31; cf. Luke 1:77). He will grant forgiveness during his ministry; he will do it more broadly when he is exalted to his rightful position of power at God's right hand. (Note that a renewed opportunity for repentance and forgiveness flows from Jesus' exaltation to God's right hand as Messiah, Lord, and Savior in Acts 2:33-36, 38; 5:31. Cf. Tannehill 1990, 39-40.)

In the KJV the second half of Luke 1:14 is translated, "and on earth peace, good will toward men." This translation is based on a group of ancient manuscripts that read *eudokia* ("good will," "favor") in the nominative case. However, today most scholars agree that the reading *eudokias* (*eudokia* in the genitive case) has better manuscript support. Adopting this reading, we could translate literally "And on earth peace among people of good will" or "favor." An ambiguity still remains, for the text does not say explicitly who is showing good will. The RSV and NRSV resolve this ambiguity by speaking of God's favor, suggesting that God is showing favor to a chosen group. There is some support in Qumran documents for this interpretation (cf. Fitzmyer 1981, 411-12), but the fact that verse 14 does not refer explicitly to God's favor leaves room for doubt (cf. Brown 1993, 678-79). An ambiguity can be a stimulus to thought. It is legitimate to consider the possibility that the phrase encompasses both God's gracious favor and a corresponding human good will awakened by God's grace (cf. Bovon 1989, 129).

The importance of the angels' message is emphasized as the narrator describes the shepherds' response. They not only sought out the child to verify the message but then "made known what had been told them about this child" (v. 17). The shepherds become earthly messengers of the heavenly messengers, enabling others to understand the full meaning of this birth (cf. Coleridge 1993, 148). Furthermore, the shepherds' praise of God (v. 20) continues the praise begun by the angels (vv. 13-14). In verses 18 and 20 what the shepherds had been told is at first a cause of amazement and then later a cause of praise for God. Thus, the narrator underscores the special significance of the angels' message for understanding Jesus' birth.

There is some uncertainty about the degree of understanding attributed to Mary in verse 19. The word translated "pondered" *(symballousa)* is understood by some to indicate that she is hitting upon the right interpretation of the things she has experienced (cf. Bovon 1989, 131). However, I think that this view attributes too much to Mary at this point (cf. Fitzmyer 1981, 398, 413). In 2:50 she does not understand something important, and *symballousa* in 2:19 is a present participle, indicating a process underway, not a completed action with clear results. To describe Mary as "pondering" these events, then, is appropriate. Even if the message of the shepherds seemed clear, there is reason for Mary to be puzzled about the great contrast between Jesus' future role and the circumstances of his birth (cf. Coleridge 1993, 155-56).

◊ ◊ ◊ ◊

The claim made about Jesus in the infancy narrative would seem very bold, perhaps ridiculous, in the context of the first century. Even though the claims of some Roman emperors to be "saviors" who bring "peace" might provoke cynicism, their power was obvious to all, while the claim that Jesus is the true peace bringing savior, whose birth is good news, would seem incredible to many. Even within the church, some whose careers and social positions gave them an investment in the status quo (such as Cornelius) might find the angels' words disturbing, for they indicate the possibility of conflict between the savior Jesus and rulers who claim the same title. The narrator is well aware that outsiders will perceive a conflict and bring charges on this basis (cf. Luke 23:2; Acts 17:7). This conflict between the claims of rulers cannot be completely avoided, unless Jesus' claims are curtailed.

For those Christians who still prayed fervently for the freedom of the Jewish people, the angels' words could be a disturbing reminder that the Messiah has not yet proved to be the savior of Israel in the full sense, for he has not yet "saved" Israel "from our enemies" (1:71). For some, however, the same words might reinforce the hope that this salvation will still come.

Presentation in the Temple (2:22-40)

2:22-27: There are some puzzling features of verses 22-24 that lead some scholars to believe that the narrator did not have accurate knowledge of Jewish ritual practice. Two requirements of the law are relevant: the purification of the mother after childbirth, which can take place forty days after the birth of a son or eighty days after the birth of a daughter (Lev 12:2-8), and the redemption of a firstborn son by payment of five shekels to the priests (Exod 13:1-2, 11-16; Num 18:15-16). The offering indicated in verse 24 is the requirement for the mother's purification from those who cannot afford a sheep and a pigeon (perhaps the majority of Jews at the time). Puzzles arise because verse 22 refers to "their purification," although the purification applies only to the mother, and because the parents bring Jesus along to present him to the Lord at the temple, although we lack evidence that this was a requirement or custom (as v. 27 may imply) for redemption of the firstborn. (See, however, Neh 10:35-36.)

The presentation of the firstborn in the temple, whether customary or not, fits the narrator's picture of what an especially devout family would do and provides the setting for words of Simeon that are central to the following scene. The story of the birth of Samuel may have been an important influence here, as it was earlier in Luke's infancy narrative. After he was weaned, Hannah brought the child Samuel to the sanctuary, giving him to the aged priest, Eli (compare Simeon), for the service of the Lord (1 Sam 1:21-28). Later Eli repeatedly blessed Hannah and her husband (1 Sam 2:20; cf. Luke 2:34). For the narrator, the presentation in the temple is a sign that Jesus is "holy to the Lord" (v. 23), that is, dedicated to the service of God, as the angel previously declared in 1:35. The special nature of that holy service will be further disclosed by Simeon.

There is strong emphasis on obedience to "the law of the Lord" in verses 22-24, and the parents' obedience to the law is again mentioned in verses 27 and 39. The setting is the temple, the center of Jewish cultic worship, where many of the ritual commands must be fulfilled. In this context the Holy Spirit is active. (The Spirit is mentioned three times in vv. 25-27.) There is no perceived conflict between law and Spirit, and the two persons that we meet in the temple (Simeon and Anna) are pure examples of religious devotion. This is not a picture of religion in decay. (The reader might regain some appreciation of what temple worship meant to Jewish families by reading E. P. Sanders 1992, 112-16.)

Simeon and Anna form a male and female pair. Both of them are devout, both are prophets (v. 36; see also the references to the Spirit in vv. 25-27), probably both are old (vv. 26, 29 probably imply that Simeon is clinging to life only so that he could see the Messiah, as promised), and both recognize the child as the Messiah. Simeon and Anna are not the first male-female pair in the narrative, for the story began with Zechariah and Elizabeth, who, like Simeon and Anna, were described as devout (1:6), and continued by balancing two annunciation scenes, one to a male parent (Zechariah), the other to a female parent (Mary). These are only the first of a series of male-female pairs in Luke (cf. Tannehill 1986, 132-36). The effect of this literary technique is to highlight the role of women, most of whom were denied public roles in ancient Mediterranean society. In 2:29-35 Simeon is quoted, while Anna's message is briefly summarized. However, in 1:5-56 the narrator favors Mary over Zechariah. Anna's message complements Simeon's, for she speaks publicly about Jesus (an unusual role for a woman; cf. Seim 1994a, 131), while Simeon speaks only to Mary and Joseph.

Zechariah and Elizabeth are also prophets, for their speech is inspired by the Spirit (1:41-45, 67-79). The devotion of Simeon and Anna, however, is characterized by a phrase not used before: Simeon was "looking forward to *(prosdechomenos)* the consolation of Israel" (v. 25), and Anna shared with the circle of those who were "looking for *(prosdechomenois)* the redemption of Jerusalem" (v. 38). These are parallel phrases reflecting the message of consolation (or comfort) for Israel in Isaiah, beginning at Isa 40:1. (For both phrases in parallel, see Isa 52:9.) Isaiah 40–66 has a strong influence on Luke–Acts and especially on Luke 2:25-38. Isaiah 40–55 joyfully anticipates the restoration of the exiles to their homeland and the rebuilding of the ruined city of Jerusalem. At the time of Jesus, Jerusalem was intact, but at the time of the composition of Luke it was again a city in ruins, and the Jewish people had suffered a devastating defeat. This situation would have a marked impact on the Lukan audience's reaction to these reminders of Isaiah's message concerning "the redemption of Jerusalem." (Fitzmyer 1981, 432, notes that documents of the second Jewish revolt [AD 132-135] were sometimes dated by the [very brief] years of "the redemption of Israel" or "the freedom of Jerusalem," reminding us of the political implications of these phrases at the time.)

2:28-32: When Simeon received the baby Jesus, he "praised God" (more literally, "blessed God," like Zechariah in 1:64, 68). The third hymn of the Lukan infancy narrative, traditionally called the Nunc Dimittis, expresses this praise (2:29-32). The scene of the presentation of Jesus in the temple deserves to be the Lukan text for Epiphany, for it is the manifestation of Jesus as savior of the whole world, including the Gentiles. While Simeon's hymn continues themes from the previous hymns (see "peace," "salvation," "light"), the inclusion of the Gentiles is something new. In the sense that it presents God's saving purpose through Jesus in its broadest scope, the Nunc Dimittis is the climax of the Lukan infancy narrative.

Simeon recognizes that he is God's "slave" (NRSV: "servant"), just as Mary did (1:38). The phrase "you are dismissing your slave" probably refers to Simeon's coming death, but it can also refer to the freeing of a slave. In this case, the two meanings converge. Through death, Simeon is being released from his long service. Simeon has been a watchman, but his task is now complete.

Seeing the baby, Simeon sees God's "salvation." Although the normal New Testament term for salvation is *sōtēria,* a feminine form, the word used here is *sōtērion,* a neuter form. The latter term occurs only four times in the New Testament, with three of those occurrences in Luke–Acts. The word is being borrowed from Second Isaiah, and the specific source is probably Isa 40:3-5 LXX, a text quoted in Luke 3:4-6 with "all flesh shall see the salvation *(sōtērion)* of God" as its climactic line. Along with this word, Simeon's hymn absorbs the inclusive perspective of Second Isaiah, in which God's servant is called to be a "light to the nations" or a "light to the Gentiles" (the Greek word means both; cf. Isa 42:6;

49:6; and Luke 2:32; Acts 13:47). Although the phrase "all peoples" in Luke 2:31 could, in another context, mean the tribes of Israel, it is explained in verse 32 by references to the Gentiles and Israel. It is equivalent to the "all flesh" of Isa 40:5. The two lines in verse 32 are roughly parallel, emphasizing that the "salvation," which is also "light," is for both the Gentiles and Israel.

It is important to remember this, for the third use of *sōtērion* in Luke–Acts is found at the end of Acts in Paul's announcement that, in light of Jewish rejection, "this salvation of God has been sent to the Gentiles" (Acts 28:28). This warning and rebuke to the Jews cannot be a satisfactory conclusion to the story of God's saving purpose for the narrator, because authoritative prophets (Isaiah and Simeon) make clear that the Jewish people should be included. The fact that the end of Acts reminds us of "this salvation of God" in a context that refers both to Jews and Gentiles provides evidence that the divine purpose as defined in Luke 2:30-32 and 3:6 is the connecting thread behind the narrative as a whole.

Isaiah 52:7 speaks of "the messenger who announces peace, who brings good news, who announces salvation." In the temple scene in Luke 2, Simeon is the messenger who announces peace and salvation. Simeon's departure "in peace" means personal fulfillment of his longing, but it also refers to Simeon's share in the corporate peace and salvation promised in Isaiah.

2:33-40: After the hymn of celebration, Simeon delivers an oracle to Mary, and the mood of this second statement contrasts sharply with the first. The "falling and rising of many in Israel" indicates social upheaval, and a "sign that will be opposed" anticipates the opposition that Jesus will encounter in Galilee and Jerusalem. The falling and rising can be understood in two different ways. Either some will fall and others will rise (as with the powerful and lowly in 1:52-53), or the same group will fall and then rise. In itself the text is ambiguous; it does not compel us to read it one way or the other. The pervasive influence of Isaiah on this passage provides some evidence that we should not exclude the possibility that those who fall (the Jewish opponents) might later rise, for Isa 51:17 LXX exhorts Jerusalem to arise, because she has drunk up "the cup of falling" (author's translation; *ptōsis* in the LXX, as in Luke 2:34), the cup of God's wrath (cf. Koet 1992, 1559-64). It is unusual for Jesus to be called a "sign" *(sēmeion)*, but there are several passages in Isaiah that connect a sign or ensign with the Gentiles (cf. 49:22; 62:10, and also C. F. Evans 1990, 219). Isaiah 11:10, 12 LXX is especially interesting, for it speaks of "the root of Jesse," and says, "in him Gentiles will hope," and then that the Lord "will raise a sign *(sēmeion)* for the Gentiles." If this is the source of the reference to Jesus as "sign" in Luke 2:34, a major cause of opposition will be the inclusion of Gentiles in Jesus' messianic kingdom (cf. Acts 13:44-45).

The saying about the sword piercing Mary's soul has elicited a number of interpretations (see Brown 1993, 462-63, who lists eight). It is probably wise for the interpreter to avoid being too specific. I agree with Brown that Mary will experience sharp pain when she recognizes that "the claims of Jesus' heavenly Father outrank any human attachments between him and his mother, a lesson that she will begin to learn already in the next scene (2:48-50)" (Brown 1993, 465). But we need not exclude reference to pain because of the death of her son and because of the conflict in Israel that he will cause both before and after his death.

Through this conflict "the inner thoughts of many will be revealed" (v. 35). The narrator later reports this happening through repeated use of the word "thoughts" *(dialogismoi)* or the related verb in scenes where Jesus exposes latent opposition and the weakness of disciples (cf. 5:21-22; 6:8; 9:46-47; 24:38).

Simeon's hymn and oracle to Mary provide Luke's audience with an important preview of, and guide to, the following narrative. The audience can now anticipate that the story concerns God's comprehensive saving purpose as it encounters human resistance.

On the figure of Anna, see p. 70. The time between the presentation in the temple and the next episode in Luke's story is bridged by a summary statement of growth in verse 40. This resembles the statement about John in 1:80, but the additional note about Jesus' wisdom prepares for the demonstration of precocious wisdom in the following scene.

◊ ◊ ◊ ◊

Gentiles in the Lukan audience may be gratified that their share in God's salvation is affirmed in Simeon's hymn. They have had to wait until the end of the infancy narrative for inclusion in the story. Even now Simeon's words make clear (to those who know scripture) that inclusion of the Gentiles does not mean a break with Judaism, for it fulfills Isaiah's prophecy. Nevertheless, the Jews and Gentiles in the Lukan community would surely recognize that it is not easy for Jews and Gentiles to form one community and that large numbers of Jews reject the Christian movement because its unrestricted welcome of Gentiles is a threat to Jewish identity. Some Christian Jews may share these concerns. For them the provocative "sign" continues, now represented by Jesus' inclusive community. Thus the tensions may be internal as well as external, as the community faces the challenge of welcoming all, while respecting diversity. (See the accusation of Judean believers against Paul that his teaching is undermining the traditions of Christian Jews [Acts 21:20-21].)

The Lukan audience may rightly wonder how to balance the two statements of Simeon. Do the somber words about the falling and rising of many in Israel and about Jesus as a provocative sign negate the joyful words about Jesus as salvation and glory for Israel? This interpretive issue relates to the larger issue of what to think of Israel in light of widespread resistance to the gospel concerning Jesus.

The inclusion of women in the story, through the prominent role given to Mary and the lesser roles given to Elizabeth and Anna, would be an indication to the Lukan audience that women are important in their community. They may be called to special service in fulfilling God's will, including the role of prophet. The aged also have a prominent role as interpreters of the unfolding events (see Elizabeth, Zechariah, Anna, and probably Simeon). In traditional societies that rely less on writing (and electronic media) than on oral communication, the elderly are the repositories of community memory and wisdom. The elderly persons in the infancy narrative represent that communal wisdom and also represent Israel's long wait for its Messiah. In the infancy narrative, however, the youthful Mary also shares in celebrating and interpreting God's work.

The Young Jesus Anticipates His Future (2:41-52)

Persons destined for greatness, it was assumed, would display their unusual ability at an early age; thus it was common for biographers to take note of their subjects' remarkable accomplishments while still young (cf. de Jonge 1977-78, 322-23, 340-41). Both Philo and Josephus, for instance, describe the remarkable intelligence of the young Moses (Philo, 287-89; Josephus *Ant.*, 2 §230). Luke's story of the twelve-year-old Jesus in the temple, however, not only ranks him with others who showed remarkable intelligence while young, it also provides a first indication that Jesus is aware of his special mission and hints at the conflict between that mission and family expectations. This scene is told in the form of an elaborated pronouncement story, coming to a climax with the pronouncement of Jesus in verse 49. (On pronouncement stories, see pp. 99-100.)

◊ ◊ ◊ ◊

It is strange that Jesus would leave his parents without informing them, when he must have known that they were about to leave for home. It is also strange that his parents would travel for a day without having located their son (even though the extended family typical of the time would permit care of a child to be shared with relatives). These events set up the exchange of mutual reproaches between mother and son later in the story (vv. 48-49). Apart from the fact that Jesus deserted his parents, the scene in verse 46 would not be surprising, for the young were expected to learn from the elders and recognized teachers. When verse 47 adds, however, that "all who heard him were amazed at his understanding and his answers" (not just his questions), it is clear that the narrator is presenting Jesus as a child of remarkable intellect and insight. Nevertheless, we should not imagine that his understanding was complete, for verse 52 indicates that Jesus continued to increase in wisdom.

The fact that Jesus is sitting among the teachers does not necessarily imply that he is already taking the role of a teacher. Still, Jesus is demonstrating the power that will later make him a famous teacher. Therefore, it is appropriate to see this scene as foreshadowing Jesus' later teaching, especially his teaching in the temple at the end of Luke (19:45–21:38; cf. Kilgallen 1985, 553-59). Note, however, that there is no indication of conflict between Jesus and the Jewish teachers at this point. Jesus' remarkable "understanding" *(synesis)* (v. 47) and growing "wisdom" *(sophia)* (vv. 40, 52) may relate not only to his vocation as teacher but also to his messianic role, for Isa 11:1-2 testifies that the "spirit of wisdom and understanding" *(sophia* and *synesis* in LXX) will rest on the Messiah.

Mary's question in verse 48, "Why have you treated us like this?" is a reproach (cf. Brown 1993, 489). Jesus' treatment of his parents would probably be more disturbing in ancient Mediterranean society than in our own. In that society (according to Malina and Rohrbaugh 1992, 300) "parents socialize their children to be absolutely loyal to their biological kin group, since every member of the family shares the family honor and one member's misbehavior shames the entire group." Family honor was especially threatened by lack of respect for parents. In Jewish society, the importance of such respect was reinforced by the command, "Honor your father and your mother" (Exod 20:12).

Jesus answers Mary with counterquestions, which may combine reproach with surprise. When his parents discovered him missing, they should have known where he would be. Jesus' second question indicates why they should have known where to search for him. Literally, Jesus says, "Did you not know that I must be in the _____ of my Father?" The blank space indicates that the Greek sentence assumes a masculine or neuter plural noun at that point but does not express it. As the NRSV footnote indicates, more than one translation is possible. The use of the Greek expression to refer to someone's house or home is well documented, and Jesus is indicating that his parents should have known the place to find him. Therefore, a location, "my Father's house," must be part of the meaning. But it is quite possible that there is a double meaning, for the same expression may refer to someone's "affairs" or "business" (hence the NRSV footnote, "be about my Father's interests"). Then Jesus is not only indicating where he can be found, but why. He already feels the calling to be engaged in his Father's business.

His parents "did not understand" what Jesus said. This note indicates that there is something enigmatic about Jesus' words. The double meaning may be part of the enigma. Also, there is a play on words between "your father" (Joseph) in Mary's statement and "my Father" (God) in Jesus' reply. Jesus' words require the listener to turn a sharp corner through a sudden redefinition of his father. Even if these things are understood, the puzzle remains as to why Jesus' calling as Son of God should require him to cause pain to his human parents. Here, also, this scene may foreshadow future events. Jesus indicates here for the first time what he "must" do (using the impersonal verb *dei,* "it is necessary"). He will speak this way again at key points in the narrative, especially when he says that he "must undergo great suffering, and be rejected" (9:22; cf. 17:25). At this point it will be clear that he cannot carry out his vocation without causing emotional pain and social dishonor to his family. Two loyalties hang in the balance. Already, as a child, Jesus indicates which must control his life, in spite of his mother's pain.

Jesus' response is softened in verse 51, which indicates that Jesus returned home with his parents and "was obedient to them." The incident in the temple is a foreshadowing of Jesus' adult ministry, not his regular behavior as a child, which would have made him a rebellious son. Just as the gap from baby to child of twelve is bridged by a summary in verse 40, so the gap from age twelve to adulthood is bridged by a similar summary in verse 52. The latter verse indicates that growth in wisdom continues to take place. Both verses 40 and 52 refer to Jesus' "wisdom," forming a frame around the intermediate story, which illustrates this wisdom. The closing verse of the chapter adds "human favor" to divine (compare v. 52 with v. 40), for Jesus has already amazed and impressed the crowds.

THE BEGINNINGS OF THE MISSION (3:1–4:44)

The Mission of John (3:1-20)

3:1-2: The elaborate dating in verses 1-2 not only provides a benchmark for relating the public ministries of John and Jesus to political history but also reminds the audience that John is a prophet, for the words are reminiscent of the introductions to prophetic books in Jewish Scripture. The date marks the time when "the word of God came to John," making this "word of God" the motive force behind his work. Placing this dating at the beginning of John's (not Jesus') ministry, thereby marking a major new segment of the narrative, unites John's ministry to that of Jesus, rather than placing John in an earlier epoch (cf. Conzelmann 1960, 22-27).

3:3-6: When the word of God came to John, he began "proclaiming a baptism of repentance for the forgiveness of sins." John is a prophetic preacher whose preaching includes a call to baptism. Ritual washings were performed by Jews to remove pollution that would defile the temple. Moreover, a number of Jewish and Christian groups of this general period, including the Essenes, emphasized ritual washing, and the practice was also well known in other religions of the ancient Mediterranean (cf. Hartman in Freedman 1992, 1.583). Since Luke connects John's baptism to forgiveness of sins, it seems to be understood as a symbolic action that washes away the pollution caused by sin. It is also a public sign of repentance.

Repentance and forgiveness are closely related in Luke–Acts. Together they form a central aspect of the message of the apostles and Paul (cf. Luke 24:47; Acts 3:19; 5:31; 26:18-20), and in Acts 2:38 they are associated with baptism, just as here. Repenting (expressed by the verb *metanoeō*) is synonymous with "turning" (expressed by the verb *epistrephō*) in Luke–Acts (cf. Acts 3:19; 26:20), and the audience was previously told that it was John's task to "turn" the people of Israel to God (Luke 1:16). There must be a decisive change in direction, for the present course of the nation and individuals leads to destruction. The destructive consequences of the present course are sometimes pictured as expressions of the anger of God, who has been personally affronted (cf. "the wrath to come" in 3:7), and sometimes in less personal terms. Although the Lukan emphasis on repentance might seem to make human action more important than God's grace, that is not the case, for repentance itself is understood as something that God "gives" (Acts 5:31; 11:18). People do not turn in a new direction of their own power.

The past holds them so tightly that something must happen to create a new opportunity. Repentance is the renewal of personal and corporate life made possible by the arrival of a special time, the time when "all flesh" can "see the salvation of God" (3:6).

"Forgiveness of sins" could also be translated "release of sins," for the noun *aphesis* and the verb *aphiēmi* have a broader meaning than forgiveness. They can be used when speaking of the cancellation of debts (11:4) and the release of prisoners (4:18). Sins (the Lukan audience may have thought) are like a debt that cannot be repaid, robbing people of happiness and independence. Restitution is due to those who have been injured, but the debt can grow huge so that people fall into debt bondage. Despair or hardened denial of responsibility could be the result, unless there is opportunity for a new start, free from this bondage.

John's "baptism of repentance for the forgiveness of sins" is a public rite of washing that represents this opportunity. It is made possible and necessary by the imminent arrival of "the salvation of God" (3:6).

At Luke 3:3 we reach a portion of Luke that begins to parallel Matthew and Mark. As in these two Gospels, Luke relates a scripture quotation to John's ministry, but Luke omits that part of Mark not derived from Isaiah and continues the Isaiah quotation farther than either Matthew or Mark (who stop with "make his paths straight"). Isaiah 40:3-5 depicts the return of the Lord to Zion. The visit of a ruler to a city required the people to decorate and repair the road of approach. In this case, the prophet envisions a radical transformation of the landscape. In Luke transformation of a landscape that obstructs travel into a straight and smooth road becomes imagery for radical repentance, and the Lord in mind is no longer Yahweh but the Lord Messiah (2:11). The shift from "the paths of our God" in the LXX to "his paths" in Luke makes this application possible. The Isaiah quotation is extended primarily in order to include the final statement, "all flesh shall see the salvation of God." This statement is a reprise of the words of Simeon in 2:30-32, where Jesus was viewed as God's "salvation" for "all peoples," both the Gentiles and Israel. The two passages together disclose the full scope of the salvation that God intends through

Jesus Messiah. "All flesh shall see the salvation of God," then, anticipates the participation of Gentiles in God's salvation. Not Gentiles only, however, for "all" embraces other excluded groups, such as the tax collectors and sinners who will soon appear in the narrative.

Near the beginning of the public ministry of key characters, the narrator likes to place a prominent scripture quotation that indicates the divine commission to be fulfilled at that stage of the story (see 4:18-19 for Jesus; Acts 2:17-21 for the apostles; 13:47 for Paul). Luke 3:4-6 has a similar function, but it not only highlights John's work of preparing the way, but also presents the full scope of the divine purpose that unifies Luke–Acts as a whole.

3:7-18: In this passage a representative sampling of John's preaching (v. 18: there were "many other exhortations") is presented in three segments, verses 7-9, 10-14, and 15-17. The first segment is a harsh warning against superficial repentance. Here we have a section of non-Marcan material shared with Matthew (usually designated Q; cf. Matt 3:7-10). Although John's words are very similar in the two Gospels, the audience is different. Words that Matthew deems appropriate for Pharisees and Sadducees are addressed to the crowds in Luke. Their function is to make the crowds aware of the need for repentance and to warn that only true repentance counts. The crowds have come to be baptized, but baptism by itself is worthless unless they "bear fruits worthy of repentance" (v. 8). The change in direction must be validated by changed behavior. Several misconceptions may suggest to people that this change is not really needed. Some may think they will escape the consequences of their actions because they "have Abraham" as their "ancestor." The promise made "to Abraham and to his descendants" (1:55) remains important in Luke–Acts, but this does not mean that God is stuck with every descendant, no matter how obstinate. God can act with sovereign freedom to "raise up children to Abraham" (v. 8). This phrase is sometimes taken as an indirect reference to the Gentiles, but it may equally well refer to someone like Zacchaeus, who is reclaimed as a "son of Abraham" (19:9). Some in the crowd may also feel that they can continue as before because they have not suffered any consequences. John, however, insists that "the ax is lying at the root of the trees" (v. 9). The evil consequences of their actions are about to strike them with devastating force. The exact form of this judgment is hidden behind the imagery of ax and tree.

The segment in verses 10-14 (found only in Luke) helps to define the "fruits worthy of repentance" demanded by John. Some specific examples of appropriate fruits are given through dialogue with three groups. John first replies to the "crowds" in general; therefore, this reply seems to have general relevance. The demand to share clothing and food is radical. Two garments are already too much if someone else has none. (The translation "coats" is misleading. The Greek refers to the *chitōn*, the "tunic," a basic garment worn next to the skin, not an extra garment for warmth.) These words could be addressed to people with very little. They complement Jesus' later words about love and sharing (6:30-36). Even for poor people, repentance means learning to share.

Two special groups are then addressed, the tax collectors and the soldiers. John's words to them may not seem so radical, since they are not asked to leave their professions. Their tendencies to be oppressive are addressed, however, and it may have been difficult to follow John's demands. The right to collect taxes (meaning tolls and customs duties) was auctioned off to the highest bidder, and the winner usually had to pay in advance. Then he had to recoup the amount plus expenses and profits. The natural result is for the "chief tax collector" to put pressure on his agents, the local "tax collectors," to gouge as much as possible from people (cf. Fitzmyer 1981, 469-70). The soldiers may fit into the same picture. They may be soldiers sent to enforce the demands of the tax collectors. Both the tax collectors and the soldiers would be under orders from superiors, who might not be pleased with their concern for the public.

In verse 16, Luke partly parallels Mark, partly Matthew; Luke then continues with verse 17, which parallels Matthew. This mixture of Marcan and Q tradition is preceded by verse 15, found only in Luke. It is a common Lukan technique to present sayings of Jesus as a response to the questions or concerns of a group or an individual. Here the same technique is applied to John. This setting reinforces the point that John is directing the messianic expectation of the people away from himself to another who is coming. Here John bears witness to the coming Messiah, who will far exceed John in power and honor. John also distinguishes between his baptism and the baptism of the Messiah, which will be "with the Holy Spirit and fire" (v. 16). The promise of baptism with the Holy Spirit is important in Luke–Acts. Jesus will repeat this promise, again contrasting it with John's baptism, in Acts 1:5. Then it will begin to be fulfilled at Pentecost (Acts 2:1-4). In Acts 2:17, however, this promise is associated with the prophecy of Joel that "I will pour out my Spirit upon all flesh." In fulfillment of this prophecy, the spread of the Spirit to new groups is reported. We are told how the Samaritans received the Spirit (Acts 8:15-17), then the Gentiles (Acts 10:44-48), and finally a group who had received John's baptism but had not heard about the Spirit (19:1-7). The reference to a baptism with "fire," as well as Holy Spirit, is ambiguous. Since the Spirit appears as tongues of fire at Pentecost (Acts 2:3), fire may be a quality of the Spirit itself. On the other hand, fire twice appears as an image of destructive judgment in the context (Luke 3:9, 17). Thus it is also possible for the audience to understand the Spirit and fire as alternative baptisms, the one for the wheat and the other for the chaff.

The last reported statement of John (v. 17) returns to the theme of judgment found in verses 7-9. The "winnowing fork" was a forklike shovel used by farmers to throw the beaten grain into the air so that the wind could blow the husks away from the grain. The Messiah, according to John, will preserve what is valuable and destroy what is worthless, just as a farmer does. This may apply to good and bad individuals or to good and bad aspects of each individual.

3:19-20: Next the narrator very briefly reports the imprisonment of John by Herod the tetrarch. It may seem surprising that this report comes here, before reference to Jesus' baptism. The narrative order does not mean that John was imprisoned before Jesus was baptized or that John belonged to a different epoch of salvation history. The narrator is turning from a section that focuses on John to a much larger section that focuses on Jesus. Before doing so, the narrator prepares for the next narrative segments in which John will figure (7:18-35; 9:7-9), even though this means skipping ahead chronologically. The same technique was used in 1:80.

Later Jesus will be presented as a rejected and suffering prophet (4:24; 13:33-34). The fate of Jesus is foreshadowed by the arrest (and later execution) of John, another prophet who disturbs the powerful and suffers the consequences. John Darr points out that the portraits of Herod and John fit a conventional literary pattern of philosopher versus tyrant and prophet versus evil king. They are playing conventional roles, and their characters would be understood in light of the convention (Darr 1992, 136, 149-60).

Key aspects of John's message return in Peter's preaching at Pentecost. The call to repentance and baptism for forgiveness of sins, with the gift of the Spirit (only anticipated by John), and the warning that people must be saved "from this corrupt generation" (literally, "crooked generation," cf. Luke 3:5) recur in Acts (cf. 2:38, 40). The Lukan audience, then, would probably recall their own encounter with the gospel and their own baptism as they heard about John. Baptism for them was a public decision with social consequences. By individuals and by families they had decided that they would no longer conform to "this corrupt generation," the society that had shaped their past, and they had publicly declared their allegiance to Jesus as Lord and to the community of his followers. This community, a marginal group within its society, had its own standards and a strong sense of cohesion, strong enough to bring together people whose contacts were normally restricted: Jews and Gentiles, women and men, poor and privileged. Repentance, then, meant a change in the community with which one identified and adoption of a new set of community standards to guide behavior. It also meant risking loss of social standing within society at large.

The Empowerment of Jesus (3:21-22)

Although there is considerable similarity between Luke 3:21-22 and Mark 1:9-11, the latter is properly titled "the baptism of Jesus," while the former is not. In Mark the descent of the Spirit and the heavenly voice occur "just as" Jesus rises out of the water. In Luke the Spirit and voice come not at the moment of baptism but afterward, while Jesus is praying. As a result, the focus of attention shifts from Jesus' baptism to the divine affirmation and empowerment in verse 22. Jesus prays to God, like any other devout person, and prayer provides the appropriate state of receptivity for the following revelation. Although Jesus was baptized by John, like the rest of the people, the narrator says nothing about the encounter of John with Jesus, and there is no indication that John recognized Jesus as the "more powerful" one that he had predicted.

The opening of heaven provides the setting for communication between the heavenly world and the world below. This communication has two aspects. First, the Holy Spirit descends in the form of a dove. The coming of the Holy Spirit is Jesus' consecration and empowerment for ministry. Although Jesus was conceived through the Holy Spirit and therefore was already a holy person, consecrated to God's service, as a baby (1:35), this special endowment with the Holy Spirit is necessary for Jesus to begin his work. The narrator makes clear that this is a permanent endowment that leads to ministry, for Jesus is "full of the Holy Spirit" in 4:1, returns to Galilee "filled with the power of the Spirit" in 4:14, and announces in 4:18 that "the Spirit of the Lord is upon me." The reference to "the power of the Spirit" indicates empowerment for ministry, as in Acts 10:38: "God anointed Jesus of Nazareth with the Holy Spirit and with power" (a hendiadys). Although Luke 3:21-22 is not explicitly a commissioning scene, since no mission is described there, consecration with the Holy Spirit does imply a mission, as 4:18-19 indicates. The meaning of the descent of the Spirit in Luke must be understood in light of 4:18-19, where Jesus says, "The Spirit of the Lord is upon me," and describes the mission for which the Spirit has empowered him. In Acts 2, also, the coming of the Spirit leads to mission. The association of the Spirit with a dove in 3:22 is a puzzle for which commentators have no convincing solution.

There is a variant reading in verse 22. Some ancient manuscripts read, "You are my son; today I have begotten you," a quote from

Ps 2:7. The reading adopted in the NRSV is more strongly attested, however, and the variant can be explained from a desire to use a psalm text that had already been given a christological interpretation (as in Acts 13:33). It is possible that the first part of the statement from heaven ("You are my Son") is nevertheless an allusion to Ps 2:7. If so, it is combined with an allusion to Isa 42:1. The words of the heavenly voice do not reflect the LXX of Isaiah, but they are close to the version of Isa 42:1 quoted in Matt 12:18, which refers to God's servant as "my beloved, with whom my soul is well pleased." Furthermore, Isa 42:1 refers to God placing "my Spirit upon him," which fits the context in Luke nicely. Ps 2:7 is addressed to God's anointed king. Isaiah 42:1 is addressed to God's servant, who is to be "a light to the nations" (Isa 42:6; cf. Luke 2:32) and "open the eyes that are blind" (Isa 42:7; cf. Luke 4:18).

Even if the audience missed the allusions to scripture, they would hear the very strong divine affirmation of Jesus. God is affirming a special relationship with Jesus and uses words that express the closest kind of familial and emotional bond. Jesus is "my Son," he is "the Beloved," and he is one with whom God is "well pleased" (an indication of God's special favor). With these words, God confirms a special relationship with Jesus and expresses confidence in him. But with the relationship goes responsibility, for the relationship implies obedience and the gift of the Spirit implies a mission. God's expressed confidence in Jesus binds God's cause to Jesus, who is now responsible for it. Jesus must respond to God's trust by doing God's will. (See Neyrey 1985, 168-70, who notes that in the Hebrew Bible and later Judaism the "designation 'son of God' . . . seems to imply a distinctive moral relationship to God," for this designation is "frequently given to the righteous and the obedient." See also Green 1995, 50.)

In 4:18-19 Jesus discloses that the descent of the Spirit and the divine declaration of sonship are to be understood as an anointing for the mission described in Isa 61:1-2. But first the devil will tempt Jesus with another understanding of his role as Son of God (4:3-13), for it could be understood as privilege rather than calling. Through struggle, Jesus must arrive at the right understanding of his position as Son of God. Only later, after his resurrection and exaltation, will he begin to enjoy the royal power associated with this title in Ps 2 (cf. Acts 13:22-23, 32-33).

Jesus' Genealogy (3:23-38)

Luke's genealogy of Jesus differs markedly from Matt 1:1-17. Luke traces Jesus' lineage to Adam (and God), not just to Abraham. Luke has more generations listed from Jesus to Abraham, and most of the names are different from Matthew's list from Jesus to David. Note that after David, Matthew traces Jesus' line through the line of kings from Solomon onward, while the ancestors of Jesus after the time of David were not kings according to Luke.

Genealogies were important for showing one's ethnic identity and because one's honor in the community depended to a considerable degree on the honor status of one's family. A long genealogy with honorable ancestors was a claim to honor in society (cf. Malina and Rohrbaugh 1992, 305, 310). The presence of David in Jesus' genealogy would add to Jesus' honor, and tracing Jesus' line back to Abraham shows his identity as a Jew. Including God in a Jewish genealogy, however, appears to be unprecedented (cf. M. Johnson 1969, 237; Kurz 1984, 177). This could be a sign of pagan influence, but we should note that the reference to Adam as son of God ties the genealogy into its context, where Jesus is addressed in the same way (3:22; 4:3, 9). Thus a comparison between Jesus and Adam is suggested.

The genealogy is cryptic, and we are left to speculate about this comparison. Tentatively, I would suggest the following: If all of Adam's descendants are also sons (or daughters) of God, simply because they are humans, son of God is no longer a title of distinction. However, son of God is a title of distinction when applied to Jesus, and it is likely that it is also a distinctive title when applied to Adam. It seems that the story in Gen 3 of Adam's disobedience and expulsion from the garden is presupposed. Adam was son of God but lost that honor through disobedience and was not able to pass it on to his descendants. Jesus is the new son of God who takes his place. He also will be tempted by the devil, as were Adam and Eve, but he will be obedient (4:1-13). This obedience will enable him and his people to recover what Adam lost (cf. Neyrey 1985, 168-72).

The Temptations of Jesus (4:1-13)

The description of Jesus as "full of the Holy Spirit" and the introduction of two of the temptations by the phrase "if you are the Son of God" recall 3:21-22. Precisely the special position Jesus was given there and the divine power that goes with it can be the occasion of temptation. Two conflicting views of what it means to be Son of God are presented in the following narrative. The devil suggests what the Spirit-empowered Son of God should do. These suggestions are rejected and, in the Nazareth synagogue, Jesus will present a different understanding of the purpose of his anointing with the Spirit. The clarity of mission revealed in 4:18-19 is gained by first rejecting the devil's alternative interpretation of what it means to be the Spirit-empowered Son of God. The references to Jesus as Son of God also encourage comparison with Adam in 3:38. One Son of God is tempted by the devil and succumbs; the other does not. However, the principal scriptural influence on 4:1-13 is not Genesis but Deuteronomy.

The scene has a clear structure. After the setting (vv. 1-2), there is a threefold dialogue between the devil and Jesus. In each case Jesus responds with a brief quotation from Deuteronomy. Each of the temptations is related to a particular setting: the wilderness, where there is no food; the kingdoms of the world; the temple. The devil's statements are more elaborate in the second and third instances, and in the third the devil argues from scripture. Jesus' responses are always short scriptural quotations. The last two temptations are in reverse order in Matt 4:1-11. The Lukan order gives the temple temptation climactic position within the threefold structure, perhaps because it corresponds to the final temptation in the Gospel, when Jesus must face death in Jerusalem. (There is a much briefer temptation story in Mark 1:12-13.)

◊ ◊ ◊ ◊

We find here a battle of wits and wills, and some interpreters have seen a similarity between this scene and rabbinic debates. In theme, however, it is related to other stories of Satan testing the faith and obedience of righteous individuals, such as Job (cf. Garrett 1989, 41-42, 127 n. 2).

Viewing the power of evil in personal form as the devil or Satan is not unusual in the New Testament or its Jewish environment. However, giving the devil a dramatic role, complete with dialogue, is unusual in the Gospels. When the narrator calls the tempter *the devil*, it is clear that his proposals are evil. Thus the line between good and evil is clearly drawn in this scene. Yet there is subtlety in the devil's proposals. They have some plausibility in light of biblical precedent and hope. The audience's challenge is to understand why these proposals are devilish. The word translated "tempted" can also mean "tested." Both are implied in this scene.

The first temptation assumes that Jesus, being full of the Spirit, has wonder-working power. The devil's proposal is plausible both because of Jesus' physical need and because there is biblical precedent: God provided bread (manna) for the people of Israel in the wilderness. Furthermore, Jesus himself will later provide bread in the wilderness (9:12-17), but not to satisfy his own hunger. Jesus replies to the devil with wisdom shaped by the wilderness experience of Israel, when Israel was tested by God and attempted to put God to the test. Israel's hunger in the wilderness served a purpose. It was to help them understand that "one does not live by bread alone" (Deut 8:3). The devil suggests that the powerful Son of God should be exempt from human needs such as hunger, but Jesus, by his reply, refuses to exempt himself from the human necessity to discipline desires and look beyond one's own needs.

Jesus not only has wonder-working power but, as Son of God, the Messiah, he will have ruling authority. After addressing the king as "my son," God says in Ps 2:8, "Ask of me, and I will make the nations your heritage, and the ends of the earth your possession" (quotations from Ps 2 appear in Acts 4:25-26 and 13:33). Again the temptation seems plausible; the devil is offering a shortcut to messianic rule. But the condition is the worship of evil. Jesus replies with Moses' words when he warned Israel not to follow other gods and forget the Lord (Deut 6:12-14). The Messiah is not exempt from the most basic demand on Israel, that it worship God alone.

The temptations, like Luke's story of Jesus, reach their climax in Jerusalem. In the first two temptations the devil has been defeated by scripture. Now the devil uses scripture in his temptation. Scripture, too, can be dangerous unless it is interpreted out of a clear commitment to the one God. The devil finds in Ps 91:11-12 God's promise to God's Son that he will be protected no matter what the danger. The devil takes the psalm literally: angels will "bear" Jesus "up" if he jumps from a height. Jesus rejects this interpretation, again quoting Moses (Deut 6:16). The Son of God has no more right than Israel did to make demands on God and manipulate God for personal purposes. This will remain true even when Jesus faces death.

The devil "departed" because he had been defeated, but the final words of verse 13 suggest that the struggle is not over. While Jesus during his ministry speaks of triumph over Satan (10:18-19; 11:20-22), the passion story will be the time of Satan's counterattack (22:3, 31, 53).

◊ ◊ ◊ ◊

Does this story have results in the rest of Luke? The clarity of purpose that Jesus shows in 4:18-19 (interpreting 3:22) would seem to depend on Jesus' rejection of the devil's Christology. It is also possible to connect the temptation story with Jesus' later statement about conquering the strong man and dividing his plunder (11:21-22), which is related to Jesus' exorcisms. The temptation story is followed by Jesus' proclamation that he has been sent to proclaim release to captives (4:18) and by stories of Jesus driving out demons (4:33-35, 41). The narrative allows, but does not require, the audience to understand these exorcisms as the result of Jesus' initial victory over the devil.

The temptation story could prompt several kinds of reflection in the Lukan audience. Jews and God-fearers may have been aware of Jewish criticism of the claim that Jesus is the Son of God. This criticism would be especially strong if they detected any tendency to worship Jesus. Many Jews would equate Christian honor of Jesus with idolatry, which is really worship of Satan or demons (1 Cor 10:19-21; cf. Garrett 1989, 40, 130 n. 17). The claim that Jesus is the Son of God would seem to conflict with the command of Moses, "Worship the Lord your God, and serve only him." The fact that God did not preserve Jesus from death on the cross would also count against Christian claims in the eyes of some. The temptation story responds to such criticism by depicting Jesus as the Son of God who fulfills his role precisely because he does not exempt himself from the obedience required of all Israel. He is able to carry out his mission because he knows that God alone must be worshiped and that not even the Messiah can substitute his personal needs and desires for God's purpose. Unless the chosen one worships and obeys God alone, wonder-working power, royal rule, and persuasive use of scripture can all be demonic. The contrast between the Spirit's purpose as described in 4:18-19 and the devil's temptations may later suggest that wonder-working power is also demonic if used for one's own benefit and not for the poor, the captives, and others in need.

Jesus is not the only person in Luke–Acts called to a mission and endowed with power. Acts presents a number of prophetic figures who speak and act with the Spirit's power, and the Lukan communities probably still honored such persons. The temptation story could be a warning to these communities that persons of Spirit-power must be held to the standard of Jesus, which in this case is also the standard of Moses in Deuteronomy.

Jesus Begins His Ministry (4:14-30)

4:14-17: As the public ministry of Jesus begins, the narrator again notes that Jesus is endowed with "the power of the Spirit" as a result of the Spirit descending in 3:22. This power of the Spirit will be manifest in Jesus' ministry. Already in the initial summary in 4:14-15 the narrator indicates widespread interest in, and approval of, Jesus.

Even though the NRSV translates the beginning of verse 15 as "He began to teach," the Greek simply says, "He was teaching in their synagogues," referring to a repeated activity over a period of time. Thus the narrator is not saying that the following scene at Nazareth reports Jesus' first public teaching. That this scene is nevertheless placed first in the narrative of Jesus' ministry is significant. It gives the audience its first impression of what Jesus' teaching was like. Placing this scene first was an important interpretive move, for it suggests that the rest of the Lukan story (Acts as well as Luke) should be read in light of this scene. There is a partial parallel to this scene in Mark 6:1-6 and Matt 13:53-58, but it occurs later in the story of Jesus' ministry and is shorter. It briefly reports the rejection of Jesus in his hometown, with the result that he did few mighty works there. There is no parallel to the words of Jesus in the Lukan scene, except for 4:24. The rejection scene in Mark and Matthew has become a scene in which Jesus announces his mission and is favorably received, yet there is a sudden shift to conflict that almost leads to Jesus' death.

4:18-21: Here Jesus is reading words from Isaiah, but these words relate closely to the Lukan portrait of Jesus and provide an interpretation of his ministry. Isaiah 61:1-2 is presented by Jesus as a statement of his own commission from God. (This is the effect of Jesus' one-sentence comment in v. 21.) In the rest of Luke we will be shown how Jesus fulfilled this commission.

Noting how words and phrases in the quotation correlate with the rest of Luke can help us understand how Isaiah is being interpreted. "The Spirit of the Lord is upon me" recalls 3:22, where the Spirit descended on Jesus (cf. also 4:1, 14). The quotation, however, serves to interpret that event as God's commissioning of Jesus for a particular task. Indeed, the descent of the Spirit was an anointing for office. The Lukan narrator is aware that the verb "anoint" *(chriō)* is related to the Jewish title *christos* ("Anointed One" or "Messiah"; cf. Acts 4:26-27, where the two words are used together). Anointed with the Spirit, Jesus is the Messiah, the king of Israel, yet his immediate function is not royal but prophetic: He is to be the bearer of good news. In contrast to the other Gospels, Luke frequently uses the verb *euangelizomai* ("announce good news") to refer to the preaching of Jesus (4:43; 7:22; 8:1; 9:6; 16:16; 20:1). That this good news is especially for the poor is also characteristically Lukan. The terms "poor," "captives," "blind," and "oppressed" may all have some metaphorical range. Yet in Luke the "poor" means first of all those at the bottom of the economic scale, who may lack even the basics for survival. Jesus in Luke will have much to say about their needs, and the beatitudes in 6:20-21 announce good news to the poor.

Jesus has also been sent "to proclaim release to the captives" (v. 18). Although the quotation follows the LXX of Isa 61:1-2 fairly closely, some editing has taken place. One phrase has been omitted and another has been inserted from Isa 58:6. The inserted phrase is translated "to let the oppressed go free" in the NRSV. This phrase also contains the word "release" *(aphesis)*. (We might translate more literally, "to send out the oppressed in release.") The insertion was evidently made in order to reemphasize this concept. The captives who are to be released probably include at least three groups. The preceding reference to the poor suggests that the captives may be people imprisoned for debt. They may also be people with physical ailments that are regarded as the result of Satan's bondage (13:16) or the devil's oppression (Acts 10:38). Finally, the term "release" is used in the phrase "release of sins" (usually translated "forgiveness of sins"). Forgiveness of sins is an important part of Jesus' ministry, and at the end of Luke, Jesus' followers are instructed to proclaim forgiveness of sins in his name (24:47). Although bringing forgiveness of sins may appear unrelated to the social ministry of proclaiming good news to the poor and of healing people, this is not the case for Luke. Forgiveness also has social consequences, for it requires acceptance of excluded people into the religious community.

"Recovery of sight to the blind" may have both a literal and metaphorical sense in the Lukan context. On the one hand, it can refer to Jesus' healing ministry, which is represented by this one example. On the other hand, sight and light are used metaphorically for perceiving revelation and sharing in salvation. In this sense, Paul, as well as Jesus, has been sent "to open their eyes so that they may turn from darkness to light and from the power of Satan to God" (Acts 26:18; cf. also Luke 1:78-79; 2:30-32; Acts 26:23).

"The year of the Lord's favor" (literally, "the Lord's acceptable year") is, in the context of Isaiah, a reference to the Jubilee year, the fiftieth year when, according to Mosaic law, family property is to revert to its original owners and indentured servants are to be released (Lev 25:8-55; note also that debts are to be canceled every seventh year according to Deut 15:1-11). The emphasis on release in Luke 4:18 relates to this, for the Jubilee year is also called the "year of release" (Lev 25:10 LXX). This remarkable social legislation was designed to give the poor a new start. It is unclear whether the Lukan narrator recognized the Jubilee background of Isa 61:1-2, but the concern for the poor that motivated the Jubilee legislation permeates Luke. (On the Jubilee and its reflections in the Gospels, see Ringe 1985, 16-90.) Although in the context of Luke "the Lord's acceptable year" may not mean a literal year, it probably does refer to a special time, the time of the approach of God's kingdom or reign as announced by Jesus (note the rephrasing of 4:18-19 in 4:43; for a fuller discussion of 4:18-19, see Tannehill 1986, 61-68).

4:22-30: The response of the congregation is at first very favorable (v. 22), but then there is a sharp shift in mood. In verse 24 Jesus states that "no prophet is accepted in the prophet's hometown." Have the people of Nazareth done anything to deserve this rebuke from Jesus?

The people ask, "Is not this Joseph's son?" (v. 22). This question should be understood in connection with verse 23, which refers to what Jesus should do in his hometown. Thus the question is not intended to denigrate Jesus but to point out that he is a hometown boy. According to the culture, this involves obligations. One must give preference to one's own family and village. (See Malina 1993, 47-70, on "in-group" loyalty in Mediterranean society.) In verse 23 Jesus expresses for the people their assumptions about his obligations. The words "and you will say" in the NRSV are not in the Greek and should be ignored. They suggest that Jesus' second statement in verse 23 is unrelated to the first, but actually the second interprets the first. "Doctor, cure yourself!" means bring the promised release to your own people, and don't allow Capernaum to get the benefits that we should have (for this application of the proverb, see Noorda 1982, 463-65). To this implied demand Jesus responds in verse 24: A prophet is not going to be pleasing to his hometown, for a prophet is not governed by in-group loyalties. Jesus, who takes the role of prophet during his ministry, is governed by the purpose of God and the precedent of scriptural prophets. Therefore, his ministry will focus not on the in-group but on the excluded. Those who cannot accept this priority will find the prophet unacceptable.

The way the scriptural prophets behaved is indicated by two incidents, one involving Elijah, the other Elisha (cf. 1 Kings 17:1-24; 2 Kings 5:1-19). In both cases the brief story-summaries emphasize that there were many in Israel who might have benefited from the wonder-working prophet, yet it was actually a Gentile who received the benefit. (The widow received food miraculously during the famine, and her son was revived by Elijah.) These incidents show that the work of a prophet is not guided and limited by in-group loyalties. Moreover, these cases provide scriptural precedent for the Gentile mission in Acts. In one sense, they are out of place, for Jesus himself will seldom minister to Gentiles. Yet the rejection Jesus will experience in Nazareth will be experienced by his witnesses in Acts, leading them to turn from Jews to Gentiles (Acts 13:44-47; 18:5-7; 28:24-28; cf. also 22:17-22). Jesus does not turn to Gentiles but to Capernaum (4:31). It is possible that the widow and Naaman had further significance for the Lukan audience. The widow was a very poor woman; Naaman was the commander of the Syrian king's army, a wealthy man of high rank. Although both are Gentiles, they could represent the social, economic, and gender diversity of the Lukan communities (cf. Esler 1987, 179-80). Elijah and Elisha will serve as models of Jesus' healing ministry later in Luke (cf. below on 7:1-17).

Once the people of Nazareth are reminded that prophets do not respect in-group loyalties, they demonstrate the truth of 4:24. Jesus is indeed unacceptable in his hometown. In a rage the people take him out to hurl him from a cliff. Jesus passes through the angry crowd and leaves. The narrator leaves us to wonder how.

◊ ◊ ◊ ◊

The scene of Jesus in the Nazareth synagogue would remind Jews and God-fearers in the Lukan audience of their own participation in a synagogue. The memory might be painful, for conflict between synagogue leaders and the followers of Jesus may have ended the possibility of synagogue attendance for the latter (cf. John 9:22).

Jesus' rejection at Nazareth would remind the Lukan audience, whether Jew or Gentile, of the conflict they face with Jews who feel threatened by the Christian movement. In particular, the angry reaction to Jesus' statements about the widow and Naaman may partially parallel the effect of Gentiles in the church (whether of low or high status) on Jewish critics of the Lukan communities. Loyalty to the Jewish community would not immediately disappear among Jews and God-fearers, but the scene of Jesus in Nazareth would urge all Christian believers to recognize the importance of carrying Jesus' benefits beyond the in-group.

The quotation from Isaiah defines Jesus' mission. This definition has implications for the early church's understanding of its own mission and its life as a community. The emphasis on good news for the poor stands in tension with the strong tendency in ancient Mediterranean society to regard the elite as those rightly favored by gods and humans. (On the elite's conviction of superiority in character and Roman law's discrimination in favor of the elite, see Esler 1987, 172-73; Garnsey 1970, 1-10, 221-23.) This attitude would not immediately disappear when people entered the community of Jesus. The Lukan audience might need repeated reminders of Jesus' orientation toward the poor and other people in need.

Jesus' Mighty Acts in Capernaum (4:31-44)

In this section, Luke parallels Mark 1:21-39, sometimes quite closely, sometimes with additions or changes. One significant difference: in Mark this material follows the call of the first disciples, but in Luke it precedes their call. This section contains four scenes united by time and place. These scenes report what happened at Capernaum on one day and the following morning.

At the beginning of this section, Jesus is teaching on the sabbath in a synagogue, and the people are astounded. These features are similar to the first part of the scene in Nazareth (4:16-22). The connection with the Nazareth scene is reinforced by the conclusion at 4:43-44. There, in a summary statement about Jesus' mission, three terms are repeated from 4:18-19: "proclaim the good news" *(euangelisasthai)*, "I was sent" *(apestalēn)*, and "proclaiming" *(kērysson)*. This statement, which differs from Mark, tells the audience that Jesus is continuing to do what he was sent to do according to 4:18-19. The statements of vocation in 4:18-19 and 4:43-44 frame the intervening material and together fill out the reference to Jesus teaching in synagogues in 4:15. The frame unifies this segment of the narrative, suggesting a comparison between Nazareth and Capernaum. This frame also suggests that Jesus' teaching in Capernaum (vv. 31-32) was similar to the message Jesus brought to Nazareth.

The suggested comparison between Nazareth and Capernaum highlights the difference between the two accounts. Jesus is rejected in Nazareth but eagerly sought out in Capernaum. (Nevertheless, when the people of Capernaum try to prevent Jesus from leaving in verse 42, they may show the same desire to keep Jesus for themselves as surfaced in Nazareth.) In Capernaum we find Jesus doing the mighty acts of healing that the Nazarenes evidently wanted (v. 23). We are told that Jesus also taught in Capernaum (vv. 31-32) but are not told the content of his teaching. The content of Jesus' teaching was sufficiently indicated in the Nazareth section, to which the Capernaum section adds the mighty acts of healing that Nazareth missed. Together the two sections present what "Jesus did and taught," as the narrator summarizes in Acts 1:1.

4:31-37: The first scene in Capernaum is an exorcism story. In exorcism stories, Jesus meets a person possessed by a demon and forces the demon to depart, freeing the person from this evil influence. At the point of exorcism, the story focuses on the interaction between Jesus and the demon, who speaks and acts through the possessed person. Jesus may sometimes also interact with an accompanying person, such as a father or mother, who speaks on behalf of the possessed person (cf. 9:37-43), but that possibility is not developed in this first exorcism story. Belief in demons (or "unclean spirits") is well attested in Jewish literature of the time and was widespread among other peoples as well. This belief is accepted in the synoptic Gospels and provides the basis for exorcism stories. In other ancient literature, demons are driven off in various ways. Noah was given medicines to ward off evil spirits

(*Jub.* 10:9-13), Tobias got rid of a demon by burning things with a repellent odor (Tobit 8:1-3), and Eleazar, by using a ring with a special root in it, drew a demon out of a man's nostrils (Josephus *Ant.* 8 §45-49). Jesus acts by his commanding word.

The demon asks, "Have you come to destroy us?" We are probably to understand that the answer is yes. The coming of God's reign is marked by the end of the power of demons and the devil (11:20). The demons can recognize Jesus. This demon calls Jesus "the Holy One of God," which repeats a theme from 1:35 and also accents the difference between Jesus and the demon, who is "unclean" (v. 33), the opposite of holy. Jesus "rebuked" the demon, which, in the context of an exorcism story, means that Jesus spoke a powerful word that subdued the demon. The amazement of the crowd is a regular part of healing and exorcism stories, but here (v. 36) the crowd comments on Jesus' authoritative "word," to which the narrator previously referred (v. 32). (This emphasis on Jesus' authoritative "word" is obscured in NRSV.) Jesus' word had authority both in his teaching and in his exorcism. This theme will continue with Jesus preaching "the word of God" in 5:1.

4:38-39: The exorcism of a man is followed by the healing of a woman, Simon's mother-in-law. The bland translation "was suffering" misses a significant nuance. Luke, in contrast to Mark, says that the woman "was seized" or "held captive" by the fever. Jesus "rebuked" the fever just as he had rebuked the demon, opposing his powerful word to its oppressive force. Then the fever "left her" or "released her," an example of "release to the captives" announced in 4:18. Thus the fever is treated as if it were a demonic power. The woman's healing is demonstrated by the recovery of her ability to serve her family and offer hospitality to her guest.

4:40-44: Two individual accounts of Jesus' mighty acts are followed by a summary of many more healings and exorcisms. In the shouts of the demons, the narrator picks up two titles from the infancy narrative, "Son of God" and "Messiah" (1:35; 2:11). In 4:41 the narrator interprets "Son of God" as "Messiah," showing that they are synonyms. Jesus does not allow the demons to reveal him. Evidently it is not yet time for Jesus to claim his messianic role.

Jesus' mission cannot be restricted to one place, where he would become the local healer. As noted above, Jesus uses key terms from 4:18-19 in summarizing his mission in verse 43. However, an important phrase is added for the first time, "the kingdom of God." The "good news to the poor" and proclamation of "release to the captives" is also "the good news of the kingdom of God," for in Jesus, God's sovereign power is appearing, bringing justice and salvation to needy people. Healings by Jesus and his disciples are to be understood as particular manifestations of God's royal rule, now appearing (cf. 10:9; 11:20). Jesus "must" proclaim this good news because this is God's calling for him (4:18, "He has sent me to . . . "). "Judea" in verse 44 probably refers to the whole of the Jewish homeland, including Galilee. This verse indicates that the synagogue preaching noted in Nazareth and Capernaum is a regular and continuing part of Jesus' ministry, and this preaching is to be understood on the model of the Nazareth scene.

◊ ◊ ◊ ◊

Members of the Lukan audience would relate stories of Jesus as healer and exorcist to their own health problems. Some of them may have experienced healing "in the name of Jesus" (Acts 3:6); others may have hoped for healing but were disappointed. The stories of Jesus as healer would encourage all in the Lukan communities to continue hoping that their health problems could be solved through the power of Jesus the healer, which continues to operate through his name. (On the "name" of Jesus in Acts, see Tannehill 1990, 39-40, 49, 53-54.) This power was conferred on Jesus' disciples (Luke 9:1; 10:9) and continues in Acts, where, among other wonders, Peter heals a lame man (Acts 3:1-10) and Paul performs an exorcism (16:16-18). Acts attests that Jesus' healing power did not depart with the earthly Jesus.

Scholars who study health issues on an intercultural basis distinguish between "disease," which reflects the modern biomedical perspective, and "illness," which refers to a socially disvalued state as defined by a particular culture (cf. Pilch in Neyrey 1991, 191-92). Modern medicine works with disease; folk healing (of which healing in the early church would be an example) works with illness.

Folk healing accepts and works within the worldview of the culture in which it is practiced; the beliefs of that culture are used as resources for healing (cf. Pilch in Neyrey 1991, 198-200). Folk healing does not distinguish (at least, in the modern scientific way) among biological, psychological, and social factors in a malady and may try to affect all of these areas at once. The stories of Jesus as healer would be understood by the Lukan audience as encouragement to use the resources of their faith for their own kind of folk healing.

A DEVELOPING MISSION CENTERED IN GALILEE (5:1–9:50)

The Call of the First Disciples (5:1-11)

This scene, in which Jesus chooses his first disciples, replaces the scene of Jesus calling four fishermen in Matt 4:18-22 and Mark 1:16-20. Luke's scene is similar to those in Matthew and Mark in the following respects: (1) the new disciples are fishermen; (2) Jesus' statement to them relates to their previous role as fishermen; and (3) the fishermen leave and follow Jesus. But Luke's story has developed in a unique way through inclusion of a wondrous catch of fish. This aspect of the story is related to John 21:1-11, which, however, has a postresurrection setting. The setting of Luke's story differs also from Matthew and Mark, which give no indication of previous contact between Jesus and the fishermen. In Luke, Jesus has already taught in Capernaum and has healed many, including Simon's mother-in-law. Simon Peter already knows something of Jesus' mission and power before he is asked to share in Jesus' work. Thus a basis has been laid for his acceptance of Jesus' call.

Luke 5:1-11 is an expanded pronouncement story, coming to its climax in the pronouncement of Jesus in verse 10. Pronouncement stories are brief narratives in which the climactic element is a pronouncement (or a pronouncement and an action) that is presented as someone's response to something said or observed on a particular occasion. Thus a pronouncement story consists primarily of a situation provoking a response and the resulting response. It is a common literary type in Greco-Roman literature, where it is sometimes called a *chreia*. (For a collection of many examples, see Robbins 1989.)

Luke 5:1-11 is an expanded pronouncement story because it contains a provision wonder. A provision wonder in the Gospels presents Jesus providing a wondrous supply of food or drink for people. Besides the stories of great catches of fish in Luke and John, there are stories of Jesus feeding crowds in the wilderness with a few loaves and fish (Matt 14:13-21; 15:32-39; Mark 6:32-44; 8:1-10; Luke 9:10-17; John 6:1-15) and of Jesus providing wine for a wedding (John 2:1-11). The provision stories tend to take on symbolic significance.

◊ ◊ ◊ ◊

Luke 5:1-11 may be divided into three parts, verses 1-3: Jesus teaching the crowd along the lake; verses 4-7: the great catch of fish; verses 8-11: the dialogue between Simon and Jesus. How do these three parts relate to one another? The first part presents Jesus engaged in the mission that he described in 4:43. In the third part we learn about Simon Peter's role in this same mission. This mission material frames the middle part, the great catch of fish. After the "catch" of fish, Jesus says to Simon, "From now on you will be catching people." Here catching fish becomes a metaphor for missionary activity. This shift to metaphorical language invites the audience to understand the great catch of fish on a second level: as a symbolic narrative of the amazingly successful mission that Jesus is starting and that Simon and others will continue. This understanding integrates the middle part with the mission theme in the rest of the scene, and also adds complexity to the scene. The great catch of fish both contributes to Simon's decision to follow Jesus and previews the success of his future mission.

The discipleship episode focuses on Simon Peter. James and John are mentioned secondarily (v. 10), and Andrew (the fourth fisherman in Mark 1:16-20) is not mentioned at all. This focus matches the central role that Peter will have in Acts 1–12 as the early church's mission begins.

As a result of their encounter with Jesus, the fishermen "left everything and followed him" (v. 11). This introduces a Lukan theme: those called by Jesus must leave everything (cf. 5:28; 14:33; 18:22-23). Although possessions are meant in some of these passages, we do not understand the radical nature of the disciples' decision unless we recognize the importance of a local social network, especially the kinship group, to people of that time. Social science criticism distinguishes our individualistic culture from the "dyadic" or group-oriented culture of the first-century Mediterranean world. People did not think of themselves as independent individuals but took their identity from a social unit, particularly the family, which required loyalty and conformity. "Group-oriented persons internalize and make their own what others say, do, and think about them because they believe it is necessary, if they are to be human beings, to live out the expectations of others" (Malina and Neyrey in Neyrey 1991, 73; cf. 72-74). "Leaving everything" means leaving the family (cf. 14:26) and leaving one's means of support. The family was the primary producing unit in antiquity. Whatever economic security there was came through the family. In leaving their families these men were abandoning family responsibilities and their own security. However, we will see later that they moved from an original family to a "surrogate family," the community of disciples (cf. 8:19-21), as the primary group (cf. Malina and Rohrbaugh 1992, 335-36). This decision did not suddenly make the disciples individuals in the modern sense, but it would take some strength and independence to decide against the group to which society gave the highest value.

In 5:1-11 Simon comes to this decision by steps of deepening involvement with Jesus. First he allows Jesus to use his boat. Then, contrary to his own judgment as a fisherman, he follows Jesus' directions and lets down his nets. The amazing catch of fish is recognized by Simon as a manifestation of divine power. This by itself does not lead Simon to follow Jesus, however. Indeed, Simon says, "Go away from me, Lord, for I am a sinful man!" The manifestation of the holy does not attract but repels, for Simon sees himself as an unworthy sinner, threatened by the holy. Simon's decision to leave all and follow Jesus can only come after Jesus' reassurance ("do not be afraid") and promise ("from now on you will be catching people"). This promise opens a new future and is equivalent to forgiveness. It enables Simon to stop viewing himself as a sinner and to become a companion of Jesus. Interestingly, the episode moves through the same three steps as the call of Isaiah (Isa 6:1-8): from revelation of the holy to confession of sin to call.

◊ ◊ ◊ ◊

The majority of early Christians did not leave their homes and families to go off preaching the gospel. Most of the Lukan audience, then, might distinguish between Simon's call and their own call. Nevertheless, this scene would encourage the Lukan audience to respect those who did leave their homes, support them with hospitality, and do their part to share the gospel on the local scene. The conflict with family suggested in verse 11 could be a problem even for those who stayed home (cf. 12:51-53). It would take some courage to stand up to family members who did not want one to join this semi-Jewish sect.

Cleansing a Leper (5:12-16)

The setting of this story "in one of the cities" reminds the audience of Jesus' plan in 4:43 to proclaim the kingdom "to the other cities also." This mission involves both preaching and healing. The crowds respond by coming both to hear and to be healed (5:15).

At this point Luke returns to the order of Mark. Luke 5:12-16 parallels Matt 8:1-4 and Mark 1:40-45. There are some noteworthy differences from Mark, however. Luke drops two expressions of strong emotion by Jesus (Mark 1:41, 43), places less emphasis on Jesus' command to speak to no one, and omits the leper's disobedience of this command.

◊ ◊ ◊ ◊

This episode shares many of the standard features of a healing story in the Gospels. As in other healing stories, Jesus encounters a person in need of healing, and the nature of the problem is briefly indicated (v. 12). Jesus responds, in this case with both touch and a word of healing (v. 13a). The healing takes place (v. 13b), it will be publicly confirmed (v. 14), and there is a public response (v. 15). The Lukan narrator, however, uses additional structuring devices. In 5:1-26 and 6:1-16 the narrator repeatedly uses the phrase *kai egeneto* or *egeneto de* ("and it happened") to indicate the beginning of a new episode. In 5:12, as elsewhere, this is followed by a brief indication of the general setting, leading to *idou* ("behold"), which serves to focus our attention on the specific person (the leper) who will precipitate the main action of the episode. The healing takes place "immediately" (v. 13), again a regular theme (cf. 4:39; 5:25; 8:44, 55; 13:13; 18:43; cf. Busse 1979, 456-58). (Both "and it happened" and "behold" are omitted in the NRSV in order to achieve smoother English.)

Knowing what is typical in healing stories (as indicated above) can help us recognize what is special in an individual story. Here the leper, in his petition, says, "Lord, if you choose, you can make me clean." The point at issue, this suggests, is not whether Jesus is able to heal but whether he will choose to heal this leper. Jesus responds, "I do choose. Be made clean." The leper is not certain that Jesus will be willing to attend to the needs of someone who is ritually unclean and excluded from society. Jesus declares that he is willing, and touching the man is an extra indication that he is not put off by the man's uncleanness. Jesus' command to the man to show himself to the priest also indicates that social isolation is a major issue in this scene. It is through a priestly ritual that the man can be publicly recognized as clean and reintegrated into society (Lev 14:1-32). Only then will the healing be complete, for the malady is not only physical but also social. The phrase "for a testimony to them" in Luke 5:14 could mean testimony to Jesus' healing power, but in connection with the cleansing ritual it probably means testimony that the former leper is now acceptable in society.

"Leprosy" in the Bible should not be identified with the disease that we now call leprosy (Hansen's disease), for it included a number of skin diseases, and in Leviticus 13–14 it even includes molds that affect clothing and houses. Thus the suffering of the leper of biblical times was due, in many cases, not so much to the severity of the disease as to the way that the leper was treated by religious society. (On ways a leper was to be marked and isolated, see Lev 13:45-46.)

Jesus will heal other lepers in 17:11-19. Lepers were one of the outcast groups in Jesus' society, along with "tax collectors and sinners" (5:30) and the street beggars mentioned in 14:21. These outcast groups were the special focus of Jesus' ministry, according to Luke.

This segment ends with a summary statement. Crowds would repeatedly gather to hear Jesus and be cured, but Jesus would repeatedly interrupt his work by withdrawing to isolated places for prayer. Jesus is not understood to be self-sufficient in Luke. He is dependent on God, and his power must be refreshed through prayer.

Challenges from Scribes and Pharisees (5:17–6:11)

In 5:17–6:11 we find a series of scenes in which Jesus or his disciples are challenged by the scribes and Pharisees. There is a growing sense of conflict in this section, culminating in the strong opposition privately expressed in 6:11.

Authority to Forgive Sins (5:17-26)

This passage has parallels in Matt 9:1-8 and Mark 2:1-12. One of the interesting differences between Mark and Luke is that Mark pictures a dirt and stick roof, which can be dug through, while Luke pictures a tile roof, whose tiles can be removed. Luke also differs from Mark in setting this scene in the presence of Pharisees and teachers of the law "from every village of Galilee and Judea and from Jerusalem." Such a gathering, representing the Pharisees and scribes of the whole Jewish homeland, not only indicates that Jesus was attracting widespread attention but also suggests that the following event is especially important for the encounter between these groups and Jesus.

The narrator first refers to "teachers of the law" before calling them "scribes" (v. 21) because "scribes" could simply refer to secretaries or recorders. These scribes are something more; they are learned in the Jewish law and recognized as teachers. The scribes and Pharisees are not to be identified with Jews in general. Comparatively few Jews belonged to the three Jewish parties, the Pharisees, Essenes, and Sadducees (cf. E. P. Sanders 1992, 14). The Pharisees, and the scribes associated with them, are especially important in the Gospels, however, for they are used to express a point of view against which Jesus' own views are defined.

Most of the material in 5:17–6:11 fits a formal type frequently called the "controversy dialogue" but also called the "objection story." In this subtype of the pronouncement story, someone objects to what Jesus or his disciples have said or done, leading to a (usually forceful) response by Jesus (cf. Tannehill 1981, 8-9). The first and last scenes in this section (5:17-26; 6:6-11) also involve healing and have characteristics of healing stories. In both cases the healing is part of Jesus' response to his critics. Although some interpreters regard a combination of two recognized literary types in a single scene as an indication of secondary conflation, both scenes are well-structured narratives.

Because the action in 5:17-26 begins with a paralyzed man and his companions on a quest for healing, and ends with the success of this quest, this scene can also be viewed as a quest story (cf. Tannehill 1986, 111-13). From this perspective, interest focuses on whether the quest will be successful, and tension arises because two obstacles must be overcome: a crowd blocks entrance to Jesus and then scribes and Pharisees object to Jesus' statement of forgiveness. However, the challenge to Jesus by the scribes and Pharisees and Jesus' response to them are very prominent in this story, so it is possible to view this scene as primarily an objection story. (The purpose of discussing literary types is not necessarily to come up with a single "right" classification but to appreciate the ways a story's formal structure can contribute to its nuances.) In verse 24 Jesus addresses both the objectors and the paralyzed man because his words and his act of healing are doing two things at once: responding to the objection in verse 21 and responding to the need of the paralyzed man, bringing his quest to a successful end.

◊ ◊ ◊ ◊

The paralyzed man's companions let him down through the roof, and Jesus "saw their faith" (v. 20). Their bold action demonstrated their faith. This is a good example of the way that the term "faith" is used in healing stories. It does not mean confession of Jesus as Son of God. It means trusting that God can help through Jesus and doing all that is necessary to secure that help. It is the opposite of passivity and shows itself in courageous action (cf. 7:50; 8:48; 17:19; 18:42).

Jesus responds to the paralyzed man by saying, "Your sins are forgiven you," which causes the objection of the scribes and Pharisees. This objection introduces conflict, heightens suspense, and focuses attention on the issue of Jesus' authority to forgive. Jesus' statement in verse 20 assumes that forgiveness of sins is the key to healing for this paralyzed man. The story need not imply that every health problem is caused by sin, only that the man's sins are a significant factor in this case.

It is not true that first-century Jews denied any role to humans in mediating God's forgiveness, for, according to Mosaic law, the priests have just such a role. There were, however, prescribed sacrifices, and repentance with restitution was important (cf. E. P. Sanders 1985, 206-8). Probably the objection is against Jesus, who is not a priest, forgiving simply by saying so. In verse 23 Jesus asks, "Which is easier . . . ?" and the implication seems to be that the healing is more difficult because it is publicly verifiable and, in this case, must include forgiveness. The healing thus becomes the way of demonstrating effective forgiveness. This is the way that Jesus puts the matter in verse 24, first addressing his critics, then the paralyzed man. Thus Jesus' claim is vindicated by the healing, according to this scene. This claim is put in strong terms in verse 24: "so that you may know that the Son of Man has authority on earth to forgive sins." This is a sweeping claim to authority that applies to Jesus' whole ministry. This scene serves to fortify this claim against doubters. Note that Jesus' authority to forgive does not await his later death on the cross.

In verses 25-26 the Lukan narrator adds to Mark by having the healed man, as well as the bystanders, glorify God. Glorifying God is a frequent feature of Lukan healing stories. God is the true source of healing and the one to be glorified (cf. 7:16; 9:43; 13:13; 17:15, 18; 18:43; 19:37). The conclusion of the scene ("amazement seized all of them, and they glorified God") seems to indicate that even the many scribes and Pharisees present were amazed and impressed. Temporarily the criticism is silenced, but it will soon reappear.

◊ ◊ ◊ ◊

It would, of course, be very important to the Lukan audience that forgiveness of sins be available through Jesus, without following the prescriptions of the Jewish law. In this and the following scenes of controversy with scribes and Pharisees, the early followers of Jesus are being taught their identity as a people separate from non-Christian Jews. Such self-definition in distinction from others is a necessary process in group formation. It enables the group to cohere and to embrace a distinctive set of values and practices. It also has its dangers, for it can build prejudice against outside groups who are seen as regular opponents. Members of these groups may no longer be viewed as human beings who must be treated honestly and respectfully. Careless reading of Luke can lead to this kind of prejudice against the scribes and Pharisees.

Feasting with Sinners Instead of Fasting (5:27-39)

A brief call story (5:27-28) is followed by two pronouncement stories (5:29-32, 33-35) in which Jesus responds to objections by "the Pharisees and their scribes" to the way that Jesus and his followers are eating and drinking. Although the two pronouncement stories are separate scenes in Matt 9:10-15 and Mark 2:15-20, they are combined as part of a continuing dialogue in Luke. The Pharisees and scribes in Luke 5:30 continue the discussion by asking Jesus about fasting. In verses 36-39 Jesus adds some metaphorical sayings, which, in Luke, are separated by a new introduction, "He also told them a parable."

5:27-35: In 5:8 Simon confessed that he was a sinner. Now Jesus calls a tax collector. Jesus' tendency to make disreputable people his disciples causes criticism in verse 30. The taxes collected by Levi included tolls or customs duties on goods being taken to market. Levi should be distinguished from an official like Zacchaeus, who is described as a "chief tax collector" and "rich" (19:2). Levi is working for one of these chief tax collectors and does not have the same opportunities to get rich. Yet tax collectors, as a class, were despised because of the burdensome taxes and because the system encouraged those who obtained tax contracts to pressure their employees into gouging as much as possible from people. In 3:12-13 John the Baptist only requires that tax collectors be fair; they need not leave their jobs. Levi, however, is abandoning his job, since he "left everything" to follow Jesus (as the fishermen did in 5:11).

"Sinners" are a distinct group of people, the outcasts of Jewish society. In 5:31-32 Jesus attempts to change negative attitudes toward them and toward his own ministry by a metaphor. Judge the situation, he suggests, from the perspective of a physician. Most would admit that a physician rightly goes to those in need of healing. Think of my ministry in the same way. Then Jesus adds a fundamental statement about his mission, "I have come to call not the righteous but sinners to repentance."

The words "to repentance" are not in Mark. This addition might seem to be an accommodation to the Pharisees' perspective, since they cannot really object if sinners are repenting. However, the Pharisees and their scribes do not see sinners mournfully repenting; they see people at a banquet. The objection to Jesus eating and drinking with tax collectors and sinners may be due less to purity rules than to the fact that these meals are celebrations, joyful parties that seem inappropriate for people who need to repent.

The narrator's decision to combine the question about fasting with the preceding scene indicates that this is the issue. Fasting accompanies urgent prayer. Especially, it is a sign of repentance for sin. If Jesus is indeed calling sinners to repentance, why are they feasting rather than fasting? Jesus defends his disciples by picturing the present situation as a wedding party, when no one fasts. His statement makes clear that the banquet in Levi's house was a celebration, not an ordinary meal. Jesus is also saying something important about repentance. Repentance does not consist of mourning and fasting. Rather, one's life is turned around through the joyful discovery of a new opportunity. The sign of repentance can be the joy of finding and being found. This point will be made at greater length in Luke 15, which begins by repeating the scene in

5:29-32. Again the Pharisees and scribes are "grumbling" because Jesus is eating with sinners. Jesus responds with parables showing that joy, especially joy at a meal of celebration, is the appropriate sign of repentance (15:7, 10, 23, 32).

The final fulfillment of the reign of God is pictured in the Gospels as a glorious dinner party (see Luke 13:28-29; 14:15-24; 22:16-18), and the banquet in Levi's house may have been an anticipation of this kingdom banquet. The wedding imagery in 5:34 also supports this connection (for the kingdom as a wedding banquet, see Matt 25:1-12; Rev 19:9). These parties with tax collectors and sinners would then have great religious significance. By celebrating with these people, Jesus indicated that they had received God's forgiveness and would share in the reign of God.

5:36-39: The sayings about the new and old garments and the new wine and old wineskins (5:36-38) relate to the issues just discussed but also to the broader context. The newness includes Jesus' claim to forgive sins (5:24), his sharing in parties with tax collectors and sinners, and also his attitude toward the sabbath (6:1-11). On all these points there are conflicts with the scribes and Pharisees, who here represent the old. Jesus, in Luke, is insisting that his community be allowed to adopt the new ways of acting that fit their new situation. The statement in verse 39, found only in Luke, is probably a sober recognition of continuing opposition because of the strong tendency to stick with the old.

◊ ◊ ◊ ◊

In 4:18 Jesus announced that he was sent to proclaim "release." This includes the "release" (or "forgiveness") of sins. The scenes with the paralyzed man and Levi show Jesus carrying out this mission. Jesus' statements that he has authority to forgive sins (5:24) and has come to call sinners to repentance (5:32) add definition to Jesus' mission by highlighting the importance of repentance and forgiveness in Jesus' continuing work. Echoes of the language of 5:20-32 in later passages will remind the audience of what they learned about Jesus here (cf. 7:34, 48-50; 15:1-2, 7; 19:1-10).

COMMENTARY

Sabbath Observance (6:1-11)

Luke continues to follow Mark here (cf. Mark 2:23–3:6; also Matt 12:1-14). The preceding controversies with scribes and Pharisees (Luke 5:17-39) are completed with two more pronouncement stories of the objection story or controversy dialogue subtype. These two scenes discuss sabbath observance.

6:1-5: Refraining from work on the sabbath is a very important part of Mosaic law and Jewish practice. It is one of the Ten Commandments (Exod 20:8-11), and in Num 15:32-36 God demands death by stoning for a man who has broken this commandment. The severity of this was mitigated by the provision that one who commits a sin unintentionally can receive atonement through a sin offering (Lev 4:27-31), and later rabbinic interpretation imposed conditions that restricted the application of the death penalty. Nevertheless, observance of the sabbath was considered to be a major aspect of God's rules for the covenant people, and Jews took the sabbath seriously, even though it cost them to do so. Even in war they were willing to fight on the sabbath only when attacked on that day, which enabled their enemies to work without opposition on the sabbath in preparing to capture the temple (Josephus *J.W.* 1 §145-47; cf. E. P. Sanders 1992, 209).

Plucking grain with the hands in someone else's field is explicitly permitted in Deut 23:25, but doing so on the sabbath is another matter. The Pharisees regard it as reaping (prohibited work), and rubbing the grain with the hands to get the husks off is considered threshing. Jesus and his disciples, on their travels, probably depended on the hospitality of others, supplemented by what they could pick for themselves in the fields. They might not have had the means to prepare sabbath food in advance, as other Jews would do.

Jesus responds to the accusation by citing the behavior of David as reported in 1 Sam 21:1-6. In 1 Samuel, Ahimelech the priest (not Abiathar, as stated in Mark) agrees to give David the holy bread. As the Gospels retell the story, however, all the attention is on David, who seems to act on his own authority in a situation of immediate need. Although the David incident does not deal with sabbath law, it provides a precedent from which to argue that the law must be flexible in cases of human hunger. To this argument is added the assertion, "The Son of Man is lord of the sabbath." Jesus here claims authority to interpret and apply the sabbath law in light of his divine commission and his insight into the will of God. This claim to authority is comparable to 5:24.

6:6-11: The healing of the man with the withered hand moves the conflict a step forward. (Luke, unlike Mark, specifies the *right* hand, i.e., the most important one.) The relation of Jesus to the scribes and Pharisees has deteriorated to the point that they are watching him in order to find a basis for bringing a formal charge against him. Jesus has already performed an exorcism on the sabbath, and news of this spread widely (4:31-37). The scribes and Pharisees now want to know whether Jesus makes a regular practice of healing on the sabbath. (This is the implication of v. 7 in the Greek.) Jesus responds not by avoiding conflict but by challenging his opponents. He orders the man to "stand in the middle" of the group, where he can be seen by the greatest number (= "stand here" in the NRSV). Then he asks his opponents a probing question that requires them to choose between these alternatives for the sabbath: "to do good or to do harm . . . to save life or to destroy it." Jesus' question is clearly argumentative, and the opponents would likely reply that failure to do good out of respect for God's law need not mean doing harm. Yet in certain situations it might. The rabbis later formally recognized that immediate danger to life overrides the sabbath restrictions (*m. Yoma* 8:6). They were probably recognizing what had been standard practice for some time. In such a case, failure to save life would destroy it. Jesus' question stretches this principle by adding as a parallel "to do good or to do harm." By implication he is arguing that the same principle can apply to situations where life is not at stake. The failure to do good is actually doing harm if an opportunity is lost. The healer who is present today may not be present tomorrow. In such situations, refusal to heal is an act with harmful consequences.

Although Luke omits Mark's references to Jesus' anger and grief, Jesus' question is still challenging and his behavior provocative. He commands the man to stretch out his hand, and as the man does so, it is restored. Thus Jesus answers his own question of what is lawful on the sabbath by healing. However, it may be significant that he does not lay hands on the man. That could be construed as work, while simply speaking is not (cf. E. P. Sanders 1990, 21). Jesus makes his provocative point, but no accusation is forthcoming. Luke considerably softens the end of the scene, for in Mark the Pharisees begin to plot Jesus' death. In Luke the scribes and Pharisees are "filled with *anoia*," which can mean madness, folly, or ignorance (the NRSV translates "fury"). Perhaps this means that they almost went crazy with frustration and anger; perhaps it is a general comment on the lack of perception shown by the scribes and Pharisees throughout 5:17–6:11. In the latter case they share the "ignorance *(agnoia)*" that the rulers and people of Jerusalem will show when they bring about Jesus' death (Acts 3:17; cf. 13:27). This is a perverse blindness, but it does not exclude the possibility of repentance. Although the Pharisees share this blindness, they disappear from Luke before the death plot in Jerusalem and are not implicated in it. The plan to accuse Jesus comes to nothing in 6:6-11, but the issue of sabbath healing will return in 13:10-17 and 14:1-6, where Jesus will defend his practice with additional argumentative questions.

◊ ◊ ◊ ◊

Jesus, by his healing, asserts that it is lawful to do good on the sabbath. This position is still compatible with observance of the sabbath rest, except on special occasions. However, it can also be taken as authorization to do anything that is judged to be good. Both this position and the claim that "the Son of Man is lord of the sabbath" (6:5) are open doors that can lead to reinterpretation of the law, eliminating sabbath observance entirely. We do not know the degree of sabbath observance in the Lukan communities. Jews among them may have wished to continue observing the sabbath, yet this might have been difficult if the majority of the local Christian group was not doing so. Acts denies that Paul taught "all the Jews living among the Gentiles to forsake Moses," as he was accused by Jerusalem believers (Acts 21:21). However, participating in a community that did not, as a whole, observe the law may have led Christian Jews to abandon sabbath observance. These sabbath passages, whatever the intention of their original narrators, contributed to the loss of the sabbath—a prime mark of the covenant people, according to Jewish Scripture—and to a final separation from Judaism.

Choosing the Twelve (6:12-16)

The choice of the twelve (cf. Matt 10:1-4; Mark 3:13-19) is preceded in Luke by a night of prayer. The comparatively frequent references to Jesus' prayer in Luke almost always precede an important new development or crisis (3:21; 5:16; 9:18; 9:28-29; 22:40-46). Jesus' prayer in 6:12 also fits the pattern of Acts, where prayer regularly accompanies appointment of people to special positions (Acts 1:24; 6:6; 13:2-3; 14:23; cf. Nolland 1989, 272).

In 6:17 the narrator will mention "a great crowd of his disciples." There are now enough of them that Jesus can select twelve for a special role. They are called "apostles." Although Paul uses this term when speaking of himself and others not named to the twelve, in Luke–Acts the term *apostles* is almost always restricted to the twelve (exceptions are Acts 14:4, 14). Furthermore, when Judas is replaced, we are told of the qualifications required: An apostle must not only be a witness to the risen Jesus but must have accompanied him throughout his ministry (Acts 1:21-22). The apostles are missionaries, but they are more. They are chosen "witnesses" who are qualified to transmit the story of Jesus' ministry, death, and resurrection to the world. The number twelve is important. It represents Israel in its wholeness, consisting of twelve tribes. The twelve apostles will be witnesses to "the entire house of Israel" (Acts 2:36) and then rule over the twelve tribes (Luke 22:29-30). But before they can perform these duties, they must serve their apprenticeship with Jesus, and there will be difficult things to learn.

The Sermon on the Plain (6:17-49)

We come now to the first large section of teaching on discipleship, the so-called Sermon on the Plain (6:20-49). The narrator makes clear that the twelve are present, plus "a great crowd of his disciples and a great multitude of the people" (the NRSV passes over the Greek article here, but "the people" *[ho laos]* is a standard Lukan phrase for the Jewish people in their covenant status; cf. Tannehill 1986, 143-44). Note that the audience consists both of disciples and others (cf. 7:1), for those not yet committed also need to know what discipleship involves. Teaching and healing occur together (as in the summary in 5:15), for "they had come to hear him" as well as be healed. In 6:19, as elsewhere, Jesus is understood to be a carrier of divine "power" that can pass from him to others (cf. 5:17; 8:46).

Most of Luke 6:20-49 has parallels in Matthew's Sermon on the Mount (Matthew 5–7; exceptions are Luke 6:24-26, 39-40). Matthew's sermon, however, is considerably longer, and there are significant differences in wording and arrangement of the material that the two sermons have in common. Both sermons begin with beatitudes, but Luke has four beatitudes balancing four woes, while Matthew has nine beatitudes and no woes. Matthew's beatitudes are in the third person ("they"), but Luke's are in the second person ("you"). The two Gospels share language but show characteristic differences. Where Luke refers to the "poor," Matthew speaks of the "poor in spirit," and where Luke refers to those who are "hungry now," Matthew speaks of those who "hunger and thirst for righteousness" (Matt 5:3, 6).

Beatitudes and Woes (6:20-26)

The Lukan beatitudes and woes are a carefully constructed set, each woe contrasting with one of the beatitudes. The first three beatitudes are also to be interpreted as a set. The poor, hungry, and weeping are not three different groups of people but three descriptions of a single group. Because they are destitute, they are also hungry and weeping. The fourth beatitude, to be sure, stands out, for it is much longer than the others and clearly refers to persecuted followers of Jesus. The "poor" in the Lukan beatitudes means the economically needy, for they are hungry and are contrasted with those who are rich and full.

Yet more is involved. To a greater degree than in the modern world, economic status in ancient Mediterranean society was valued less for its own sake than as a factor in honor status. (On honor and shame as "pivotal values of the Mediterranean world," see Malina and Neyrey in Neyrey 1991, 25-65.) The rich stand out not just because they have possessions but because they have power and honor in society. The poor are those who can no longer maintain a position of respect in society. Either they lose the economic means for decent living and then are excluded from respectable society, or they are excluded and then lose their means of support. The result is the same: They are both economically deprived and socially marginalized. (On the social aspect of poverty, see Green 1994a, 59-74.) There are probably large areas of overlap among the "poor," the "sinners," and the disabled among whom Jesus ministers. When Jesus speaks the beatitudes, he is announcing to these people the happy news that they have been chosen by God to share in God's kingdom, which will end their hunger and exclusion.

According to verse 20, Jesus spoke the beatitudes as "he looked up at his disciples." The beatitudes are relevant to the disciples, for the call stories indicate that they "left everything" to follow Jesus (5:11, 28), thus joining the ranks of the poor. We should not assume that the introduction in verse 20 is restricting the beatitudes to the present group of disciples, however. Jesus may focus on the disciples not only because they are poor but because they must minister to the poor. Furthermore, statements elsewhere do not limit concern for the poor to those who have already become disciples (cf. 1:52-53; 7:22; 14:21). In 16:19-25 poor Lazarus is not comforted because he is a follower of Jesus. Jesus, however, would like to comfort the poor now, not after death, by enabling them to believe in God's kingdom for them, which may mean living as disciples. Thus, through the beatitudes Jesus is carrying out the mission announced in Nazareth of bringing "good news to the poor" (4:18).

Each beatitude is matched with a woe directed to the rich, who are also the socially honored ("all speak well of you," v. 26). It may seem strange that the rich are treated so roughly here, but there is an underlying conviction that those who hoard what the poor need are held responsible before God. The beatitudes and woes present the same reversal of situation through God's intervention proclaimed in the Magnificat (1:51-53). The woes would seem to say that there is no hope for the rich, but later teaching about riches in Luke will show that this is not entirely true. There is a possibility of repentance for the rich, although the way of discipleship will be costly (18:18-27).

The beatitudes also apply to Jesus' followers who are socially excluded "on account of the Son of Man" (v. 22). Exclusion could be a powerful weapon, for it meant loss of honor in society at large, which would be deeply felt by ancient group-oriented persons. There would probably be economic consequences, for the ability to earn a living was dependent on social relationships.

◊ ◊ ◊ ◊

Those in the Lukan audience who were poor may have been comforted by the beatitudes. Insofar as they had already experienced acceptance and received material support through the community of Jesus, these beatitudes would ring true, not only for the future but also for the present. Those in the community who were relatively wealthy, however, could hardly be comfortable while hearing these words. Their reactions might range from anger to anxiety about their place in God's kingdom.

The Love of Enemies (6:27-36)

The introductory phrase "I say to you that listen" indicates that the following teaching is directed to all those who "had come to hear (or "listen to") him" (v. 18). Although Matthew's sermon separates the command to turn the other cheek and the so-called Golden Rule from the command to love enemies (cf. Matt 5:38-42, 43-48; 7:12), these are placed together under the heading of love of enemies in Luke. This heading provides the theme for Luke 6:27-36, and the warnings against negative judgment of others in 6:37-42 are related. Thus, love of enemies is the central theme of the Lukan sermon.

Jesus' teaching in this Lukan sermon has a careful formal pattern in which the series of four parallel utterances predominates. There are four beatitudes and four woes. The command "love your enemies" is followed by three similar commands that clarify its implications. There is also a foursome in verses 29-30. In the Greek, the saying about the cheek begins in the same way as the saying about giving, and the saying about clothing begins the same way as the saying about taking away goods (forming an *abab* pattern). The rather lengthy "if" clauses in verses 32-34 drop back to three, but repetitive emphasis continues. The summary in verse 35a, which repeats the command "love your enemies," contains three commands, but verses 37-38a return to a pattern of four (two negative commands and two positive).

Thus, there is strong use of repetitive patterns, which provide emphasis and also suggestively expand an initial utterance. The language tends to focus on specific actions in specific situations, but the implications are not thereby limited. A series of situations is mentioned, and more could easily be added. This patterned use of language stimulates hearers to imagine additional instances that fit the pattern, instances that reflect their own situations.

Jesus' teaching uses forceful and imaginative language, which is to be clearly distinguished from legal language. Legal language must try to provide clear definitions in order to regulate external behavior. Forceful and imaginative language is not concerned with clear definitions. Thus it is not at all clear when we should act as indicated in verse 29 and when there might be good reasons for not doing so. Offering the other cheek when struck and giving up one's tunic (the basic garment = "shirt" in the NRSV) as well as one's cloak are examples of surprising action that may or may not fit situations faced by the listeners. (The generalizing "anyone," used twice by the NRSV in v. 29, is not in the Greek.) Forceful and imaginative language is not concerned primarily to regulate external behavior but serves to stimulate moral insight by challenging the ruts in which people move. Such language succeeds when it stimulates the moral imagination to imagine the possibility that breaks out of these ruts. It can change action by working through the imagination, challenging old assumptions and suggesting a new possibility while trusting the hearer to work out the details. Luke 6:27-36 is a carefully crafted attempt to awaken the imagination so that radically new ways of relating to enemies will result. (On imaginative language in this passage, see further Tannehill 1975, 21-28, 67-77.)

◊ ◊ ◊ ◊

The composition begins with four brief commands, for which "love your enemies" sets the pattern. The following three commands reinforce the first and also suggest how love of enemies might be expressed. The four commands form an open-ended series. Other commands of the same pattern could be added, for there are certainly other ways in which love of enemies might be expressed. The reference to "those who hate you" in verse 27 is probably a reminder of verse 22. The "enemies" to be loved are, in part, those who have excluded the community of Jesus. With the command to pray for enemies, see Luke 23:34; Acts 7:60.

In the next part, the command to love enemies is sharpened by some radical examples (vv. 29-30). Offering the other cheek and one's basic garment is not to be understood as passivity in the face of aggression. Passivity would mean doing nothing. Offering the other cheek is doing something provocative. It risks greater harm in order to make a (nonverbal) statement, which requires the aggressor to take a second and more careful look at the one who is being victimized, with the possibility of a change in relationship (for better or worse). The result might simply be a struggle of wills. However, since verse 29 is explaining the command "love your enemies," the purpose must be to find the good not only for oneself but for the enemy. The normal concern for self-protection is laid aside for this purpose. In verse 30 the same lack of self-concern is required in responding to those who threaten one's possessions, first the beggars and then the robbers.

The so-called Golden Rule in verse 31 may seem much less radical, since it works with the principle of reciprocity. The principle of reciprocity (do to others as they do to you = love your friends and hate your enemies) was widely accepted in the ancient world (cf. van Unnik 1966, 284-300) and represents the attitude that Jesus is challenging. Both the Golden Rule and verses 32-35 attack this principle. (On the connection between the Golden Rule and vv. 32-35, see Betz 1995, 591, 599.) We are not to do to others as they do to us but as we would want them to do to us. This turns reciprocity into a guide to proactive goodness, free of calculations concerning our past treatment by others. The following verses provide further support. Three rhetorical questions are used to underscore the difference between what Jesus expects and the normal practice of reciprocity (vv. 32-34). The choice of lending for the third example reflects the special Lukan interest in the disposal of possessions (there is no parallel in Matthew).

Following the forceful language of verses 28-34, the composition returns to the commands of verse 27 and repeats them as the main theme (except that lending is now included). Finally, a crowning argument and motivation are added, "Your reward will be great, and you will be children of the Most High" (v. 35). Love of enemies does not lead ultimately to suffering and misery but to great reward, and that reward consists of being "children of the Most High," with the great inheritance that follows. Disciples are properly children of God because they are acting as God does. God's kindness and mercy extend to the ungrateful and wicked, including the disciples. We should copy God's mercy rather than limiting love as humans do. (Note that Luke ends the section with "be merciful, just as your Father is merciful," while Matt 5:48 has "be perfect.")

◊ ◊ ◊ ◊

The willingness of the Lukan audience to accept Jesus' teaching of love of enemies may have been increased by their own experience of a community in which Jews and Gentiles, poor and rich, had joined in mutual support. To some extent Jesus' way of loving enemies had worked, although a diverse community is likely to have persistent tensions. However, the experience of exclusion, indicated in verse 22, would make love of the excluders very difficult. These people might be leaders of the local synagogue, as well as family members, former patrons, and former friends. Differences in deeply-held religious beliefs often breed hatred and violence, but the community of Jesus is being told that it must find ways to love these enemies.

A listener with a critical mind might ask whether the Lukan narrator is showing love of enemies in portraying the scribes and Pharisees. Are they being presented as negative stereotypes that simply serve to make Jesus look good? In my opinion, it is possible, but not necessary, to understand them in this way, and the modern reader should be alert to this danger. (On this issue, see Tannehill 1994, 424-33.)

The experience of meeting and worshiping with a Roman soldier or official in a Christian community (such as Cornelius in Acts 10) might have led some Christian Jews to believe that love of their national enemies, the Romans, was possible. These Jews might have hoped that Zechariah's prophecy that Jews would be "saved from our enemies" (1:71) would be realized, not by armed rebellion but by transforming the enemy through love. Some might have seen this happening through conversions of Romans. Others might have recalled from recent events that offering the other cheek was sometimes the best political action, for on at least two occasions the willingness of Jews to offer their lives in nonviolent resistance had changed the policy of Rome (cf. Josephus *J.W.* 2 §169-74, 195-201). Armed resistance, on the other hand, had brought disaster.

Do Not Judge (6:37-42)

Some interpreters divide the sermon differently, placing verses 27-38 together in one section and making verses 39-49 the final section (cf. Nolland 1989, 274-75). Admittedly, there is no major break between verses 36 and 37, for verse 36 is a transitional verse. Not judging is an important aspect of being merciful as God is merciful. It is doubtful, however, that there is a break at verse 39. The introductory words "he also told them a parable" need not indicate a change of topic, for similar statements are used when the narrator introduces strongly metaphorical material that provides an additional comment on preceding teaching (cf. 5:36; 12:16; 13:6; 21:29). The part about the speck in the eye (vv. 41-42) appears to relate closely to verses 37-38. If so, the enigmatic sayings in between are probably related also.

◊ ◊ ◊ ◊

The use of carefully crafted, forceful language continues in verses 37-38. Four parallel commands are given, two in the negative and two in the positive. These are brief and rhythmic. In each a single verb is used twice, first in the active and then in the passive. ("Do not *judge,* and you will not *be judged."*) This technique holds together, like the pin in a hinge, what we do and what we will receive. The use of the same word makes the point that the latter will match the former. Religious zeal can make people judgmental, for they feel responsible for enforcing God's standards. Their efforts are supported by a sense of justice; it is just that evil be condemned. This tendency is here countered by another vision of justice. You will receive what you give. That is justice, but it speaks against the demand for justice through condemning others.

Generosity in treating others is encouraged by description of the measure that God would like to use. In the Greek the description of the promised return appears thus:

metron kalon pepiesmenon sesaleumenon hyperekchynnomenon

measure good pressed down shaken together running over

The descriptions move from the shortest and mildest to the longest and strongest so that the listener feels the overflowing generosity in the words themselves. These emphatic words about not judging may have been important for the internal life of the church, particularly because of the differences between Jews and Gentiles, but they can also be taken as additional instruction on how believers should treat their enemies, the nonbelievers who exclude them.

Although verses 39-40 are difficult to interpret, it is best to try to understand them in context. One possibility is the following: Those who wish to judge others set themselves up as guides to the blind, but they are actually blind themselves (see the following image of a log in the eye). The teacher (Jesus) does not condemn those whom these disciples condemn. In condemning, they try to set themselves above their teacher instead of becoming like their teacher—a very foolish attitude for disciples.

The saying about the log in the eye in verses 41-42 is rather close in wording to its parallel in Matt 7:3-5, which directly follows Matthew's shorter version of the saying that begins "do not judge." In Luke, too, the two sayings are probably connected. In verses 41-42 extreme language is used to attack the deep-seated tendency of persons to minimize their own faults and maximize the faults of others. A single image—having something in the eye—is developed in a contrast of small and great that is extended to hyperbole. Hearers are to imagine the impossible, having a log in the eye, and then must compare this with the speck in the other person's eye that attracts their attention. Through very forceful language that is designed to stick in the imagination, those who want to judge and guide others are warned that they may be publicly shamed. Twice they are confronted directly (using the second person) with accusing questions that reveal what all can see but them: the ridiculously large log in the eye. Then they are called hypocrites and told to concentrate on their own problem first. Confidence in their judgment of others is undermined by awareness that their vision may be blocked by a log in the eye. Although such accusatory language might primarily produce anger and defensiveness if applied to an individual, those who overhear it being spoken to no one in particular may become more aware of their own vulnerability and distorted vision, making them less likely to judge others. Where the NRSV has "neighbor," the Greek reads "brother," a common way of addressing fellow believers. Thus, at some point in its life, this saying probably spoke to the desire of some believers to control and correct others.

Concluding Exhortations (6:43-49)

The sermon closes with two sets of exhortations of a general kind. The sayings in verses 43-45 can cut two ways. On the one hand, they can serve as a call to action. Since the "tree is known by its own fruit," people must show good fruit in order to be known as good trees. Good fruit means acting as indicated in verses 27-42. On the other hand, verses 43-45 also show that concentration on action alone is not enough. Good action has its origin deep within the self, in the heart. Only if one's fundamental commitments and values are good will truly good action be possible.

In verses 46-49 we find Jesus' concluding challenge to his audience. This challenge is tied to the narrative context by verse 47. The large audience "had come to hear him" (v. 18). Now the crucial question is whether they will not only come and hear but also act. The consequences of acting or not acting are indicated by the simile of the houses with and without a foundation. Only the person who listens and then acts is like a secure house with a solid foundation. The nature of the future test is hidden behind the image of an overflowing river. The testing may occur both in this life and at the final judgment. This conclusion to the sermon leaves open the question of whether the disciples in the narrative will not only hear but act on Jesus' words. Outside the narrative it poses the same question to the Lukan audience.

The Faith of a Centurion (7:1-10)

Luke's story of the centurion differs significantly from the parallel stories in Matt 8:5-13 and John 4:46-53. Only in Luke does the centurion or official send delegations to Jesus rather than having direct contact with him. Luke 7:1-10 is a quest story, a more elaborate kind of pronouncement story in which a person other than Jesus plays a prominent role. A quest story is concerned with the success or failure of a person who is seeking a benefit from Jesus. A central dialogue addresses an issue crucial to the quester's success (cf. Tannehill 1986, 111-12, 114-16). In Luke 7:1-10 we are told much about the centurion in a few verses, and he has the longest speech in the scene (vv. 6-8). He is meant to be an impressive character. When a successful quester is praised by Jesus, as in verse 9, he or she tends to become a model for others. The centurion is a model of faith for all, but the fact that he is a Gentile and a centurion is also important in this scene.

The first three scenes of chapter 7 (7:1-23) are related to 4:16-30. Note that the summary of Jesus' ministry in 7:22 begins with "the blind receive their sight" and ends with "the poor have good news brought to them." These are aspects of the mission Jesus announced in 4:18. Furthermore, 7:23 adds a blessing on those who do not take offense, as the people of Nazareth did in 4:28-30. In 4:25-27 Jesus referred to Elijah and a widow and to Elisha and Naaman the Syrian. These references not only have a function in the Nazareth scene but also provide scriptural precedents for Jesus' healing ministry. The audience's appreciation of 7:1-10 is enriched through comparison with Elisha and Naaman, and their appreciation of 7:11-17 will be enriched through comparison with Elijah and the widow (cf. below). This is not to say that the story of Jesus and the centurion was simply constructed as a parallel to the Elisha story. Yet hearers who remember the Elisha story (having been reminded of it in 4:27) can note interesting similarities and differences with 7:1-10 that will contribute to their understanding of the concluding statement in verse 16 that Jesus is "a great prophet" (like Elijah and Elisha). Both Naaman (cf. 2 Kgs 5:1-19) and Luke's centurion are officers in a foreign army who seek healing (Naaman for himself, the centurion for his slave). In neither case do the officers meet the prophets before healing takes place, instead conversing through messengers (a feature distinctive of Luke's version of the Gospel story). In both cases the healing takes place at a distance from the prophet (cf. Ravens 1988, 287). There is, however, an interesting difference between Naaman and the centurion. Naaman is proud and at first rejects Elisha's instructions; the centurion is remarkably self-effacing and trustful.

After the introduction of the centurion and his slave's need of healing, the scene is structured through the sending of two delegations to Jesus. The focus of the scene is on the centurion and on Jesus' response to him. The healing is noted only briefly in verse 10, its primary function being to reinforce Jesus' favorable response and bring the centurion's quest to a successful end. The scene is an interesting example of negotiation on the part of a centurion who is very sensitive to the social barrier between himself and a Jewish holy man. First the centurion sends Jewish elders to Jesus. He apparently assumes that a recommendation from Jewish leaders is necessary for a Jewish healer to consider the case of a Gentile at all. The elders support their recommendation of the centurion by saying, "He loves our people, and it is he who built our synagogue for us." The centurion is a patron of the local Jews, and, according to current understanding of patron-client relations, his patronage establishes a lasting relationship with the beneficiaries, requiring reciprocal support from them. The elders are fulfilling their obligation to the centurion by speaking in his behalf to Jesus. (On patron-client relations, see Moxnes in Neyrey 1991, 241-68; Malina and Rohrbaugh 1992, 326-29.)

Apparently Jesus sees no problem in healing the centurion's slave, for he goes with the elders to the centurion's house. Now, however, the centurion realizes that there may be another issue. It may be presumptuous of him to ask a Jewish holy man to defile himself by entering the dwelling of a Gentile. (Dwelling places of Gentiles are unclean, according to *m. Oholot* 18:7.) Hence, a second delegation is sent. The words the delegation speaks are the centurion's, and they form the longest speech in this episode. Although the elders vouched for the centurion's worthiness in verse 4, the centurion declares that he is not worthy either to have Jesus enter his house or to come directly to Jesus. For the sake of his slave and out of respect for Jesus, the centurion is laying his honor aside. Furthermore, it is not necessary for Jesus to come to the house. He can simply speak the word. The centurion then draws an analogy between Jesus' command and his own experience as a military officer. The centurion works in a chain of authority, subordinate to his commanders but superior to soldiers under him. Because of this chain of authority, his commands are effective. The centurion's humility is not based on doubt of his own abilities. He has authority in his own context, but now he needs help. He assumes that Jesus works in a similar chain of command. Because Jesus is set under God's authority and acknowledges that authority, he can command with divine authority in healing. The analogy is drawn from the experience of a soldier. A person in another line of work might use a different analogy.

Hearing this, Jesus "was amazed," as the crowds are often amazed following a healing. He responds with strong words of praise: "I tell you, not even in Israel have I found such faith." Jesus is not denying that there is faith in Israel. In fact, his statement assumes that one should find faith in Israel. But the centurion's faith is extraordinary, and it is found where one would not expect it, in a Gentile soldier. His faith consists of his determination to surmount the social barrier between Jew and Gentile (as the paralytic's friends showed faith in circumventing the crowd by opening the roof in 5:17-20). He also shows faith by his willingness to lay aside his own honor, by his trust in Jesus' healing power, and perhaps also by his insight into Jesus' divine authority.

Jesus is willing to help Gentiles, but it is not yet time for the Gentile mission by Lukan reckoning. The lack of direct contact between Jesus and the centurion is a sign of this situation. Jesus will enter Gentile territory in 8:26-39, and he will enter a Samaritan village in 9:51-56, but both times Jesus will be rebuffed. When the Gentile mission must begin, Peter will encounter another centurion, Cornelius (Acts 10). This time the social barrier will come down. Contact through intermediaries will give way to direct contact. Peter will enter Cornelius's house, eat there, and baptize Gentiles.

◊ ◊ ◊ ◊

Gentiles in the Lukan audience would rightly understand this scene to be an invitation to share in the community of Jesus and the reign of God. Perhaps we can be more specific: The scene affirms that soldiers in the service of Rome and its client rulers may share in the benefits of Jesus. The story also challenges both Gentiles and Jews to show faith equal to the centurion's.

Both this centurion and Cornelius are remarkably pro-Jewish. Cornelius, we are told in Acts 10:2, "gave alms generously to the [Jewish] people and prayed constantly to God." The Jewish elders testify in Luke 7:5 that the centurion "loves our people, and it is he who built our synagogue for us." Following the Roman-Jewish war, it may have been difficult for either Jews or Gentiles to believe that there was a centurion who loved the Jewish people. This centurion may be not only a model of faith but also a model for other Gentiles of the proper attitude toward Jews. Furthermore, from the perspective of the Lukan audience a centurion who "loves" the Jewish people is someone who loves his enemies, as Jesus commanded in the preceding sermon (6:27).

A Widow and Her Son (7:11-17)

This scene, found only in Luke, fits at this point in the narrative because it forms a pair with 7:1-10 and because it prepares for 7:22 by providing a case of resurrection of the dead. In 7:1-10 Jesus acts on behalf of a Gentile man; in 7:11-17 he acts on behalf of a Jewish woman. The effect of the former is to affirm God's saving work for Gentiles (particularly soldiers); the effect of the latter is to affirm God's saving work for Jews and women (particularly widows). In both cases the rest of the community is encouraged to recognize this affirmation. Furthermore, these two scenes are related through their common connection with the mighty acts of Elijah and Elisha mentioned in Luke 4:25-27. Once again, the Lukan scene is not simply a copy of the scriptural story, but there are sufficient similarities to jog the memories of persons well-versed in scripture. In 1 Kgs 17:10-24 the prophet Elijah encounters a widow at the gate of the city. Later he raises her dead son. In the LXX account the son makes a sound as the first sign of his return to life. Then Elijah "gave him to his mother," words that are repeated exactly in Luke 7:15. (In 2 Kgs 4:8-37 there is a similar story of Elisha reviving a woman's [not a widow's] dead son. He is evidently her only son.)

Jesus, then, was not the only one to whom resurrection stories were attributed. According to Jewish tradition, such a thing might be done by a "great prophet" like Elijah (cf. Luke 7:16). Outside the Jewish and Christian tradition, there is a story of Apollonius of Tyana reviving a bride who had died at her wedding (Philostratus *Life of Apollonius,* book 4, chap. 45).

In spite of the connections between 7:1-10 and 11-17, the latter is formally a healing wonder, while the former is a quest story, that is, a type of pronouncement story.

◊ ◊ ◊ ◊

The mention of disciples and a large crowd in verse 11 reminds us of 6:17. It appears that many disciples and a large crowd not only listened to Jesus' sermon but accompanied him on his travels. As one crowd meets another at the gate of the city, the narrator introduces pathos into the scene. The setting is a procession of mourners. The death is particularly grievous because the dead man "was his mother's only son, and she was a widow." Mourning for an only son or child is used as an image of extreme grief in Jer 6:26; Amos 8:10; Zech 12:10 (cf. Bovon 1989, 362). Since the woman had already lost her husband, the loss of her only son is not only a second family tragedy but also ends her main economic support.

"A son was a mother's lifelong protector and her ultimate social security" (Malina and Rohrbaugh 1992, 329-30). In contrast to many healing stories, no one in this scene requests Jesus' help. He takes the initiative out of compassion for the widow. The reference to Jesus having compassion on the widow is unusual. Except in special cases, the narrator avoids attributing emotions to Jesus. (Luke lacks many of the references to Jesus' emotions found in Mark; cf. Fitzmyer 1981, 95.) Jesus is acting for the widow's sake. He has compassion "for her," and when her son is revived, he "gave him to his mother," a further indication of the mother's stake in what is happening.

This revival of a dead man is followed by a crowd reaction that goes beyond the ordinary. To be sure, the statement that they "glorified God" following Jesus' mighty act fits a common Lukan theme, but two additional statements by the crowd are added. First, "A great prophet has risen among us!" Here Jesus is recognized to be a great wonder-working prophet like Elijah, Elisha, and, perhaps, Moses (cf. Acts 3:22-23; 7:37). This is an important insight about Jesus. Although it is something less than recognizing Jesus as Messiah, Jesus does take the role of a prophet during his earthly ministry, not only in his teaching and healing but also in facing death (Luke 13:33-34). Second, in Jesus' ministry "God has visited [NRSV: "has looked favorably on"] his people." These words pick up a theme from the Benedictus, where Zechariah spoke prophetically of God having "visited" his people, bringing redemption. (The same Greek verb, *episkeptomai,* is used in 1:68, 78, and 7:16.) That prophecy is now being realized in Jesus' ministry. These strong statements by the crowd are followed by an equally strong statement about the spread of Jesus' fame. Although the NRSV translates "throughout Judea" in verse 17, the narrator has previously used the term "Judea" to mean the land of the Jews, including Galilee (cf. 4:44). That seems to be the case here also. Otherwise it is hard to understand why events that took place in Galilee should be discussed mainly in Judea. Then "all the surrounding country" indicates that Jesus is becoming known as a great prophet even beyond the Jewish homeland. We have reached a high point in the public recognition of Jesus as a healing prophet. This view circulating among the people will now provoke inquiries by John the Baptist and Simon the Pharisee.

◊ ◊ ◊ ◊

The Lukan audience might take note of the fact that Jesus showed special concern for a widow. Acts indicates that the early church made special provision for the support of widows (6:1; 9:39). In Acts 9:36-43, Peter repeats the miracle of Jesus by reviving Tabitha (or Dorcas), who worked closely with widows to provide clothing for them and who may have been a widow herself. Jesus' compassion for a widow would encourage the Lukan audience to help widows in their community, perhaps imitating the good works of Tabitha, and it would encourage widows to hope in the Lord's compassion, even in difficult times (cf. 18:1-8).

John and Jesus (7:18-35)

This section is a collection of material in which John the Baptist is repeatedly mentioned. Most of this material is also found in Matthew, and in the same order (Matt 11:2-19).

John's Question for Jesus (7:18-23)

The question of John and reply of Jesus form a pronouncement story, which Matthew offers in a shorter version.

◊ ◊ ◊ ◊

There has been no indication in Luke that John recognized Jesus as the fulfillment of John's prophecies. Therefore, John's question does not represent the weakening of previous belief but the hopeful exploration of a possibility. The possibility occurs to John because of his disciples' report concerning "all these things" that Jesus has been saying and doing. John raises a question that others, too, will raise concerning the implications of Jesus' work for an understanding of Jesus himself and his future role.

John asks whether Jesus is "the one who is to come *(ho erchomenos)*." Commentators are divided as to what this implies. Some understand it as a reference to the returning Elijah of Mal 3:1-2;

4:5, who will be a fiery reformer (cf. Fitzmyer 1981, 664, who believes Jesus rejects this role). Others see here a general eschatological expectation, not an expectation for a specific figure (cf. Nolland 1989, 328-29). I think that this phrase, whatever it may have meant at an earlier stage, is applied in Luke to the Messiah. John's question is linked to his earlier statement that "one . . . more powerful than I is coming" (3:16). John is responding to the people's question whether John "might be the Messiah" (3:15); therefore he is referring to the Messiah in 3:16. There is a further link: the word translated "wait for" in 7:19 *(prosdokaō)* is also used in 3:15 to express the people's expectation. Furthermore, the phrase in question *(ho erchomenos)* returns in 19:38, and there the expected figure is identified as "the king," that is, the Messiah.

The NRSV translation of 7:21 ("Jesus had just then cured") could mean that Jesus performed these healings before John's disciples arrived. Literally, the text reads, "In that hour he cured," and the point is that he performed these cures in the presence of John's disciples. They are eyewitnesses of Jesus' healing ministry and can report what they have seen to John. The fact that there are two of them fits the requirement for reliable witness in Deut 19:15.

In verse 22 Jesus indicates what the messengers are to tell John in a series of short phrases that, in the Greek, consist only of plural nouns followed by third-person plural verbs (plus one conjunction). The repetition of the same types of words in the same order has a marked rhythmic effect. Use of this formal pattern required reformulation of the scriptural passages that stand in the background.

It is important to recognize the scriptural background, for this gives Jesus' response in 7:22 its full significance. There is a group of texts in Isaiah that list, in a series, some of the same disabilities as Luke 7:22 and proclaim that these disabilities will be eliminated at the time of God's redemption (Isa 29:18-19; 35:5-6; 42:18). Isaiah 61:1 must be added to the list, for it includes reference to good news for the poor. Isaiah 26:19 speaks of the resurrection of the dead. However, the references to lepers and the dead in 7:22 probably reflect the mighty acts of Elijah and Elisha for the widow and Naaman, figures mentioned in 4:25-27 and allusively recalled in 7:1-17. The list of Jesus' works in 7:22, then, not only shows that he is a great prophet like Elijah and Elisha but reveals that the time of God's redemption, prophesied in Isaiah, is being realized through Jesus' ministry.

John asks concerning an eschatological figure called "the one who is to come." Jesus responds by pointing to the fulfillment of eschatological expectation. He does not give an explicit answer to John's question, and the answer he does give may puzzle John. These are acts that might be expected of a prophet in the time of fulfillment but not of the Messiah. For the narrator this is probably not a problem. The one sent to "bring good news to the poor" is also the one whom the Lord "anointed" according to 4:18, where Isa 61:1 is quoted. The Messiah appears in the role of a prophet during his earthly ministry. But John and others may not make the same connections.

The reference to good news for the poor is a clear reference back to Jesus' announcement in Nazareth, and the blind receiving their sight is also related to 4:18. The blind and the poor are the first and last items in the list of 7:22. Placement of these items in positions of emphasis shows that the fulfillment of Jesus' announced task in 4:18 is especially in mind. We have here a retrospective summary of Jesus' ministry showing that Jesus has been fulfilling the commission from God that he publicly accepted in Nazareth.

The favorable impression Jesus made in Nazareth quickly turned to rage. The final verse of the scene—a beatitude, but also a warning—tells John and the Lukan audience that Jesus may still cause offense. Jesus may offend because he does not fit one's expectations, and there are other, more specific, reasons for offense, as the Lukan narrative indicates. One can only rejoice in Jesus' fulfillment of the scriptural promises if one can move beyond this offense.

Jesus' Comments About John (7:24-35)

Jesus continues by discussing the role of John the Baptist and the criticism that some make of John and of himself. Except for verses 29-30, this section parallels Matt 11:7-11, 16-19, with small variations.

Jesus both praises John and clarifies John's role by declaring that he is a prophet, "and more than a prophet." John's preeminence over other prophets is explained by the scripture quotation in verse 27. This quotation is based on Mal 3:1, but the references to "you" and "your" are not found there. The quotation has been adapted so that the messenger prepares not for the coming of God (who is speaking) but for another figure, addressed as "you." This adaptation may have been facilitated by Exod 23:20, which begins in the same way and includes "you" (meaning, in context, the people of Israel). In the context of Luke, this adaptation of Mal 3:1 is understood to present God speaking to the Messiah about John the Baptist, the messenger who will prepare the Messiah's way (cf. 1:17, 76; 3:4). In identifying John with Malachi's "messenger" (*angelos*, which could also be translated "angel"), there is also the strong suggestion that he is the returning Elijah of Mal 4:5-6 (cf. Luke 1:17). John is greater than all before him (7:28) because he, by his call to repentance and his witness to the coming one, directly prepares for the messianic time of salvation when God's promises will be fulfilled. The second half of verse 28, however, qualifies the high ranking of John: even "the least in the kingdom of God is greater than he." This statement emphasizes the wondrous nature of the kingdom of God, in which John does not yet participate.

It is probably appropriate to put verses 29-30 in parentheses, as the NRSV has done, because they are a comment of the narrator that interrupts the short speech of Jesus in verses 24-28, 31-35. A sharp contrast is made between "all the people," who accepted John's baptism, and the "Pharisees and lawyers," who did not. In rejecting John's baptism the Pharisees and lawyers also "rejected God's purpose for themselves." "God's purpose" or "plan" *(hē boulē tou theou)* is a key theological concept in Acts, which here appears in Luke. It is the divine will and power that leads events forward so that "all flesh" may "see the salvation of God" (3:6). Special people are called to serve God's purpose (cf. Acts 13:36). Opposition may seem to defeat God's purpose, but that opposition is anticipated and the seeming defeat will contribute to God's purpose (Acts 2:23; 4:28). Although humans cannot ultimately defeat God's purpose, Luke 7:30 indicates that they may reject

"God's purpose for themselves," that is, reject their own share in God's saving purpose. In spite of this sharply negative judgment on the Pharisees and lawyers, the narrator does not eliminate the possibility of a better response from them (see the discussion of 7:36-50).

Luke 7:31-35 is addressed to people who reject both John and Jesus, for opposite reasons (vv. 33-34). They are called "the people of this generation" (v. 31). The narrator has limited the application of this phrase by verses 29-30. "All the people" acknowledged the justice of God at work in John. They cannot be "the people of this generation" who declare that John "has a demon." That leaves the Pharisees and lawyers as critics of John and Jesus at this point.

There are difficulties in relating the saying about the children in verse 32 to verses 33-34. The most common explanation presently is that Jesus is like the children who said, "We played the flute for you," and John is like those who said, "We wailed." In neither case were the critics willing to respond. This explanation, however, does not fit the introduction to the children's words, which says that "the people of this generation" (not Jesus and John) are like children calling to one another, "We played the flute. . . . " In spite of common opinion, Jesus and John may be the implied objects of the accusations in verse 32, just as they are in verses 33-34 (cf. Linton 1976, 171-77). The children of this generation are like children playing at festivals and funerals who accuse John and Jesus of not joining in. John does not join the festival dances because (in the critics' view) he is always fasting. Jesus does not join the mourning because (in the critics' view) he is always feasting. This reading fits a previous passage. The accusation of eating with tax collectors and sinners, reflected in 7:34, first appeared in 5:30, where, as part of the same scene, it was followed by the question of why Jesus' disciples are eating and drinking rather than fasting (5:33). The same reproach is directed at Jesus in 7:32-34. He is not participating in the fasts of the Pharisees that express their mourning for Israel's sin. Fasting was an important practice of the pious, but one should not fast on sabbaths and festivals (cf. Jdt 8:6). Therefore, John could also be accused. Because of John's and Jesus' sense of a special time and a special calling, neither fits the standards of the Pharisees and lawyers for a good Jewish life.

Jesus is different from John because he comes "eating and drinking." Moreover, he is accused of being "a glutton and a drunkard." Jesus is not eating in the ordinary way, which would cause no comment. His meals are parties; they are celebrations. A second reproach concerns the people with whom Jesus shares these parties, the "tax collectors and sinners." Putting these two reproaches together, we see that Jesus was celebrating at festive meals with those that religious society had marginalized. Since the consummation in the kingdom of God was pictured as a festive meal (13:29; 14:15; 22:16, 18), Jesus' festive meals appear to be a promise and foretaste of this despised company's share in God's kingdom.

The wisdom of God is personified in Prov 8:1–9:6 and in other Jewish writings (Wis 7:22-30; Sirach 24). A similar view of wisdom is reflected in the saying that she is "vindicated" and has "children." In the Lukan context, wisdom is probably a near synonym to God's purpose (7:30). In spite of the scoffing words of those who cling to the ways of "this generation," wisdom will have many children. In them God's wise plan is vindicated as it reaches fulfillment.

The Woman in the Pharisee's House (7:36-50)

Scholars disagree on whether Luke 7:36-50 is based on the same incident as the rather different story in Matt 26:6-13, Mark 14:3-9, and John 12:1-8. The woman anoints Jesus' head in Matthew and Mark, but John 12:3 shares with Luke the details of the woman anointing Jesus' feet and wiping them with her hair.

Luke 7:36-50 is a rather lengthy pronouncement story. It has also been called a "symposium," a table conversation at a banquet, which became a recognized literary form (cf. Bovon 1989, 386; Steele 1984, 379-94). Two persons other than Jesus have prominent roles, a woman who provokes the dialogue and a Pharisee with whom Jesus discusses her behavior. As in parables with three characters (e.g., the prodigal son, Luke 15:11-32), the three persons in this scene represent different positions, thus enabling the story to explore and clarify an issue.

In 5:30 the Pharisees and scribes objected to Jesus' fellowship with tax collectors and sinners. This attitude reappeared in the scoffing words of 7:34. These scenes, plus the negative remark about the Pharisees and lawyers in 7:30, might lead the Lukan audience to believe that the scribes and Pharisees are hard-hearted opponents of Jesus for whom there is no hope. Now, however, the narrator inserts a scene showing that Jesus has not given up hope. Jesus seeks to bring insight to a Pharisee while responding to the dramatic action of a woman. The woman says no words, but she speaks by her actions. Jesus first defends her and then responds directly to her in verses 48, 50.

◊ ◊ ◊ ◊

Discussion with the Pharisees has not ended. Indeed, one of them is willing to invite Jesus to dinner, evidently because he has heard the claim that Jesus is a "great prophet" (7:16-17) and wants to find out for himself (cf. v. 39). Where the NRSV says that Jesus "took his place at the table," the Greek says he "reclined." Jews had adopted the Greco-Roman practice of eating a formal dinner or banquet while reclining on couches with the head next to the table and the feet sticking out. That is why the woman can approach Jesus' feet. Her actions are emotionally charged and bold. She enters a home where she is not welcome, disrupts the banquet, and publicly behaves with improper intimacy.

There is a significant gap in the narrative, for we are not told what caused the woman to come to Jesus with her ointment. If this act of grateful love is the result of forgiveness, as the parable in verses 41-42 implies, she must have already been offered forgiveness, presumably through Jesus. But we are not told that part of the story.

The Pharisee is offended by what he sees. The woman is a sinner who doesn't belong at the dinner. Jesus cannot be a prophet, for he obviously doesn't know the nature of this woman. Jesus responds not with condemnation but with corrective teaching. First, Jesus addresses the Pharisee by name, "Simon." It is unusual for a character who appears in a single Gospel scene to be named. The use of the name is a sign that the conversation is moving to a personal level. It also helps the audience to think of the man as an individual and not just as another Pharisee. Next, Jesus uses a parable, which can provide an imaginative bridge leading hearers to judge a situation from a new angle. Jesus asks Simon to make a judgment about the two debtors in the parable (v. 43), testing to see if Simon agrees so far. Then he turns back to the woman whom Simon called a sinner and asks him to look at her again: "Do you see this woman?" (v. 44). Simon addressed Jesus as "teacher" in verse 40, and since that time Jesus has been acting as teacher. But the woman can also be Simon's teacher, if he is willing. From her he can learn about the powerful love that comes from forgiveness.

Jesus ticks off a series of contrasts between the treatment he received from the woman and from Simon. The narrator has withheld, until this climactic point, both Jesus' reaction to the woman's striking behavior and information about Simon's reception of Jesus. Now Jesus makes three contrasts between the woman's reception of Jesus and Simon's. We do not have evidence that foot bathing, kissing, and anointing the head were required for normal hospitality. Nevertheless, in comparison with the woman's actions, Simon's welcome of Jesus looks decidedly cool.

In verse 47 Jesus draws a conclusion that unites his observations about Simon and the woman with the preceding parable. There is an ambiguity in the Greek of verse 47. It would be possible to translate, "Her many sins have been forgiven because she has shown great love," understanding her love as the basis for receiving forgiveness. This, however, contradicts both the parable, where forgiveness leads to love, not vice versa, and the final statement in verse 47 (little forgiveness leads to little love). It seems necessary, then, to understand "because she has shown great love" as providing the reason why Jesus is sure that she has been forgiven, connecting this phrase with the beginning of the sentence, "therefore, I tell you." The sense then would be, "Therefore, I tell you, her sins, which were many, have been forgiven, (and I can tell you this) because she has shown great love." The implication of the NRSV translation is similar. Simon is being shown the value of the woman's experience, not just for her but for him. It is valuable not because Simon also has many sins (no such accusation is made), but because

Simon can learn about the depth of God's forgiveness and its powerful effect through the experience of the woman. If Simon can accept her, the woman's experience can revitalize Simon's understanding of God.

There is a major gap at the end of the scene. We are not told how Simon responds to Jesus' words. Jesus has carefully led him toward a judgment about the woman that is different from his initial one. The scene leaves Simon poised on the threshold of decision. He may finally accept Jesus' teaching, or he may not. Simon is more than a negative stereotype. It is quite possible to view him as an open character who might change. Thus the Pharisees are not completely reduced to negative stereotypes in Luke (cf. Tannehill 1994, 424-33).

At the end of the scene Jesus turns to the woman, showing that he is not just concerned with Simon, for whom the woman can provide a lesson, but also with the woman herself. Jesus' statement "your sins are forgiven" may be puzzling at this point, for the story assumes that the woman's grateful love shows her previous experience of forgiveness. Nevertheless, reassurance of forgiveness may be important, since the woman must face people who share Simon's negative attitude. Jesus also speaks about her faith (v. 50). As in 5:18-20, faith was demonstrated in bold action.

Jesus' assurance of forgiveness creates a question in the minds of the other dinner guests. This question is a milder version of the questions that follow Jesus' words of forgiveness to the paralyzed man (5:20-21). It reminds the Lukan audience of that occasion, when he proclaimed his authority on earth to forgive sins. The question "Who is this?" will become a repeated theme in the narrative, leading up to the christological revelations in 9:20, 22, 35. (See the questions in 8:25; 9:9, 18.)

◊ ◊ ◊ ◊

A Lukan audience that contained despised classes as well as people of good social standing would find food for thought in this passage. The passage insists that the "sinner's" forgiveness and acceptance is important for the whole community. Both the socially marginal and the established are encouraged to value this experience as being central to the community's purpose and as a source of religious vitality. The community is also being encouraged to remain open to those labeled "sinners."

The audience may also understand this scene as part of the painful dialogue with the community's Jewish parent, for whom the Pharisees have become representatives. In this context it is important that Simon is presented as an open character, who might still learn from Jesus and accept what he is saying. Through the figure of Jesus the Lukan communities are shown a way to state their case without allowing the dialogue to dissolve into mutual recriminations. Presenting Simon as an open character also permits members of the Lukan communities to recognize their similarities to Simon. Those in a favorable social position may be no more eager than Simon to associate with the outcasts, but Jesus upsets normal social rules and makes the sinful woman the guide and test of the community.

Jesus Travels with the Twelve and the Women (8:1-3)

The summary statement of Jesus' preaching ministry in verse 1 is a reminder that Jesus is doing what he said he must do in 4:43. Luke 8:1 and 4:43-44 share key terms, *kēryssōn* ("proclaiming") and *euangelizomenos tēn basileian tou theou* ("bringing the good news of the kingdom of God"). The two verbs are drawn from Jesus' announcement in Nazareth (4:18). Thus Jesus is steadily carrying out the mission announced in 4:18, 43-44, now even to villages (only cities were mentioned in 4:43).

By mentioning the twelve, the narrator is preparing for their mission in 9:1-6. Presently they are learning from Jesus by accompanying him; soon they will be sent out on their own. More surprising is the reference to a group of women traveling with Jesus and the twelve. Here also the narrator is preparing for a later development. Women who follow Jesus from Galilee will see the Crucifixion, they alone will witness the entombment, and the first report of Jesus' resurrection will come from some of them (23:49, 55; 24:1-11). These women supplement the witness of the twelve at a crucial point in the narrative. When the apostles are listed again in Acts, the women are also mentioned (Acts 1:13-14). These women, at least those who are named, are to some extent female counterparts of the twelve. We are not told, however, that they preach (although it is not impossible that the seventy sent on mission in 10:1 included women). The statement in verse 3 that they "provided for them [or "were serving them"] out of their resources" allows us to understand them as a women's auxiliary, which many today would view as an inferior role. (Turid Seim, however, notes the positive importance in Luke of the serving role here attributed to the women. Women are presented as important examples of service. However, they do not share the task of "serving the word" [Acts 6:4] because women are not accepted as credible witnesses. [Cf. Seim 1994a, 87-88, 96, 251-55.])

It is possible that the pictured arrangement reflects the division widespread in ancient and traditional societies between women, who work within the household, and men, who are expected to handle public affairs. Without wishing to defend this as appropriate for today, I would note that this arrangement gave considerable responsibility to women. Their work was essential to family survival, in many cases. The family was a production unit, and larger households could be the equivalent of a small factory, with a woman as its manager. In the ancient world the division of labor could be used to support the authority of women, for it could be asserted that women are the appropriate rulers of households, where men should not interfere. Furthermore, the tendency to understand early churches on the model of households enabled women to assert their right to leadership within the churches. (On this paragraph, cf. Torjesen 1993, 40, 53-87; cf. also Malina and Rohrbaugh 1992, 348-49).

The reference to Joanna, wife of Herod's steward, is noteworthy. She came from a higher social rank and, if she still had access to family resources, could contribute much more than gathering and cooking food. She could be a patron of the group, providing financial support and contacts with important people. To the Lukan audience she may represent female patrons known to them, like Lydia in Philippi (Acts 16:14-15, 40), women who had an important role in development of local churches and considerable influence in them.

Even if verses 2-3 do not break with traditional gender roles in all respects, the idea of women wandering through the countryside with an itinerant preacher and his band would be shocking. Maintaining a woman's sexual honor was very important to her husband and family. Prolonged contact with males outside the family would threaten the honor of the woman and her family (cf. Malina and Neyrey in Neyrey 1991, 44).

The Parable of the Sower and Related Sayings (8:4-21)

At this point Luke rejoins the order of Mark after the Q material and special Lukan material in 6:20–8:3. Luke offers a shorter version of the parables discourse in Mark 4:1-34 and Matt 13:1-53. The parable of the mustard seed, omitted here, will appear in Luke 13:18-19. Luke simplifies and unifies the scene, omitting the withdrawal to privacy in Mark 4:10. At the end of the scene Jesus' mother and brothers appear (8:19-21). This pronouncement story occurs earlier in Matthew and Mark. The Lukan setting of this story highlights the thematic connection between hearing and doing the word of God in 8:21 and the parable of the seed and soils.

The crowds have been witnessing Jesus' healing and hearing his teaching for some time. In 6:43-49 Jesus began to warn the crowds and disciples that simply listening to him is not enough. The present scene reinforces that message. The word is only effective if it takes root and grows. That depends on whether the listener will "hold it fast . . . and bear fruit with patient endurance" (8:15). Steady commitment is necessary if the word is to grow and produce fruit. The interpretation of the parable in verses 11-14 warns of conditions that prevent this growth.

8:4-10: Jesus first speaks a parable, and then, after a brief comment to his disciples, provides an interpretation. The interpretation need not be viewed as the only application of the parable. The interpretation focuses on a particular set of hindrances to the growth of the word of God in its hearers. If the situation changes, other hindrances might need to be mentioned. Furthermore, the interpretation, in its concern with exhortation, neglects the note of triumph in the phrase "it produced a hundredfold" (a very high yield). The parable, when considered apart from the interpretation, can be understood as simply listing some of the obstacles that a farmer faces when sowing, thereby acknowledging that there will be problems, yet the parable insists that the good soil will produce abundantly. Viewed in this way, the parable uses the peasant farmer's trust in a future harvest to provide reassurance in the face of obstacles that may appear overwhelming to disciples.

When asked about this parable (not about parables in general, as in Mark 4:10), Jesus first makes a sharp distinction between disciples, to whom it has been given to know the secrets (or "mysteries") of the kingdom, and the others, for whom Jesus' message remains only parables. Jesus' message is in parables "so that" the latter group may not perceive nor understand. ("So that" translates *hina,* which basically expresses purpose, "in order that." However, it sometimes expresses result, and the NRSV understands *hina* in that sense here.) It is important to recognize that verse 10 contains a free quotation of Isa 6:9, part of a passage that will be quoted more fully in Acts 28:26-27. According to Luke, the presence of people for whom Jesus' words are only parables, revealing no mysteries, fulfills this scripture. They see and hear superficially, without the message taking on lasting meaning for their lives. The fact that this faulty seeing and hearing fulfills scripture means that it is anticipated in God's plan, which will not be thwarted by it. It does not mean that God's last word about such people has been spoken. Even the more powerful accusation of deafness and blindness in Acts 28:26-27 does not eliminate hope for change (cf. Tannehill 1990, 346-53). Luke's omission of the last line of the comparable quotation in Mark 4:12 ("so that they may not turn again and be forgiven") supports this view.

8:11-18: The explanation of the parable begins by identifying the seed with the word of God. Although this term can refer to the church's missionary preaching (Acts 4:31), in this context it refers to the preaching and teaching of Jesus (cf. Luke 5:1). The following verses provide further comment on the two kinds of people in verse 10. Jesus' parables do not automatically and easily reveal mysteries of the kingdom. This revelation comes only to those who hold the word fast in a good heart and allow the word to bear fruit with patient endurance (v. 15). There must be long-term personal commitment and a willingness to let Jesus' word shape heart and action. Those who do not hold the word fast in a heart open to its meaning will find little in Jesus' parables.

Three specific forms of failure are mentioned. In some cases the word never gets a chance to start growing. This failure is attributed to the devil, the anti-godly power present in the world. In some cases the word is received joyfully, but times of testing reveal a lack of sustaining root. In some cases the word is "choked by the cares and riches and pleasures of life." "Cares" and "pleasures" are related to "riches," for riches provide pleasures and seem to be the solution to worries about economic security. The warnings about falling away in times of testing and about cares, riches, and pleasures apply to the disciples as well as the crowd. Although testing may cover more than persecution, persecution is included, and Jesus will repeatedly seek to prepare his disciples for it (cf. 9:23-26; 12:4-12; 21:12-19). The conflict between discipleship and the desire for financial security is also a repeated topic of teaching to the disciples (cf. 12:22-34; 14:33; 16:1-13; 18:18-30). The explanation of the parable provides norms by which the Lukan audience can assess persons in the narrative as well as themselves. The disciples in Luke will fall short, at least when they face their greatest test in the passion story.

By omission of Mark's introductory "he said to them," Luke ties the following three sayings (vv. 16-18) more closely to the preceding verses, and noting connections with verses 10-15 will help us interpret them. The lamp must go on the lampstand, where it can be seen, for the sake of "those who enter." That is, guests who are coming to the house will be able to find their way in if they can see the light. There is a missionary concern here, and it balances the reference in verse 10 to those who do not truly see. Outsiders are not to be forgotten. By speech and action one must be a light that enables such people to see and enter the house. The next verse promises that the hidden will be disclosed. In verse 10 it is the secrets of the kingdom that are hidden from some. Disciples should not assume, however, that this situation is permanent. Taking a proverb that may have originally warned that guilty secrets have a way of coming out, Jesus promises that the secrets of the kingdom, presently hidden to many, will be disclosed. The third saying (v. 18) is related to the references to listening or hearing in verses 10-15. In some cases listening does not bring understanding nor does it enable the seed to take root and grow, but others hear the word and hold it fast in a good heart. So much depends on "how you listen." Furthermore, true listening is cumulative. Through holding fast to what has been given so far, disciples will be able to accept the teaching that will follow and grow in understanding, but those who are like the rocky and thorny ground will find that the faith they thought they had will vanish.

8:19-21: Without a change of time or place, the narrator introduces Jesus' mother and brothers in order to say something further about hearing the word of God. Luke 8:19-21 is a short version of a pronouncement story found also in Matt 12:46-50 and Mark 3:31-35. It is integrated with the preceding discussion by the substitution of "word of God" for "will of God" in Mark. The short Lukan version loses some of the dramatic power of Mark, and the contrast between the biological family and the family of disciples is not as sharp. Nevertheless, the pronouncement story is still constructed through using the phrase "mother and brothers" in the normal, literal sense and then introducing a second sense that is surprising in the context. In doing so, Jesus highlights a new family bond that takes precedence over the birth family. "Those who hear the word of God and do it" are members of this new family. (Fitzmyer 1981, 722-25, understands v. 21 as praise of Jesus' biological family. Against this view, see Tannehill 1986, 212-13.)

◊ ◊ ◊ ◊

This story shows a typical lack of biographical interest. We are neither told whether Jesus' mother and brothers finally got to see him, nor whether they supported Jesus' ministry. Mary is presented favorably in Luke's infancy narrative, and Jesus' mother and brothers will reappear as part of the postresurrection community in Acts 1:14. Luke 8:19-21 and a related dialogue in 11:27-28 may disturb this positive image, for they could be understood to show lack of respect by Jesus for his mother and family. The narrator was willing to risk this because 8:19-21 makes a point that is important for the Lukan audience. In a culture in which the typical person was not an independent individual but was embedded in a group, the primary group (the family) defined identity and obligations, and provided status and support systems (cf. Malina and Neyrey in Neyrey 1991, 72-73). Following Jesus, however, could require a break with one's family, and the resulting conflict in families is clearly reflected in other Lukan passages (12:51-53; 14:26; 18:29-30; 21:16). For those alienated from their families, the Jesus community became a surrogate family (cf. Malina and Rohrbaugh 1992, 335-36). New parents, brothers, and sisters could be found within the community, which provided a new support system for those who had lost family support. This little scene, then, adds a further challenge to the preceding exhortation to hold fast the word. Like Jesus, the Lukan audience would be expected to willingly give priority to the family that finds its unity in hearing and doing the word of God.

Stilling a Storm for the Disciples (8:22-25)

This scene, which has parallels in Matt 8:23-27 and Mark 4:35-41, is both a rescue wonder and an epiphany. As a rescue wonder, it shows the disciples being rescued from the threatening water by divine power. Other rescue wonders are found in Acts 12:1-11 and 27:1-44. As an epiphany, the story reveals Jesus as the bearer of mysterious divine power, including the Creator God's power over the waters. This focus on Jesus appears in the concluding question, "Who then is this?"

◊ ◊ ◊ ◊

The disciples' words as they wake Jesus are more respectful than in Mark but less prayerful than in Matthew. Their words could be taken as an expression of despair. Jesus responds to their need, rebuking the wind and waves as if they were demons, but he then also chides the disciples with the question "Where is your faith?" Through lack of faith in a time of testing, they have come dangerously close to being like the rocky people who "believe only for a while and in a time of testing fall away" (8:13). The disciples' concluding question about Jesus shows their amazement at his power but also reveals their inadequate understanding of him. The question "Who then is this?" is part of a larger plot line, for it will be repeated by Herod in 9:9. Later Jesus will pose the same question about himself, asking first for the judgment of the crowds and then of the disciples (9:18-20), which will lead to the revelations about Jesus in 9:20-22, 35. The disciples are being taught that they must not lose faith in the rescuing power of God, whether before or after death. (For faith even at the moment of death, see 23:46; Acts 7:59.) They are also being led to more powerful affirmations about Jesus.

This scene could take on broader significance for those acquainted with the Psalms. There, danger of drowning functions as a symbol for any extreme danger (Pss 18:16-17; 69:1-2, 14-15). God is viewed as sleeping when divine help seems absent (Pss 35:23; 44:23; 59:4-5; 121:3-4; cf. Bovon 1989, 425), but the psalmist proclaims God's power to calm the threatening sea (Pss 89:9; 107:23-32). The drama of human need and divine help is played out in this imagery, which could be applied to many situations. The communities of Jesus believed that through Jesus, the rescuing power of the God who can calm the sea was available to them in their various needs.

Exorcism of the Man with "Legion" (8:26-39)

This elaborated exorcism story shows Jesus confronting demons, as in 4:31-37, but it differs from that brief scene by extending the dialogue between Jesus and the demons, providing vivid descriptions of the possessed man before and after the exorcism, and adding an extensive appendix that clarifies Jesus' relation both to the people of the country and the former demoniac. The Lukan account follows Mark 5:1-20 fairly closely, while Matt 8:28–9:1 offers a shorter version with two demoniacs.

The place name is somewhat uncertain, since the manuscripts divide among three options. It is most important to recognize that Jesus has entered territory with a large Gentile population. The presence of a herd of swine, forbidden food for Jews, is a sign of this.

8:26-33: The vivid description of the possessed man's condition is divided between verses 27 and 29. He wore no clothes and did not live in a house. That is, he was dehumanized, living like a beast. He lived in the tombs, unclean places for Jews. He was also beyond human control, even with chains and shackles. Yet, like other demons, the demon speaking through him immediately recognizes who Jesus is, "Son of the Most High God" (cf. 4:41). When Jesus asks for a name, the man replies "legion." Probably the chief significance of this name is to show that Jesus is faced with a massive concentration of demonic power, although some interpreters take "legion" as code for the Roman occupying forces that oppress the land (cf. Theissen 1991, 110). In the latter case, the story of driving out legion takes on political significance.

The demons want to escape being sent into the abyss. The abyss was regarded as the place of imprisonment and punishment of demons (cf. Rev 20:1-3). This word was also used in the LXX to translate the Hebrew $t^e h\bar{o}m$, the flood or watery deep (cf. Böcher in Balz and Schneider 1990, 1.4). It may be that Jesus' permission for the demons to enter the swine, which rush into the lake and drown, tricks the demons, which end in the abyss (represented by the lake) after all. However, this point is not clearly made in the story. One technique of exorcism is to remove the demon from the person to another creature or object (cf. Twelftree 1993, 75). In this case the large herd of swine provides a new home for the many demons, and the herd going berserk visibly demonstrates the demons' new location. The plunge of the swine into the water removes the demons from the land, whether permanently or temporarily. This story, told from a Jewish perspective, puts no value on the swine and is not concerned about the owner's loss.

8:34-39: Considerable attention is given to the effect of this event, not only on the man freed of demons but on the whole region. That the man is now "clothed and in his right mind" shows the change from his former condition. The fact that he is sitting at Jesus' feet may indicate the beginning of discipleship. The reaction of the people, however, is not joy or amazement but simply "great fear" that leads them to ask Jesus to leave (v. 37). Luke, in contrast to Mark, emphasizes that this was the reaction of "all the people of the surrounding country." As a result, Jesus departs. Jesus has entered Gentile territory and has performed a fabulous exorcism, but this will not be the start of an extended mission by Jesus, for these people are not ready to receive him. This response contributes to uncertainty about the long-range effect of the drowning of the pigs in the lake. Is the purging of the land permanent or is there danger of return (cf. 11:24-26)? The Gentile mission must wait until the apostles are commissioned to go to Gentiles and are empowered with the Spirit (cf. 24:47-49). As Luke presents it, Jesus was ready to help Gentiles, but they were not ready for him. Jesus will encounter a similar rebuff from the Samaritans (9:51-56).

The man freed of demons wants to accompany Jesus, but Jesus sends him away. The man who did not live in a house (*oikia*, v. 27) is to return to his house (*oikos*, v. 39), which will complete his return from the inhuman world to human society. By doing so, he can be Jesus' representative among a people that wants Jesus to leave. The shift from "how much God has done" to "how much Jesus had done" in the execution of Jesus' command does not indicate disobedience. The mighty acts can be ascribed to both God and Jesus, for they are deeds of power "that God did through" Jesus (Acts 2:22). Although there is no indication that a community of believers results, the man's proclaiming prepares for later mission in the area.

◊ ◊ ◊ ◊

The Lukan audience might first have related this vivid exorcism story to cases of demonic possession in their own community in hope that through the name of Jesus some of their friends and family might be freed from unclean spirits. Later passages in Luke may have encouraged the audience to take a broader view. Jesus and his representatives not only help individuals but are conducting a general campaign against demons and Satan, and they have the power to conquer these inhuman enemies (10:17-19; 11:14-22).

The setting of this exorcism among Gentiles might also catch the attention of the Lukan audience. According to some Jewish authors, the pagan gods are demons (*Jub.* 1:11; 22:17; *1 Enoch* 19:1; 99:7; 1 Cor 10:19-20). Some interpreters believe that the story of the Gerasene demoniac is a midrash on Isa 65:1-4 LXX, understood as an accusation against Gentiles (cf. Sahlin 1964, 160-62). Although the description there of Gentiles offering incense to demons, sleeping among the tombs, and eating swine's flesh is striking, it is difficult to believe that the special features of this story are all derived from this text. Nevertheless, this general way of thinking suggests that some Gentile members of Lukan communities might have been encouraged to understand, and so have experienced, their conversion as release from the power of demons. Although preaching to Gentiles in Acts does not label the many gods as demons, they and their images are rejected firmly as "worthless things" from which people must repent (Acts 14:15; 17:29-30). The more strident label of "demons" is dangerous, but there is a sense in which gods possess their worshipers, sometimes with destructive consequences. This story, then, could both represent individual conversions and be a sign of hope for the purging of demons from pagan culture as a whole.

Jairus's Daughter and the Woman with a Hemorrhage (8:40-56)

This passage is parallel to Mark 5:21-43. There is a shorter version in Matt 9:18-26. Luke 8:22-56 (in parallel with Mark) offers a series of wonder stories of various types: the calming of the storm, a major exorcism, and now a resurrection and a healing of a woman with a bloody flow. As the disciples observe these events, they are being prepared for their own ministry of exorcism and healing (9:1-2; 10:9, 17), which will continue in Acts. The story of the hemorrhaging woman, however, is more than a healing story. The healing takes place early in the scene (v. 44), and the main focus is on Jesus' response to a woman who has violated purity rules in order to find healing. The story of the hemorrhaging woman is inserted into the story of Jairus. The encounter with the woman causes a delay that increases the gravity of the situation; the daughter who was dying is now declared dead. The interweaving of the two stories also suggests comparisons among the key characters.

◊ ◊ ◊ ◊

Jairus is a synagogue leader, a person of prominence in Jewish society. Although Jewish leaders, such as the scribes and Pharisees, when operating as a group, generally oppose Jesus, this is not always true of individuals. Jairus comes not to debate but to find help for his daughter. He lays his dignity aside and falls at Jesus' feet. Luke increases the sense of pathos by adding that he is asking help for his "only" daughter, a detail that may remind hearers of the previous story of the widow whose "only son" had died (7:11-17). Luke offers two resurrection stories with the genders switched: a mother and her son; a father and his daughter.

The woman touches the fringe of Jesus' cloak and her hemorrhage stops. The fringe (or tassels) on Jews' cloaks was to remind them of "all the commandments of the LORD" so that they would do them (cf. Num 15:37-39). But the woman is violating a purity commandment by touching this fringe. Women are ritually unclean for seven days when they have a menstrual discharge. If the discharge continues, the impurity continues, and this impurity can be transmitted to others (Lev 15:19-31). Purity was crucially important when going to the temple, lest the temple be defiled. There were probably Jews who did not worry about issues of purity at other times. Yet maintaining ritual purity was valued as a sign of devotion (cf. E. P. Sanders 1990, 164, 270-71). The little scene uses the word "touch" four times, for this is the crucial action that both heals and conveys impurity. Following the healing, Jesus asks, "Who touched me?" No one is willing to admit doing so, especially not the woman, who realizes that she may be publicly rebuked for defiling a holy man. That is why, when Jesus persists and the woman fears discovery, she comes forth "trembling." Her impurity may also explain why she did not come to Jesus openly with her need.

In verse 47 the woman stops hiding and makes an open confession "in the presence of all the people." She is ready to receive Jesus' rebuke. Instead, Jesus praises her faith, demonstrated in entering the crowd (where she should not be) and in touching Jesus. "Your faith has made you well" (or "has saved you"), he says. The verb *sōzō*, "save," is frequently used in healing stories to refer to release from physical affliction (cf. 8:36, 50; 17:19; 18:42; Acts 4:9; 14:9), suggesting that these healings are part of the "salvation" for "all flesh" (3:6) that God is bringing through Jesus (a point obscured by the translation "made you well"). As in 5:19-20, faith has been demonstrated by bold action that refuses to stop at barriers. Jesus' encounter with the hemorrhaging woman ends with the same words used to commend another woman who transgressed social rules (cf. 7:50).

Jesus challenges Jairus to match the woman's faith. After saying to the woman, "Your faith has saved you," he tells Jairus, "Only believe [i.e., "have faith"], and she [the daughter] will be saved" (vv. 48, 50). Luke has added "and she will be saved" to indicate better the connection with the woman's story. Thus the story presents a low-status woman, one who has been ritually unclean for twelve years, as a model for a high-status man, a synagogue leader, just as Simon the Pharisee was asked to learn from the sinful woman (7:36-50).

In verse 52 Jesus says that Jairus's daughter is sleeping, contrary to the belief of all. The word for "sleeping" here is sometimes used in the New Testament to refer to death that is temporary because it will be followed by resurrection (cf. Eph 5:14; 1 Thess 5:10). When Jesus says, "Child, get up," and the narrator says, "She got up at once," two Greek verbs *(egeirō, anistēmi)* are used that are commonly used of the resurrection of Jesus and the final resurrection of others (11:32; 20:37; 24:6-7). This language makes it easy for the Lukan audience to take this story as a prefiguration of what Jesus, as the "Author of life" and "first" of the general resurrection (Acts 3:15; 26:23), will do for believers when he returns with royal power.

◊ ◊ ◊ ◊

The Lukan audience would not only find hope of healing and resurrection in these stories but also encouragement to keep their communities open to contrasting sorts of people. A man and a woman, the former prominent in Jewish society, the latter excluded from the temple and a source of pollution to others, are accepted and helped by Jesus. Therefore, they must also be accepted in the community of Jesus' followers. The synagogue leader is not rejected as an opponent, yet such people must be willing to join a community that includes persons judged unclean. Society's leaders are also being asked to recognize that the faith of lowly people can provide a challenging example for those of higher social status. Peter, too, had to adjust to this new reality (Acts 10:28; 15:9).

The Mission of the Twelve (9:1-6)

9:1-2: In 5:11 Peter, James, and John began to follow Jesus. In 6:12-16 the twelve were chosen as apostles. They were given instruction through the sermons in 6:20-49 and 8:4-21, and they witnessed Jesus' mighty acts in 8:22-56. Now the twelve are ready to share in Jesus' work. At this point Jesus gives them power and authority to cure diseases and cast out demons (v. 1), and commissions them to proclaim the kingdom of God and heal (v. 2). Their preaching mission fits Jesus' own. Just as they are sent to "proclaim the kingdom of God" and bring "good news" (9:2, 6), so Jesus was sent to "proclaim the good news of the kingdom of God" (4:43-44; cf. 4:18; 8:1). The preaching is accompanied by healing and exorcism, for these are indications of the reign of God powerfully effective in the present (cf. 10:9; 11:20).

There are parallels to this passage in Mark 6:7-13 and Matt 10:1, 7-11, 14. Luke alone has a second mission discourse (10:1-24) in which seventy (or seventy-two) are sent out. Thus the disciples' mission is not restricted to the twelve, even during Jesus' ministry. The twelve have the honor of being sent first, but the second sending is more fully developed and concludes with a section of rejoicing at the powerful signs of God's reign in this mission (10:17-24). In contrast, 9:1-6 ends by simply noting that the apostles fulfilled Jesus' command. Thus the emphasis falls on the second sending, to which the sending of the twelve is preliminary. Both of these are preliminary to the worldwide mission that Jesus will announce in 24:46-49.

That the twelve are now able to preach good news and cure diseases does not mean that they are ready for their later mission in Acts. They still have much to learn, and their faith must grow. The narrator will soon show that they are sometimes unable to use the authority over demons granted by Jesus (cf. 9:40).

9:3-6: Jesus gives detailed instructions to the twelve. His words in verse 3 are strange, for Jesus prohibits items that could be very useful in dealing with the difficulties of a journey. The bag is a traveler's bag for supplies, which could also be used for begging. The wandering Cynic preachers were known for their ability to survive with very little from the culture that they were attacking, but they at least carried a staff and a bag for begging (cf. Crossan 1991, 74-88, 338-39). As a result of Jesus' prohibitions, the apostles are completely dependent on whatever hospitality they will receive in the villages. In verse 4 the twelve are told that they are not to move from house to house, perhaps looking for better accommodations or begging from door to door. When offered hospitality, the apostle should share the family's meals and lodging, as if he were a relative from another village, until it is time to go. The need for food and lodging requires the apostle to live with people and share their lives. Perhaps this sharing enables the seed of the good news to take root and grow in a new place.

Yet this will be a tough life, for the apostles cannot be sure of welcome. The third instruction (v. 5) concerns the times when they will find no welcoming homes in a town. The gesture of shaking the dust off one's feet is probably a prophetic sign. It is a solemn sign of separation. It recurs not only in 10:11 but also in Acts 13:51 and, in the variant form of shaking out one's clothes, in Acts 18:6. In the last passage, the gesture is accompanied by a statement, borrowing language from Ezek 33:4, that Paul's responsibility has been fulfilled. Now he can turn elsewhere, and those who have rejected him must take the consequences of their rejection of a prophet's word (cf. Tannehill 1990, 223). Probably the gesture of separation in Luke 9:5 has similar significance. It is to be "a testimony against them" (or "to them"), a notable sign that will testify after the apostles have left.

Herod Is Perplexed (9:7-9)

Unlike the parallels in Matt 14:1-2 and Mark 6:14-16, this brief scene does not introduce the story of John the Baptist's death, which is absent from Luke. Also, Herod in Luke does not identify Jesus with the risen John, as in Matthew and Mark. In response to reports about Jesus, he simply asks, "Who is this about whom I hear such things?" The question "Who is this?" has been voiced before (5:21; 7:49), most recently by the disciples (8:25). The claims about Jesus to which Herod is reacting are repeated in 9:19, immediately before Peter's confession. The narrator is using Herod's question to prepare for important disclosures about Jesus. We should keep this leading question in mind as we examine the following narrative, especially 9:10-45 (cf. Fitzmyer 1981, 757-58).

The three claims that people make about Jesus all identify him with past prophets. Although the Lukan audience was told already in 1:32-33 that Jesus is the Davidic Messiah and Peter will soon come to the same conclusion (9:20), the identification of Jesus as a prophet is not to be dismissed as a sign of blindness. From what the people have seen and heard so far—Jesus' teaching and healing—they can reasonably conclude that he is a prophet (cf. 7:16). Even Jesus describes himself as a prophet (4:24; 13:33-34). Although the identifications of Jesus with John, Elijah, or another scriptural prophet go too far, these guesses show some insight; Jesus does carry on John's call to repentance and forgiveness (cf. 3:3), both Jesus and the narrator have suggested similarities between Jesus and Elijah (4:25-26; 7:11-16); and the reference to "one of the ancient prophets" could suggest that Jesus is the prophet like Moses, which will be affirmed in Acts (3:22; 7:37; cf. Deut 18:15). The last of these identifications uses, in contrast to Mark, the verb *anistēmi* ("raise up, arise"), the verb applied to the prophet like Moses in Deut 18:15.

◊ ◊ ◊ ◊

Herod continues to play a role in the story of Jesus. He is curious about Jesus but is also a potential threat to him. His statement "John I beheaded" shows the audience how he treats meddlesome prophets, and those familiar with the traditional theme of conflict between prophets and rulers (cf. Darr 1992, 149-58) would have additional reason for apprehension. Herod is cited as a threat to Jesus in 13:31. His desire to see Jesus (9:9) is finally fulfilled in the passion story (23:6-12). There Herod is disappointed in his hope to see Jesus perform a sign, and he adds to the contempt being heaped on Jesus.

Feeding a Multitude (9:10-17)

There are no less than six versions of the feeding of the multitude in the wilderness: Matt 14:13-21; 15:32-39; Mark 6:32-44; 8:1-10; Luke 9:10-17; and John 6:1-15. The second account in Matthew and Mark is missing in Luke. It is part of a major omission that includes all the material found in Mark 6:45–8:26. As a result, the Lukan narrative moves directly from the feeding of the five thousand to Peter's confession, a significantly different sequence.

This story is a provision wonder (cf. Tannehill 1995, 63), similar to Jesus providing wine for a wedding (John 2:1-11) and great catches of fish (Luke 5:4-7; John 21:1-11). There are stories of wonderful provision of food in the early church's scripture (manna in the wilderness [Exodus 16]; Elijah and the widow [1 Kgs 17:8-16]; Elisha feeds a hundred with twenty barley loaves [2 Kgs 4:42-44]). The last of these stories is closest in detail to the Gospel story, but the manna in the wilderness played a greater role in Israel's memory.

◊ ◊ ◊ ◊

The crowd welcomed Jesus in 8:40, and the twelve were dependent on the welcome of local people on their mission (9:3-5). Now Jesus welcomes the crowds (9:11). Indeed, he will be host at a meal provided for them all. Thus there are hints of reciprocal hospitality in the narrative.

The twelve have an important role in the feeding of the crowds. The feeding is linked to the mission of the twelve by verses 10-11 and by the reference to "the twelve" in verse 12 (Matt 14:15 and Mark 6:35 have "disciples"). The work of the apostles is not over when they return from their mission. People gathered by the mission must now receive care. The twelve recognize the crowd's need for nourishment but are taken aback when Jesus says, "*You* give them something to eat." (There is emphasis on "you" in the Greek.) The task is impossible for the twelve by themselves, but just as Jesus made possible the great catch of fish when Peter was first called to the task of "catching people" (5:1-11), so he will now enable the twelve to feed the people who have been gathered. The disciples are given the tasks of organizing the crowd into eating groups and of distributing the food that Jesus provides, with the result that "all ate and were filled." In verse 17 the narrator emphasizes that there were exactly twelve baskets of food left over. ("twelve" is the last word of the sentence in Greek, a position of emphasis.) Each of the apostles now has a supply for future nourishment of those gathered through their mission.

In 12:41-46 Jesus equates the image of feeding with congregational care. He speaks to Peter about the "manager" who is "put in charge" to give others "their allowance of food at the proper time" (12:42). The image refers to the responsibility of church leaders for those in their care. The feeding of the five thousand, I believe, has the same symbolic overtones. Support for this view also comes from 22:24-27, where Jesus, in his farewell discourse, asks the apostles to understand themselves in the future as table servers.

Although we are not told how the food multiplied, there is detailed description of Jesus' actions with the food in verse 16. The significance of these actions appears when we note that they are very similar to Jesus' actions at the Last Supper (22:19) and the Emmaus meal (24:30). This similarity ties these three meals together and also relates them to the early church's meal celebrations, which in Acts are called "the breaking of bread" (2:42). Probably these actions would be familiar to the Lukan audience, who would find here an anticipation of the church's meal celebrations, even though Jesus in Luke 9 is sharing food with people who do not recognize him as Messiah. (In 9:18-19 we will be reminded of the crowds' opinions about Jesus.)

The scene also gains depth of meaning through the eschatological associations of meals in Luke. The statement in verse 17 that they "ate and were filled" uses the same verb *(chortazō)* as the beatitude in 6:21. ("Blessed are you who are hungry now, for you will be filled.") This is a beatitude for those who will receive the kingdom of God (cf. 6:20). The expected time of fulfillment will be a time of abundance that can be pictured as a joyful banquet (cf. 12:37; 13:28-29; 14:15-24; 22:16, 18). The abundant food for the five thousand not only anticipates the church's meals but also this eschatological meal.

◊ ◊ ◊ ◊

At the Emmaus meal the disciples' "eyes were opened, and they recognized" Jesus (24:31). The feeding of the five thousand in Luke is framed by questions about Jesus' identity (9:9, 18-19), and immediately following this scene Peter confesses for the first time that Jesus is the Messiah. We are not told explicitly how he came to this new insight. Jesus' mighty acts in Luke 8:22-56 may have contributed, but the Lukan frame for the feeding scene suggests that the feeding has an important role in this new development. If so, Peter understood the feeding as more than the solution to a temporary problem. Only when understood as an anticipation of the eschatological banquet would this meal lead to the conclusion that Jesus is the Messiah, the expected ruler who brings the time of fulfillment. The connection between Messiah and meal is supported by 22:29-30, where Jesus speaks of eating and drinking "at my table in my kingdom."

Social science criticism calls attention to the experience of limited good in Mediterranean society. People of that time and place quickly learned that valuable things were in short supply, and if some people hoarded them, others would go without (cf. Malina and Rohrbaugh 1992, 324). Except for a privileged few, scarcity was a fundamental reality. The feeding of the five thousand, however, proclaims abundance. The communities of Jesus are encouraged to hope that the messianic kingdom will bring an abundance in which all can share. In the meantime, the community meals would serve as temporary signs of this future hope. The picture in Acts of the Jerusalem church—a community that shared resources, so that "there was not a needy person among them" (4:34)—also suggests how believers could share the eschatological abundance in advance. We do not know whether any of the Lukan communities followed this suggestion.

Peter's Confession and Jesus' Passion Teaching (9:18-27)

9:18-20: In Luke the next scene is preceded by prayer, a sign that something important is about to happen. Jesus' question to the disciples elicits the same answers as in 9:7-8. Because of his preaching and healing, the crowds think of Jesus as a prophet. But now Jesus puts the question to his disciples, and Peter responds by declaring that Jesus is "the Messiah of God." The Lukan audience was told this already in the infancy narrative (cf. 2:11), but this confession is a new level of insight for Peter and the other disciples. Jesus is indeed a "great prophet," as the crowds proclaimed (7:16), but there is more to his story. He is the promised Messiah.

9:21-22: Immediately Jesus commands the disciples to tell no one. Unlike Matthew and Mark, the Lukan narrator attaches the first passion announcement (v. 22) to the command to silence as part of the same sentence, implying that the passion announcement explains why the disciples must tell no one. It will be dangerous to proclaim Jesus as Messiah, and it is not yet time to do so. Furthermore, the disciples themselves do not understand what it means for Jesus to be the Messiah. Rejection and death do not fit their expectation. The lack of understanding is not immediately apparent because Luke omits Peter's rebuke of Jesus and Jesus' harsh rebuke of Peter following the passion announcement (cf. Matt 16:22-23; Mark 8:32-33). Luke has tightened the sequence of Peter's confession, passion announcement, and discipleship teaching in 9:18-27. In the process Peter is spared, but the Lukan version of disciple resistance to Jesus' way of suffering will soon follow (cf. 9:44-45).

The announcement of rejection, death, and resurrection is a sharp revision of expectations concerning the Messiah. The narrative has been subtly revising traditional expectations since the story of Jesus' birth. We have been told that Jesus brings salvation for Gentiles as well as Jews (2:30-32) and that he will be opposed in Israel (2:34). He has introduced himself as Isaiah's herald of good news to the poor (4:18) and has been presented as a healing prophet.

He has preached love of enemies rather than conquest (6:27-36). The narrative leads its audience in "progressive discovery" of what kind of Messiah Jesus is (cf. Brawley 1990, 44-51). Now Jesus announces something new, that he "must" suffer and die. The word translated "must" is an impersonal verb in Greek (*dei*, "it is necessary"). It is used repeatedly of a divine necessity that Jesus must accept and obey (2:49; 4:43; 13:33; 17:25; 22:37; 24:7, 26, 44). Thus the passion announcement is a further disclosure of Jesus' mandate from God, the program of action that he must obediently fulfill. As such, this announcement must be added to Jesus' statements about his mission in 4:18-19, 43. But the disciples do not understand why Jesus' mission must include rejection and death. It may also have been difficult for the Lukan audience to understand, for there is hardly any reference to an atoning death in Luke–Acts (possible exceptions are Luke 22:19-20; Acts 20:28).

9:23-27: The necessity of suffering applies to the disciples as well as to Jesus. When the first disciples were called, they "followed" Jesus (5:11). In 9:23 Jesus begins to explain what following means from this point on. Those who "want to continue coming after me" (the NRSV says "want to become my followers") must deny themselves and take up their own crosses. Luke adds "daily," which suggests a broader application than the single event of death by persecution. Repeatedly one must be willing to accept death and dishonor, like those who are crucified.

The sayings in verses 24-26 are each connected to the preceding by "for" (twice omitted in the NRSV), an indication that they support and interpret the fundamental teaching about cross bearing in verse 23. The first of these sayings is an aphorism that connects, in paradoxical fashion, the antithetical ideas of saving life and losing it. The paradox emphasizes the strangeness of the assertion, thereby taking the opposing view seriously. People have clear ideas of what saving life means; it does not mean losing it. Yet Jesus here asserts the opposite. This is a jolting challenge to those who think they know what they are doing in acting for their own security (cf. Tannehill 1975, 98-101). In verse 25 gaining the whole world is the extreme case of acquiring wealth. Wealth and security might seem to go together, yet neither makes sense if one loses one's very self. In verse 26 being "ashamed of me" means refusing to honor Jesus by confessing one's loyalty to him under social or judicial pressure. There is an exact balance between this action and the action of the Son of Man in a future confrontation. Reuse of the term "ashamed" suggests that the Son of Man's rebuff is fair and appropriate, since it matches the crime. Social science critics have called attention to the importance of honor and shame in the ancient Mediterranean world (cf. Malina and Neyrey in Neyrey 1991, 25-65). To be ashamed of Jesus is to shame him rather than honor him. It is likely to happen when one wants to maintain one's own place of honor within a culture that rejects Jesus' claims. Thus two competing honor systems are reflected in this verse.

The final saying of this sayings chain differs from Mark 9:1 by the omission of the words "has come with power" at the end. While Mark seems to anticipate the final manifestation of the kingdom in power, the Lukan statement is more ambiguous. Although the return of the Son of Man in glory would be a manifestation of the kingdom of God, this did not happen during the lifetime of those "standing here." The Lukan statement makes it possible to think of Jesus' appearance in glory at the transfiguration (the next episode) or of his ascension and sending of the Spirit, which are associated with his enthronement at the right hand of God (cf. 22:69; Acts 2:33-35). Since Jesus' enthronement as Messiah and Lord is an aspect of the kingdom of God, the early church's preaching about Jesus can be described as preaching the kingdom of God (cf. Acts 8:12; 19:8; 20:25; 28:23, 31).

◊ ◊ ◊ ◊

Unlike the disciples in the story, Jesus' statement about his coming death would not be startling news to the Lukan audience. Nevertheless, the following sayings about discipleship would be difficult, for they had direct relevance to the lives of early believers. Even if there was no official persecution, the believers were a small minority that aroused the suspicion of both the Jewish community and the dominant Greco-Roman culture. Choices between honor in society and making a little money, on the one hand, and honoring

Jesus, on the other, would have been necessary, and occasionally the choice might have been life threatening. The natural tendency was to try to have it both ways, but these severe sayings indicate that such a plan would not ultimately work.

Jesus' Transfiguration (9:28-36)

Luke's transfiguration scene, which has parallels in Matt 17:1-9 and Mark 9:2-10, is basically a divine affirmation of Jesus. The description of his heavenly glory, the association of Jesus with Moses and Elijah, and the divine pronouncement at the end all contribute to this. This scene can be called an epiphany story; it reveals Jesus as the glorious Son of God. Therefore, it can serve as a preliminary experience of the coming in glory and appearance of the kingdom mentioned in 9:26-27. It is important to recognize, however, that this epiphany story is linked to the mandate of suffering announced by Jesus for himself and his followers in 9:22-26. The strong desire of the Lukan communities to honor Jesus as God's Son is here used to underscore the necessary place of suffering in God's way for Jesus and his disciples.

9:28-31: Once before, a voice came from heaven affirming Jesus as "my Son" (see 3:21-22). Jesus' sonship is being reaffirmed as Jesus enters a new stage of his work, but this time the message is directed not primarily to Jesus but to three apostles. Just as before, the experience of the divine voice comes in the context of prayer. Jesus' conversation with Moses and Elijah can also be understood to hint at the role of scripture in Jesus' understanding of God's purpose. The transfiguration experience may be extraordinary, but it occurs in the context of the ordinary practices of a devout Jew, who, through prayer and scripture, seeks God's will.

Moses and Elijah appear in glory because they are part of the heavenly world, and for brief moments Jesus now shares this heavenly glory. The significance of Moses and Elijah in this scene is not easy to specify, for there are a number of possibilities that make sense in the Lukan context. Moses and Elijah may represent scripture, especially as witness to God's unfolding purpose (cf. 24:27, 44: "Moses and all the prophets"). Aspects of the Moses story probably have special importance. Moses in Luke–Acts is understood not just as the giver of the law but as the prophet-leader (cf. Bock 1994a, 616-19) who was the "liberator" or "redeemer" (*lytrōtēs;* Acts 7:35) of his people and who announced that "God will raise up for you a prophet like me" (Deut 18:15; Acts 3:22; 7:37). The parallels between Jesus and Moses as prophet-redeemers who encounter rejection are developed in Acts 7:33-41, 51-53. The appearance of Moses in Luke 9:30 might cause listeners to note features of the transfiguration story that recall the story of Moses. Moses, too, ascended a mountain and heard the voice of God from a cloud (Exod 24:15-16; 34:5), and Moses' face shone from his encounter with God (Exod 34:29). Furthermore, "listen to him" in Luke 9:35 repeats the instructions concerning the prophet like Moses in Deut 18:15, and in Luke 9:31 Jesus talks with Moses about Jesus' coming "exodus" (*exodos* = "departure" NRSV).

Elijah, a miracle-working prophet, provides a scriptural model for Jesus' ministry (cf. Luke 4:25-26; 7:11-17), but he may also be important as the one scheduled to appear just before the time of fulfillment (Mal 4:5), providing closure to the scriptural prophets' work. Furthermore, the "exodus" that Jesus shares with Moses will involve being "taken up" (Luke 9:51) as Elijah was (2 Kgs 2:11).

Only Luke indicates the subject of the conversation among Jesus, Moses, and Elijah: "his exodus, which he was about to accomplish at Jerusalem" (author's translation). The Greek word *exodos* can mean departure from life, but, with Moses present, the scriptural connotations of this word are clearly important. Jesus' exodus will be a journey to liberation (cf. Ringe 1983, 92-99; Garrett 1990, 656-80) that will establish his kingdom for his people. This exodus will involve not merely Jesus' death but also his resurrection and ascension. The statement in verse 31 can be supplemented by verse 51, another glance forward to Jerusalem, which anticipates Jesus' ascension. Jesus' death, resurrection, and ascension are part of one process by which Jesus is able to "enter into his glory" (24:26) and take his throne at the right hand of God. In the transfiguration there is a brief anticipation of this future glory, assuring both Jesus and his disciples that there is triumph beyond the suffering that they must face. Jesus must "accomplish" or "fulfill" this exodus "at Jerusalem," which will soon be his destination (v. 31).

9:32-36: In verse 32 the narrator's attention shifts to the three disciples, especially Peter. Peter, John, and James see the three glorious figures, even though they are very sleepy. Peter is fascinated by what he sees and makes a proposal, "not knowing what he said" (v. 33). The proposal is inappropriate because the disciples do not really understand what is going on. In particular, they don't understand Jesus' exodus, as verses 44-45 will make clear. Peter wants to build three *skēnas,* temporary shelters such as tents or the huts made from branches for the feast of booths. It may be that the booths of the feast had taken on eschatological significance as heavenly dwellings (cf. 16:9 [again *skēnas*] and Bovon 1989, 499). Peter apparently thinks that Jesus has already arrived in glory, which would eliminate the need for an exodus involving suffering and death.

The voice from the cloud, directed to the disciples, corrects Peter's misunderstanding. The highest titles of authority, appropriate for God's Messiah, are applied to Jesus. (For "chosen" applied to the Messiah, see 23:35; for Son of God applied to the Davidic Messiah, see 1:32-33; 4:41; 22:67-70; Acts 9:20-22; 13:22-23, 32-34.) Then the divine voice commands, "Listen to him!" These words recall the prophet like Moses, who must be heeded (they repeat the command in Deut 18:15 LXX, with its inverted word order). The principal application in context is to Jesus' teaching about suffering and death in 9:22-26, but this command is also a preface to all Jesus' teaching of disciples on his journey to Jerusalem, teaching designed to prepare them for their tasks when he is no longer with them. Peter has recognized Jesus as the Messiah. The voice from the cloud points to the necessary consequence: They must recognize the authority of his teaching, the regulations of his kingdom. This will be difficult because of the content of these teachings. When the voice has spoken, Peter's prized scene vanishes. There is no Moses, no Elijah, no voice, no glory, only Jesus alone, with his mind set on his exodus in Jerusalem (cf. Nolland 1993, 497).

The Disciples' Weaknesses (9:37-50)

The sequence of events in this section follows Mark 9:14-40, but in Mark there are distinct changes of location before the second passion announcement and the discussion about greatness, dividing the section into separate scenes. In Luke these divisions are absent. The second passion announcement comes while people are marveling at Jesus' works, especially the preceding exorcism, and the discussion about greatness follows immediately without change in time or place. So Luke 9:37-50 forms a single scene (cf. Busse 1979, 252-53). The topics may seem to shift abruptly, but there is continuity in that weaknesses of the disciples are being exposed. They are not yet ready to assume full responsibility for Jesus' mission. Jesus, on his journey to Jerusalem, must urgently prepare them.

Failure as Exorcists (9:37-43)

The Marcan version of the exorcism of the boy with an unclean spirit (Mark 9:14-29) is considerably more elaborate than Matt 17:14-20 or Luke 9:37-43. Luke lacks both the concluding discussion with the disciples and the discussion with the father about faith. Luke's version is a basic exorcism story with little elaboration except at two points: (1) The father's request for help is long in comparison with other elements of the story. It contains vivid description of his son's suffering. Pathos is increased by the statement that his son is his "only" one (not stated in Matthew or Mark). This is the third story of a parent and child in need (cf. 7:11-17; 8:40-42, 49-56). These stories fit a common pattern. In each case the son or daughter is the "only" one (cf. 7:12; 8:42; 9:38). (2) The man indicates that Jesus' disciples were unable to cast the demon out, and Jesus replies with a strong reproach of a "faithless and perverse generation." Since Luke's story gives no attention to the faith of the father, and since this reproach immediately follows reference to the disciples, Jesus seems to regard the disciples as the prime example of a "faithless and perverse generation" at this point.

This phrase is reminiscent of Moses' reproach of the people of Israel in Deut 32:5, 20. The twelve were given "power and authority over all demons" in 9:1. Therefore, the nine who did not accompany

Jesus up the mountain should have been able to cast out this demon, but the disciples are showing the same faithlessness and perversity that repeatedly characterized Israel, according to scripture. This robs them of power. Furthermore, Jesus knows that his time is growing short. He says, "How much longer must I be [more literally, "will I be"] with you?" Strengthening the disciples is now an urgent matter.

Failure to Understand the Passion Announcements (9:44-45)

First Jesus heals the boy, then he turns to his disciples and insistently repeats his announcement of his coming rejection. He does this while everyone is still marveling over all his mighty works, including the exorcism that has just taken place. There is a sharp shift of mood here. Everyone else is rejoicing in amazement, but Jesus turns to his disciples and says with vehemence, "Let these words sink into your ears," then indicates that the Son of Man whose deeds are so powerful will have no power to escape his human enemies. In comparison with Matt 17:22-23 and Mark 9:30-32, the emphasis shifts from the passion announcement itself (shortened in Luke) to the failure of the disciples to understand (expanded in Luke). Mark's statement that the disciples did not understand and were afraid to ask is strengthened by adding that the matter "was concealed from them, so that they could not perceive it." This addition may suggest that forces greater than the disciples are at work (Nolland 1993, 514, suggests that the blindness is Satan's work; cf. the role of Satan in the passion narrative: 22:3, 31, 53). However, the disciples are not being excused. They are supposed to understand, as Jesus' command "let these words sink into your ears" makes clear. The three disciples on the mountain were told to "listen to" Jesus. Now Jesus himself demands that they listen, but they do not understand.

This failure will persist. It will be highlighted again in 18:34 and will continue into Easter day (cf. 24:25). Only when the risen Messiah opens the Scriptures to his disciples do they begin to understand that it was "necessary that the Messiah should suffer these things and then enter into his glory" (24:26; cf. 24:25-32). The problem is not the meaning of Jesus' words. The fact that the disciples were afraid shows that they grasped some of the implications. But they could not understand how rejection and death could fit into God's saving plan through Jesus. The narrator makes the Lukan audience wait to discover how Jesus' rejection and death take on meaning, and even later the audience must struggle along with the disciples.

A series of false attitudes is linked to this failure of the disciples to understand Jesus' death (cf. Tannehill 1986, 253-74). Some of these false attitudes appear in 9:46-50.

Desire for Greatness and Jealousy of Others (9:46-50)

Without any change of scene (contrast Mark 9:33), the Lukan narrator juxtaposes the disciples' argument about greatness with their inability to understand the passion announcement. Jesus' crucifixion means rejection and public humiliation (see the emphasis on rejection in 9:22 and the emphasis on mocking in 18:32 and 23:35-39). Those fascinated by greatness will find a crucified Messiah incomprehensible. This appears to be one facet of the disciples' problem.

Jesus seeks to correct the disciples by placing a child by his side and making this child his representative. The test that he poses is whether they will "welcome" or "receive" this child, that is, whether they will recognize him or her as important enough to be shown the respect due an honored guest. Children lacked power and status. Young children were under the care of women or servants and were part of the female world (cf. Malina and Rohrbaugh 1992, 300). Although a father should take a hand in disciplining his son (Prov 3:11-12; Sir 30:1), the counsel of the wise regarded chatting with children as a waste of time (m. Abot 3:10). Yet Jesus makes the child his representative by saying, "Whoever welcomes this child in my name welcomes me." Here a formula applied to the emissary or missionary (cf. 10:16; Matt 10:40; John 13:20) is surprisingly applied to this child. Accepting the child can be equated with accepting Jesus because Jesus will be robbed of power and status through the Crucifixion, thereby becoming child-like.

The child also represents "the least among all of you," that is, whoever seems insignificant. The disciples must learn that such people, being Jesus' representatives, are really "great" (the NRSV has "the greatest," but the Greek removes the idea of comparison at this point).

Just like the failure to understand Jesus' death, the desire for greatness is more than a momentary defect. The disciples' refusal to welcome children in 18:15 will show their failure to accept Jesus' teaching. At the Last Supper they will again argue over who is greatest, and Jesus will again try to change their attitude (22:24-27). The passion setting of 22:24-37 supports the previously suggested connection between Jesus' disgraceful death and his rejection of society's concern with greatness.

The statement of John in 9:49 is introduced as an answer or response to what Jesus has been saying about the child. Thus John recognizes a possible connection between the child or the least and the irregular exorcist that the disciples tried to stop. John and the others are so convinced of their own importance that they feel only those who "follow with us" can be legitimate (despite the fact that some of the disciples failed as exorcists and were rebuked by Jesus in 9:40-41). Again Jesus corrects the disciples' jealous desire for status and control. They should be willing to recognize that the powers of God's kingdom are at work beyond their own circle. Jesus says, "do not stop" the exorcist, and this command will be repeated when the disciples try to prevent the children from coming to Jesus (18:16).

◊ ◊ ◊ ◊

Since the apostles will be the leaders of the early church, some of the problems of church leadership can be addressed through the portrait of the apostles (cf. especially 22:24-30). The Lukan audience would have probably caught on to this quickly and would have related Jesus' teaching to the leaders of their own communities. Some church leaders might have felt threatened by what they were hearing, wishing to protect their authority. However, they might also have been reminded of the special importance in Jesus' community of those who are least in the eyes of society, and they might have considered whether such people were being neglected. Also, the discussion of the independent exorcist might have called to mind rival groups within the early Christian movement. Partisans in church conflicts were often not as open-minded as Jesus in verse 50. Jesus' response to John might have caused some reconsideration.

An Expanded Mission as Jesus Journeys to Jerusalem (9:51–19:44)

Luke 9:51 begins a major new section of the Gospel in two senses. First, Luke here departs from the material in Mark that Luke has generally been following since Luke 8:4 (with a major omission of Marcan material between Luke 9:17 and 18). A fairly large amount of Luke 9:51–18:14 has parallels with Matthew and a small amount with Mark, but in Matthew and Mark the material is located in other contexts. At 18:15 Luke rejoins the narrative found in Matthew and Mark. Much of the material in Luke 9:51–18:14 is unique to Luke, and all of it is unique as an ordered narrative.

Second, Jesus now begins his journey to Jerusalem, which he will finally end in 19:45, when he enters the temple. (The end point of the Jerusalem journey is disputed, but note that in 19:28-44 Jesus is still journeying, and the narrator carefully marks the final stages through repeated references to "coming near" [using *engizō* in 19:29, 37, 41; cf. Denaux 1993, 385].) The Jerusalem journey section of Luke is long. It may seem strange that Jesus makes no discernible progress toward Jerusalem until he approaches Jericho in 18:35. This anomaly is due to the use of traditional material that was not originally attached to locations on the way to Jerusalem. Nevertheless, there are occasional reminders that Jesus is traveling to Jerusalem (13:22, 33; 17:11; 18:31; 19:11, 28) as well as reminders of the rejection, death, and resurrection that will happen there (12:49-50; 13:33-34; 16:31; 17:25; 18:31-33; 19:14). These reminders encourage the Lukan audience to make connections between the teaching being presented and the events that lie ahead.

There are a few healing stories during the Jerusalem journey (11:14; 13:10-17; 14:1-6; 17:11-19; 18:35-43), but in most scenes Jesus is teaching. Jesus is preparing his disciples through teaching, while also challenging the crowd and debating his opponents.

Rejection in a Samaritan Village (9:51-56)

The Jerusalem travel narrative begins, "And it came to pass when the days of his assumption [or "ascension"] were being fulfilled. . . . " The NRSV translation "drew near" misses the implication of fulfillment of prophesied events necessary to complete the plan of God. These events, already mentioned in 9:22, 31, have their climax in Jesus' "assumption" *(analēmpsis),* that is, his being taken up to heaven to sit at the right hand of God (Acts 2:33-35). (The related verb *analambanō,* "take up," is used of Jesus' ascension in Acts 1:2, 11, 22.) Since the statement in verse 51 speaks of the "*days* of his assumption," it does not refer to an isolated event on a particular day but to a period of time, with Jesus' transfer to power and glory as the climax. This time period will also include Jesus' death and resurrection. Thus the term has much the same scope as Jesus' "exodus" (NRSV: "departure") in 9:31.

"He set his face" expresses Jesus' determination as he turns toward the place of suffering, but it may also suggest the coming conflict between Jesus and Jerusalem, resulting in Jesus' death and eventually in Jerusalem's destruction (19:44). This phrase is used in Jer 21:10; Ezek 6:2; 13:17; 21:2 in speaking of God or the prophet as they speak words of judgment, sometimes against Jerusalem. The word "face" is repeated twice in Luke 9:52-53, for the first sentence of verse 52 is literally "and he sent messengers before his face." This is a reference back to the biblical quotation in 7:27: "See, I am sending my messenger before your face, who will prepare your way before you." This quotation was applied to John the Baptist, who is now dead. The new application of the quotation suggests that the disciples are taking over the function of John the Baptist as the forerunners of Jesus who "prepare" (NRSV: "make ready" [v. 52]) for the coming of Jesus. John's function is not finished. The missionaries must prepare for Jesus' coming in each town (cf. 10:1) by preparing people to welcome him.

The quote in 7:27 is an adaptation of Mal 3:1 (see p. 132), which is linked in Malachi with the sending of the eschatological Elijah (Mal 4:5). John the Baptist, Jesus, and Jesus' disciples share characteristics of Elijah. The disciples are "messengers" who are sent "before" Jesus' "face," like John and Elijah, but Jesus will be "taken up" into heaven as Elijah was (cf. 2 Kgs 2:10-11, which in the LXX uses *analambanō* as in Acts 1:2, 11, 22). Another reminder of Elijah is found a few verses later (Luke 9:54), and 9:51-56 may be a reworking of themes from 2 Kgs 1:1–2:6, in which Elijah calls down fire from heaven and then journeys with his disciple, Elisha, to the place of Elijah's assumption into heaven (cf. Brodie 1989, 96-109).

The messengers sent to the Samaritan village may simply have been arranging for lodging and food, but the designation of them as "messengers" like John and Elijah hints at something more. This is the beginning of a mission strategy that will be described more fully in 10:1-20. In 10:1 Jesus sends many more pairs of disciples ahead of him to places where he would go, and their task is not just to arrange hospitality, but to preach the kingdom of God and to heal. The Samaritan village, however, refuses to receive Jesus "because his face was set toward Jerusalem." Pilgrims passing through Samaria for Jerusalem aggravated the religious controversy between Samaritans and Jews, for Samaritans refused to recognize the Jerusalem temple, having their own sanctuary on Mt. Gerizim. When the Samaritan village refuses to welcome Jesus, James and John want to do what Elijah did when he encountered troops from Samaria: call down fire from heaven to destroy them (cf. 2 Kgs 1:2-14). Jesus, however, rebukes them, and they simply travel on to another village. Jesus refuses to follow Elijah at this point. He has, after all, preached the love of enemies (6:27-36).

◊ ◊ ◊ ◊

When he instructs the seventy, Jesus tells them what to do when a town will not receive them (10:10-12). At that time Jesus warns of a future judgment, but it is wrong for disciples to think that they can bring down judgment immediately. This is not their proper function, and it ignores the possibility of future repentance. Jesus does not give up hope for Samaritans. He will use Samaritans as positive examples in 10:29-37 and 17:11-19, and Samaria will be an area of successful mission in Acts 8.

It is striking, however, that Jesus' journey to Jerusalem begins with a rejection scene. His ministry in Galilee also began with rejection (4:23-30). In fact, he has been rejected in Galilee (see also 10:13-16), rejected by Gentiles (8:37), rejected by Samaritans, and will be rejected in Jerusalem (9:22; 19:41-44). Yet rejection does not end the mission to any of these groups, and the word will bear great fruit in some areas where there was initial rejection.

James and John's suggestion is an abuse of the power that Jesus has given to them. It broadens the portrait of defective disciples begun in 9:45-50. In 10:1-12 Jesus will give careful instructions to his messengers, in part to prevent such abuses.

The Difficult Demands of Discipleship (9:57-62)

In this section we find three brief pronouncement stories. They make a set because in each case Jesus is talking with a would-be disciple about the requirements of following him on his itinerant ministry. Furthermore, there are a number of repeated words or phrases that tie the three brief dialogues together. Each pronouncement story ends with the challenging word of Jesus, which means that we are not told whether the would-be disciple was able to accept Jesus' condition or not. There is no interest in these inquirers as individuals. All emphasis is on the challenging words of Jesus, which, however, gain part of their force from contrast with proposals that seem at first to be either praiseworthy (v. 57) or reasonable (vv. 59, 61).

The first two of these pronouncement stories have parallels in Matt 8:18-22. In Luke this section joins 9:51-56 to form an introduction to 10:1-20, the mission of the seventy (or seventy-two). Jesus is gathering new followers as he travels to Jerusalem, followers who could participate in the mission described in 10:1-20 if they are able. But the requirements of this task are severe. According to 9:57-62, following Jesus means leaving home and family in order to share Jesus' travels and mission. Many later believers in Jesus were not followers in this sense.

◊ ◊ ◊ ◊

The first person tells Jesus, "I will follow you wherever you go." He sounds eager and fully committed, but Jesus does not take his statement at face value. He does not encourage him but warns him. He does so with a threefold statement in which a pattern is set by the first two instances (the foxes and birds) in order to emphasize the contrast with the third instance (the Son of Man). The statement is also rhythmical, which supports the pattern and contrast. A rhythm of three beats per line results when the most important words are emphasized in speaking. The following translation preserves the word order of the Greek and displays the rhythm:

1.	Foxes	holes	have,
2.	and birds	of the sky	nests;
3.	but the Son	of Man	has not
	where	the head	to lay.

How strange and difficult the homeless life of Jesus is, when even foxes and birds have lodgings. His followers must be willing to share this homelessness. It may seem surprising that Jesus accents the negative so strongly, since the story implies that he did sometimes receive hospitality (10:38-42). The rejection in the Samaritan village, however, indicates that this will not always be the case. Jesus presents the eager applicant with homelessness because only someone willing to endure such privation will persist as Jesus' follower.

A second person is willing to follow, but has a pressing family obligation—the burial of his father. The proper burial of one's parents was a duty of prime importance in ancient Mediterranean society, including Jewish society. It was part of fulfilling the commandment to honor one's father and mother (Exod 20:12). It ranked high among the works of love in Jewish piety, so much so that normal religious obligations could be laid aside for this purpose (cf. *m. Berakot* 3:1; *m. Nazir* 7:1; Tob 6:14; also Hengel 1981, 8-15). We must assume that the father is dead or near death, for Jesus does not reply by saying that there will be time enough for burying the father later. Instead he declares that this central obligation of religious and family piety must be set aside in order to go and proclaim the kingdom of God. Since the man is offering one of the best excuses possible, the effect of Jesus' specific and extreme command is to invalidate all sorts of excuses for delay (cf. Tannehill 1975, 163).

Jesus makes his point with dark wit, using a play on words. It is appropriate that the dead take care of the dead, for they belong to the same group. He does not explain who he means; it is only clear that those who can proclaim the kingdom of God are not among these dead and thus have a different duty. The command to go and proclaim the kingdom anticipates the instructions in 10:9, 11.

The third person, like the first, declares that he will follow but, like the second, wants first to perform a family duty. Saying farewell to his family shows them proper respect. While Jesus replied with poetic words involving contrast in the first case and a play on words in the second, he here uses a metaphor. The metaphor provides a filter for seeing the situation in a new way. Saying farewell may seem like the necessary thing, but, seen through the metaphor, it is looking back while plowing, a sure cause of a crooked furrow. When Elijah called Elisha (who was plowing), the latter said, according to the LXX, "I will kiss my father, and I will follow after you" (3 Kgdms 19:20 = 1 Kgs 19:20). Although Elijah's response is somewhat obscure in both the Hebrew and the LXX, apparently the request to first go home is denied, for instead Elisha sacrifices his oxen and follows Elijah. As Josephus tells the story, however, Elijah permits Elisha to say farewell to his parents (*Ant.* 8 §354; cf. Hengel 1981, 16). The pronouncement story plays with the well-known story of the call of Elisha, turning the plowing into a metaphor, and choosing the harsher alternative: the man's request is denied.

◊ ◊ ◊ ◊

The second and third of Jesus' responses are very harsh. It is doubtful that the Lukan audience would have used them as regulations for ordinary life. Only a minority of them would have been traveling missionaries who would have had to leave home. Even such missionaries would probably return, if possible, to bury a dead father or to say farewell to family. These observations do not imply that Jesus' words were empty of meaning. They continue to show

how much can be demanded when one recognizes that Jesus' call
to the kingdom has first priority. Furthermore, difficult issues of
home and family (the subject of the three pronouncement stories)
could arise even for believers who were not traveling missionaries.
The extended family was the social and economic base of ancient
people (cf. Malina and Rohrbaugh 1992, 335-36). Sons and daughters could lose their family home and be ostracized from the family
if parents opposed their new faith (cf. 12:51-53; 21:16). This could
produce a social rootlessness similar to the situation of the wandering missionary, for which the surrogate family of the church would
have to compensate.

The Mission of the Seventy-two (10:1-24)

The Jerusalem journey is the last and most intensive phase of
Jesus' mission outside Jerusalem. Near the beginning of this journey,
a much larger group than the twelve is sent out. They are to prepare
the way for Jesus, but this involves more than arranging hospitality.
They are to conduct a mission of preaching and healing, just as the
twelve did (9:1-6). More space is given to this second mission than
to the mission of the twelve, and while the return of the twelve elicits
only a bland comment (9:10), the return of the seventy(-two) is
accompanied by strong statements of success and joy (10:17-24).
Thus we have climactic parallelism; the second mission narrative is
a grander version of the first. Although the twelve will have an
important role in Acts as interpreters of the Jesus tradition, and
Peter will be an important preacher, others will take the initiative
in mission at key points (cf. Tannehill 1990, 102-5, 113, 146-47).
The mission of the seventy(-two) already hints at the importance of
these others.

Instructions for the Mission (10:1-16)

There are parallels to Luke 10:1-16 in Matt 9:37-38; 10:7-16,
40; 11:20-24. Matthew 10, like Luke 10:1-16, is a mission discourse, but it concerns a mission of the twelve, not seventy(-two),
and the material is arranged differently.

10:1-4: There is strong manuscript support for both the readings "seventy" and "seventy-two," making it difficult to know which is the original reading. Perhaps seventy-two should be given the edge because it is a less common number; therefore it is easier to explain a change from seventy-two to seventy by copyists (cf. K. Aland in Metzger 1971, 151). There is a second, related point of debate. Does the number have special significance because it alludes to a passage of scripture? The supposed number of peoples of the world, according to Genesis 10, is seventy or seventy-two, depending on whether one follows the Hebrew or the LXX. Moses appointed seventy elders as his helpers in Num 11:16-30, but after the Spirit rested on them, two others (Eldad and Medad) also received the Spirit. Thus the seventy or seventy-two may be patterned after the Spirit-filled assistants of Moses, or their number may anticipate the world mission. Both suggestions fit Lukan concerns, for both Spirit-filled messengers and world mission anticipate Acts.

Jesus sent them in pairs "before his face" (NRSV: "on ahead of him"). This phrase is important because it is a reminder of 9:52 ("he sent messengers before his face") and 7:27, a scripture quotation applied to John the Baptist. Disciples have now been given the role of going before Jesus and preparing his way, as John did previously (cf. Tannehill 1986, 229-30, 233-35). The messengers, as they announce the kingdom of God, are preparing for Jesus' arrival, which might be understood on two levels: Within the story setting, it is assumed that Jesus will travel to each of the places where the pairs of missioners have worked. Within the situation of the Lukan communities, however, Jesus' workers are understood to be preparing for his coming in glory (cf. the parables of servants and their absent Lord in 12:35-48; 19:12-27).

Jesus' representatives are being sent "like lambs into the midst of wolves" (v. 3). This is not a warning to protect themselves. It introduces the prohibitions in verse 4, which increase the travelers' vulnerability by denying them normal provisions for travel. Since they will have neither money purse nor a travel bag with food and clothing, they will be completely dependent on whatever hospitality local people may offer. Except for the bag, the list of prohibited items differs from 9:3, but the general effect is the same. The prohibition of greetings on the road is puzzling. When the mission-ers enter a house, they should give a greeting, as verse 5 indicates. Then, if welcomed, they should stay. Perhaps the mission requires contact with people in their homes and towns, while brief contacts on the road are insufficient.

10:5-12: The sentences in verses 5, 8, and 10 begin in similar ways, but the first refers to houses, while the second and third refer to towns. The description of the home-based mission in verses 5-7 is striking. The missioners are seeking hospitality in a home, not a handout or a single meal. They are to "remain in the same house" (v. 7) and share the family's food over a longer period of time. They are not to act or think of themselves as beggars but as laborers who deserve their pay. In effect, they become temporary members of the household. Being members of the household and repeatedly sharing meals may be necessary to transmit what they have come to bring. (As to the meals, John Dominic Crossan understands this "com-mensality" to be a basic strategy for building an egalitarian com-munity; cf. Crossan 1991, 341-44.)

What they have come to bring is already indicated by the initial greeting, "Peace to this house!" This is a standard greeting, yet Jesus makes a point of it, suggesting that it has special significance. The next verse supports this view, for it indicates that the peace greeting will be effective. It will either "rest on" the person greeted, or it will return on the greeter. It is a word of power that conveys peace to one person or another. "Peace" in Luke–Acts refers to the messianic salvation offered to individuals and to the people of God in its corporate life. Peace has a significant place in the anticipations of salvation for Israel in the infancy narrative (1:79; 2:14, 29). The emphasis on peace in 10:5-6, near the beginning of the Jerusalem journey, is matched by the return of this theme at its end, although Jesus then will mourn Jerusalem's failure to accept peace (19:38, 42; cf. Swartley 1992, 161). In Acts 10:36 God's message to Israel is summed up in the phrase "preaching peace by Jesus Christ." In the mission of the seventy(-two) the peace of the Messiah's kingdom is being established at the grass roots, in the homes and towns of common people, not from the top down.

When the focus shifts from homes to towns in verses 8-12, the peace greeting is replaced by the statement, "The kingdom of God has come near to you." The meaning is basically the same, for the kingdom of God includes the peace of the Messiah's kingdom. The instruction to "eat what is set before you" may indicate that food should not be refused because of purity regulations. The announcement of the kingdom of God is accompanied by healing, as in the mission of the twelve (9:2). Healing is one of the ways that people are experiencing the kingdom near to them.

The approach of the kingdom with the arrival of Jesus' representatives is a special opportunity that must be accepted while it is available. Rejection brings a prophetic warning. A public gesture, with accompanying announcement, is to be performed in the "streets" (plateias = the broad streets as distinct from the alleys; places of maximum visibility). The action of wiping dust from the feet is a formal act of separation. "Even the dust" implies that everything else that connects the messengers to the town is being removed. However, they do leave one thing behind, the knowledge that "the kingdom of God has come near." This claim is reinforced as the messengers leave, keeping open the possibility of the town's later recognition of this crucial visitation. Continued rejection of God's rule will have dire consequences in the final judgment. This point is made strongly through declaring that such a town is worse than Sodom, the corrupt city punished by God in Gen 19:1-29, which later became a symbol of divine judgment (Isa 1:9).

10:13-16: The threat of dire consequence is reinforced by prophetic oracles against three towns where "deeds of power" (or "mighty acts," dynameis) have been performed without proper response. There are prophetic oracles against Tyre and Sidon in Isaiah 23 and Ezek 28:2-23, and verse 15 is based on Isa 14:13, 15, part of an oracle against Babylon. The words in Luke show a careful attempt to be as forceful as possible. They recall cities denounced as evil in scripture but make them look good by comparison with the towns now being denounced. The forceful language used is more than a prediction of the future. It is meant to crack the complacency of these towns, and all others like them. It is prophetic warning that is still trying to bring the accused towns to repentance by causing complacent people to see their situation differently through powerful words that can capture the imagination (cf. Tannehill 1975, 122-28).

It may seem surprising that Capernaum is included in the towns denounced. When rejected at Nazareth, Jesus turned to Capernaum, where he performed the first mighty acts recorded in Luke (4:31-41; cf. also 7:1-10). The crowds there are obviously impressed, for they do not want Jesus to leave (4:42). In 10:13-15, however, it becomes clear that Jesus' deeds of power should produce more than amazement and adulation. They should produce repentance, for they disclose the approach of God's reign, which brings blessing or judgment. Since the description of John's preaching in 3:3-14, the words "repent" or "repentance" *(metanoeō, metanoia)* have been infrequent (only in 5:32). From 10:13 on they will become more important. The present denunciation of unrepentant towns will be followed by severe warnings of the need for repentance in 11:29-32, 12:54–13:9, and 13:23-30. As Jesus turns toward Jerusalem, his words become urgent as he seeks a full response to his deeds and message.

The mission discourse closes in verse 16 with a saying that underscores the authority of the missioners as Jesus' representatives. The missioners bear heavy responsibility, since they represent Jesus and the God who sent him, and the choice made by respondents is a grave one.

◊ ◊ ◊ ◊

Members of early churches doubtless shared their faith in Jesus with those around them. Only a few of them, however, became traveling missionaries, like the seventy(-two). The travelers were risk takers, since traveling was difficult and a reception uncertain. The words of Jesus to the seventy(-two) would be important not only to those who risked travel with meager supplies and little assurance of support but also to local believers who might offer them hospitality. Finding a home that would offer food and shelter, and support for the mission, was a key to starting a local community, and hospitality for traveling "apostles and prophets" was important even after churches were well-established (cf. *Didache* 11:3-6). Thus many in the Lukan audience would see their role in the providers of food and shelter, who thereby share in the messianic peace that the travelers bring.

Celebration at the Return of the Missionaries (10:17-24)

The return of the seventy(-two) is depicted as a time of rejoicing and praise. First, they rejoice and Jesus responds. Then Jesus rejoices in thankful prayer to God, followed by a beatitude addressed to the disciples.

◊   ◊   ◊   ◊

10:17-20: The seventy(-two) rejoice because the demons are subject to them "in your name." The name of Jesus is an important theme in Acts (cf. Tannehill 1990, 49, 60-61). It represents the power and authority of Jesus as Messiah, which is available to Jesus' representatives and is a potential source of salvation for all (cf. Acts 2:21; 3:16; 4:7, 12). The salvation available through Jesus' name includes healing and expulsion of demons (cf. Luke 9:49; Acts 3:16; 16:18).

Here, however, the subjection of demons is placed in an eschatological context, for it is associated with the fall of Satan from heaven, a part of the end events. Satan's place in heaven represents his power, including power to accuse people before God (cf. Job 1:6-12; Zech 3:1). The end of Satan's power is celebrated in the New Testament (John 12:31; Heb 2:14), and victory over Satan can be pictured as his fall from heaven (Rev 12:7-9). Susan Garrett notes that victory over Satan is the result of the death (or death and resurrection) of Jesus in the New Testament texts just cited (cf. Garrett 1989, 51-52). This may also be the case in Luke 10:18, but we cannot be certain. Jesus could be reporting a vision of a future event, connected with his death and resurrection, but his statement is prompted by the disciples' report of their present power over demons. This power is at least a clear sign of Satan's imminent fall, if not the result of the fall itself.

The authority given Jesus' messengers is expressed in graphic language in verse 19. It is authority "over all the power of the enemy," represented by dangerous "snakes and scorpions." "Nothing will hurt you" can also be translated "In nothing will he [the enemy] hurt you" (taking *ouden* as an adverbial accusative). The second translation fits the later narrative better, where it is clear that Jesus, as well as the disciples, are indeed subject to physical injury through persecution, even though they may be protected from Satan's power. Furthermore, Jesus cautions the disciples in verse 20 that their power as exorcists is not the essential thing; rather they should rejoice that they have been enrolled as citizens of heaven. (On the scriptural imagery, based on the practice of preparing lists of citizens in cities or kingdoms, see Fitzmyer 1985, 863-64.) The disciples should not be too proud of their power as exorcists but should rejoice in the salvation that they share with all of God's people. It is possible that their citizenship in heaven is also the result of the fall of Satan, who can no longer exclude people by his accusations (Rev 12:10-11; cf. *T. Levi* 18:10-12, which relates the binding of Beliar and authority to trample on wicked spirits to opening the gates of Paradise; cf. C. A. Evans in Evans and Sanders 1993, 43).

10:21-22: Jesus responds to the disciples' rejoicing with his own rejoicing and prayer of praise to God (v. 21). The Greek words translated "rejoiced" and "thank" are often found together in the LXX Psalms (cf. 9:2-3; 32:1-2; 66:4-5; 70:22-23; cf. Nolland 1993, 571). Thus Jesus is adopting the language of the psalmists as he turns in praise to God. This praise is for God's revelation, shared not with the "wise and the intelligent" but with "infants." Just as in the Magnificat (1:51-53), God is praised as one who overturns human expectations and destroys human distinctions. Status is a factor in openness to the revelation. Those recognized as authorities through their knowledge of sacred traditions have a stake in things as they are. A new revelation would be disturbing. Not so with those who are "infants" in knowledge. To be called "infants" is not, in itself, a good thing. Paul and the author of Hebrews want the infants in their communities to grow up (1 Cor 3:1-3; Heb 5:12-14; cf. Eph

4:14). But it is God's "gracious will" or "pleasure" to break through to such people, and God has done so in revealing "these things" to the disciples. In context, "these things" probably refer to the manifestations of God's royal power in the work of Jesus and his disciples.

Both the theme of revelation and the address of God as father connect verse 22 with verse 21. In verse 22, however, the focus shifts from those who receive the revelation to the special relation between God as father and Jesus as son that makes the revelation possible. "Father" and "son" are terms of intimacy here. Father and son "know" each other as others cannot know them. Therefore, the son can reveal the father in a special way. This is also a relationship of trust, for "all things have been handed over to me by my Father." If this refers to universal rule, it seems premature, for elsewhere Christ's universal rule is associated with his resurrection-exaltation (Matt 28:18; Phil 2:9-11) and is fully realized only at his return in glory (1 Cor 15:23-28). It may, however, refer to the full knowledge of God that makes possible the special relationship described in verse 22.

The designation of God as "father" may, from the cultural context, carry connotations of ruling authority, but it also connotes an intimacy and love that can be trusted. The son here claims a unique relation with the father, but the relation is not solely for his own enjoyment. He is able to reveal this father God to others, and in his teaching on prayer in 11:1-13, he will do so. There he will teach the disciples to address God as father and to trust God as a father who wants to give good gifts to his children (cf. also 6:36; 12:30, 32). Trust in God as a reliable father is expressed by Jesus at his death (23:46). It is important to recognize that references to God as father in Luke carry these connotations of intimacy and trustworthiness.

10:23-24: Jesus closes with a beatitude that continues the theme of revelation (vv. 23-24). The disciples are blessed because of what they see, namely, the fulfillment of what many prophets and kings longed for. Here the prophecies of the time of salvation and of the king who would renew David's line are called to mind. (Luke has "kings," while the parallel in Matt 13:17 has "righteous people.") The context suggests further that the disciples are blessed because they see the manifestations of the kingdom revealed to infants and know the father God revealed through Jesus the son.

Jesus and a Lawyer Discuss Love of Neighbor (10:25-37)

Matthew 22:34-40 and Mark 12:28-34 present the double love commandment, as does Luke 10:25-28. However, in Matthew and Mark the dialogue is introduced by a question concerning the "great" or "first" commandment, it is Jesus who cites the double love commandment, and there is no following parable. Luke differs in each of these respects.

The indication that the lawyer was testing Jesus and the later statement that he wanted "to justify himself" suggest that the man is suspicious and unreceptive. He could be dismissed as one of the "wise" to whom God's revelation has not been given (cf. v. 21). Yet Jesus does not respond to the lawyer's suspicion with hostility; instead, Jesus is presented as a skillful teacher who can lead his suspicious partner to agreement while delivering a challenging message. In verse 37 the lawyer interprets the parable correctly, and Jesus presents his final challenge. The lawyer may or may not "go and do likewise," but, having come to understand love of neighbor in a new way through the parable, new ways of acting are made possible. The scene ends with this possibility rather than with rejection by the lawyer. Thus this dialogue with a lawyer qualifies the possible impression of verse 21 that those who value Jewish wisdom are hopelessly closed to the new revelation.

◊ ◊ ◊ ◊

The lawyer's question (v. 25) is an important one, for it concerns sharing the ultimate blessings of God's kingdom. Jesus believes the answer can be found in the law; therefore, the lawyer can answer his own question. The lawyer answers so well that Jesus only needs to agree. Thus the first part of the dialogue emphasizes the common ground between Jesus and this Jewish lawyer. There is agreement on these central matters: that love of God and neighbor is the core of the law and that living in this way will bring eternal life. In

18:18-23 Jesus, in discussion with a Jewish "ruler," proceeds in the same way. The common ground in central commandments of the law is first established before introducing something that is distinctive. (On 10:25-37 and 18:18-23 as variations of a single "type-scene," see Tannehill 1986, 170-71.)

The command to love God completely, with full engagement of the basic aspects of one's being, is found in Deut 6:5. These words have a central place in Jewish piety, being used in daily prayer (cf. E. P. Sanders 1992, 195-96). The quotation of Lev 19:18 ("You shall love your neighbor as yourself") as a summary of Jewish teaching would also cause no surprise (cf. E. P. Sanders 1992, 231-34, 257). Both commands begin, "you shall love," which makes it easy to fit them together in one command that embraces both the relation to God and to humans. The Lukan narrative, in which the double love commandment is presented by the lawyer, acknowledges that this is Jewish teaching. Jesus accepts the view that these commands mark the path to eternal life. The following discussion will not change this. It remains within the Jewish context and proceeds by scriptural interpretation. In the commandment what is the meaning of the term "neighbor"?

Both love commandments are forceful. One must love God with one's whole being. One must love the neighbor "as yourself." Modern psychology has made us aware that some people do not love themselves, which tempts us to understand Lev 19:18 as advocating love of self as well as neighbor. That is not the point of the ancient commandment. Rather, it assumes that normal people love themselves, indeed, love themselves strongly; therefore, this self love can be made the standard for a full love of neighbor.

The term translated "neighbor" *(plesion)* means one who is near. It is not a natural way of referring to everyone, nor does Lev 19:18, read in context, imply love of everyone (but note the extension to the resident alien in 19:34). Therefore, even if the lawyer feels a need to justify himself, his question is legitimate. When he asks, "Who is my neighbor?" he is asking, "Who is close enough to me that I must respond with love, as the commandment says?" Jesus answers by telling a story.

The man who is robbed, beaten, and left "half dead" is in desperate need of help. The audience is told nothing about him except for his need. The focus on his need alone would create sympathy for him and a desire for a helper to appear. The story proceeds by presenting a series of possible helpers. Here we meet the "folkloric triad" (cf. Brawley 1990, 219), the common narrative device of presenting a series of three in which the third instance will either be the strongest form of the pattern established by the first two, or contrast with it (recall the three little pigs). The first two, even though they are persons of importance in religious society, are failures as helpers. The priest may have feared ritual defilement through a corpse, for Lev 21:1-3 commands that a priest not defile himself through the dead except for his nearest of kin. This, however, is not an adequate excuse, for the man was not, in fact, dead, and the Mishnah (cf. *m. Nazir* 7.1) views a neglected corpse (such as a body abandoned by the road) as a special case. Even a high priest is permitted to contact uncleanness because of a neglected corpse (cf. Scott 1989, 195-96). The first two failures build suspense for a third traveler, who may be the hoped-for helper and the hero of the story.

The first word of verse 33 (in the Greek) is "Samaritan"—a surprise—but we must wait until the last word of the verse (*esplanchnisthē;* "he was moved with pity" or "had compassion") to learn that he is the expected helper. The Samaritan is a surprise because there is a jump in categories—priest, Levite, and Samaritan do not make a logical sequence—and because hatred between Jews and Samaritans would not lead a Jew to expect a Samaritan to show compassion. Priest, Levite, and lay Israelite would make a logical sequence and would confirm the expectations of some Jewish hearers, suggesting that priests and Levites lack compassion, while the lay Israelite truly fulfills the law. The surprise of the Samaritan gives the story a different and disturbing impact.

The enmity between Jews and Samaritans is an important historical fact assumed by this story. As Scott recognizes (Scott 1989, 192), it would be a different parable if told without explanation to Gentiles, who would probably feel no enmity for Samaritans. However, we should note carefully the Lukan context. A parable about a Samaritan is being told to a Jewish lawyer. The parable works when the audience is being told about its enemy.

A Jewish audience would probably assume that the injured man on the Jericho road was a Jew, since there is no indication that he is an alien. When stripped of his clothes, it would probably be impossible to recognize his ethnic identity or status. To the Samaritan it makes no difference. He moves to the injured man's side and begins to help.

The description of the Samaritan's actions in verses 34-35 is surprisingly detailed. The Samaritan's compassion is not just a feeling but a series of concrete actions in which the Samaritan expends himself and his resources to meet the need of the injured man. The Samaritan does, to be sure, travel on the next day, but only after he has made provision for the man's continued care. Extensive efforts are made to be really helpful.

◊ ◊ ◊ ◊

Although the lawyer and other members of Jesus' Jewish audience might have expected to identify with the hero of this story, the appearance of the Samaritan makes this very difficult. If this were a story of a Samaritan who had been robbed and beaten and of a compassionate Jew who helped him, it would be a striking example for Jews of love of enemies. The present story does stretch love of neighbor until it becomes love of enemy (as in 6:27-36), but it is more unsettling. The lawyer and other members of a Jewish audience may no longer know where to find themselves in the parable. They must reexamine themselves in relation to all of the characters, which will require deeper reflection. Since the Samaritan is definitely not their representative, they may have to admit to themselves that they are like the priest and Levite, who pass by on the other side. Or they may come to see themselves in the injured man, in dire need of help. Or if they are finally willing to risk following the Samaritan into a love that asks no questions about ethnic or religious identity, they must first be willing to be taught by their enemy what love of neighbor means.

The Gentiles in the Lukan audience would need to appreciate what this parable would mean for a Jew so that they could translate it to their own cultural experience.

Hospitality with Martha and Mary (10:38-42)

Although many have understood this story to affirm women's roles in the church, some recent interpreters deny this. Elisabeth Schüssler Fiorenza and others have argued that there is a hidden agenda in the story. Martha is distracted with "much service" (*pollēn diakonian;* NRSV: "many tasks"). Since the word *diakonia* is applied to the roles of preacher-leaders in Acts, Luke's intent in telling this story is to discourage women from exercising these leadership roles and instead to adopt the passive, silent role of Mary in this scene (cf. Schüssler Fiorenza 1987, 1-12; 1992, 52-76; for a response see Seim 1994a, 97-107, 112-14).

This pronouncement story does reflect on women's roles in the early church, but the issue at stake, in my opinion, is a different one. The passage is introduced in verse 38 by a reminder of the theme of travel and hospitality that characterizes the beginning of the Jerusalem travel narrative. As Jesus and his messengers travel, they seek hospitality in homes and villages. Sometimes they are welcomed (10:5-8), sometimes not (9:52-53; 10:10-12). Martha does welcome Jesus and his band. She is evidently head of her own household, since there is no reference to a husband or father in her decision to open her house. Not only does she demonstrate the right response in welcoming Jesus, but she also represents many people who played an important role in the early spread of the gospel. Those who offered hospitality to traveling missionaries enabled the word to take root in a new location and often became patrons or patronesses of house churches. With this came a position of influence in the life of these churches. (With Martha compare Lydia in Acts 16:14-15, 40.)

In this setting of hospitality, *diakonia* means caring for one's guests, especially through providing a meal. It does not refer to an established "ministry" of preaching and leadership. The noun *diakonia* in verse 40 cannot be distinguished in meaning from the verb form in the same verse, and the verb *diakoneō* is consistently used in Luke of domestic service, such as providing food, something that women or slaves were expected to do (4:39; 8:3; 12:37; 17:8), or it is used of Jesus and the disciples when they take this same servant role (22:26-27).

Martha objects both to the behavior of her sister and to Jesus' lack of concern. Her objection should be taken seriously, for she is providing a valuable service to her guests, and she doubtless needed the help. By her objection, however, she is also trying to force her sister back into the expected woman's role. Jesus responds to Martha by defending Mary's right to leave the job of serving the meal in order to listen to Jesus. Mary is seated at Jesus' feet, like a disciple with a teacher (cf. 8:35; Acts 22:3), listening to "his word" (NRSV: "what he was saying"). Mary is silent as she listens to Jesus. We should be cautious about concluding that she is a silent and passive woman, however. Pronouncement stories are told very briefly. They do not give complete character portraits. The story does not require us to infer from the few words about Mary that she is only and always a listener. The scene itself suggests that she is not passive, for she has taken bold action in leaving her expected role of serving dinner in order to listen to Jesus. Furthermore, the larger Lukan narrative makes clear that listening to the word is only a first step. One must not only listen to Jesus' word (or the word of God) but also do it (6:47; 8:21), and in 11:27-28 Jesus will make this same point to a woman who has the too-limited view that a woman's greatness depends primarily on bearing a great son. Thus Jesus' teaching elsewhere in Luke suggests that Mary, if she is really listening to Jesus, cannot remain a passive listener.

This does not necessarily mean that she will preach in public. It has been rightly noted that only men preach in public in Acts. The church in Acts silently accepted a cultural limitation. The missionary preachers are Jesus' "witnesses," and it is important that witnesses be respected and credible to the public. Because of cultural assumptions about women, they could not qualify (cf. D'Angelo 1990, 449-50; Seim 1994a, 162, 254-55). Nevertheless, the story of Martha and Mary defends the freedom of women, not just because Mary takes the role of a disciple but also because she is affirmed in her decision to neglect domestic duties in order to grow as a disciple.

The importance of hospitality for traveling missionaries shows that Martha's role must also be respected. However, she is "worried and distracted by many things" and has forgotten that really "there is need of only one thing." Unfortunately, there are a number of textual variants in verses 41-42. In particular, there is an important group of manuscripts that read, "There is need of few things, or one." This reading may refer to the meal. Martha should simplify the meal so that it can be prepared without overburdening herself. Even one dish is sufficient. This could still be the meaning of the shorter reading adopted in the NRSV. However, it is likely that the one thing needed is equivalent to the "better part" (or "good portion") that Mary has chosen. Then the one thing needed is listening to the Lord's word.

◊ ◊ ◊ ◊

In 10:5-9 receiving the messengers seemed equivalent to receiving the message. The story of Martha and Mary adds a qualification to that simple assumption: The task of hospitality may actually distract one from the message. Hospitality was very important to the early church, but this story cautions that preoccupation with arrangements can lead one to lose contact with the community's real purpose. This is especially apparent when a woman cannot graciously allow a sister to spend time listening to the Lord's word.

Instruction in Prayer (11:1-13)

11:1-4: Jesus, according to Luke, repeatedly withdraws for prayer (3:21; 5:16; 6:12; 9:18, 28). Since the disciples recognize the importance of prayer for Jesus, they now ask him to teach them about this also. This request provides the opportunity to introduce the Lukan version of the Lord's Prayer, which is significantly shorter than the more familiar version in Matt 6:9-13.

In 10:21-22 Jesus addressed God as "father" in prayer. He will do so again in his prayers during the passion story (22:42; 23:46; and 23:34, if it is an original part of Luke). Now he teaches his disciples to address God in the same way. When God is viewed as father, it is assumed that God both has the power to help and the desire to help. Within the society known to the New Testament, "father" connotes ruling authority within the family. Therefore, it is not surprising that the beginning of the prayer can move easily from God as "father" to a reference to God's "kingdom" (cf. D'Angelo 1992, 628). It is also assumed that the father is bound by love and loyalty to his family. This aspect of the image is stressed by the simile of the father who can be trusted to give good gifts in verses 11-13. It will be stressed again in 15:11-32 (the parable of the compassionate father) and in 12:30-32, where, in language that recalls 11:2-13, the disciples are assured that God the father knows their needs and takes pleasure in giving. Luke 12:30-32 provides assurance of God's answer to the second and third petitions of the prayer in 11:2-4.

The traditional translation "daily" bread is something of a guess. There is no certain use of the word *epiousios* in any ancient source, independent of the Lord's Prayer. Various hypotheses concerning its derivation yield various translations: (1) bread for today (hence, "daily bread"); (2) bread for the coming day; (3) bread for subsistence, that is, essential or necessary bread (cf. Fitzmyer 1985, 904-6). Many people in the ancient world lived at a subsistence level and would readily pray for food each day. This may have seemed even more important for a wandering band with no continuous supply of food. Both the petition for bread and the teaching about the ravens and the lilies (12:22-31) may be designed, first of all, for those who shared this itinerant life.

In verse 4 the petition for forgiveness is followed by assurance that we also forgive others. A necessary connection between these two forms of forgiveness is also assumed in 6:37-38. Luke, unlike Matthew, refers first to "our sins" and then to those "indebted to us." The latter phrase could refer to forgiveness of loans as well as wrongs. The final petition seems to assume that God might lead disciples to a "time of trial" (= *peirasmos*, "testing," "temptation"), which they must avoid. However, neither Jesus nor his followers escape testing (cf. 4:1-13; 8:13; 22:28; Acts 20:19), which includes persecution. Judging by the Gospel narrative, the answer to this petition comes not in the form of immunity but as strength to endure and recover.

11:5-10: The Lord's Prayer is followed by teaching on prayer, consisting of two similitudes drawn from village and family life (vv. 5-8, 11-13), separated by a rhythmic exhortation (vv. 9-10). The first similitude is unique to Luke, but verses 9-13 parallel Matt 7:7-11.

Although the NRSV begins with "suppose," verses 5-7 are actually a long and involved question that begins "who of you . . ." and expects the answer "no one." The man's request for bread, even if inconvenient, will not be refused. The situation described might well seem humorous to first-century listeners, as they picture someone struggling out of bed in spite of his angry retort. The similitude cannot be understood allegorically as a depiction of God. Rather, it presupposes the "how much more" type of argument found in verse 13. The scene also presupposes the importance of hospitality in village life. To be unable to offer a meal to a guest would be a cause of great shame. (On honor and shame as "pivotal values of the Mediterranean world," see Malina and Neyrey in Neyrey 1991, 25-65.) It is assumed that a friend would lend bread to prevent such shame, but asking for it at midnight is an extreme case. Evidently there is only one room in the house, or only one sleeping room, with the whole family bedded down together. Getting up in the pitch dark will disturb the whole family. In spite of this, the request will be honored, if not for friendship's sake at least because of "his *anaideia*." Interpretation of this term is difficult. In spite of the NRSV, "persistence" is not quite accurate, for *anaideia* really means "shamelessness," the negative quality of one who offends social standards. Some interpreters think this refers to the shamelessness of the sleeper in the eyes of the village if he does not get up and help his friend (cf. Nolland 1993, 626). The alternative is to apply "his shamelessness" to the one asking for bread, with the assumption that, even though the man is preserving his honor by feeding his midnight guest, he is acting shamelessly by rousing a family out of bed. Part of the problem is a confusion of pronouns in verse 8, which leaves uncertain who is meant by "*his* shamelessness."

In support of the second reading, it might be noted that shamelessness, even though a negative quality in society, is not necessarily so in the Gospel tradition. The "faith" commended in healing stories is a boldness that refuses to be stopped by social proprieties (see above on 5:20 and 8:47-48), and the widow who approaches the unjust judge (another example of prayer) is not only persistent but bold, even impudent (see below on 18:1-5). Although it is true that human requests of God may show ignorance and pettiness, this passage seems to deal with a different problem: an unwillingness to ask, out of fear or deference. The following verses (vv. 9-10) speak to the same issue.

In verse 9 rhythmic repetition is used for emphatic effect. The commands "Ask, search, knock" are synonymous. Each command is followed by a promise, forming a short, two-beat line with accent on the verbs. (*"Ask,* and it will be *given* you."*) This pattern is repeated three times. Then verse 9 is supported by verse 10, which repeats most of the key verbs and falls into a similar rhythmic pattern. The whole is urgent and emphatic. These verses appear to be addressed to people who are fearful, because they see themselves as unworthy, or passively resigned, because they believe that nothing can change. The claims made here are extravagant. Particularly the "everyone" in verse 10 seems incredible. Obviously many requests made to humans are not answered positively, and the same seems to be true of requests to God. Yet Jesus insists that God is ready to respond, and people must seize the opportunity to present their requests. The point of "everyone" may be to show that even outcasts, not just those with religious qualifications, are invited to present their requests (cf. Bailey 1976, 135).

11:11-13: The hearers are again asked to give their judgment by responding to a question, but this time they are to compare themselves not with the asker but with the one being asked. Since God can be addressed as "father," the request is placed in the context of the family. The similitude presumes that the strong bond of loyalty in families of that time and place would lead a father to respond to his son's requests with good will. (The Greek refers to a father and son in v. 11, for which the NRSV has substituted the gender-inclusive terms "anyone" and "child.") Even though the hearers are "evil" in comparison with God, they could not imagine that they would act in an evil way toward their own children. How much more with God the father.

Surprisingly, Luke refers to a particular gift of God in verse 13, the "Holy Spirit" (Matt 7:11 simply says "good things"). The disciples will not receive the Spirit until Pentecost (Acts 2:1-4), but verse 13 indicates in advance the importance of this special gift. It will come after prayer (Acts 1:14; 4:23-31; 8:14-17; 9:11, 17). The similitude in Luke 11:11-13 refers to a father who gives good gifts, particularly the Holy Spirit. These terms prepare for later theological motifs, for the Holy Spirit is repeatedly called a "gift" (Acts 2:38; 8:20; 10:45; 11:17) and the "promise of the Father" (Luke 24:49; Acts 1:4; cf. 2:33). In Rom 8:15-16 and Gal 4:6 the Spirit is cited as witness that the believers are God's children, who can address God as Abba, Father. In both Luke–Acts and Paul's letters, the experience of a new, closer relation to God through the Spirit lies behind this connection between the Spirit and God as Father.

Jesus Responds to Challenges from the Crowd (11:14-36)

Controversy dominates this section, which contains a sharp attack upon Jesus. The attack comes from some of the crowd (v. 15), while others in the crowd show their skepticism by demanding a sign from heaven (v. 16). In Matthew and Mark these attitudes are expressed by the scribes and Pharisees, not the crowd (cf. Matt 9:34; 12:24, 38; 16:1; Mark 3:22; 8:11). The crowd has responded to Jesus with excitement and amazement, but the inadequacy of their response is beginning to show. In 10:13-15 Jesus condemned certain towns for their failure to repent. Now it appears that parts of the crowd are turning against him. Jesus will respond with harsh warnings and words of judgment (11:29-32; 12:13-21; 12:54–13:9; 13:22-30). Jesus appears here as a prophet of judgment, addressing people who have become blind and deaf.

Mark 3:22-27 contains a shorter version of the Beelzebul controversy. Matt 12:22-30 not only shares the Marcan material but also contains most of the additional material found in Luke. Luke's version of the saying about the strong man (vv. 21-22) differs significantly from both Matthew and Mark.

11:14-23: The brief exorcism story in verse 14 introduces the controversy over Jesus' exorcisms in verses 15-22. Two negative comments by two segments of the crowd follow this exorcism. Jesus will reply to the first in verses 17-26 and to the second in verses 29-32. He will argue that his exorcisms indicate that the kingdom of God has come (v. 20), but those who demand a sign are clearly looking for something greater than the exorcism they have just witnessed.

Beelzebul is the name of a Canaanite god. Pagan gods were viewed as demons (*Jub.* 1:11; 22:17; *1 Enoch* 19:1; 99:7; 1 Cor 10:19-20). Beelzebul is here given the role of "ruler" of demons and is identified with Satan in verse 18. The accusation in verse 15 is an attempt at social control through labeling Jesus as a tool of Satan. If he can be stuck with such a label, his influence can be eliminated, even if he does have extraordinary power. (On "deviance labeling" as a social mechanism, see Malina and Rohrbaugh 1992, 353-54; Malina and Neyrey in Neyrey 1991, 97-122.)

Jesus replies as follows: First, he explores the consequences of the charge. If Satan's power is being used against the demons, there is civil war in Satan's kingdom. Such a divided kingdom "becomes a desert" or "is laid waste," as in the destruction of war. It is absurd, of course, to think that Satan is destroying his own kingdom, but it is interesting that even the opponents' charge supports Jesus' claim that this is an eschatological time in which Satan's power is collapsing (cf. 10:18). Thus Jesus catches the opponents in a dilemma. Second, verse 19 suggests the unfairness of the charge. There are others performing exorcisms, but they are not being accused in the same way. ("Your exorcists" [NRSV] is literally "your sons"—probably a way of referring to a group of exorcists not aligned with Jesus and more acceptable to those accusing him. For a story of a Jewish exorcist, see Josephus *Ant.* 8 §46-48.)

Having robbed the accusation of its initial plausibility, Jesus turns, third, to an alternative interpretation of his work. If the accusation of a Satanic source crumbles, the other possible source of power is "the finger of God." (This, like God's "arm" [1:51] and "hand" [1:66], is a biblical image for God's power. See Exod 8:19, where Egyptian opponents are forced to recognize that Moses and Aaron's mighty acts are done by "the finger of God.") Jesus draws a further consequence: If by the finger of God, "then the kingdom of God has come to you." Jesus is doing what he instructed his messengers to do in 10:9, interpreting the mighty acts of healing and exorcism as signs of the promised time of salvation. To view them only as cures of a few lucky people or proofs of Jesus' power is to miss their real significance. Key passages have already placed Jesus' and the disciples' healing work in the large context of God's saving purpose, revealed by scripture (cf. 4:18-19; 7:22; 10:23-24). Now this work is explicitly taken as a manifestation of God's powerful rule bringing an end to Satan's power.

Fourth, Jesus' claim is transformed into imagery through the similitude of the strong man (vv. 21-22). The rulers of the two "kingdoms" mentioned in verses 18 and 20 (Satan and God) are represented by a strong man and a stronger man who overpowers him. Luke's version of the strong man depicts him as a fully armed soldier. When overpowered, he loses his armor as well as his property. Thus Satan, the strong man, has lost his power to fight, and his property is being plundered through exorcisms. The time of Satan's defeat is not specified, and it is possible that this similitude simplifies what, in the rest of Luke–Acts, is a more complex struggle. Fifth, Jesus challenges members of the crowd to show active support (v. 23). There are some who are clearly against him, and there are others who are uncommitted. In the new situation of growing polarization, commitment is necessary. The aphorism in 11:23 is severe, while the related aphorism in 9:50 is tolerant. Although they seem to conflict, the truth of such aphorisms depends on whether each is spoken in an appropriate situation.

11:24-26: The point of verses 24-26 in context is obscure, but placement of these words here suggests that they are an additional comment about Jesus' exorcisms, the subject of verses 14-22. However, there is a sharp shift in mood. Although verses 20-22 give maximum importance to Jesus' exorcisms by associating them with the coming of God's kingdom and the overpowering of the strong man, verses 24-26 sound a cautionary, even pessimistic note. In this case, the departure of the unclean spirit does not finally lead to improvement; rather, "the last state of that person is worse than the first." The cause of this disaster is not indicated. Even the reference to the house being "empty," and so unguarded, found in Matt 12:44, is absent in those manuscripts of Luke that probably give the original reading. Our only clues as to cause come from the context. Perhaps this disaster is likely among those who, after being freed from unclean spirits by Jesus, refuse to make the commitment to be "with me" (v. 23) or to "hear the word of God and obey it" (v. 28). The claims to victory over demonic power in verses 20-22 do not fit easily with the resurgence of demonic power in verses 24-26. Here, as in other parts of the Gospels, the listener is left with the task of seeking the truth behind statements that seemingly conflict, but may balance and qualify one another.

11:27-28: Not only in verses 27-28 but elsewhere (cf. 12:13, 41), variety is introduced into some of the long discourses through an interjection by a member of the audience. The interjection may suggest a new topic or may lead to clarification, but it does not indicate that the discourse is over. In this case, a woman makes a laudatory statement about Jesus' mother. Indirectly it also reflects favorably on him. The woman's statement is similar to statements about Mary in the infancy narrative (1:42, 48). Nevertheless, Jesus corrects the woman's beatitude with another. The correction need not imply that the woman is entirely wrong, only that her statement is inadequate to the present situation. The statement is by a woman about a woman and presupposes an understanding of how a woman may achieve blessing: by being the mother of a great son. Jesus responds with general language (in the Greek, masculine participles used in a generic sense) because his message has general relevance. Yet it is significant that he is responding to a woman. A principal effect of his words is to challenge and invite women to aim for a different kind of blessedness, the blessedness of "those who hear the word of God and obey it" (cf. 6:47; 8:21).

11:29-32: In verses 29-32 Jesus replies to the second negative response in the crowd, the demand for a sign from heaven (v. 16). There are four versions of this text, including a short version in Mark 8:11-12 in which Jesus rejects the request for a sign without mentioning the sign of Jonah; a version in Matt 16:1, 4 in which Jesus refers to the sign of Jonah but does not explain it; and a longer version in Matt 12:38-42 that explains the sign of Jonah by relating it to Jesus' death and burial.

If the skeptics in verse 16 understood Jesus' exorcisms as Jesus explains in verse 20, they would have a sign of God's royal power at work through Jesus. But they demand something more than the exorcism witnessed in verse 14. Jesus responds in verse 29 with strong words of condemnation, calling these people an "evil generation" or "clan" (*genea* can refer to any large group linked by common origin). He then rejects their request. To be sure, he offers the sign of Jonah, but this is not the kind of sign they wanted. In relating the sign of Jonah to Jesus, Matthew and Luke use different parts of the Jonah story. Matthew 12:40 compares the death and burial of Jesus to Jonah's time in the belly of the sea monster; Luke 11:30 refers to Jonah as a sign to the people of Nineveh, where he did not relate his adventures at sea but announced God's coming judgment (Jonah 3:4). Jonah was less a preacher of repentance than a prophetic preacher of judgment; repentance and mercy were unwelcome results for him (Jonah 4:1-3). Jesus will immediately assume this role of preacher of judgment in verses 31-32 (cf. Nolland 1993, 653-54). The future verb "will be" in verse 30 is appropriate, for this is largely a new role for the Lukan Jesus. Although he has previously warned people of the consequences of future action, he has seldom condemned people for their present condition or past action. (Exceptions are found in 6:24-26 and 10:13-15; rebukes of this "generation" are found in 7:31-35 and 9:41, but these passages do not announce coming judgment.) From this point on, Jesus' words are interspersed with severe threats to the unresponsive.

As in 10:12-15 the words of judgment in verses 31-32 are reinforced by comparison with scriptural figures. In this case, Jesus' audience is compared unfavorably with outsiders who were responsive. The "queen of the South" is the queen of Sheba (cf. 1 Kgs 10:1-13; 2 Chr 9:1-12). The queen of the South came to hear "the wisdom of Solomon," and the Ninevites heeded "the proclamation of Jonah." Jesus' words are also wisdom (2:40, 52; 7:35) and prophetic proclamation, but the neuter form *pleion* ("something greater") in both verses 31 and 32 gives a mysterious, indefinite quality to the important thing that Jesus' audience is missing. They and the Lukan audience must struggle to define it. The words of judgment in verses 31-32 sound final, but so did Jonah's announcement in Nineveh. The Jonah story suggests that repentance could still change the verdict.

11:33-36: The discourse ends in verses 33-36 with a combination of sayings found separately in Matt 5:15 (cf. Mark 4:21; Luke 8:16) and Matt 6:22-23. This final section asks the audience to consider what is necessary for a lamp's light to illuminate as it should. The "eye" is viewed as a crucial factor; it is "the lamp of your body." Although an external lamp may give light, the eye, the internal source of light, must cooperate if the person is to be illuminated. The emphasis on the eye here seems to show awareness that human perception is selective and interpretive, being influenced both by our culture and by our individual commitments. Due to this conditioning, the eye either admits the light of God's word or does not. The NRSV refers to the eye as either "healthy" or "not healthy." The first of these terms translates *haplous,* which basically means "single," in contrast to divided or deceitful. Singleness of heart or eye is a way of speaking of a life that is completely focused on God, a devotion not mixed with other concerns (cf. *Testament of Issachar* 3:5; 4:1-6, and Garrett 1991, 96-100). The eye that is single in this sense is open to God's illumination, enabling the self to be "full of light." Although there is a warning in verse 35, the discourse ends on a positive note in verse 36 (contrast Matt 6:23). The audience, including the opponents and skeptics, is invited to seek this single eye; then the external lamp can fully do its intended job. In the next section, however, Pharisees and lawyers are presented as examples of those who lack singleness of heart and eye (cf. Garrett 1991, 103).

Woes to Pharisees and Lawyers (11:37-54)

The issue of washing to remove cultic impurity before eating appears in Matt 15:1-3 and Mark 7:1-8, but the words of Jesus in this section of Luke have their closest parallel in Matthew 23, where they occur in a different order and with variations in wording.

Jesus also dined with a Pharisee in 7:36-50, and he will do so again in 14:1-24. Although there is tension between Jesus and his dining partners, including the host, in all of these scenes, neither of the other scenes approaches the degree of conflict in 11:37-54. In responding to the Pharisee's implied criticism in verse 38, Jesus makes sweeping statements of harsh censure that go far beyond the initial issue of washing before eating. The meal setting makes Jesus' behavior even more provocative and scandalous, for he is offending against the social rules of hospitality. Although an invitation may sometimes be a test of the social acceptability of a stranger, all signs of disrespect and hostility between host and guest must be avoided (cf. Gowler 1993, 220-23). Yet Jesus calls the Pharisees "fools" and pronounces woes on the Pharisees and lawyers present. This offense against hospitality can escape censure from the first-century audience only because Jesus is presented as being "prominent" and a "limit breaker," that is, one who is superior to normal social rules, who, therefore, can do things normally forbidden (cf. Gowler 1993, 227-28). The strong words of Jesus in this section reflect the struggle for leadership within Jewish communities between the Jesus movement and the leaders represented by the Pharisees and lawyers. They also reflect the socially disruptive character of the Jesus movement, which was often not willing to conform quietly in order to preserve polite society.

Jesus addresses "you Pharisees" and "you lawyers." It is easy to take his words as valid descriptions of all Pharisees and their successors, which would contribute to anti-Jewish prejudice. Therefore, it is wise to remember that the narrative itself does not authorize such a generalization. Jesus is addressing a specific dinner party. His words may have wider implications but only for those who share the faults being described. Such people may include the believers in the Lukan communities. These Pharisees and lawyers are being used as negative examples of what Jesus' followers, too, must avoid. This is made clear by the application that follows in 12:1. Jesus, now speaking to the disciples, warns, "Beware of the yeast of the Pharisees, that is, their hypocrisy." The term "hypocrisy" serves as a summary of the charges made in 11:39-44. Some of the specific issues in 11:39-44 may no longer be problems in the Lukan communities, but the underlying danger of hypocrisy is still real.

11:37-44: Washing the hands to remove ritual impurity was important before handling food to be eaten by priests, and there is also evidence for the practice on sabbaths and other holy days. It is not clear, however, that this was expected at every meal (cf. E. P. Sanders 1992, 437-38). Nevertheless, in this narrative the Pharisee expects Jesus to join the others in washing. Jesus' response accuses "you Pharisees" of a false understanding of cleanness before God. In verse 39 Jesus contrasts the "outside" of dishes with the "inside" of people. The former may be clean, but, in this case, the latter is not, for they are "full of greed and wickedness." *Harpagē* is not just greed but rapacity, or predatory greed. When this greed is present, external cleansings are useless. But there is a cure, the giving of alms (v. 41). The NRSV translates, "So give for alms those things that are within." It is not clear what this means. There is an alternative translation: "But concerning the things within (i.e., the greed and wickedness of v. 39), give alms, and see, all things are clean for you." Jesus is saying, then, that the particular antidote for the predatory greed that is defiling these Pharisees is alms giving. Jesus will urge his disciples to sell their possessions and give alms in 12:33. In contrast, Pharisees will be portrayed as "lovers of money" in 16:14. This is a kind of hypocrisy, for apparent devotion to God is used to hide devotion to greed.

The tithe (v. 42) was the tenth of agricultural produce that was to be given to support the Levites and priests. (There were also additional tithes; cf. E. P. Sanders 1992, 146-49.) Paying the tithe carefully could indicate devotion to God, but not if the person were to "neglect justice and the love of God." The word translated "justice" *(krisis)* often means judgment, and could refer here to the judgment of God. But the concern with predatory greed in verses

39-41 supports the translation "justice." Then "justice and the love of God" come close to being a summary of the double love commandment in 10:27 (cf. Fitzmyer 1985, 948). For love of God these Pharisees substitute another love, according to verse 43. They love being given special honors by humans. It is clear that this disease infects the followers of Jesus also, for Jesus must correct his disciples who want to be the greatest (9:46-48; 22:24-27). In part he does so by warning them about the scribes (20:46) with words that expand on 11:43. Such desires are another form of hypocrisy, for a life apparently devoted to God hides a desire for human honors. Such people "are like unmarked graves" (v. 44). Although they take special care to be clean before God, they are actually defiled and are a source of defilement to others, who do not recognize the danger.

11:45-54: A lawyer regards Jesus' words as insulting, not only to the Pharisees but to himself. ("Teachers of the law" or "scribes" have been associated with the Pharisees since 5:17, 21; the lawyer belongs to this group.) This interjection prompts Jesus to pronounce three woes on the lawyers comparable to the three woes on the Pharisees in 11:42-44. The shorter two reflect the position of the lawyers as respected interpreters of Jewish law. In both verses 46 and 52 they are accused of failing their responsibility as teachers of the people. On the one hand, they load heavy burdens on the people without being willing to assist them with their load; on the other hand, they have locked people out from true knowledge of the essentials of the law (the knowledge that the lawyer in 10:25-37 partly demonstrated). Between these two woes there is a longer and stronger accusation (vv. 47-51). It is probably significant that it is applied to the lawyers and not to the Pharisees, for the scribes who are part of the Jerusalem council will have a role in Jesus' death, while the Pharisees disappear from the story after Jesus' arrival in Jerusalem. The theme of the persecution and killing of the prophets appears a number of times in Luke–Acts (Luke 6:22-23; Acts 7:52), including passages in which Jesus identifies himself as one of these prophets (Luke 4:24; 13:33-34). Luke 11:47-51 is the harshest statement of this theme.

It may seem strange that building tombs for the prophets is taken as testimony that these lawyers approve of the deeds of their ancestors who killed the prophets. This is a provocative and ironic inversion of the apparent meaning of tomb building. This accusation gains force through what is said in verses 49-50: This generation continues the policy of its ancestors by killing and persecuting the prophets and apostles sent to it. Therefore, building tombs for prophets cannot be a way of honoring them; it must be a way of celebrating their deaths (cf. Nolland 1993, 667-68). In verse 49 the Wisdom of God is cited. (For wisdom personified and speaking, see Proverbs 8; Sir 24:1-22.) The NRSV ends the quotation of Wisdom's words at the end of verse 49, but they probably continue into verse 51. This is not a biblical quotation but a prophetic interpretation of the hidden providence of God, which, in this case, leads to judgment. The current persecutors of the prophets—here represented by the lawyers who oppose Jesus—are judged to be the representatives of a continuous group whose accumulated debt of wickedness, down through the centuries, is finally coming due.

In verse 50 the phrase translated "may be charged with the blood of all the prophets" is literally "the blood of all the prophets may be sought." To seek the blood of someone from someone is a biblical way of speaking of the death penalty for murder (cf. Gen 9:5-6; 2 Sam 4:11-12; Ezek 3:18-19, passages that, in the LXX, use the same Greek verb). Abel, of course, was the first person murdered in biblical history (Gen 4:8). The identity of Zechariah is less certain. The stoning of Zechariah, son of Jehoiada, in the temple is reported in 2 Chr 24:20-22. (In the present order of the Hebrew Bible, 2 Chronicles is the last book, matching Genesis as the first.) But the parallel in Matt 23:35 refers to Zechariah, son of Barachiah, a biblical prophet (see Zech 1:1) whose violent death is not recorded. In either case, there is a considerable gap until the time of Jesus. A third possibility is Zechariah, son of Baris, who was murdered in the temple by the Zealots, according to Josephus *J. W.* 4 §334-44. This was after the time of Jesus and shortly before the destruction of Jerusalem by the Romans. In any case, the current representatives of a group that has consistently opposed the prophets are held liable for an extensive history of murder.

The response of the scribes and Pharisees in verses 53-54 represents a new, higher level of hostility, resulting in greater danger for Jesus. This hostility does not lead directly to Jesus' death, but it does raise the issue of how one can face arrest and death, something Jesus will discuss in 12:4-12.

A Discourse in the Light of Coming Crises (12:1–13:9)

This section is a rather lengthy discourse by Jesus that is segmented by shifts in topic and in the group addressed. A massive crowd is present, but part of the time Jesus is addressing his disciples in the presence of the crowd. Three times there are interjections from listeners, to which Jesus responds. These give the impression that Jesus is speaking *extempore* rather than presenting a prepared speech. These bits of dialogue also help the Lukan audience to keep the narrative audience in mind while listening to Jesus. In much of the Jerusalem travel narrative, there is a rough rotation among three groups who repeatedly appear as Jesus' audience: the disciples, the crowds, and the religious leaders. Having just addressed the scribes and Pharisees in 11:37-54, the next section is devoted to the disciples and the crowd. Jesus first speaks to his disciples about hypocrisy and the need for fearless confession in spite of the threat of death (12:1-12). Then he is interrupted by someone in the crowd and speaks to the crowd (12:13-21). Turning to the disciples, he speaks to them about the same topic: possessions (12:22-34). He continues to address the disciples but begins to speak of the tests disciples face as they wait for the Lord's coming (12:35-53). Finally, he warns the crowd that they also must be alert and ready, particularly through repentance (12:54–13:9).

Hypocrisy and Persecution (12:1-12)

This section is more closely linked to the preceding than the bland term "meanwhile" indicates. The Greek begins, "in which things" or "times" (the noun must be supplied). Jesus is speaking in the situation of intense hostility described in 11:53-54 and warns the disciples that they must not share the hypocrisy of which he accused the Pharisees in 11:39-44. The metaphor of "yeast" implies that it can spread throughout the community if allowed to do its work. The attempt to conceal something will not finally succeed, according to verse 2, and this general warning is applied to the disciples in verse 3 (note the "you"; a version of v. 2 is applied differently in 8:16-17). The chief concern is things the disciples have "said" that they might want to conceal. These things could be various kinds of shameful or unkind remarks, but the continuation in verses 4-12 suggests that verse 3 may refer to believers who are willing to express their faith privately but not in public, out of fear. This is a kind of hypocrisy that can infect the community of Jesus. It is the public pretense that they are no different than the majority. It will not work for long, Jesus says.

We may note the following parallels: Luke 12:1 with Matt 16:6 and Mark 8:15; Luke 12:2-9 with Matt 10:26-33; Luke 12:10 with Matt 12:31-32 and Mark 3:28-30; Luke 12:11-12 with Matt 10:19-20 and Mark 13:11. There is another version of Luke 12:11-12 in Luke 21:14-15.

When Jesus first announced his coming death in 9:22, he also warned his followers that they must be willing to lose their lives for his sake (9:23-25). Having provoked hostility from the scribes and Pharisees (11:53-54) and having recalled the deaths of the prophets (11:47-51), he now addresses the fear that remarks about death and persecution can cause. The verb "fear" (*phobeomai*) is used five times in verses 4-7, and it will return in verse 32. The verb "worry" (*merimnaō*) is also used frequently (vv. 11, 22, 25, 26). Jesus is addressing the disciples' fears and worries, especially their fear of death and their worry about food and clothing.

In verses 4-7 Jesus first tries to replace one fear with another. ("Do not fear . . . But I will warn you whom to fear.") A fearsome God has authority to cast into hell. Then Jesus shifts abruptly to emphasize God's care for even the least creatures and God's great care for the disciples (vv. 6-7). These different descriptions of God have the common goal of overcoming fear of human opponents. The word translated "hell" is literally "gehenna," a word derived from Hebrew. It originally referred to a valley near Jerusalem where there was burning rubbish. Later it designated a place of fire where sinners would be punished (cf. Fitzmyer 1985, 959-60).

The Lukan Jesus continues to address the fears of his followers in verses 8-9. These verses present a balanced reciprocity. The Son of Man in the heavenly court will either acknowledge or deny his followers, depending on whether they have acknowledged or denied him. Public acknowledgment is required, even though this may be dangerous. There is an assumed bond of loyalty here; to deny Jesus is to be disloyal. The two forms of the word "deny" in verse 9 are not found later in Luke until the prediction and story of Peter's denial (22:34, 57, 61). Peter denies *knowing* Jesus, that is, denies that he is his friend and follower. The same kind of denial is probably meant in 12:9. Jesus nevertheless intercedes for Peter (22:32), and he recovers. It is possible that 12:10 follows 12:9 in Luke partly because the first half of verse 10 allows forgiveness for someone like Peter. Another version of verses 8-9 is found in 9:26, where it also demands public loyalty to Jesus even when there is threat of death.

The offer of forgiveness in verse 10 to "everyone" (whether a follower like Peter or an outsider) who speaks against the Son of Man is a sweeping grant of amnesty, but it serves primarily to set off the one thing that cannot be forgiven: blasphemy against the Holy Spirit. The Lukan setting (which differs from Matthew's and Mark's) suggests that this possibility arises because of persecution. It is not entirely clear, however, whether the one who blasphemes the Holy Spirit is the persecutor who rejects the witness of the Spirit in the public confession of the persecuted (cf. v. 12 and Stegemann 1991, 65-77), or whether the blasphemer is the disloyal disciple who refuses the guidance of the Spirit in the hour of trial and denies any relation to Jesus. The second possibility is more likely. Luke 12:10 is speaking of a disloyal disciple who, in the threatening situation where the Spirit will be most active (cf. vv. 11-12), refuses to be led by the Spirit and instead publicly reviles the Spirit given through Jesus. Blaspheming is something more than denying knowledge of Jesus. It involves public vilification of Jesus and the Spirit as proof that one is not a follower. Persecutors could try to force Jesus' followers to do this (cf. Acts 26:11).

The threats in verses 9-10 are accompanied by a promise in verses 11-12. The Spirit will help the disciple to speak before threatening authorities. The "synagogues" had their own judicial procedures and could hand out punishment (cf. Acts 22:19; 2 Cor 11:24). The "rulers" and "authorities" for the Lukan communities would probably be local magistrates, who would be Gentiles. What the Holy Spirit teaches when brought before such authorities could be something very simple: to say that I am a loyal follower of Jesus. But the parallel in Luke 21:12-15 and related stories in Acts suggest that more is in mind. Interrogation by authorities is a special "opportunity to testify," and it is important that it be done with impressive "wisdom" (21:13-15). But that is more likely to happen through the inspiration of the Spirit than through the prepared speech of the Greco-Roman orator. In particular, the Spirit inspires boldness of speech in spite of opposition. When Peter and John are brought before the Jerusalem council, Peter, as promised in Luke 12:12, is "filled with the Holy Spirit" (Acts 4:8). The speech that follows is brief, but it is a sharp and clear witness to the power of Jesus Messiah. The council is amazed at the "boldness" of Peter and John, even though they are "uneducated" (Acts 4:13). When Peter and John return to the community of believers, they pray for the ability "to speak your word with all boldness," in spite of threats (Acts 4:29). The answer is a renewed outpouring of the Spirit, resulting in bold speech (Acts 4:31). These scenes provide a narrative example of the situations anticipated in Luke 12:11-12.

◊ ◊ ◊ ◊

The possibility of being interrogated before officials, being beaten, and even killed was real. It is difficult to know to what extent Jews, on the one hand, and Gentiles, on the other, were involved in such actions. The bitter opposition of many Jews needs to be understood in light of the threat that the Jesus movement posed to Judaism at this time. Judaism had lost its cult center, the Jerusalem temple, in AD 70. At the very time that Judaism faced this crisis, some followers of Jesus were questioning other fundamentals unifying Judaism: the law and the place of Jews as God's special people. Furthermore, after the Roman-Jewish war, the continuing presence of messianists (like followers of Jesus Messiah) in the synagogues would arouse the suspicions of Roman officials. And when the Jesus people left the synagogues, they had a way of taking Gentile supporters of Judaism (the so-called "God-fearers") with them, robbing the synagogue of important financial and social support. The resulting conflict could be bitter, and each side might try to use the local magistrates to its own advantage. Roman authorities had their own reasons for suspicion. New religious movements, they feared, could threaten the social order and disrupt families. The warnings and promises in 12:4-12 would speak to the Lukan communities as they faced these conflicts.

Concerns About Possessions (12:13-34)

A request from a member of the crowd provides a way of changing the subject in the midst of Jesus' discourse. In this section Jesus teaches first the crowd and then the disciples about possessions and the physical needs of life. Other sections of extensive teaching about possessions in the travel narrative (16:1-31; 18:18-30) are also split between teaching that is directed to outsiders and that which is directed to followers. Jesus' teaching on this subject is not just for those who follow him.

12:13-21: Since Torah contains laws of inheritance (Num 27:1-11; 36:1-9; Deut 21:15-17), a religious teacher might be asked to settle disputes about it. Jesus, however, refuses this role. Instead, he takes the request as an occasion to warn the crowd against greed, primarily through a parable. The man in the parable is already rich; then he has a bumper crop. The simple introductory statement in verse 16 leads to interior monologue, which occupies most of this short story. The decisive event in the story is not an external action but an internal decision. The interior monologue allows the audience to observe the man deliberating and highlights his decision as the crucial event. In verse 17 the man poses the question, "What should I do" with the abundant crops? His answer to this practical question will be crucial.

In verse 18 his answer begins to appear. It could be viewed as a prudent decision. He is preparing for the future, perhaps so that he can generously share with others in times of need. The next verse, however, shows no concern for others. He only anticipates his own enjoyment over many years, using a well-known formula for hedonistic living (cf. Scott 1989, 135-36). Versions of this formula in Jewish tradition include awareness of the shortness of life: "Let us eat and drink, for tomorrow we die" (Isa 22:13, quoted in 1 Cor 15:32); and when someone says, " 'I have found rest, and now I shall feast on my goods!' he does not know how long it will be until he leaves them to others and dies" (Sir 11:19; cf. Wisdom 2:1-9). God declares the man a fool. He is a fool because he is thinking of his own pleasures and behaving as if there is no God (cf. Ps 14:1). He is also a fool because he has forgotten how the saying goes, "Let us eat and drink, *for tomorrow we die.*" The saying applies strictly in his case; he will die during the night that begins the new day. Therefore, his grand plans are worthless.

Probably the man is being condemned not only because he has forgotten about death and God but also because of his greed (cf. v. 15). There was another option for use of his abundant crops. He could have become a generous benefactor. Sirach contrasts the "fool" who is taken captive by gold with the rich man who is blessed. The latter is generous, and "the assembly will proclaim his acts of charity" (Sir 31:5-11; see also Malina and Rohrbaugh 1992, 324-25, 359 on the social conviction that accumulation of goods should be condemned because it deprives others, unless the rich man is a generous benefactor).

Of course, not every rich man dies before he can begin enjoying himself. Jesus tells another story about a callous rich man in 16:19-31. The story begins with the rich man doing just what the man planned to do in 12:19: enjoy himself ("be merry" in 12:19 and "feasted" in 16:19 both translate the verb *euphrainō*). The judgment on the second rich man is just as clear, although it is not revealed until his self-indulgent life is exchanged for punishment.

A generalizing conclusion is added in verse 21, contrasting two ways of being rich. There are those who store up goods "for themselves," and there are those who are "rich toward God." Being rich toward God requires proper use of possessions, that is, not being greedy (v. 15), not keeping things for oneself. As a conclusion to the section, verses 33-34 will explain further how one may substitute savings in heaven, where they are really safe, for earthly savings. (The verb *thēsaurizō,* translated "store up treasures," simply means "store up" or "save" and can apply to the rich man's grain as well as to gold.)

12:22-34: Next Jesus turns to the disciples and applies his teaching about possessions to them. They are living on quite a different economic level from that of the rich man. Jesus is now addressing people who gave up what security they had when they "left everything and followed him" (5:11, 28). Their problem is not in dealing with abundance but in finding the basic needs of life: food and clothing. A parallel to 12:22-31 may be found in Matt 6:25-33.

The basic argument is similar to 12:6-7: God cares for all creatures; God cares even more for you. But in 12:22-31 the argument is considerably elaborated, making it more forceful and challenging. This section begins with instruction not to worry, which is applied to two concerns, food and clothing. In verses 29-31 the basic instruction returns, "Do not keep striving . . . and do not keep worrying," followed by the contrasting command to strive for God's kingdom. Within this envelope structure (the conclusion returns to the beginning) is placed the material about the ravens and lilies, the part about the ravens responding to the need for food and the part about the lilies to the need for clothing.

A simple command cannot stop people from worrying about their basic needs. Then as now the consciousness of many people is so dominated by worry and their actions so dominated by anxious striving that these concerns define reality for them. They cannot imagine any other way to live. Change requires a basic challenge to one's sense of reality that awakens the imagination to view the world differently. This is what Jesus attempts through forceful and imaginative language. He points first to the ravens and then to the lilies. These are ordinary creatures and seem an unlikely source of revelation. But Jesus urges his audience to "consider" the ravens, that is, look at them thoughtfully, and then he notes something that makes their life seem remarkable in comparison to human life. For them there is no lengthy process of growing and storing food (including building barns, as the rich man planned in v. 18), "yet God feeds them." They get along as well as humans do, but with much less anxious preparation. Ravens are unclean birds according to Torah (Lev 11:15; Deut 14:14), but God's care for them is mentioned in scripture (Ps 147:9). The choice of ravens to make the point may accent God's indiscriminate goodness.

In verses 27-28 Jesus goes through the same argument a second time, except that this section is longer and the diction more emphatic than in verse 24. The repetition with emphasis adds force and imaginative power to the language, which is moving toward a climax. Again there is a contrast with human life: Lilies do not toil or spin to make their clothing. Yet their clothes outshine even Solomon's. This does not mean that these flowers are especially important. In verse 28 the splendid flowers are called "grass" that will soon be used as fuel for the oven. God's extravagance shows in the splendid garb given to such ephemeral plants. Then comes the application, "How much more will he clothe you—you of little faith!"

The argument will be convincing only if the ravens and lilies become resonant images for a reality that extends far beyond them. This can happen if they work in the audience's imagination to remind people of their own encounters with the goodness and beauty of creation, a goodness and beauty that was there before human attempts at management. This goodness and beauty is also the basis of human life. Humans may sow seed and spin thread, but prior to human work is the goodness of God that feeds and clothes the birds and flowers. This goodness persists even when disciples are not able to obtain food and clothing in the normal way. Birds and flowers testify to the fundamental goodness that makes life possible and that also makes it possible for disciples to find release from worry, even though they have few resources. Thus Jesus not only commands the disciples not to worry but seeks to make possible what he commands through a gift of freedom. By new recognition of God's goodness and care, the disciples can be freed from anxious striving for food and clothing (v. 29) so that they may strive instead for God's kingdom (v. 31) (on 12:22-31, see further Tannehill 1975, 60-67).

The renewed reference to God as "your Father" (v. 30) supports the emphasis on God's care (cf. 11:2-3, 9-13). Between the statements about the ravens and the lilies, verses 25-26 indicate the futility of worry. The noun *hēlikia* can mean "stature" as well as "span of life," and the word translated "a single hour" normally means "cubit" (about eighteen inches). Since adding eighteen inches to one's stature does not seem like "so small a thing" (v. 26), the translators understand verse 25 to refer to a small amount of time added to one's life.

In verse 32 the Lukan Jesus picks up the theme "do not be afraid" from 12:4-7 and adds a further word of assurance. The kingdom for which they must strive will be their Father's gracious gift. The Father's "good pleasure" refers to a gracious decision in their favor. The same term was used of God's choice of Jesus, announced following his baptism (3:22). The assurance is followed by a concluding command that brings the teaching about possessions home to the Lukan audience. We were told that the first followers of Jesus "left everything and followed him" (5:11, 28). Nevertheless, they might still have possessions at home that could be sold. Probably the main concern here, however, is the communities of believers who do not leave home on mission. They have possessions that can be sold in order to give "alms" or "charity." (The Greek word *eleēmosynē* refers to a contribution to the needy given as an act of mercy.) The reference to *selling* possessions indicates that substantial properties are in mind, not just spare money. In this way those with possessions are being asked to share the same risk and show the same trust as those who left home without any sources of food and clothing. They, too, will need to learn the lesson of the ravens and the lilies. Acts 2:44-45 and 4:32-37 illustrate the community of sharing that could result. (On almsgiving as a symbol of Luke's "vision of a new society," see Moxnes 1988, 113-23.)

By selling your possessions and giving alms, Jesus says, you will be exchanging forms of wealth that are always at risk for wealth that is secure. Purses wear out and leak coins, thieves steal, and moths destroy clothing (luxurious clothing was an important kind of wealth for rich people). However, what is stored in heaven, with God, is secure. Verse 34 adds an additional consideration in support: the place where one's wealth is stored indicates the orientation of the heart. Those with earthly wealth invest their hearts in earthly things; those with heavenly wealth invest their hearts in God (cf. 16:13). The challenge to sell possessions and give alms will reveal which is the case.

Responsible Servants (12:35-48)

Jesus continues talking to the disciples, but the topic shifts to the need for eschatological watchfulness. The shift is not quite as abrupt as it may seem, for detachment from possessions and worries is an important part of preparation for the Lord's coming. Thus in 21:34 disciples are warned lest their hearts be "weighed down with . . . the worries of this life [cf. 12:22], and that day does not catch you unexpectedly" (cf. also 8:14). The exhortation to be ready for the return of the Lord in 12:35-48 is complemented by further eschatological teaching in 17:20–18:8 and 21:7-36 (cf. also 19:12-27). Luke 12:35-36, 38 are distantly related to Mark 13:33-37. There is a closer relation between Luke 12:39-46 and Matt 24:43-51.

Readiness for the appearance of the Lord or the Son of Man is the theme of this section. There is a difference between verses 35-40, where readiness alone is stressed, and verses 41-48, where readiness means faithful fulfillment of an assigned responsibility in the interim. Throughout, however, disciples are warned to be constantly ready because humans do not know the time of the Lord's appearance. He is likely to appear unexpectedly (vv. 40, 46). In Acts 1:6-7 Jesus states as a principle that knowledge of God's timing is not granted to Jesus' followers. There are a few indications in Luke 12:35-48 that, from the point of view of his disciples, the Lord's coming has been delayed (vv. 38, 45). Nevertheless, the Lord's coming still functioned as a strong motivation for present faithfulness. It had not become a remote event that was no longer a concern of first-century believers (cf. Carroll 1988, 53-60). It could catch believers off guard at any time, but those whom the Lord would find faithfully watching and working are repeatedly called "blessed" (vv. 37, 38, 43).

◊ ◊ ◊ ◊

"Be dressed for action" is a free translation of the biblical phrase "Let your loins [or "waists"] be girded." When working or running, the loose robe could be belted to keep it out of the way. The returning master will also "fasten his belt" for work, according to verse 37. The NRSV translates "master" when the text refers to a parable character, but "Lord" when there is a direct reference to Jesus (as in vv. 41-42). It is, however, the same Greek word *(kyrios)*, and the double use of the term shows that the "master" is a rather transparent stand-in for the Lord Jesus returning in glory. The comparison of the Son of Man to a thief breaking into a house (vv. 39-40) is striking. Here a negative social role provides an image for the Son of Man, whose unexpected arrival can have destructive consequences for some.

Most striking, however, is the description of the master's behavior with his faithful slaves in verse 37. A role reversal takes place, for the master has the slaves "sit down to eat" (literally, he makes them "recline," as at a banquet) and then serves them. The expected social roles are indicated in 17:7-10, which shows that a master would not even allow his hard-working slave to eat before preparing and serving supper to the master. Jesus, to be sure, does take the role of table servant in 22:27, but in the context of his imminent death. That the Lord who returns in glory still takes the role of servant for his people suggests that this is now an indelible part of his character. The image of the eschatological banquet is in the background. This image will be important in immediately following chapters (13:28-30; 14:15-24; 15:22-32). The eucharistic experience of the early church may also be a factor (cf. 22:14-20; 24:30-31).

Peter asks concerning the application of "this parable" in verse 41, but Jesus does not give a direct answer. Since the two audiences being addressed in Luke 12 are the disciples and the crowd, "us" in verse 41 could refer to the disciples and "everyone" to the crowd. Then verses 47-48 would indicate that the teaching applies primarily to the disciples, who know the master's will, and only secondarily to the crowd. However, this view does not account for the fact that Jesus' response to Peter introduces a "manager" (or steward) who is in charge of other slaves. He is responsible for feeding them (a role given to the twelve in 9:12-17; see also 22:24-30). Thus when Peter refers to "us," he probably means those who will be leaders in the early church, like the twelve. "This parable" probably refers to verse 39, and Peter's question is prompted by the reference to the "owner of the house" (*oikodespotēs*, more precisely "master of a house" or household). Peter's question and Jesus' response suggest a special application of verses 39 and 42-47 to those who have leadership responsibility in early churches, which are understood by analogy with households.

Jesus first describes the "faithful and prudent manager" who does his master's will (vv. 42-44). A beatitude is pronounced, and there is a promise of greater authority for faithfulness. The situation is similar to verses 36-37*a*, except that the task assigned involves responsibility for other slaves. In contrast to verses 42-44, verses 45-46 describe a possible negative outcome. The manager is a slave but has authority over other slaves, not an uncommon arrangement in the ancient world. The delay in the master's return becomes a test of the manager. If he is not committed to his task, his interim authority gives him the opportunity to become self-indulgent, wasteful, and abusive of others. When the master unexpectedly returns, the punishment will be extreme: The master "will cut him in pieces." (The NRSV has the literal translation, while the RSV weakened it to "punish him.") Being put with "the unfaithful" probably refers to his lot at God's judgment after death. The warning to abusive church leaders is severe.

In verses 47-48 a gradation of responsibility and punishment for failure is introduced. These verses serve as a conclusion to the section that began in verse 35. The translation "did not prepare himself" can be misleading. The Greek simply says "did not prepare." This is a reference to the servants who were supposed to be ready for their master's return in verses 36-38. "Do what was wanted," in turn, refers especially to the master's charge to the manager in verse 42. During the master's absence, the manager was given a specific responsibility. He "knew what his master wanted." This situation increases liability and punishment in case of failure. The rule in verses 47-48 provides some excuse for those outside the church and for those within the church who have had little opportunity to learn. However, it is tough on those with knowledge and those who have been given special responsibility and power. These concluding verses may enable us to answer Peter's question in verse 41. The teaching in verses 39-48 applies to all, but especially to those with knowledge and power, the leaders of the communities. To them "much has been entrusted," and "more will be demanded."

Division in the Family (12:49-53)

Here Luke's Jesus suddenly shifts to a passionate statement about his own mission. He expresses the tension that he feels because of an incomplete task, giving the narrative a new sense of straining forward (cf. also 13:32-33). In the context of the Jerusalem travel narrative, the fire and baptism that have not yet been kindled or completed must relate closely to the rejection and death that awaits Jesus in Jerusalem. Note that Jesus does not speak of the baptism of others but of a baptism that he himself must undergo. As in Mark 10:38, baptism seems here to be a symbol for death. "Baptize" probably retains its original sense of dip, immerse, or plunge, and this is a life-threatening immersion in water or fire. Although there is no immediate preparation for Jesus' statements in verses 49-50, they fit the general context of the journey and remind the audience of the goal of this journey. The following verses go on to relate the rejection that Jesus will face to the family conflict disciples must face. Family separation and conflict are painful issues for disciples (cf. 8:19-21; 9:59-62; 14:26; 18:28-30; 21:16), so Jesus rounds off his words about facing death and renouncing possessions in verses 4-34 by addressing these issues. Matthew 10:34-36 presents a different version of verses 51-53, but verses 49-50 have no canonical parallel.

The Greek emphasizes the key words "fire" and "baptism" by placing them first in the sentences, and the two sentences have a parallel construction. The parallelism suggests that there is some connection between the fire and the baptism. Baptism and fire are also connected in 3:16, where John the Baptist announced the one who "will baptize you with the Holy Spirit and fire." It is possible that Jesus' baptism in 12:50 is also a baptism with fire, which he must undergo as he brings fire on the earth. The fire in verse 49 is probably a threatening image of judgment, but not necessarily of final judgment, nor need it result only in destruction. We might think of the refiner's fire that purges away impurities, as in Mal 3:2-3 (note the reference to Mal 3:1 in Luke 7:27).

Like the statement in verse 49, the question in verse 51 concerns what Jesus has come to do. The answer is likely to be a surprise. Jesus has, indeed, come to bring peace according to 1:79; 2:14 (cf. also Acts 10:36). Yet the immediate reality is division. In 19:42 Jesus will mourn because the peace intended for Jerusalem is being rejected by it. Similarly, the peace that Jesus' messengers brought to homes (10:5-6) is being replaced with division in families, because of the conflict that Jesus' mission produces. The division is developed in concrete and graphic language through a rhythmic series of pairs, beginning with "three against two and two against three" and extending through a series of family relationships. The closest family ties break in mutual animosity, and the pain of this is reinforced by the rhythmic repetition. Moreover, "I have come" or "I came" statements (implied in v. 51) frequently are used to announce a fundamental purpose of Jesus' mission, as in 5:32 and 19:10. For Jesus to say "I have come to bring . . . division" is very disturbing. It implies, at least, that family conflict is now a necessary consequence of Jesus' mission. It is stated so strongly in order that disciples may face this reality and make their decision for discipleship with full awareness of the pain ahead. Otherwise, commitment is likely to collapse when the disciple bangs into hard reality (on 12:49-53, see further Tannehill 1975, 143-47).

Warnings for a Time of Crisis (12:54–13:9)

Jesus turns again to the crowds. His tone is urgent and severe. He seems to be reacting to a potentially disastrous failure to respond to his message. He warns the crowds that this is a critical time (12:54-56), a time requiring urgent action (12:57-59), repentance (13:1-5), and fruit-bearing (13:6-9).

12:54-59: Two specific cases of accurate weather prediction are cited in verses 54-55; this ability is generalized in verse 56a; and then a contrasting failure is cited (cf. Tannehill 1975, 128-33). The reference to weather prediction serves purely as a foil to the failure; therefore, Jesus speaks as if these cases of weather prediction were easy and reliable. Clouds that form over the Mediterranean (the west) may bring rain to the Jewish homeland. The wind that blows in from the south comes from hot desert areas. The point appears in verse 56, where Jesus draws a sharp contrast. Those who can do so well on the weather should be able "to interpret the present time." Jesus' closing question is provocative. It suggests that there is something very significant about the present time but does not say what that significant reality is. Clearly, however, Jesus is not talking about a future time that will affect other people, but the present time of the people being addressed. This is the time when they are confronted with Jesus' message and a crucial response is demanded. "The present time" *(kairos)* has the same significance for the people addressed as "the time *(kairos)* of your visitation" for the people of Jerusalem in 19:44. It is the crucial time when the hearers must respond to Jesus' call or let a great opportunity slip away.

The transition in verse 57 probably indicates that, since they know how to interpret earth and sky, they should be able to judge what is right in the present situation. The need is underscored with a parable that is directly applied to Jesus' audience by using the second person ("you"). The hearers are to imagine themselves being dragged off to court, evidently because of nonpayment of debt. There is only a little time to make a settlement on the way. Failure to do so will bring disaster; they will be thrown into debtor's prison. The need to act now to avoid disaster is the primary point. Possibly the parable also encourages settlement with all those one has wronged (see the parallel in Matt 5:25-26 and Matthew's context). Luke Johnson, however, suggests that the parable in Luke relates directly to the narrative situation. Jesus and the crowds are "on the way," and in the limited time left the crowds must make every effort to settle with their accuser—the prophet Jesus—in order to escape the judge and disaster (cf. L. T. Johnson 1991, 209).

13:1-5: Although some interpreters regard 13:1 as the beginning of a new section, there is no change of time or location, and those who bring the report about Pilate do not represent a new group. They are members of the crowd, and Luke's Jesus continues to address this crowd, as he has been doing since 12:54. Interjections from the audience have already occurred at 12:13, 41 of this discourse. The report at 13:1 is a third case. Furthermore, 13:1-9 develops the challenge and warning in 12:54-59.

Two reports of deaths in Jerusalem are developed into a twofold warning that follows a repetitive pattern. In each case there is a question requiring the audience to make a judgment about the people who were killed. The questions ask whether there is a connection between degree of sin and suffering in these cases, a view that might fit the theology of some. Jesus, however, rejects such a connection and turns these news items into warnings to his audience. Those killed were no worse than you are. You must repent in order to escape the same fate.

Jesus cites the second case himself, but the report of Pilate killing Galileans in the temple is brought to him by others. A common purpose of telling atrocity stories is to arouse people to condemn the perpetrator. Failure to show sympathy for the victims and join in the condemnation can be taken as a sign of disloyalty to the nation (cf. Bailey 1980, 75-76). If that was the purpose of those who brought the report, surely they were disappointed or angered by Jesus' response.

Jesus is on his way to Jerusalem. When he approaches the city, he will indicate that there is a connection between his rejection and death there and the coming destruction of Jerusalem by the Romans (cf. 19:42-44). Traveling to Jerusalem (and with the Lukan audience's awareness of the fate of Jerusalem) it is likely that "you will all perish as they did" means something more than "you, too, will perish." The catastrophe of the Roman-Jewish war is hovering in the background. At that time, both Galileans and Jerusalemites suffered and perished through attacks by Roman troops (as in 13:1) and through the collapse of walls and buildings (as in 13:4; the destruction of Jerusalem will not leave "one stone upon another," according to 19:44 and 21:6). The minor catastrophes discussed in 13:1-5 could be taken as omens of the great catastrophe to come.

(For omens of the destruction of the temple, see Josephus *J. W.* 6 §288-309.)

13:6-9: Jesus adds the parable of the fig tree to the warnings in 12:54–13:5. The threat that an unproductive fruit tree will be cut down was already part of the Baptist's message (see 3:9). This will be the fate of those who do not "bear fruits worthy of repentance" (3:8). The barren fig tree in Luke 13 represents the large Jewish audience that has been listening to Jesus but has not responded with repentance or the deeds that are the fruit of repentance. Now Jesus speaks like John the Baptist, but in a parable. The dialogue between the owner and the gardener allows expression of the owner's indignation, leading him to call for the tree's removal, but it also allows for a temporary check of this plan by the subordinate figure. There is still a chance for the people to repent and produce fruit. The gardener has not given up hope and is willing to work hard to help the tree produce. But there is only one more chance to avoid catastrophe. The parable is open-ended. The gardener ends his statement by balancing positive and negative possibilities. So Jesus, at the end of the discourse that began in 12:1, leaves the crowd hanging between these two possibilities.

Release from Bondage on the Sabbath (13:10-21)

Sabbath healing stories combine features of healing stories with features of pronouncement stories involving controversy. The story of the bent woman has enough in common with the sabbath healings in 6:6-11 and 14:1-6 to regard them as three developments of the same pattern or "type-scene" (cf. Tannehill 1986, 171). To be sure, it differs from these other two sabbath healings in that the healing is completed before the controversy appears. However, this sequence fits the normal sequence of an objection story (a subtype of the pronouncement story; cf. Tannehill 1995, 56-59). In objection stories a statement or action by Jesus or his disciples provokes an objection from critics, to which Jesus responds (cf. 5:29-32; 6:1-6). Here the healing is the provocative action, to which the leader of the synagogue objects. There is similarity between Jesus' responses in 13:15 and 14:5. These two sabbath healings form a pair in which a woman, then a man, is featured. (This is also true of the pair of parables in 13:18-21.)

13:10-17: "A spirit that had crippled her" (NRSV) is literally "a spirit of weakness." "Weakness" can refer to various sorts of diseases and ailments. Even though Jesus does not address the spirit, as in an exorcism, attributing the woman's condition to a spirit relates her to other persons possessed by evil or unclean spirits (cf. 4:33, 36; 6:18; 7:21; 8:2, 29; 9:42). This view is strengthened in verse 16, where her condition is described as bondage to Satan, the evil power behind the demons (cf. 11:15-18). The woman is another person on the margins of Jewish society, just like the hemorrhaging woman (8:43-48), for she has been afflicted by an evil, unclean spirit for eighteen years (cf. Seim 1994a, 41-43). It is Jesus' task to free her from Satan's bondage and restore her to her rightful place as "a daughter of Abraham."

The description of the woman as daughter of Abraham is unusual (cf. Seim 1994a, 43-48). It is placed first in the Greek sentence (v. 16), a position of emphasis. This description will be matched in 19:9 by Jesus' insistence that Zacchaeus is "a son of Abraham," a point that Jesus makes against the crowd, which rejects Zacchaeus as a "sinner." Similarly, it is probable that Jesus insists the woman is a daughter of Abraham because she has been robbed of her rights as a member of the covenant people, since she is identified as the bearer of an unclean spirit. Her physical position—bent over—can be taken as symbolic of her social position, just as Zacchaeus's short stature can represent his vulnerability before the crowd.

Abraham has an important place in Luke–Acts (cf. Seim 1994a, 49-54). Abraham represents the originating covenant and promise given to the Jewish people. This promise is still valid, but its realization requires radical transformation. When the promise to Abraham is first cited in Luke, it is preceded by Mary's celebration of God bringing down the powerful and lifting up the lowly (1:52-55). In 3:8 people are warned that God is not limited by human calculations of membership in Abraham's family. The future fulfillment of the promise for Abraham and others in the kingdom of God will mean that some who are last will become first and the first last (13:28-30; cf. 16:22-31). Thus the promise to Abraham will be realized only through social upheaval, which includes rein-stating people like the bent woman and Zacchaeus as participants in the promise.

The healing and the following discussion of healing on the sabbath are united by the theme of freeing or releasing someone from bondage. When Jesus heals, he says, "You are set free from your ailment" (using the verb *apoluō*). In verse 16 he explains that the woman had been "bound" by Satan; therefore, it was necessary for her to "be set free from this bondage" (using *luō apo*). The analogy in verse 15 is relevant because it concerns freeing an animal that was confined ("untie" in the NRSV translates *luō*, which could also be translated "free" or "release"). This language puts a specifi-cally Lukan perspective on Jesus' healings, for, on the one hand, it agrees closely with the summary statement in Acts 10:38 (Jesus "went about . . . healing all who were oppressed by the devil") and, on the other hand, it fits Jesus' proclamation of "release to the captives" in his inaugural sermon (Luke 4:18). One of the kinds of captivity from which Jesus frees people is Satanic oppression in the form of physical ailments, but this may be accompanied by social oppression through being stigmatized.

Jesus' healing on the sabbath, however, meets resistance from the leader of the synagogue, who cites the sabbath commandment. His words are directed to the crowd, not directly to Jesus, which suggests that the crowd, although recently criticized for lack of response to Jesus, is much more willing to accept sabbath healing than the synagogue leader is. In his response, Jesus is addressing the synagogue leader but also others like him, since he uses the plural "hypocrites." This term, which is much less frequent in Luke than in Matthew (used only in Luke 6:42; 12:56; 13:15), is probably explained by the following argument, which points to an inconsis-tency between the critics' position on the woman and on animals. Jesus' argument implies that what holds in the less important case of releasing animals must surely hold also in the more important case of the woman. Two points of contrast increase the force of the argument. She is a daughter of Abraham, not an ox or a donkey, and she has been waiting eighteen years, not the comparatively brief time the animals must wait. Her release is long overdue. Indeed, it is a compelling necessity. (The verb *dei*, "it is necessary," is used in v. 16.)

The Mishnah makes clear that animals may go out on the sabbath (*m. Shab.* 5.1-4). Tying and untying knots are listed as forbidden work (*m. Shab.* 7.2), but exceptions are made for some kinds of knots (*m. Shab.* 15.1-2). It is not certain that these regulations were in force in the first century. The argument in verses 15-16 clearly assumes that people did release their animals (whether by untying them or by opening stall doors) and take them to water on the sabbath. Therefore, Jesus' "opponents were put to shame" when their self-centered inconsistency was publicly exposed, according to the story. Most opponents, of course, would respond by denying that the case of the animals and the case of the woman are really comparable. For Jesus in Luke, however, release of this daughter of Abraham is an immediate necessity and entirely appropriate to the sabbath (a day that, according to Deut 5:12-15, commemorates Israel's release from bondage; cf. Hamm 1987, 27-28).

13:18-21: The parables of the mustard seed and yeast are not placed in a separate scene; instead they are presented as additional comments by Jesus on the healing of the bent woman, as the "therefore" in verse 18 shows. The smallness of the mustard seed was proverbial. The contrast between the small seed and the great "tree" that results is probably a factor in Luke, even though Luke does not mention the smallness of the seed, as Matthew and Mark do (cf. Matt 13:31-32; Mark 4:30-32). Mustard plants are also difficult to control once they are established. According to Pliny, "When it has once been sown it is scarcely possible to get the place free of it, as the seed when it falls germinates at once" (Pliny, *Natural History*, 19.54.170; cf. Scott 1989, 380). The Mishnah forbids planting mustard seed in a garden, because this vigorous plant would threaten the required separation of kinds of plants (*m. Kil.* 3.2; cf. Scott 1989, 374-75). Nevertheless, this gardener "tossed" (*ebalen*) a mustard seed into his garden. It grew vigorously and even became a "tree." This is an exaggeration that reflects scriptural pictures of a king or kingdom as a great tree. The birds nesting in its branches are part of this picture (cf. Ezek 17:22-23; 31:3-6; Dan 4:10-12, 20-22). Vigorous though it may be, for a small mustard seed to grow into a mighty tree of empire is quite a transformation!

A woman's parable is added to the man's (as in Matt 13:31-33). (The NRSV translates "someone" in Luke 13:19, but *anthrōpos*, which can mean simply "person," means "man" when it is paired with *gynē,* "woman"; cf. 15:4, 8; 22:56-58.) Leaven, since it was prepared by letting bread rot, was frequently used as a symbol of moral corruption (cf. 12:1 and Scott 1989, 324-25; the translation "yeast" is somewhat misleading, since ancient people did not have the modern form of yeast). Jews had to clean leaven out of their houses during the feast of unleavened bread. But people did make leavened bread on other occasions, probably because they liked it, and it may be that the only point of the leaven here is its power to permeate the dough (cf. 1 Cor 5:6; Gal 5:9). Where the NRSV translates "mixed in with," the Greek says that the woman "hid" the leaven "in three measures of flour." Three measures of flour is a very large amount, about thirty-six quarts, or more than a bushel (cf. Fitzmyer 1985, 1019). As with the mustard seed and "tree," the large result emphasizes the power of the leaven.

◊ ◊ ◊ ◊

Jesus has been encountering resistance and lack of response. The Lukan audience probably knew this experience also. The parables of the mustard seed and leaven suggest, however, that events such as the freeing of the bent woman from Satan's bondage represent the power of God's kingdom in their midst. The kingdom starts as a small seed tossed into a garden or as leaven hidden in dough, but it will show its power to grow and permeate the whole. Such assurance is important, for the promises of salvation in Luke are sweeping. It would be easy to lose faith in them. The narrative points believers to small events in their local communities as being signs that Satan's power is ending and the kingdom is appearing. The freeing of a daughter of Abraham from Satan's power, like Jesus' and the disciples' exorcisms in 10:17-18 and 11:20, is offered as an example of such signs.

The Danger of Missing the Kingdom Banquet (13:22-30)

There are scattered Matthean parallels to this section. See Matt 7:13-14, 22-23; 8:11-12; 19:30; 20:16; also Matt 25:10-12. The opening verse reminds the Lukan audience that Jesus is on the road to Jerusalem. He is using this journey as an opportunity to teach in as many towns and villages as possible. Jesus' response to a question becomes the occasion for another prophetic warning to the crowd, supporting what was said in 11:29-32 and 12:54–13:9. Jesus' initial answer seems to affirm the truth that few are being saved, for "many" will not be able to enter the narrow door. The emphasis lies, however, on the urgent message to bend every effort to be among those who enter the door.

◊ ◊ ◊ ◊

The grammatical structure of verse 25 is awkward in the Greek. It is possible that most of verse 25 is actually part of the last sentence of verse 24 ("Many . . . will try to enter and will not be able when once the owner of the house gets up . . . 'Lord, open to us'."). "Then in reply" appears to start a new sentence in the Greek. Thus verse 25 indicates why many will not be able to enter. They will realize too late that they want to join the banquet, and they will find the door already shut. Then they will appeal to their past association with the host (who, in v. 26, is clearly Jesus). He taught in their towns, and they had meal fellowship with him. This is an attempt to establish themselves as friends who deserve to be invited to the banquet. But the master will reject their appeal, repeating his initial statement "I do not know you, where you come from" (to translate more literally). (Knowing a person's origin is a significant part of knowing the person.) This statement doesn't mean the master knows nothing about these people. It is a repudiation of the claimed relationship and the obligations of friendship that go with it. As previous warnings have made clear, it is not enough to listen to Jesus' teaching and invite him to dinner. People must recognize the special demands of the time (12:54-57) and respond with the fruits of repentance (13:1-9).

In verses 28-30 the important gathering behind the door becomes the banquet in the kingdom of God. (Where the NRSV translates "eat" in v. 29, the Greek says "recline," the normal practice at a banquet.) The prophets will be there, along with the ancestors of Israel, for the banquet is for faithful Israel, and the kingdom fulfills promises made long ago. But many of those listening to Jesus may be "thrown out." The people who come from all directions fulfill scriptural promises of the regathering of scattered Israel in the time of salvation (cf. Ps 107:2-3; Isa 11:11-12; 43:5-6). It is possible that the narrator reinterprets these promises to apply to Gentiles. However, Luke–Acts also shows a concern for the restoration of the Jewish people. The apostles are to rule over the restored twelve tribes (22:30). The people from many lands addressed by Peter at Pentecost (Acts 2:5-11) are all "devout Jews" who represent the Jewish diaspora, and only secondarily the Gentiles. Through their representatives in Jerusalem, Peter is offering salvation to "the entire house of Israel" (Acts 2:36). Perhaps the people in Luke 13:29 are both restored Israel and the Gentiles who will accompany Jews into the kingdom of God. The present concern, however, is that many who met Jesus personally will not be part of this group. They are the "first" who will end up "last." The final verse of the section fits with earlier indications of radical reversal of status (1:51-53; 2:34; 6:20-26).

This section complements 14:15-24, which also addresses the issue of who will share in the kingdom banquet.

Jesus Anticipates Rejection in Jerusalem (13:31-35)

We cannot be sure of the Pharisees' motives in warning Jesus about Herod. They could be acting out of genuine concern for Jesus, or they could be trying to get Jesus to leave their territory. Even if their concern is genuine, they ironically misunderstand Jesus' situation. There is a play on the word "go" *(poreuomai)* in the text. The Pharisees tell Jesus to "go" (NRSV: "get away") in order to save himself. Jesus tells them to "go" and speak to Herod, then reveals in verse 33 that it is indeed necessary for him to "go" (NRSV: "be on my way"), but in so doing he is not escaping death but traveling to the appointed place of his death.

Probably the narrator intends us to take the danger from Herod seriously. Herod beheaded the prophet John (9:9), thus aligning himself with the persecutors of the prophets, and Jesus does not respond to the Pharisees by accusing them of lying about Herod's intentions. Rather, he says that, whatever Herod's intentions, the role of prophet-killer is reserved in Jesus' case for Jerusalem.

Jesus speaks boldly in response to Herod's threat, calling him a "fox." The original audience might interpret Jesus' response in the context of a traditional "type-scene" of bold philosopher confronting tyrant, or bold prophet confronting king. "Fox" could indicate that Herod is cunning or weak, but the Lukan portrait of Herod suggests that the term expresses his role as a destructive predator (cf. Darr 1992, 139-62). The verb that the NRSV translates "I finish my work" can also be translated "I am finished" or "I am brought to my goal." Although some interpreters would see a reference to Jesus' death here, the three days mentioned in verse 32 must be the same as the three days in verse 33. They are days of journeying toward Jerusalem and do not cover the whole time until Jesus' death. In verse 32 Jesus is either saying "on the third day I am finished" with my healing ministry in Herod's territory (Herod Antipas was tetrarch of Galilee and Perea), or "I am brought to my goal," namely, Jerusalem. The latter option would carry an indirect reference to Jesus' death, of which Jerusalem will be the site.

The theme of the rejection and killing of the prophets returns in verses 33-34 (cf. 4:24; 6:22-23; 11:47-51; Acts 7:52) with specific application: Jesus is the prophet and Jerusalem is the killer. "Must" in the NRSV translates *dei,* a term frequently used of a necessity imposed by God's hidden purpose. That "it is impossible for a prophet to be killed outside of Jerusalem" is an exaggeration, making the point that Jerusalem especially, as symbolic center and seat of authority, is responsible for the deaths of the prophets. Thus it is the appropriate site of Jesus' death.

Although verses 31-33 are unique to Luke, verses 34-35 have a close parallel in Matt 23:37-39. There is a shift in verses 34-35 because here Jerusalem is being directly addressed in words of lament. Using an emotionally charged double address ("Jerusalem, Jerusalem"), the city is indicted for its crimes. Nevertheless, the speaker is emotionally tied to Jerusalem. In words of unfulfilled yearning, Jesus compares himself to a hen anxious to protect her brood against predators. This is what "I desired" *(ēthelēsa)*, but this desire found no response ("you did not desire it" *[ouk ēthelēsate]*; NRSV: "you were not willing"). These words of lament anticipate 19:41-44, where the lament aspect is even clearer (Jesus weeps over the city).

Although Jesus is the speaker in verses 34-35, some features of these verses are easier to explain if we understand Jesus to be speaking prophetically, so that the "I" in verses 34-35 is not only Jesus, but also God (or the wisdom of God, as in 11:49). "How often" in verse 34 is puzzling in the Lukan context, since Jesus has not yet conducted any mission in Jerusalem. Although Jesus' ministry to this point might be understood as an effort to gather Jerusalem's "children" (in the broad sense of the Jewish people), this does not explain the refusal that has already taken place, in which Jerusalem must have participated. If Jesus, as a prophet, is speaking God's words, however, verse 34*b* refers to the long history of God's dealings with Jerusalem. The imagery would also fit the scriptural imagery of God's wings as a place of refuge (Ruth 2:12; Ps 17:8; 36:7).

Such prophetic speech may also help to explain verse 35. The time when Jerusalem will say, "Blessed is the one who comes," is not the time of Jesus' entry into Jerusalem. Although this greeting recurs in 19:38, the narrator indicates in verse 37 that it is the "multitude of the disciples" accompanying Jesus who greet him in this way, not the people of Jerusalem. To understand the entry into Jerusalem as the fulfillment of 13:35 would also rob this verse of importance, for Jesus would merely be saying that Jerusalem will not see him until he arrives there, a thought that hardly justifies the emphatic language being used. What, then, is meant by "you will not see me"? If it refers to Jesus, it must mean, "you will not see me properly," that is, as Messiah. The words fit better, however, if they refer to God (cf. Ezekiel's vision of the departure of God's glory from the temple, Ezek 10:18; 11:22-23). Then verse 35 is speaking of the departure of Jerusalem's divine protector, who will not return to Jerusalem until it is willing to welcome its Messiah, "the one who comes in the name of the Lord."

This view fits with verse 35*a*. "Your house" may mean specifically the temple (cf. 6:4; 19:46), or the city as a whole. In any case, saying it "is left to you" means that it is no longer mine; God is withdrawing from it, leaving it exposed to its enemies (cf. Jer 12:7; Josephus *J. W.* 6 §299-300). Within the context of Luke, this passage anticipates the destruction of the city and the temple by the Romans in AD 70, for it is the first of a series of texts in which not only Jerusalem's failure but the consequences (conquest by an enemy and complete destruction) are announced (cf. 19:41-44; 21:5-6, 20-24; 23:28-31). The repeated references to this event show its importance to the narrator.

◊ ◊ ◊ ◊

It may seem strange that the narrator should be so concerned with these events when addressing communities far from the theater of war and containing large numbers of Gentiles. But just as the first destruction of Jerusalem in 586 BCE could be understood as a lesson to the people of God in later times, so the followers of Jesus in the eastern Mediterranean had something to learn from the march of the people of God toward disaster, which in Luke is attributed to failure to repent, resistance to the prophets, and especially the rejection of Jesus, their prophet-Messiah.

"Blessed is the one who comes in the name of the LORD" is a quotation from Ps 118:26 and was used as a greeting to pilgrims coming to Jerusalem for the festivals. Although Jesus will not be welcomed by Jerusalem but instead will be crucified, verse 35 holds open the possibility of another coming of the Messiah to Jerusalem when he will be welcomed. "Blessed" is a welcoming greeting. It does not express mourning or fear, as one might expect if the returning Messiah were a fearful judge (cf. Allison 1983, 75-76). In Acts 3:19-21 Peter tells the people of Jerusalem that, although the Messiah they rejected must remain in heaven for now, their repentance can still result in the sending of their Messiah in order to fulfill all God's promises to them. As interpreted in Luke, the central promise of God is that the Messiah will bring salvation for both Gentiles and Jews (2:30-32; 3:6). This lament over Jerusalem includes a continuing hope that a restored Jerusalem will find this salvation.

A Discourse on Dinner Invitations (14:1-24)

The opening paragraph (14:1-6) should remind the reader of two types of scenes previously encountered in Luke: scenes in which Jesus is invited to a meal with a Pharisee (7:36-50; 11:37-54) and scenes in which Jesus answers objections of opponents about his healing on the sabbath (6:6-11; 13:10-17; on Lukan "type-scenes" see Tannehill 1986, 170-71). The meal setting will be important in 14:7-24, but first the narrator deals one last time with the issue of healing on the sabbath. The encounter in 14:1-6 shows similarities to both of the previous sabbath healings. In all three Jesus responds to his critics by asking questions that they do not answer. Jesus' question in 14:3 can be understood as a reminder of the more forceful question in 6:9. His second question in 14:5 resembles the question in 13:15, and its placement—after the healing—is the same. Thus 14:1-6 summarizes and concludes the arguments about sabbath healing.

The Man with Dropsy (14:1-6)

The scene begins ominously, for the "leader of the Pharisees" and the other "lawyers and Pharisees" (v. 3) "were watching him closely." This statement repeats a verb *(paratēreō)* used in the first sabbath healing controversy (6:7), which ended with the angry opponents discussing "what they might do to Jesus" (6:11). Furthermore, Jesus' previous meal with scribes and Pharisees ended with the hostile opponents "lying in wait for him" (11:53-54). In light of this previous information, the motive for the invitation seems suspect and the situation dangerous. However, nothing comes of this threatening situation. The Pharisees and lawyers are reduced to silence, for they cannot counter Jesus' arguments. A Jew who believed that Jesus and his followers were a fundamental threat to the sabbath would probably not give in so easily. Jesus, to be sure, is not denying that sabbath observance is important but only asserting that healing is important enough to be included among those things one must do, sabbath or not.

Dropsy involves abnormal retention of fluids, causing swelling. It can have a number of causes. Today it is more commonly called edema. The argumentative question in 14:5 refers either to a child and an ox or to a donkey and an ox. There is good manuscript support for both of these readings. The former combination is frequently preferred because it is the more difficult reading, making it easier to explain a later correction by copyists. However, it also introduces some confusion into the argument, since 13:15 and 14:5 otherwise depend on the point that a human being is more important than a farm animal (cf. Nolland 1993, 744, for defense of the second reading). In 14:5 Jesus speaks of an animal (or a child) falling into a well (*phrear*, a deep pit or shaft, usually a well for water; the parallel in Matt 12:11 lacks this term). Just as there was a connection in 13:15-16 between releasing the woman and releasing an animal, it is possible that there is an implied connection between falling into a well and having dropsy. The Greek term translated "dropsy" is formed on the word for water and means something like "waterlogged." There may be another connotation of dropsy that is significant, however. While the body is swollen with fluid, dropsy is accompanied by an unquenchable craving for drink. Hence this disease became a metaphor for insatiable desire, viewed as a moral failing (cf. Braun 1995, 30-42). Jesus cures this man with dropsy, and then turns to the Pharisees and lawyers, who are driven by their own insatiable desire for places of honor. Can he cure them by his teaching?

How to Choose Places at the Dinner (14:7-11)

Jesus' discourse in 14:7-24 is given in the setting of a meal and also concerns meals, more specifically, invitations to dinner parties (the verb *kaleō* in the sense of "invite" is a key word in this section). The idea of a dinner party functions on three levels in this scene: (1) the dinner party as setting for Jesus' discourse; (2) Jesus' discourse about (human) dinner parties; (3) the dinner party as metaphor for the joyful kingdom of God (cf. v. 15). The interplay among these three levels adds to the richness of this scene. The scene may reflect the custom of the symposium, a dinner and drinking party that included after-dinner speeches. The symposium could be the setting for philosophical discussion or merely for witty remarks. (On Luke and the symposium, see de Meeûs 1961, 847-70; Steele 1984, 379-94; and Smith 1987, 613-38.) In Luke 14, however, Jesus alone is allowed a speech. The narrator is interested only in Jesus' discourse, leaving us with the impression that the others cannot match Jesus' wisdom (cf. Darr 1992, 106).

Jesus' discourse is divided into three sections (vv. 7-11, 12-14, 15-24) with the addressee indicated in each case. (On 14:7-24 see further Tannehill 1992b, 1603-16.) The first two sections are a formal pair, for Jesus twice makes a strong contrast using the same formal pattern: "When you . . . , (negative command about dinner behavior), in case . . . , but when you . . . , (positive command followed by a promise), for (rationale for the promise)." "The places of honor" in verse 7 are literally "the first couches." The couches on which the guests reclined during a banquet were arranged in an order that indicated the rank of each guest (cf. Smith 1987, 617-20; Nelson 1994, 53, 57). Choosing a place of honor shows the desire for special honor that Luke associates with the scribes and Pharisees (11:43; 16:15; 20:46), a desire that was probably widespread in ancient Mediterranean culture (cf. Malina and Neyrey in Neyrey 1991, 25-65).

Jesus warns that the attempt to gain the place of honor can actually lead to its opposite: the shame of being moved to the lowest place. On the other hand, those willing to take the lowest place will be honored. Jesus' comments sound like good advice for avoiding shame and getting ahead in human society (see the similar advice in Prov 25:6-7). However, these comments are more than that in the present context. It may seem strange that Jesus' instruction in verses 8-11 is called a "parable" in verse 7, but this designation suggests that it has a second level of meaning. It applies also at God's table, as verse 11 indicates. The sweeping statement of reversal in verse 11 may not always apply in human affairs, but it is the rule in God's kingdom, and the action of God is described in the passive verbs ("will be humbled"; "will be exalted"). This second level of application is supported by the parable of the great dinner in 14:15-24, in which a similar reversal interprets the kingdom of God.

Whom to Invite (14:12-14)

The issue of social status carries over into verses 12-14, where instructions are given on whom one should invite to dinner. A formal dinner was a way in which an elite family (the kind of family who could afford such a dinner) proclaimed and maintained its elite status. The guest list was important, for the invitation indicated that one was accepted as a member of the elite. Family members and important people of the community needed to be honored in this way, and they would be expected to reciprocate. Jesus' instructions in verses 12-14 conflict with this social function of dinners. It might be a source of honor for someone to give charity to the poor, but it is quite another thing to invite them to a social function in place of family and people of wealth, and eat with them (cf. Braun 1995, 119-20). By doing this, the host is dishonoring family and rich neighbors and in their place is honoring the poor; or, in the eyes of the elite, the host is dishonoring himself by identifying with the poor. Therefore, verse 11 may apply to what follows as well as to what precedes. Those who invite family and people of status are exalting themselves by proclaiming their place in this group. Those who invite the poor and crippled are humbling themselves.

Invitations among the elite follow the principle of balanced reciprocity (cf. Neyrey 1991, 372, 385). Those honored by an invitation are expected to return the favor. This expectation cannot be a motive for inviting the poor, who "cannot repay you." To be sure, reciprocity is maintained, but it is now in God's hands. It is removed as a factor in human social relations. To the promise of reward in the resurrection is added, in 16:19-31, the threat of punishment after death for the rich man who is not generous to the poor.

Jesus promises the host who invites the poor, "You will be blessed." In the sermon on the plain Jesus pronounced blessings on the poor and woes on the rich (6:20-21, 24-25). Now the Lukan audience learns that there is a way for the rich to be blessed, but it requires them to humble themselves by identifying with the poor.

This is likely to offend family, friends, and rich neighbors, with the resulting risk of losing one's elite status and perhaps one's share of the family wealth.

Luke 15 will reintroduce the familiar contrast between the Pharisees and scribes, on the one hand, and the tax collectors and sinners, on the other. In Luke 14 the contrast is made on a different basis, even though some of the same people may be involved. It is a contrast of the wealthy elite with the poor. (The crippled, lame, and blind, unless their families could support them, would be beggars.) The "leader of the Pharisees" and those at his party represent the people of status and wealth. (On class divisions in 14:12-24 and accompanying social expectations, see Rohrbaugh in Neyrey 1991, 125-49.) The teaching in 14:7-24 is social criticism of the elite, but it also indirectly instructs the Lukan communities, especially those members who have some status and wealth. This will become apparent in verses 25-33 when Jesus returns to teaching about discipleship and requires the same break with family and possessions that would result if a rich man radically changed the guest list at his parties, as Jesus directs in verses 12-14. In verses 18-20 also, ties to property and family are seen as obstacles to accepting God's invitation. In the Lukan communities a person of status and wealth could lose both by identifying with a group of nobodies and by undertaking to care for these people. But that is what Jesus asks in Luke.

The Parable of the Great Dinner (14:15-24)

The parable of the great dinner tells of a man who has prepared a banquet and then faces a major social embarrassment because those expected to come all excuse themselves at the last minute. The three specific excuses used in verses 18-20 build suspense and dramatize the problem, leaving the man with a social crisis. The focal point of the parable is the man's response to the crisis. Rather than abandoning his plans, he makes a surprising decision, one sure to cause gossip; he decides to replace people of property and social standing with those at the bottom of the social pyramid. He even insists that his slave go out to such people a second time so that the banquet hall will be full. There is a rather different version of this parable in Matt 22:2-14.

◊ ◊ ◊ ◊

The Lukan parable is placed in a double frame that suggests two different applications. The inner frame consists of verses 15 and 24 and the outer frame of verses 12-14 and 25-33. The remark in verse 15 serves to shift the level of thought so that the discussion of dinners can now be related to the banquet in the kingdom of God. God is the host of this banquet, and the crucial question is Who will participate in it? The parable of the great banquet can be understood from this perspective. However, in verses 12-14 Jesus was talking to a human host about the people he should invite to a dinner, and the list of those to be invited in verse 13 is the same as those in the following parable (v. 21). With this introduction, the parable of the great dinner becomes the story of a human host who actually did bring the poor to dinner, as Jesus instructed in verses 12-13. It not only suggests that this can be done, but also explores what might lead a wealthy person to such radical action. The whole story can be understood from this second perspective. The parable gains in richness as it shifts in meaning, depending on which part of the Lukan context guides interpretation at the moment.

Viewing the parable from the first perspective, we note that the remark in verse 15, associating the dinner motif with the coming kingdom of God, provides a significant setting for the following parable. Jesus does not reject this remark, which fits the image of the kingdom banquet elsewhere in Luke, but warns that, due to the response he is receiving, there may be a surprising reversal. Those one would expect to be at a great dinner will not be there because they turned down the invitation. On the other hand, people who could never expect to attend a great dinner—the beggars in the streets—find themselves at the banquet table. The parable is a warning to those with whom Jesus is eating, as verse 24 shows. They, like those first invited in the parable, may be excluded from the banquet. It is not entirely clear whether the master in the parable is still speaking in verse 24 or whether Jesus is commenting on the parable. The phrase "my dinner" fits best if spoken by the master in the parable, but the introductory phrase "for I tell you" uses a plural "you" in Greek, although the master appears to be speaking only to his slave. In any case, this is a warning similar to Jesus' warnings to the unresponsive crowd in 11:29-32, 12:54–13:9, and 13:23-30. These earlier warnings are here brought home to the lawyers and Pharisees as Jesus tells of people who turned down the invitation and then were excluded from a dinner that was important after all, since it represents the banquet of the kingdom.

The parable is both bad news and good news, bad news for those who turn down the invitation and good news for those brought in from the streets. These two groups have clear social profiles. Those who turn down the invitation are people with property and family ties. They place these interests ahead of the invitation. They have a social position befitting a great dinner, but at the last minute they excuse themselves to tend to their own business. Their last-minute excuses are a major social affront to the host, who decides to go ahead with the dinner anyway and angrily orders his slave to get the beggars from the streets. These are people at the bottom of the social pyramid. The Lukan audience might want to see themselves in those brought in to the party, but not all would fit the social profile. The parable is proclaiming good news to a specific group.

The master insists that his house must be filled. There is an additional gathering of people from outside the city in verse 23. Because of the importance of the Gentile mission in Acts, these people are often viewed as representatives of the Gentiles. This is possible, but verse 23 may simply emphasize the master's determination in a way that shows knowledge of the ancient city. There was an outcast group not permitted to live in the city who, nevertheless, stayed close to it because they could sell their services to city-dwellers (cf. Rohrbaugh in Neyrey 1991, 144-45). Inclusion of them reinforces the social reversal.

When the invitations are understood as invitations to the kingdom banquet, as verse 15 suggests, the parable becomes a commentary on Jesus' ministry. The scribes and Pharisees, who represent people of high status in Jewish society, have been rejecting the invitation, but those at the bottom of the social scale have responded eagerly to Jesus' healing and preaching. Of the four groups listed in verse 21, three are also listed as beneficiaries of Jesus' work in 7:22 (cf. 4:18). There is, however, one aspect of the parable that does not fit well either with the ministry of Jesus or the Lukan understanding of God. The master in the parable turns to the outcasts only because he is angry at being snubbed by his social equals. When we understand the parable in light of verse 15, this aspect of it must be accepted as an indication that the man is a man, not simply a representative of God. The cause of his invitation to the poor is irrelevant to the application of the parable.

The situation is different, however, when we consider the parable in the wider frame of verses 12-14 and 25-33. Now the parable is understood to encourage persons with resources to invite the poor to their homes for banquets, as Jesus instructs in verses 12-14. This would be one way of giving up one's possessions, as Jesus demands in verse 33. The close relation of verse 13 to verse 21 in the parable is clear, but the parable does more than repeat the command in verse 13. The parable relates how a man of high social standing and wealth came to give a banquet for the poor, when that wasn't his original intention at all. The story fits the situation of someone who is attracted to the Jesus movement but has not made a full commitment. Word of this man's interest in this largely lower-class group could lead to social signs of disapproval, including the refusal of a dinner invitation. The surprising fact that all of the man's social peers excuse themselves can be understood as a coordinated act of ostracism. In this case, however, the effort to correct deviant behavior pushes the man over the brink. He makes a clean break with his old life by inviting the poor into his house and to his table. The parable reflects the problem that a relatively rich believer might have when trying to keep one foot in each of two social worlds (cf. Rohrbaugh in Neyrey 1991, 140-47). It also suggests the solution, but this solution requires the radical discipleship that Jesus demands in the next passage.

At various times, each of the two readings of the parable discussed above could become dominant, depending on the current needs and concerns of the early church.

Further Demands of Discipleship (14:25-35)

Here Jesus again addresses the crowds about discipleship. In doing so, he continues to discuss with a different audience an issue that surfaced in the great dinner parable, namely, the danger that attachment to family and property will prevent people from responding to his call (cf. 14:18-20). In verses 26-33 there are three challenges to discipleship that end with a common refrain: "cannot be my disciple." (The NRSV rearranges v. 33, obscuring the refrain shared with vv. 26-27.) These three verses refer to three kinds of sacrifice that disciples must be willing to make. Jesus has already talked about these three issues, but here his language is very sharp, for hating one's family, carrying one's cross, and taking leave of all one's possessions are made conditions of discipleship. In the early church the traveling missionaries were most likely to make these sacrifices, but the believers who stayed at home might face circumstances in which the same demands would be made of them.

There are a whole series of antifamily sayings in Luke (cf. 8:19-21; 9:59-62; 12:51-53; 18:29; 21:16). The demand that one "hate" one's family is perhaps the strongest. (The parallel in Matt 10:37 only forbids loving family "more than me.") In the ancient world the terms love and hate referred less to emotions than to behavior that either honored or dishonored someone else. Hating one's family meant doing something that injured them, particularly by disgracing them. Life was family centered, and the honor of the family was very highly valued. Every family member was expected to protect the honor of the family. If some members joined a suspect movement and abandoned their home, this brought disgrace on the family, particularly if done in disobedience to the patriarch (cf. Malina 1993, 2-3, 79). Such persons showed hatred for the family and also disobeyed the command to honor father and mother (Exod 20:12). The list of injured family members in 14:26 includes the wife, unlike Matt 10:37 and Mark 10:29. The result is a contrast with 14:20, where the banquet invitation is refused because "I have married a wife" (to translate literally). The wife reappears in 18:29

in a list of those who have been abandoned by disciples, suggesting that this is a purposeful Lukan addition.

One must hate "even one's own life" (NRSV: "even life itself"). This remark prepares for verse 27, where a second terror faces the disciple: carrying a cross to execution. Personal safety must also be sacrificed for discipleship. Carrying a cross is part of following Jesus, as he previously made clear in 9:23. Jesus is on the way to Jerusalem and, by extension, can be viewed as already carrying his cross. The journey motif, reintroduced in verse 25, also influences the wording of verse 33, Jesus' third demand for disciples. There "give up" all possessions is literally "say farewell to" all possessions, as when one departs on a journey. In 12:33 Jesus asked disciples to sell their possessions and give the proceeds away as charity. But the disciple might not have the opportunity. One of the consequences of disgracing the family could be loss of any share in the family wealth.

Between verses 27 and 33 two brief parables are inserted. They advocate considering one's resources before beginning a project that might end in shame or defeat. In the context, considering one's resources must mean considering whether one is willing to sacrifice everything else in order to be a disciple of Jesus.

The harsh demands in verses 26-33 may seem inhuman, but discipleship also has its rewards. Those who leave home and family are promised that they will "get back very much more" in 18:29-30. This reward includes the gift of a surrogate family to replace the one lost (cf. 8:19-21).

The saying about salt in 14:34-35, understood in context, is probably an additional comment about disciples. Normally salt is good for seasoning and preserving. But if (strangely) it loses its saltiness, it is worthless. The same would be true of a discipleship involving no commitment or sacrifice.

Parables for Pharisees and Disciples (15:1–17:10)

This long section of seventy-three verses is presented as a discourse of Jesus given on a single occasion. It is similar to the slightly shorter (sixty-eight verses) discourse in 12:1–13:9. In both cases Jesus shifts from one set of addressees to another as he continues to speak, and there are occasional references to comments or questions from the audience. The two scenes differ in that Jesus shifts between the crowd and the disciples in 12:1–13:9 but between the Pharisees-scribes and the disciples in 15:1–17:10. In both cases the disciples are present to hear what Jesus says to others, for they, too, must learn from this teaching.

Rejoicing When Sinners Are Found (15:1-32)

The first two verses provide a pronouncement story setting for the three parables in this chapter. The parables are presented as Jesus' response to the grumbling of Pharisees and scribes at Jesus' association with tax collectors and sinners. This situation functions as a type-scene in Luke (cf. Tannehill 1986, 170-71), since it is a basic situation that occurs several times, with variations. The narrator can recall the situation, when needed, as the setting for appropriate teaching. In particular, the narrator is recalling the banquet in Levi's house and Jesus' exchange with the Pharisees and scribes then (5:29-32). Then as now the Pharisees and scribes "complain" or "grumble" (= *gongyzō* and *diagongyzō*, which come from the same stem), their objection is similar, and Jesus' response will refer to the righteous, the sinner, and repentance (5:32; 15:7), as well as to those who "have no need" of a physician or repentance (5:31; 15:7). Thus Luke 15 offers a much more extensive reply to the kind of complaint made in 5:30 (cf. also 7:34). Note that the accusation of *eating* with tax collectors and sinners is carried over from 5:29-30 to 15:2, even though there is no further reference to Jesus eating in Luke 15.

There is a version of the parable of the lost sheep in Matt 18:12-14, but the rest of Luke 15 is unique. In Luke the lost sheep is the first of three parables that share common themes. The lost sheep and lost coin are also very close in structure. They form a pair of parables that differ primarily in presenting male and female characters. The prodigal son is a much more fully developed narrative, yet it retains the themes of the lost being found and of public rejoicing. The rejoicing in the parables contrasts with the grumbling of the Pharisees and scribes.

15:3-10: A hundred sheep is a fairly large flock, but this need not mean that the shepherd is prosperous. The sheep may belong to his extended family. The lost sheep parable contains a contrast that is not carried over to the parable of the lost coin, between the many and the one. The shepherd is willing to "leave" the ninety-nine to go after the one, and, in the application, "there will be more joy" over the one than over the ninety-nine. The question in verse 4 presumes that the shepherd is acting as a shepherd normally would. There is no suggestion that he is acting foolishly by leaving the ninety-nine, who, at present, appear to be safe. Yet there is some risk for the shepherd in focusing all his attention and effort on the lost sheep. When he finds it, a neighborhood celebration is fitting. Calling friends and neighbors and saying "rejoice with me" means that the shepherd is organizing a party.

Because the shepherd's behavior will strike the majority of the audience as appropriate, Jesus can argue in verse 7 for a similar response to the repentant sinner. The reference to the "ninety-nine righteous persons who need no repentance" is ambiguous. There are references to righteous persons in Luke (cf. 1:6; 2:25; 14:14; 23:50). Thus verse 7 may simply be emphasizing how great heaven's joy over one sinner will be; it will exceed the joy for ninety-nine righteous persons. However, if the Pharisees claim to be among the righteous, the term "righteous" becomes ironic, for the Pharisees' claim will soon be challenged. Jesus will accuse the Pharisees of falsely justifying themselves before others (i.e., claiming to be righteous to attract human honor; cf. 16:15; 18:9-14).

Neither the sheep nor the coin seems an obvious image for repentant sinners, for neither the sheep nor the coin does anything. They are simply found. However, verses 7 and 10 can provide significant insights into the Lukan understanding of repentance. Repentance is more an experience of being found by a concerned seeker than the product of human effort. And its public sign is joy at the gift of new life rather than doleful remorse. The same notes were sounded in 5:29-34 (which are parts of one scene in Luke). There, in response to Jesus' call, the sinners were celebrating. The Pharisees and scribes thought they should be fasting and making penitential prayers instead, but Jesus defended joyful celebration as the appropriate sign of repentance. The seeking shepherd mirrors Jesus' role, for Jesus will later summarize his own mission by speaking of the Son of Man who seeks the lost (19:10).

The seeking shepherd mirrors Jesus' role but also represents God, for the shepherd is an established image for God in scripture (Ps 23:1-4; Ezek 34:11-16). Such is not the case for the anxious housewife of Luke 15:8-10. Yet the two parables are parallel, and the housewife must also be taken as an image of God and God's prophet-Messiah. Since this feminine image is much more unusual, it would attract notice. The "friends and neighbors" in verse 6 are masculine, but those in verse 9 are feminine, which accurately reflects social behavior. Many women would associate almost entirely with their own families or with other women. The details in verse 8 emphasize the woman's diligent efforts. The lost coin is important to her. Her simple house probably lacks windows, so the lamp and broom will help her find the coin in the dark.

◊ ◊ ◊ ◊

These parables help to define the character of God and the mission of Jesus. In presenting God and Jesus as searchers for sinners, they also require the Lukan audience to show a similar concern and to rejoice when the lost return to God's people.

15:11-24: The parable of the father and his two sons is unusual for its character development. None of the three principal characters is a cardboard cutout. Each is allowed to express strong emotion and to present a basic attitude in speech so that his position can be understood. It would be possible for members of the audience to identify with any one of the three. There is also artistry in the phrasing of the story, especially in the short speeches, as when the father, at the end, replaces the elder son's phrase "this son of yours" (v. 30) with "this brother of yours" (v. 32). Vivid detailing also adds to the dramatic impact of the story at key points (cf. vv. 15-16, 22-24).

Parables are often built upon a basic contrast. In this parable the situation is more complex than usual because there is a struggle between two contrasts. The parable begins, "There was a man who had two sons." This beginning suggests that the two sons will represent the main contrast. This, indeed, is the way the elder son wants to tell the story; for him it is the story of a prodigal son and a faithful son, and the contrasting ways that they have been treated by their father (vv. 29-30). The way the narrator tells the story, however, suggests that the basic contrast is between the father and the elder son. It is the story of two contrasting responses to the younger son's homecoming. The conflicting responses are highlighted at the end, as the father tries to persuade the elder son.

Although there is ongoing discussion among commentators concerning the laws and customs of inheritance presupposed in verse 12, the situation seems to be this: It was unusual for a father to divide his property prior to the time of his death. Sirach 33:19-23 warns against this. It was even more unusual for a son to ask for and be given the right to dispose of family property while the father was still living. Indeed, such a request would probably be viewed as a disgraceful thing, an act that dishonored the father (cf. Bailey 1976, 161-69). Instead of refusing, the father complies. All through the story he acts in ways that show remarkable disregard for his own rights and honor. In dividing the property, the elder son would receive a double portion, in this case two-thirds of the estate (Deut 21:15-17). With the elder son, the more normal situation seems to prevail. The property is assigned to the elder son, but the father retains control of it and has the right to use any produce (*m. B. Bat.* 8.7). Thus the father gives the orders to kill the fatted calf, although he also assures the elder son that "all that is mine is yours" (v. 31). In granting the younger son a share of the property and allowing him to leave, the father is not only losing property but also his son, whom he regards as "dead" and "lost" (vv. 24, 32), since he never expects to see him again.

The younger son gathers his wealth, selling any land he has inherited, leaves his family, and then squanders his inheritance. "Dissolute living" may include devouring the father's "property with prostitutes," as the elder brother says in verse 30, but the narrator avoids details in verse 13, leaving the audience to speculate whether the elder brother exaggerates. The narrator reserves the details for the stage at which the younger son hits bottom. Hunger drives him to take a job tending pigs, unclean animals for Jews. The "pods" in verse 16 are carob pods. There is a kind of carob pod with a sweet pulp that both animals and people can eat. However, the wild carob, which is bitter and lacks nourishment, may be meant (cf. Bailey 1976, 172-73), or verse 16 may indicate that the younger son was not even allowed to eat the pig's food. In any case, he is starving and has been completely degraded.

Then we are allowed into his thoughts through a monologue as he decides that he must return home. He rehearses three short statements to his father, all of which end with the same Greek word (vv. 18b-19). They include a confession of sin and recognition that he has forfeited his position as son. Yet he plans all this because he is dying of hunger. The privilege of overhearing the younger son's thoughts does not clear up a basic ambiguity about him, for we are not told directly that he is remorseful but only what he proposes to say to his father in order to obtain help (cf. Ramsey 1989, 37-41). His return home may be motivated entirely by self-interest rather than any real feeling for the injury he has done to his father. In this story the narrator is not interested in separating true repentance from false. Nor does the father probe his son's motives. For him it is enough that the lost son has returned.

We have little basis for reading the father's character until he sees his returning son in verse 20. His response is described in a rush of verbs that move rapidly from seeing to running, embracing, and kissing. By these actions the father gives an emotional welcome before the son speaks a word. The father does not wait for explanations, confessions, or promises. Nor is he concerned with the restoration of his own damaged honor. It has been suggested that running to meet the son while he is still at a distance also has the purpose of protecting the son from the scorn of the rest of the village, who would remember the way that he had treated his father and make their feelings known (Bailey 1976, 181-82).

After being strongly welcomed, the returning son makes his speech, except that the last part, the proposal that was the purpose of it all, is omitted. (Some important manuscripts do include "treat me like one of your hired hands," but the addition is easily explained from a copyist's desire to match v. 19.) This omission may be due either to the father's interruption in verses 22-24 or to the son's awareness that the request is no longer appropriate because he is receiving a son's welcome. In any case, the son is not being received as he expected. His best hope was to be hired as a laborer, for he was not worthy to be a son. He is being received as a son, nonetheless. The father pays no attention to the declaration of unworthiness, turns to his slaves, and barks out orders for full public honors to be granted to his son. The best robe, the ring, and the sandals are all signs that the father honors the returnee as his son, and making the slaves clothe him in this way ends any uncertainty as to how they are to treat him. The fatted calf was a young bull or steer kept for a celebration. Meat was not part of the daily diet. The whole animal would have to be eaten in a short time or the meat would spoil, so the father is expecting a large group. Perhaps the whole village will be invited. The father is not planning a quiet family gathering but is making a public gesture to proclaim his acceptance of his son so that the whole community will follow suit. (Note that when the father states the reason for the party in v. 24 he explicitly refers to the prodigal as "this son of mine.") All of this is done without requiring any period of testing or acts of public penance from the wayward son.

The call to celebrate fits the calls to "rejoice with me" in the two previous parables, and the reference to the son as "lost" and "found" fits these parables better than the story of the prodigal, where there is no searching for the son. The father's role is to wait for one who will be "found" only when he returns home. The story of the prodigal supports the remarkable connection in Luke between repentance and joy. As in 5:29-34 and 15:3-10, the sign of repentance is not fasting and mourning but joy demonstrated in communal celebration. In the prodigal son this celebration is preceded by the son's return home and confession (with no probing of his motives).

15:25-32: A separate scene contrasts the elder son's reaction to the homecoming with his father's. The elder son's anger is expressed by his refusal to join the party. When he refuses to come in, the father comes out, just as he ran out to his younger son in order to bring him back to the family. In coming out to plead with the elder son, the father is ignoring his own dignity and position. The son's refusal to join a party at which the father is host dishonors his father, just as the younger son dishonored the father by his premature request for a share of the property (cf. Bailey 1976, 195-96). The elder son is allowed to state his case in strong words that accuse the father as well as the younger son. Here the issue of the parable is posed most sharply. The party with the fatted calf becomes the focus of complaint, and the elder son draws the contrast between himself and the younger son as clearly as possible. The father does not treat his sons fairly, for the one who stayed home and worked for his father has never been given even a small party ("young goat" and "my friends" indicate a smaller party than the one in progress). Yet the son who disgraced his father and wasted his property is now received with this big celebration.

The elder son's reference to "this son of yours" (picking up the father's phrase in v. 24) both recognizes that the younger brother is being received as a son and expresses refusal to receive him as a brother. The claim to have never disobeyed the father's command sounds a bit hollow in light of the present refusal to join the party, but the claim to have slaved for his father for years should not be discounted. Yet what counts for the father is the unity of the family. Again the father shows that he is unconcerned about his property and honor; instead, he is concerned about his sons. He responds to the elder son not with rebuke and rejection but with reassurance and persuasion. The one part of the complaint that he contests is the implication that he does not care about his elder son. He begins with "child" (*teknon;* NRSV: "son"). This form of affectionate address, used even of adults, reaffirms the family relationship. "You are always with me" indicates that the father appreciates the elder son's past loyalty and wants a close relation to continue. "All that is mine is yours" assures the elder son that the younger son's return will not affect the prior inheritance agreement. Then the father pleads with the elder son to recognize that the return of a lost brother requires just this kind of celebration. In making his final plea, the father substitutes "this brother of yours" for the elder son's designation "this son of yours." The key is whether the elder son will recognize the father's other son as his brother.

The story breaks off with the conflict unresolved. The elder son has given no affirmative response, but it is possible that, out of love and respect for his father, he will be persuaded by his father's words.

◊ ◊ ◊ ◊

The Lukan introduction to the chapter suggests that the younger brother represents the tax collectors and sinners, while the elder brother represents the Pharisees and scribes. This parable modifies the picture of bitter conflict between Jesus and the latter group. Here Jesus responds to conflict with persuasion, as the father does in the parable. Jesus' effort shows that he hasn't given up on them. He wants them to recognize the Jewish outcasts as their kin, as part of the family of Israel, and join the celebration of their return. Scripture speaks of Israel as God's son (Exod 4:22; Jer 31:9, 20; Hos 11:1). The parable develops this imagery, but the son has been split in two. Israel will be restored and the joy of God complete when the one son accepts the other as his brother.

Inclusion of this carefully crafted and comparatively long parable reflects the narrator's judgment that it is important not only to Jesus' audience, but to the Lukan audience as well. The strong characters in the parable would continue to invite members of the Lukan audience to identify with the wayward son, or to proclaim and imitate the grace of the loving father, or to recognize themselves in the elder brother. The parable could also speak to the early church's difficult relation to Judaism. Although it might be possible to reinterpret the parable by viewing the younger son as a Gentile, the parable would lose some of its power, for it relies on the belief that elder and younger son will recognize each other as family. The parable would remain powerful for a church that looked back on its history with Judaism as a split within a family. Then those who had inherited Jesus' mission to the outcasts could understand it as a powerful appeal to their brothers and sisters who have refused to accept Jesus and his mission. But those inclined to dismiss the elder son would also be reminded of the father's words to him, "You are always with me."

Making Friends by Means of Wealth (16:1-13)

Jesus is now speaking "to the disciples also." Although omitted from the NRSV, the "also" is significant, for 16:14 will make clear that the Pharisees of 15:2 are still listening (cf. Nolland 1993, 796-97). The teaching about wealth in 16:1-13 is important for the disciples but also provokes a reaction from Pharisees who are "lovers of money."

16:1-9: An estate manager (or steward) is being fired because he has been charged with squandering his master's property. Since the narrative does not say that the manager did squander the property, only that he was charged with the crime, we cannot be sure whether the charge is true or not. Evidently it is not important to the interpretation of the parable whether the manager was actually dishonest in his past dealings. The manager has no chance to defend himself, and the plot moves quickly to the question of what he can do to rescue himself when he is losing his job. At this point the narrative moves into soliloquy (vv. 3-4), allowing the audience to observe a decision in process. Having the manager pose the question "what will I do?" and then discuss his options helps the audience to appreciate the manager's problem and builds interest in the resulting decision. Several alternatives are rejected by the manager. Suspense is maintained in verse 4, for even when a decision is made, we are told only the purpose to be achieved, not the course of action. We learn the chosen course of action only as the plan is put into effect (vv. 5-7). All of this focuses attention on the manager's problem and remarkable solution. It is clear that the manager is the central character of the parable, not the master. Interpretations of the parable, then, must be primarily reflections on the manager.

Verses 5-8 raise questions that have produced conflicting interpretations. The questions include: (1) What exactly is happening in verses 5-7? (2) Why would the manager be commended (v. 8)? (3) Who is commending him?

There is dispute about what is happening in verses 5-7 because some interpreters believe that the manager is not swindling his master by reducing the debts. Rather, he is deducting the amount added to the bill for interest (contrary to laws against usury in

Torah) or for his own commission (cf., e.g., Fitzmyer 1985, 1097-1101). (For prohibitions of charging interest to fellow Israelites, see Exod 22:25; Lev 25:35-37; Deut 23:19-20.) The master might want to take credit for the righteous act of removing interest, and he would not lose if the manager deducted his own commission. However, there are reasons for doubting this interpretation. According to verse 5, the debt is owed to the master. There is no reference to the manager's commission. In verse 8 the manager is called "dishonest" (or "unjust"). Although this description might be due to the charges in verse 1, we have noted that the narrative avoids taking a stand on whether those charges were true. However, right before verse 8 the parable shows the manager reducing the amounts due his master. It is likely that this action is the reason for calling the manager dishonest. Furthermore, John Kloppenborg provides a number of indications that a first-century audience could not assume, without further clarification, that the amount of the reduction represented interest or commission. The amounts may represent payments for leased land rather than loans; the amount of the reductions do not fit what is known about current interest rates; managers were paid in various ways, so one could not assume that this manager earned commissions on business deals (cf. Kloppenborg 1989, 479-86).

The short time the master has given for the manager to finish his accounts provides time enough to alter the debt certificates, providing a nice benefit for the debtors. The debts are large, so the manager is dealing with people who run substantial operations. The manager assumes that the debtors will follow the social rule of balanced reciprocity; the benefit received requires a benefit in return (on balanced reciprocity, see van Unnik 1966, 284-300; Neyrey 1991, 371-72). The expected benefit for the manager is indicated in verse 4. He hopes that a number of people will provide temporary hospitality while he gets his feet on the ground. The debt certificates should be in the debtor's handwriting as a guarantee of authenticity. That is why the manager has the debtors rewrite them.

If, as I have argued, the manager is swindling his master by reducing what is owed him, why would the manager be commended in verse 8a? With this question is entangled the additional issue of who is doing the commending. The NRSV translates "his master" in verse 8, but *ho kyrios* can be translated either "the master," meaning the master in the parable, or "the Lord," meaning Jesus (cf. 7:13; 10:41; 11:39; 12:42; 13:15). Since the master in the parable has already been called *kyrios* three times, it would be an awkward shift for *kyrios* to mean Jesus in verse 8. Yet there is some awkwardness in any case. If *kyrios* refers to the master of the parable, we have not been told how he learned of his manager's maneuver or why he reacted in this surprising way.

Fortunately, our understanding of the parable does not depend heavily on deciding who is commending the steward. It is quite important to note that the steward is being commended, for otherwise he would appear to be a negative example. When we discover that he is being praised, we must search for the reason. Note that the commendation in verse 8 is carefully qualified. The manager is commended, but he is also described as being dishonest and the reason for the commendation is specified: "because he had acted shrewdly." Thus a distinction is drawn between his dishonesty, which is not being commended, and his shrewdness, which is. Then verse 8*b* supports the distinction by indicating that the manager was shrewd, yet was one of "the children of this age."

Was the manager really shrewd, that is, could he have gotten away with it? And would the master have commended him? Surprisingly, yes is a possible answer to both questions. The manager may have known that honor was more important to his master than wealth. In this respect, the master would be typical of his time and place. (Cf. Malina and Neyrey in Neyrey 1991, 34: "Money, goods, and any sort of wealth are really a means to an honorable name, and any other use of wealth is considered foolish.") The master would have two problems with honor: (1) A master who cannot control his subordinates is dishonored. It would not be good for this master's reputation to let it be known that his manager had swindled him. (2) Trying to take back a gift is a dishonorable thing. The alternative is to ratify the reduction of the debts and take credit for it (cf. Piper 1992, 1651). There is humor in the story that should not be missed. The rogue builds his future by doing what he was accused of doing in the first place.

Even though verse 8*a* might be the narrator's summary of Jesus' position (if one takes *ho kyrios* as "the Lord"), verse 8*b* must be words of Jesus (*hoti,* translated "for," could simply introduce the quotation). There is a gentle chiding in verse 8*b*. The "children of light" should learn to be as shrewd in their own affairs as the manager in his. The main application of the parable is found in verse 9. The emphasis on the manager's shrewdness in verse 8 doesn't require an application only to the management of wealth. Jesus has been warning of an approaching crisis, and the point of the parable could simply be resourceful response to this crisis. In verse 9, however, the management of wealth becomes the focus of concern. The manager is taken as a positive example for the disciples, who are to "make friends" with wealth as the manager did. This means reducing or canceling debts (cf. 6:34-35), or selling possessions and giving alms, as the disciples were instructed in 12:33. As in 16:4, hospitality is expected in return, but now this consists of welcome "into the eternal homes" (literally, "tents" or "booths"). Alms are for the poor, and they are the ones who most need cancellation of debts. They, like Lazarus, will be comforted after death by Father Abraham (cf. 16:22-23). They are in a position to "welcome you into the eternal homes"; hence the need to treat them as friends. (Some might view "they" in v. 9 as a reference to the angels, but in context it refers to the "friends" made with wealth.) This need not mean that the poor take the place of God as decider of final destiny. Rather, it can mean that God consults the poor, and considers one's use of wealth, in rendering judgment. The parable in 16:19-31 will depict the fate of people who fail to make friends among the poor with their wealth.

"Dishonest wealth" is literally "the mammon of wrongdoing" or "injustice." "Mammon" is derived from a Hebrew or Aramaic term for wealth (cf. Fitzmyer 1985, 1109). It will be used again in verses 11 and 13. "Dishonest" is probably too narrow a translation for *adikia*. When applied to the manager in verse 8, it refers to his dishonesty, but when applied to the disciples and others in verse 9, it means more than wealth gained by specific acts of dishonesty. It indicates that wealth in this present world is part of an unjust system that oppresses the poor. Therefore, giving it to the poor is the proper antidote. The same applies to verse 11.

16:10-13: The use of "unjust wealth" is still the subject of verses 10-12. It might seem that verses 10-12 are applying the parable in a different way than verse 9. Although the manager is a positive example in verse 9, he may appear to be a negative example in verses 10-12, since he was unfaithful with his master's wealth. This reading, however, does not fit the context. Instead, being faithful with unjust wealth probably means canceling debts and giving wealth away. One is counted faithful when one follows Jesus' command to sell one's possessions and give alms (12:33). If one fails to do so, one is "unjust" (NRSV: "dishonest"). "The true riches" (literally, "what is true") and "what is your own" must refer to the eternal reward previously mentioned in verse 9.

Finally, a saying found also in Matt 6:24 is added in verse 13. Here the faithfulness required in verses 10-12 is equated with the service of a slave. That service cannot be divided between two masters. Mammon is just such a competing master. Service of mammon is a form of idolatry, which must be rejected in order to serve God.

Response to the Pharisees (16:14-18)

Although Jesus has been teaching his disciples, the Pharisees also have been listening and now scoff at what they hear. In verses 14-15 the Pharisees are called "lovers of money" and described as "those who justify yourselves in the sight of others." Desire for money and for human honor are considered together because wealth was valued primarily as a means to high social position. "Lovers of money" *(philargyroi)* is a standard charge against those being rejected as false teachers (cf. Moxnes 1988, 6-8; L. T. Johnson 1991, 249-50). The Pharisees in Luke have become stereotypical representatives of those who possess and value wealth and human honor, although it is doubtful that this is a historically accurate picture. ("Few Pharisees were socially and financially prominent," according to E. P. Sanders 1992, 13.) Characterizing Jesus' opponents in this way has become a literary means of warning the Lukan audience against false values. It is consistent with earlier Lukan descriptions of the Pharisees (cf. 11:39, 43; 14:1, 7-14).

To be "righteous" or "just" *(dikaios)* is good, but to "justify" *(dikaioō)* oneself "in the sight of others" is not. It implies a desire to be recognized as just and religious by humans, who can be manipulated, rather than by God, who knows the heart. The deceptiveness of human claims to righteousness will be noted again in 18:9, 14, with application to a Pharisee. God is not deceived, and God's values are the opposite of humans. The honor and wealth "prized by human beings" are "an abomination" with God. An idol is called an "abomination" *(bdelygma)* in the LXX (cf. Deut 27:15; 29:16; 32:16; Isa 44:19, and L. T. Johnson 1991, 250). Therefore, verse 15 may develop the suggestion in verse 13 that wealth (along with human honor) is a false idol that some people serve.

It is difficult to understand why verses 16-18 are placed in their present setting and equally difficult to discern a train of thought. In the Greek the first sentence simply says, "The law and the prophets until John." Something must be supplied, but the NRSV's addition of "were in effect" may be misleading. It implies that the law was no longer "in effect" afterward, yet verse 17 seems to state the opposite: The whole law remains in effect. An important change takes place when Jesus proclaims the kingdom of God, but this does not mean that the law is obsolete. To be sure, Acts will later show that the law, which remains valid for Jews, is applicable to Gentiles only in a limited way (Acts 15:5-29). "Everyone tries to enter it [the kingdom] by force" is a possible translation of verse 16c, but it is also possible to take *biazetai* as a passive, which yields this sense: "Everyone is forced into it" or "is pressed to enter it." I think the passive sense works better with "everyone" as subject (cf. Fitzmyer 1985, 1117). It is not true that everyone is trying to enter the kingdom themselves, yet all whom Jesus encounters are being pressed by him to enter.

The saying about divorce in verse 18 has parallels (with variations) in Matt 5:32; 19:9; Mark 10:11-12 (cf. 1 Cor 7:10-11). Its relation to the Lukan context is puzzling. However, if we note that the law in question here is the law of adultery (Exod 20:14), the strict construction adopted could be evidence that nothing implied by the law is being dropped (v. 17). Addressed to the Pharisees, there may be an implied accusation: those teachers who permit divorce as a way of obtaining a new mate are encouraging adultery (cf. *m. Git.* 9:10). The issue of obedience to the law and the prophets will reappear at the end of the following parable (vv. 29-31). Perhaps verses 16-18 are inserted here in order to raise this issue in advance.

The Rich Man and Lazarus (16:19-31)

The dominant concern of Luke 16 reappears in this section, which returns to the issue of the responsibility of wealthy people for the poor. The parable of the rich man and Lazarus expands on verse 9 by showing what will happen to those who do not make friends among the poor through their wealth. In verse 9 there was reference to "the eternal homes," but in verses 22-31 a more detailed picture of the postdeath situation appears. Jesus is still addressing the Pharisees who are "lovers of money" and who ridicule his teaching about wealth (v. 14). The parable is a warning to them and to all Jews with wealth. The story is told from a Jewish perspective in order to speak to this audience. "Father Abraham" has a prominent role, and he points to "Moses and the prophets" as the needed guide to a share in a blessed afterlife.

The story is related to previous teaching in Luke. In 3:8 John the Baptist warned that claiming "we have Abraham as our father" (NRSV: "ancestor") would do no good without fruits worthy of repentance. The rich man repeatedly appeals to father Abraham, but to no avail. The story also illustrates Jesus' beatitudes and woes in 6:20-21, 24-25. The poor are blessed, while the rich have received all the good things they can expect. What Lazarus desires (16:21), the hungry are promised in 6:21 (both verses use *chortazō;* passive = "eat one's fill"), and the consolation or comfort denied the rich in 6:24 is granted to Lazarus, according to 16:25 (using Greek words from the same root). In 14:12-14 Jesus showed people of wealth how, by sharing with the poor, they could "be repaid at the resurrection of the righteous." The parable of the rich man and Lazarus shows what will happen to people of wealth who do not follow such advice.

◊ ◊ ◊ ◊

In spite of verse 25 the parable does not imply that the rich man is condemned simply because he is rich, since the afterlife has to even out earthly discrepancies. Close attention to verses 19-21 shows the reason for the rich man's punishment. The rich man and Lazarus are introduced in a way that emphasizes the contrast between them. The one lives a life of luxury, the other of misery. Lazarus's misery is depicted through reference to his sores (evidently ulcers or oozing sores, which attract the dogs) and his hunger. If the rich man and Lazarus lived in two different places and then their different destinies after death were depicted, the outcome would result from their earthly circumstances alone. Lazarus, however, is laid at the gate of the rich man. He can easily be seen by the rich man when entering or leaving. Lazarus "longed to satisfy his hunger with what fell from the rich man's table." This suggests a course of action for the rich man. It indicates the least that he could do, if he were concerned. The rich man is punished not simply because he is rich, but because he does not respond to Lazarus's need. He has the means but not the will to help. This failure also indicates that he did not listen to Moses and the prophets.

It is unusual for a character in a parable to be named. The name Lazarus is a shortened form of the Hebrew or Aramaic name 'El 'āzār, which means "God has helped" (cf. Fitzmyer 1985, 1131). The name may anticipate the situation after death.

The scene after death makes God's judgment clear. God, however, does not appear openly but is represented by Abraham. Where the NRSV translates "to be with Abraham" (v. 22) and "by his side" (v. 23), the Greek says, "to the bosom [or "chest"] of Abraham" and "in his bosom." More freely, we might refer to Lazarus being "in the arms of Abraham." These phrases indicate the warmest welcome and continuing care. They may also suggest a banquet scene in which Lazarus is lying next to Abraham on the banquet couch (cf. John 13:23 RSV). The change in Lazarus's situation before and after death is strongly depicted, but Lazarus remains a passive figure. The dialogue takes place between the rich man and Abraham. The parable may comfort the poor, but it is primarily designed to challenge the rich. God's concern for the poor is demonstrated in the story of Lazarus, who also represents a (lost) opportunity for the rich man.

Pathos develops through the rich man's three requests, each of which is rejected. Here the audience is shown the tragedy of a concern that appears too late. In all three cases Abraham is addressed as "father," for the speaker is a Jew, a member of Abraham's family. Abraham recognizes him as his "child" (v. 25) but cannot grant his request. The first request is minimal—a bit of water on the tongue—but even this is not possible. The rich man asks Abraham to "have mercy" *(eleēson)* even though he failed to show mercy on Lazarus by giving alms *(eleēmosynē;* cf. 11:41; 12:33, and L. T. Johnson 1991, 252). The request to "send Lazarus" shows that the rich man recognizes Lazarus from his former life. Apparently, the rich man did notice Lazarus lying beside the gate, but made no response to his need. Abraham reminds the rich man that the present situation compensates for former injustice and declares that nothing can be done now about the rich man's situation.

Unable to help himself, the rich man tries to help his brothers, who evidently live the same luxurious and callous life as he formerly did. Introducing the brothers at this point turns attention to people who can still repent and escape the place of torment. The parable is a warning to just such people. Abraham denies that a special messenger from the dead is needed, for "they have Moses and the prophets." Lazarus is not needed to deliver the message, because scripture has already done it (and this parable is doing it again). The rich man pleads, but Abraham is sure that those who do not heed Moses and the prophets will not respond "even if someone rises from the dead." Some commentators find here a reference to Jewish rejection of the message of the risen Messiah in Acts. There may be such a reference, but it is secondary to the main point that the Jewish Scriptures contain a clear and sufficient call to help the poor. For the author of Luke, Deut 15:1-11 and Isa 58:6-7 may be important, for traces of these passages are found in Acts 4:34 and Luke 4:18, but the range of relevant passages is much broader (cf. L. T. Johnson 1991, 253). According to the parable, the fate of wealthy Jews depends on their response to the call of Moses and the prophets to help the poor.

◊ ◊ ◊ ◊

The Lukan communities, even though composed of Gentiles as well as Jews, recognized Moses and the prophets as their scripture. This story about a rich Jew who ignored the poor and did not listen to scripture could be transposed to the life of the early church. There it would call believers who were relatively wealthy to care for the poor. (On the poor and the rich in the Lukan community, see Esler 1987, 164-200.) Acts 2:44-45 and 4:32-37 present a picture of a church that shared possessions. However, it is unlikely that people always sold and shared their possessions readily. Within the church, the story of the rich man and Lazarus could become a very strong word of warning to Christians who ignored the poor so that they could enjoy their own possessions.

Concluding Instruction to the Disciples (17:1-10)

Jesus' discourse continues as he addresses issues that will arise in the community life of his followers. First, all disciples are addressed (vv. 1-4), and then the apostles (vv. 5-10).

◊ ◊ ◊ ◊

"Occasions for stumbling" translates *skandala*, which refers to things so offensive that they cause people to fall away from faith. There may be an offense that is inherent to the gospel (1 Cor 1:23), but adding to that through one's own actions or words is here judged very harshly. The parallel passages in Matt 18:6-7 and Mark 9:42 refer to "these little ones who believe," but Luke has simply "these little ones." Luke's phrase doubtless includes believers who are vulnerable to damaging words and actions, but others, such as the poor who have not yet believed the good news, may also be included.

The warning about causing another to stumble is supplemented by guidance on the healing of relationships in verses 3-4. When a member of the community "sins against" another, it is taken seriously. The one who has committed the offense is to be rebuked and repentance is expected. But all the emphasis in verse 4 is on repeated willingness to forgive such persons when they say they repent. Even with repeat offenders, the possibility of forgiveness must never be removed. The appeal here to the forgiver is balanced by warnings elsewhere that repentance must be real (cf. 3:8-9; Acts 26:20). The number "seven times" is less than the "seventy-seven times" in the parallel passage in Matt 18:21-22, but Luke says "seven times a day," which provides a continuously renewing account.

The introduction of the apostles at verse 5 suggests that issues related to church leaders will be considered in verses 5-10. In verses 5-6 Jesus does not respond to the request for an increase of faith by somehow granting them more faith, but instead praises the power of faith. In a strong hyperbole, Jesus indicates that even tiny faith can do marvelous things. It is not clear why the apostles ask now for an increase in faith, nor is it clear what exactly is meant by faith. When Jesus is arrested and executed, there will be great danger that the apostles' faith will give out (cf. 22:31-32), but there is no indication that this crisis is in mind in 17:5-6. It is somewhat more likely that faith here is associated with wonder-working power, as in the related passages in Matt 17:19-20; 21:18-21; Mark 11:20-24 (cf. also 1 Cor 13:2 and the description of Stephen as a "man full of faith" who "did great wonders" in Acts 6:5, 8). Such power was lacking in Luke 9:40-41, but in Acts the leading missionaries perform miracles just as Jesus did. Wonder-working power can lead to adulation and pride, which makes the following short parable relevant.

The parable is based on the ancient practice of slavery. Ancient slavery, unlike American slavery, was not based on race, and manumission was common after a considerable length of service. The kind of service one was asked to perform made a great deal of difference. Working in the mines was horrible, working as a house slave was generally much better, and there were slaves who were given important management responsibility as trusted agents of their masters (cf. Osiek 1992, 174-76). Slavery becomes a useful image at this point because slaves are not wage earners who can demand pay or favors in return for performing their duty.

Jesus first asks the apostles to put themselves in the position of a slave owner and consider what such a person would normally expect from a slave. The owner in the parable may have only one slave, who must both work in the field and serve meals. The parable relies on the audience recognizing that a slave would neither be invited to dine with the master nor encouraged to relax when there was work to do. Nor would a slave receive thanks for performing the regular duties. (Verse 9 may refer to a concrete favor that someone may earn, rather than verbal thanks.) In verses 7-9 the apostles are asked to consider the ways they would behave as masters, but in verse 10 there is a twist. In relation to God they are like the slave, who works out of duty, not as a wage earner, and who receives no honor or special favor for performing that duty.

◊ ◊ ◊ ◊

Paul Minear has argued that plowing, tending sheep, and serving meals are images for the work of apostles and prophets in the early church (Minear 1974, 84-85). There is evidence to relate these functions to the early church's missionaries and community leaders. In Luke–Acts they are described as slaves of God (Acts 4:29; 16:17) who shepherd the flock (Acts 20:28) and plow (Luke 9:62) and who perform a "service" (*diakonia;* Acts 1:17, 25; 6:4; 20:24; 21:19). All of these leadership roles are presented in the parable as the duty owed by a slave to the master, not a basis for honor or favor. This parable is a prelude to Jesus' instructions to the apostles at the Last Supper. There, too, Jesus tells those who will be leaders in the church that they must renounce the desire to be recognized as great and instead must be "like one who serves," giving up claims to honor and privilege (see 22:24-27).

In 12:37 the returning master does what no normal master would do, according to 17:7-8. He himself serves his slaves the meal. However, 17:7-10 warns that no slave can regard such surprising treatment as wages due.

The Samaritan Leper (17:11-19)

Again the audience is reminded that Jesus is on the way to Jerusalem (cf. 9:51; 13:31-35). The description of his course puzzles the commentators, for he does not seem to be traveling in the direction of Jerusalem. We should remember, however, that Jesus' journey is not a direct march but is combined with a missionary campaign designed to cover many towns (cf. 10:1; 13:22). The mention of Samaria explains the presence of a Samaritan later in the scene.

This scene shares some features with the healing of the leper in 5:12-16. (See the commentary on that passage for discussion of the biblical meaning of leprosy, which is not necessarily equivalent to what we now call leprosy.) Jesus responds to the lepers' call for mercy by telling them to show themselves to the priests. It is through priestly examination and ritual that healed lepers are accepted back into society (Lev 14:1-32). In contrast to Luke 5:13-14, Jesus sends the lepers off to the priests before they have been cleansed. They are cleansed on the way. Perhaps it took some faith for the lepers to begin the journey to the priests before the healing.

The healing is the first part of the story, but the emphasis is on the second part, which ends with two significant comments by Jesus. This is a pronouncement story in which a healing story serves as part of the provoking event that calls forth Jesus' comment. More specifically, this is one of the quest stories, which are especially frequent in Luke. (On quest stories, a subtype of pronouncement stories, see p. 123, and Tannehill 1986, 111-12, 118-20.) There are six scenes in Luke that report successful quests by people who have some characteristic that would seem to disqualify them. They are people on the margin of religious society. One of these is the Samaritan leper. Part of the message of the story is that a leper, who is also a Samaritan, can be included in Jesus' saving work.

But the story is saying more, for Jesus contrasts the Samaritan's response to his healing with that of the other nine. When Jesus at the end says, "Your faith has made you well," the Samaritan's faith evidently includes more than a bold reaching out for help (as in 5:19-20), for the immediately preceding verses focus on the return of the Samaritan to praise God and thank Jesus. The Samaritan shared with the other lepers sufficient faith to respond to Jesus' command in verse 14, but his faith, unlike theirs, has blossomed into joyful praise of God and gratitude to Jesus, who makes God's saving power available. The story highlights the Samaritan's response to the healing. Then Jesus comments in verse 18 that the Samaritan alone returned and gave praise to God. Why is it necessary to *return* and praise God? Presumably God could be praised elsewhere. Yet it is assumed in the story that praising God and thanking Jesus should go together. This scene, like 7:36-50, shows an interest in the bond of gratitude that can arise between Jesus and those who benefit from his work. It also suggests that the salvation the Samaritan has received is more than physical healing or an end to social isolation; it is a powerful experience of God, whose saving power is present in Jesus.

◊ ◊ ◊ ◊

The audience is not told that the man is a Samaritan until the end of verse 16. Hearers are allowed to form a positive impression of the man's response before the ethnic factor is introduced. For some the result would be a disturbing challenge to their negative stereotype of Samaritans. For others this turn in the story might provide an affirmation of their own inclusion. In verses 17-18 Jesus contrasts the one leper with the nine in a way that implies criticism of the nine. Unfortunately, the benefits of Jesus do not always produce the powerful experience of God and gratitude to Jesus demonstrated in this story of the Samaritan. Jesus speaks from a Jewish perspective, even calling the Samaritan "this foreigner," but it is the Samaritan who is commended for his faith, making him a model for others.

In 18:35-43 a blind beggar calls out, "Have mercy," as the lepers did, and to him also Jesus will say, "Your faith has saved you" (exactly the same statement in the Greek as the one translated "Your faith has made you well" in 17:19). The blind man addresses Jesus as "Son of David" and is evidently a Jew. The formula "Your faith has saved you" occurs four times in Luke (7:50; 8:48; 17:19; 18:42) and is applied to two women and two men, a Samaritan and a Jew. All four are thereby held up as models.

An Eschatological Discourse (17:20–18:8)

As in previous discourses, Jesus addresses more than one party: first the Pharisees (17:20-21) and then his disciples (17:22-37). Probably 18:1-8 continues the discourse to the disciples. The eschatological teaching here is supplemented by two other major sections of such teaching, 12:35–13:9 and 21:5-36.

The Kingdom Among You (17:20-21)

The question of the Pharisees in 17:20 introduces the topic of the future coming of God's kingdom and the Son of Man. The phrase "things that can be observed" in Jesus' reply is literally "observation" *(paratērēsis)*. This term was used concerning observations made by doctors for the purposes of diagnosis and prognosis, and also for observations of the stars, which were sometimes thought to predict the future (cf. Nolland 1993, 852). The Lukan use of the related verb may be important for understanding this verse, for the narrator indicates repeatedly that Jesus' opponents are "watching" or "observing" him with hostile intent (6:7; 14:1; 20:20). The Pharisees are among those who watch Jesus closely and suspiciously. When Jesus says, then, that the kingdom "is not coming with observation," he may not be denying any observable signs of the kingdom (a denial that fits poorly with 11:20 and 21:25) but rather saying that the close but suspicious scrutiny practiced by the Pharisees will not detect the kingdom. In fact, it has not, for the kingdom is right under their noses, yet they have not seen it (cf. Darr 1992, 112-14).

The last statement depends on the interpretation of verse 21, which is disputed. Jesus' reply ends with the statement, "Look, the kingdom of God is *entos hymōn*." This could mean "is within you" or "is among you" or "will be (suddenly) among you." Although the verb is present tense, some argue that the last view is most appropriate to the context, since Jesus goes on to speak (v. 24) of a sudden, future event (cf. Nolland 1993, 853-54). However, Jesus is speaking to two different audiences in verses 21 and 24, and we should not assume that he is making the same point. Furthermore, this view requires reading something into verse 21 that is not clearly stated. The translation "within you" is not widely supported in current scholarship. This translation seems to imply that the kingdom is an inward, spiritual reality and that it is found within the Pharisees. Neither of these views fits the Gospel perspective. The best option, then, is "among you," understood to indicate that the kingdom is within the circle of their experience even though the Pharisees' "observation" has failed to detect it. The Pharisees are challenged to give up their calculations and suspicious scrutiny and to see what can now be seen if one looks with different eyes. (For the kingdom as present in Jesus' work, see 11:20.)

Warnings Concerning the Coming Son of Man (17:22-37)

Much of Luke 17:22-37 has parallels in Matthew 24, but the material is arranged differently there. In 17:22 Jesus turns to the disciples. When the Pharisees asked about the coming kingdom, they needed to be shown what they were missing at that time. The disciples need a different kind of eschatological instruction. Their problem is described in verse 22. Jesus and the disciples will be separated (cf. 5:35), which will cause them to "long to see one of the days of the Son of Man." Their desire will make them vulnerable to false claims to fulfillment (v. 23), but the future coming of the Son of Man will not be a local and limited affair that people will need to advertise. It will be sudden and unmistakable, like lightning that flashes across the whole sky.

A reminder of Jesus' passion announcements (9:22, 44) is inserted at verse 25, where it may seem out of place. So far, the disciples have not understood these announcements (9:45). Jesus now returns to this theme because it has eschatological relevance. In 19:11 the narrator will indicate that Jesus' followers expected "that the kingdom of God was to appear immediately," that is, when Jesus arrived in Jerusalem. This expectation ignores and contradicts Jesus' statements that he must suffer and be rejected in Jerusalem. The inability to comprehend the necessity of Jesus' suffering leads to premature expectation of messianic fulfillment (cf. Tannehill 1986, 257-61). The Lukan churches, of course, would know that Jesus had suffered and had been rejected. However, the portrait of resistant disciples presented in Luke would still be relevant to the churches, for there would be continuing temptation to think that fulfillment will come easily and without suffering. Jesus must again correct premature expectation in Acts 1:6-7, and Acts 14:22 warns the churches that "it is through many persecutions that we must enter the kingdom of God."

In verses 26-30 two biblical stories—Noah and the flood (Genesis 6–8), and Lot and the destruction of Sodom (Genesis 19)—are used as similes in order to crack open the comfortable shell formed by the rhythms of ordinary life. Although Genesis emphasizes the sinfulness of those destroyed, Luke refers simply to people engaged in ordinary activities, unaware of the sudden destruction that is coming. Luke does so in an artful way that is able to engage the hearer imaginatively (cf. Tannehill 1975, 118-22). A rhythmic pattern is established in verse 27 as four verbs in the imperfect tense (indicating continuous repetition of the activity) describe ordinary life. Conjunctions are omitted, heightening the sense of rhythmic repetition in the verbs. To translate literally, "They were eating; they were drinking; they were marrying; they were being given in marriage"—except that all of this is conveyed by four words in the Greek. Then the rhythm is interrupted by the coming of the flood.

The same pattern recurs with the story of Lot. The rhythmic series of verbs begins in the same way ("They were eating; they were drinking"); then other activities are introduced, enlarging awareness of the web of ordinary life, and the series of four verbs is expanded to six. Suspense builds and holds a bit longer as hearers anticipate the interruption. Then the rhythm ends with Lot's flight and Sodom's destruction. The section on Lot both repeats and intensifies the section on Noah. The effect is to make the audience more sharply aware of the rhythms of ordinary life, which make up most of its fabric; but now this is awareness with a difference. The rhythm leads to anticipation of its cutoff point. Ordinary life is no longer a closed and secure world.

The nature of the interruption is not specified. It is hidden behind the biblical images. But it is destructive for those whose life is wrapped up in the activities of heedless people. The disciples are being warned along with others, for 8:14 and 21:34 view involvement in concerns of ordinary life as dangerous for disciples. Marriage and activities that produce income are cited in 17:27-28. Emphasis on these concerns fits earlier warnings that ties to family and possessions can stand in the way of discipleship (e.g., 14:26, 33).

We should probably understand verses 31-32 as extending the application of the Lot story (cf. v. 32) with a special focus on possessions. The parallel to verse 31 in Mark 13:14-16 concerns the need for Judeans to flee hastily to the mountains at the time of great tribulation, but Luke seems to be concerned with the seductive power of possessions that might prevent one from joining Lot on the road to safety. In verses 34-35 the imagery shifts from escaping a world entirely focused on its ordinary activities to a separation between individuals seemingly engaged in the same ordinary activities. The difference between individuals is revealed when one is taken and the other left. Here again both genders are included, for, according to the Greek text, the people in question are masculine in verse 34 and feminine in verse 35. These verses share the theme of suddenness with verses 24-32, but the people involved are making no attempt to escape. If we nevertheless carry the theme of escape over from verses 26-32 to verses 34-35, being "taken" would indicate deliverance. This, however, is not certain. Furthermore, there is nothing here about escaping a period of tribulation that is coming on the rest of the world, as in the current doctrine of the rapture.

Verse 37 is even more puzzling. (Verse 36, which parallels Matt 24:40, is absent from the best manuscripts of Luke.) "They" (presumably the disciples; cf. v. 22) ask, "Where, Lord?" Are they asking where some will be taken or where the others will be left? Jesus appears to avoid a straightforward answer. Although his words might refer to the Son of Man and his followers, who are attracted to the Son of Man as vultures are to carrion (cf. Nolland 1993, 862-63), the gruesome image more likely refers to the death of those who are not chosen.

The Persistent Widow (18:1-8)

The end point of the discourse that begins at 17:20 is somewhat unclear. Probably 18:1-8 should be included in the preceding discourse because it has an eschatological orientation that fits 17:20-37. Note especially the reference to the coming of the Son of Man in 18:8, which ties the parable of the widow and the judge to 17:22-30. However, the reference to prayer in 18:1 also relates the parable to the story of the Pharisee and the tax collector praying in the temple (18:9-14).

◊ ◊ ◊ ◊

According to the narrator, Jesus is teaching his disciples "to pray always and not to lose heart." The verb translated "lose heart" *(enkakeō)* can also be translated "despair." Its opposite is persistence, but also boldness or courage. The widow presented here as an example is not only persistent, but also bold, even brash. She is a demanding, "uppity" woman (cf. Donahue 1988, 184). She resembles the man who gets his neighbor out of bed because he needs three loaves of bread (11:5-8), but the fact that she is a woman makes her behavior even more striking. The widow, having lost the protection and economic support of her husband, was likely to be poor and vulnerable to exploitation. Therefore, Torah insists that justice must not be denied to a widow (Exod 22:22-24; Deut 24:17 LXX; 27:19). This widow, however, is more than the stereotypical victim who needs help. She keeps demanding justice even though the situation seems grim.

There may be another side to widowhood that would influence the way that the Lukan audience understood this parable. Widows were sometimes supported in the early church so that they did not need to remarry in order to survive. (Widows were not necessarily old, since most women were married when they were quite young.) A widow supported by the church would have greater freedom from family demands than she had as a wife, and this would permit her to devote herself to prayer (cf. 1 Tim 5:5). It is not clear whether there was already a recognized order of widows in the Lukan communities, but Acts 6:1 and 9:36-43 may provide hints of this. In addition to the widow in the parable, there is another widow in Luke who is an example of persistent prayer, namely Anna, who is also a prophet (2:36-38). These widows may represent the role of certain widows in the early church. They are more than victims in need of help; they are examples of outstanding devotion. (On widows in the early church, especially in Luke–Acts, see Seim 1994a, 229-48.)

The parable presents an extreme case. The judge does not care about the teaching of Torah urging justice for the widow, for he "neither feared God nor had respect for people." Therefore, when the widow asks for justice, her case at first looks hopeless. But even an unjust judge cannot hold out against this widow. As in other parables, a soliloquy allows us to witness a decision being made. The judge changes his mind when he realizes what a bother this widow will be. The translation of the last part of verse 5 is uncertain. The NRSV's "wear me out" is an attempt to translate *hypōpiazō*, which literally means "strike under the eye" or "give a black eye to." It is a term applied to boxers, not a term one would normally apply to a widow. It is probably not meant literally (partly because the present subjunctive implies repeated action), but a forceful phrase is needed for translation. Perhaps "that she may not keep battering me" will do. The picture would probably strike the audience as comic.

There is also a translation problem in verse 7. In the NRSV the verse contains two questions. Some interpreters take the second as a statement, "He is forbearing with them," pointing to the use of *makrothymeō* and words of the same root in the LXX to express God's patient forbearance with wayward Israel (cf. Exod 34:6, and Horst in Kittel and Friedrich 1967, 4.376-81). Although God may, indeed, need to show forbearance even toward "his chosen ones," that does not seem to be the point here. The NRSV translation has the advantage of fitting the context, with both parts of verse 7 leading to the answer in verse 8*a*.

In the context of the parable, the widow's request, "Grant me justice," would probably relate to a financial matter. In the larger context, her request relates to the disciples' longing in 17:22, a longing for the return of the victorious Son of Man and the fulfillment of God's promises. The instruction "to pray always and not to lose heart," then, has a specific focus. It is prayer for justice in an unjust world and for the vindication of believers who criticize the world's values and face the world's ridicule and persecution. This prayer is part of seeking a transformed world.

The argument works by the principle "how much more." God and the unjust judge are distinct, for the parable does not present God as uncaring. Yet the two are analogous because they are both in the position to grant a request. The choice of a remarkably unjust judge for the parable can have an interesting and useful effect. Although the Gospels want to affirm that God does care, many cries for justice find no immediate answer. Thus in the present experience of believers, God appears to be like the unjust judge. This passage allows expression to that experience, while denying that this is the truth about God. It also supports faith by arguing that even an unjust judge will yield to the persistent and courageous seeker for justice.

◊ ◊ ◊ ◊

According to verse 8, God "will quickly grant justice." The narrator is aware that the time between the exaltation of Jesus to heaven and his victorious return seems long, so that some may "lose heart." That is a main reason for the inclusion of this parable at this point. Yet Jesus claims that God's justice will come "quickly." In this passage, hope for the victorious return of Jesus in the near future is still alive. The experience of delay has not caused the postponement of hope to the distant future (cf. Carroll 1988, 94-96, 166). The early churches believed that faithfulness and endurance were required now because at any time the returning Lord could break into their lives and demand an accounting.

The concluding question in verse 8 nevertheless shows awareness of the tendency of faith to falter as time passes. Will Jesus' followers maintain their faith as injustice continues in the world, or will they "lose heart" and be unprepared for the coming of the Son of Man? As the church gradually learned that its expectation would not be fulfilled "quickly," this question became even more acute.

The Pharisee and the Tax Collector (18:9-14)

This parable is not primarily about prayer, although it does have implications about how one should approach God in prayer. It primarily concerns true and false claims to righteousness. It is a further defense of Jesus' ministry to tax collectors and sinners, one that more aggressively attacks the attitude of some of his critics. This parable is unusual in that the labels of the two characters correspond to named groups within the Gospel narrative.

◊ ◊ ◊ ◊

In the opening verse the narrator specifies the audience for whom this parable is intended. Probably Pharisees are in mind (cf. 15:2;

16:15; 18:10), but it may be significant that the narrator does not speak explicitly of Pharisees in verse 9. The Pharisees' false attitudes may appear in others, including the disciples. Elsewhere the Pharisees and scribes are used as negative examples in warnings to the disciples (12:1; 20:45-47). In 18:14 the scene ends with a general statement about "all who exalt themselves," whether Pharisees or not. The disciples show a disturbing desire to be recognized as greater than others (9:46-48; 22:24-27), which Jesus tries to correct by placing special value on the "child" or the "youngest." Yet immediately following the parable of the Pharisee and tax collector, the disciples reject children. They show the same attitude of superiority and exclusion as the Pharisee in the parable.

Pharisees and tax collectors are important groups in Luke, and anyone who has listened to Luke to this point will have a general impression of what they are like and how they react to Jesus' message. This need not mean, however, that every Pharisee and tax collector will fit the mold. It is wise to remember that the parable concerns a particular Pharisee and a particular tax collector. Nevertheless, the parable picks up on previous stories of Pharisees and tax collectors that contrast the righteous and sinners (5:29-32; 15:1-7) and adds a new twist: it redefines what it means to be righteous.

Although a clear judgment is made about the two parable characters in verse 14, it is important to look carefully at the story in order to understand why such a judgment is made. Since the Pharisee is giving thanks to God, his prayer may seem at first to be the prayer of a devout person. Yet thanksgiving turns into self-praise, developing the picture of the Pharisee as one who trusts in himself (cf. v. 9). Even more clearly, the prayer shows that this Pharisee "regarded others with contempt." In thanking God he dwells on those to whom he feels superior. Being righteous separates him from others. It means being different from and better than other people, who can then be dismissed with pejorative terms.

Position and body language are significant in the description of the tax collector. He stands "far off" and beats his breast, an expression of remorse and repentance. The Pharisee's prayer is comparatively long; the tax collector's is very short. The verb translated "be merciful" is *hilaskomai,* a rare word in the New Testament. The word fits the temple setting, for it can refer to expiation of sins through a sacrificial offering (cf. Heb 2:17, and Bailey 1980, 153-54). The Lukan parable highlights the prayer rather than the sacrifice, but a sacrifice may have accompanied the tax collector's prayer. In any case, the temple is viewed as an appropriate place for the tax collector to ask God for forgiveness.

The tax collector is declared to be "justified" rather than the Pharisee. The term "justified," from the verb *dikaioo,* is related to the word "righteous" *(dikaios)* in verse 9, and if English permitted it, we could say that the tax collector was "righteoused." This means that the tax collector was accepted as righteous by God on the basis of his prayer. Thus in verse 14 relationships are overturned. The Pharisee who trusted that he was righteous is replaced by the tax collector who is declared to be righteous because of his earnest prayer for forgiveness. The outcome is a reversal of normal social judgments. This reversal is emphasized and generalized by the concluding maxim about exalting and humbling. This maxim was already used in 14:11 in connection with table behavior. Here it is related to the varying ways that people approach God and speak of fellow humans.

Children and the Kingdom (18:15-17)

At this point the Gospel of Luke returns to the sequence of Mark, from which it departed at Luke 9:51. This passage is a close parallel to Mark 10:13-16 (cf. Matt 19:13-15). Luke, however, specifies that the children were "infants." If Jesus, in Luke, regards these infants as important, it is not because of anything they can do. They are too young to do much at all. It is also unlikely that the infants are highlighted because of appealing qualities they might have (e.g., their innocence or openness, views that probably reflect modern sentimentality). Rather they are introduced because of their lowly status. They are powerless and have no right to claim attention in the public world dominated by adult males. This is demonstrated by the disciples' negative reaction to their presence.

It was important, of course, for a man to have children, particularly sons who would be his heirs. Nevertheless, "in the ancient

Near East the aged were shown great respect or even veneration, but children were usually held in very low regard" (Nelson 1994, 38). Children were part of the women's world. Girls were raised entirely by women, and boys lived mostly in the women's world until the age of puberty (cf. Malina and Rohrbaugh 1992, 300). To be sure, Sirach urges fathers to give attention to their children—for the purpose of discipline. An undisciplined child is a threat to a father's honor (cf. Sir 7:23-24; 22:3-6; 26:10-12, and Malina 1993, 74). Sirach also warns against playing with one's child or giving a youth authority too soon (30:9-11). Children did not share in the world of male power and status—until a son reached the proper age. Thus, there is continuity between Luke 18:15-17 and the preceding verse. Those "who humble themselves" are becoming childlike in status. This applies both to the tax collector and to those who stoop to give attention to children.

The end of verse 16 can be translated as in the NRSV, or it can be translated, "The kingdom of God is [one] of such," that is, a member of this group, the children. The choice depends on the interpretation of verse 17, which is open to at least three readings: (1) "Whoever does not receive the kingdom of God as a child receives. . . . "; (2) "Whoever does not receive the kingdom of God as one receives a child. . . . "; (3) "Whoever does not receive the kingdom-of-God-as-child. . . . " (i.e., the kingdom that is childlike). Interpreters generally favor the first interpretation, while the third is a neglected possibility (proposed in Tannehill 1983, 104-5). The construction in the Greek is the same as Luke 17:6 ("faith as a grain of mustard seed") and nearly the same as Mark 4:30-31 (the kingdom of God "as a grain of mustard seed"). If the kingdom can be compared to a mustard seed, it can also be compared to a child. This comparison would fit its present lack of power and status in the world. This third view provides an easier sequence of thought in verses 16-17. The common view requires a shift between these two verses. In verse 16 children are being received, but in verse 17 they are the receivers (they model the act of receiving). The view I favor maintains a constant perspective of receiving children (including the childlike kingdom) throughout. This is also the perspective in the similar saying in 9:48.

Jesus would be saying, then, that people cannot enter the great and glorious kingdom unless they can reject the world's values and welcome the kingdom that now appears without status and power. The disciples' behavior in this scene, however, shows that they failed to hear Jesus' command to receive the child in 9:48 and still accept the world's judgment that status and power are proper concerns. Once again Jesus challenges their views.

Jesus, the Rich Ruler, and the Disciples (18:18-30)

This passage follows Mark 10:17-30 fairly closely, although there are some significant differences (cf. also Matt 19:16-29). In Luke 18:18 there is no indication of a change of place, as there is in Mark. Therefore, there is less of a break between the new scene and 18:15-17. The new focal character is described as a "ruler" *(archōn)*. He makes a clear contrast with the little children, for he has the power, status, and wealth that the children lack. Although the term "ruler" is vague, the other rulers whom Jesus encounters in Luke are religious authorities (8:41; 14:1; 23:13, 35; 24:20). Probably this ruler is also a religious authority. The little we learn about him from his question and statement in verses 18 and 21 indicates his religious concern and commitment.

18:18-27: The ruler asks exactly the same question as the lawyer in 10:25, and there are other similarities between the two scenes. In both cases the law is cited as a preliminary answer, but obtaining eternal life is made to depend on an interpretation of the law, or on an additional requirement, that goes beyond the normal understanding of life under the law. There are also differences in the two scenes. The lawyer began by testing Jesus, but at the end there is no indication that he rejected Jesus' new teaching. The ruler seems more open at the beginning (he addresses Jesus as "good teacher"), but when confronted with Jesus' call to follow, he sadly recognizes that he cannot comply.

Luke 18:18-30 is a quest story (a type of pronouncement story; cf. Tannehill 1986, 111-12, 120-22) which has been extended by dialogue (vv. 24-30). The initial question expresses the ruler's quest for eternal life, while verse 23 indicates the outcome: at least for now, he is not prepared to do what he must to obtain what he seeks. All the other questers in Lukan quest stories succeed, but they come from oppressed and excluded groups. Thus, quest stories show how the powerful are brought down and the lowly lifted up (cf. 1:52).

Jesus' rejection of the ruler's term "good," on the one hand, seems rude, and on the other, may disturb Christian believers. (This exchange, present in Mark 10:17-18, is modified in Matt 19:16-17.) However, Jesus' response is a sign of radical devotion to God, who alone is to be praised in this way. Jesus' response fits with 4:8, where Jesus affirmed that the command to worship God alone applies to himself as well as to others. In verse 20 Jesus will quote from the Ten Commandments. It is possible that verse 19 shows Jesus' obedience to the first two of these commandments (you shall have no other gods; you shall not make an idol; Exod 20:3-6). Jesus refuses to claim honors that belong to God alone.

Among others, the command "Honor your father and mother" is cited. There is no effort to reconcile this command (which meant obeying parents and caring for them in their old age) with the fact that Jesus' followers have been leaving their parents for the sake of the kingdom (cf. 18:29).

Establishing in verse 21 that the ruler is a good Jew who obeys the commandments enables Jesus to say that this is not enough. In verse 22 Jesus adds the radical requirements of discipleship. The call to follow is preceded by the command that the ruler sell what he owns and distribute the proceeds to the poor. The emphasis on this requirement fits with the fact, disclosed later, that this ruler was "very rich," but this is not a special requirement for him. In 14:33 Jesus made this a requirement for all his disciples. The command as found in Mark is intensified in Luke 18:22 by adding "all." The command, although brief, provides some indication of why the ruler should sell what he owns. First, the proceeds are to be distributed to the poor. Their need is a just claim on the ruler's wealth. They have been unjustly deprived in the past, and the ruler must do what he can to correct this injustice. Second, the reference to treasure in heaven recalls previous contrasts between earthly and heavenly treasure (12:21, 33-34) and the related saying about not serving two masters (16:13). Earthly treasure lures one away from

God. It captures the "heart" (12:34) and becomes a competing master (16:13). Therefore it must be replaced with heavenly treasure. Thus the renunciation of wealth is not merely required because the ruler must leave home in order to follow Jesus.

Only in verse 23 are we told that the man was "very rich." This information explains why he "became sad" when faced with this stringent requirement. Such a decision is very hard for a rich man, as verses 24-25 will emphasize. Unlike Matthew and Mark, however, there is no indication that the rich man leaves after Jesus' call to follow. The scene continues, and the comments in verses 24-30 are made in the presence of the rich ruler. They include the statement that the impossible—a rich man giving up his wealth—is indeed possible with God (v. 27). Thus the rich ruler's quest is unsuccessful at verse 23 because he cannot accept Jesus' challenge, but verse 27 points to a continuing possibility for him and others.

First, however, verses 24-25 emphasize the difficulty—indeed, the human impossibility—of Jesus' requirement. The difficulty for a rich man has been illustrated by the story of the ruler; now it is forcefully expressed in general statements. Verse 25 supports verse 24 with a vivid image of the impossible: a camel, the largest animal in the region, passing through the tiny eye of a needle. The scene begins in verse 18 with a question about inheriting eternal life. In verses 24-25 Jesus speaks of entering the kingdom of God, and the response in verse 26 will refer to being saved. These three phrases are approximate synonyms. The respondents in verse 26 seem to assume that if it is impossible for a rich man, it is impossible for all, thinking, perhaps, that the rich have an advantage, being the objects of God's favor and being able to act as benefactors. The reference in verse 27 to God's possibilities should not be used to undercut all that has been said about wealth. Serving both God and mammon remains an impossibility. The relevant possibility is that people with property will be changed and will demonstrate that change by sharing their wealth with others.

18:28-30: Here the Lukan audience is encouraged to believe that such freedom from possessions is a real possibility, for it was demonstrated by Jesus' first followers. Peter speaks for this group and indicates that they have responded in a way that fits Jesus' requirement of the ruler. When the first followers were called, they "left everything" (5:11, 28). The NRSV translation "left our homes" in 18:28 fits the next verse, but the larger context suggests that it may be too narrow. They left *ta idia* ("what was ours"). Jesus responds with a promise. They will not lose but will gain, both in the present time and in the age to come. The reward in the age to come is eternal life, what the rich ruler sought. The reward in the present time is "very much more" than they sacrificed. Luke 18:30 is shorter than Mark 10:30, with a resulting loss of clarity. Nevertheless, the idea is probably similar. The natural family that one had to leave is replaced by the larger surrogate family of Jesus' followers (cf. 8:19-21). The list in verse 29 focuses more on family than on property. Luke's list is shorter than Mark's, but Luke adds "wife," as in 14:26 (cf. Matt 10:37). The emphasis on leaving family may seem to be a shift of focus, but in the ancient Mediterranean world, leaving family would probably also mean leaving property, which would remain with the family. In that society, great value was placed both on family and on retaining family property (cf. Malina and Rohrbaugh 1992, 384). The Lukan audience would no doubt feel the pain of the disciples' sacrifice, but Jesus assures his followers that this is a small matter compared to the rewards they are already receiving.

Announcement of the Passion (18:31-34)

In Mark this is the third in a sequence of passion announcements that occur about a chapter apart (Mark 8:31; 9:31; 10:33-34). It is misleading to call it the third passion announcement in Luke, however, for after the early announcements in 9:22, 44, there have been other references to Jesus' coming death (12:50; 13:33-35; 17:25). The narrator does not allow too much time to pass without a reminder of what Jesus faces in Jerusalem.

◊ ◊ ◊ ◊

Instead of speaking of what "must" happen, as in 9:22, Jesus speaks of the accomplishment of "everything that is written . . . by the prophets." These are alternate ways of referring to the divine purpose that is guiding these events (cf. Acts 2:23; 4:28), for scripture is understood as a revelation of the divine purpose. While 9:22 highlighted the role of the Jewish "elders, chief priests, and scribes," 18:32 emphasizes the role of the Gentiles. In both cases more than Jesus' death and resurrection is mentioned, and these extra details show that Jesus' death will involve rejection and shaming (cf. also 17:25). The process of shaming is expressed by the words, "He will be mocked and insulted and spat upon." The crucifixion means a contemptuous rejection of Jesus in which both Jewish leaders and Gentiles have a role.

Luke 18:31-34, like 9:44-45, ends with strong emphasis on the failure of the disciples to understand Jesus' passion announcement. In both passages the narrator hammers at the point by stating it repeatedly. There is a partial Marcan parallel to 9:45 (Mark 9:32), but none to 18:34. We can understand the remarkable emphasis on this point if we recognize that this failure is tied to a series of defects that the disciples must overcome if they are to become powerful witnesses for Jesus. This failure means that the disciples (1) do not understand God's plan in scripture nor God's ironic way of working in the world (cf. 24:25-26); (2) have premature expectations of the immediate enjoyment of messianic salvation (cf. 19:11); (3) are not ready to suffer and be rejected like Jesus (cf. 22:31-34); and (4) are not willing to humble themselves as Jesus will be humbled (cf. 22:24-27; also Tannehill 1986, 253-54).

In 18:34 the sentence "What he said was hidden from them" is sometimes understood to say that God was hiding it from the disciples. This may be so, but the disciples are not thereby relieved of responsibility. A similar reference to something "hidden from your eyes" is found in 19:42, but it does not relieve Jerusalem of responsibility. Furthermore, Jesus clearly regards it as important for the disciples to understand his passion announcements (cf. 9:44: "Let these words sink into your ears"). Insight will finally come when the risen Messiah is able to open the minds of the disciples to understand God's plan as laid down in scripture (cf. 24:26-27, 32, 44-46).

A Blind Beggar (18:35-43)

From this point until Jesus' entry into the temple, the narrator carefully notes Jesus' location, marking segment by segment Jesus' approach to Jerusalem and the temple. The parallels to this scene in Matt 20:29-34 and Mark 10:46-52 indicate that Jesus is leaving Jericho, but in Luke Jesus is approaching that city. In the next scene he will enter it (19:1), still on the way to Jerusalem and now moving directly toward that goal.

◊ ◊ ◊ ◊

The blind man is a beggar and therefore contrasts in social position with the rich ruler (18:18-23). Some continuity in this section of Luke is suggested by the repeated theme of salvation. The question "Then who can be saved?" in 18:26 is partially answered by 18:42 (the beggar is told "Your faith has saved you") and 19:9-10 (Zacchaeus is told that salvation has come to his house).

In 18:37 Jesus is called the *Nazōraios,* which may be a variant spelling of Nazarene (= person from Nazareth), but the origin and original meaning of the word are obscure (cf. Fitzmyer 1985, 1215-16 for the possibilities). The blind beggar calls out, "Have mercy," as the ten lepers did in 17:13. The story of the lepers featured a Samaritan. It is now balanced by the story of the blind beggar, whose Jewish thought world appears in his use of the title "Son of David." This title fits the Davidic messianism so strongly expressed in the Lukan infancy narrative and in the mission speeches to Jews in Acts. God will give to Jesus "the throne of his ancestor David" (literally, "his father David," 1:32; cf. 1:69; 2:11; Acts 2:29-32; 13:22-23). This reference to Jesus as Son of David is the first of several references to Jesus' royal office as he approaches Jerusalem (cf. 19:12, 38) and as he is crucified (cf. 23:35-38). It is the first public announcement of Jesus as the Davidic Messiah during his adult career, for Peter's confession was followed by a command to silence (9:20-21; cf. Kingsbury 1991, 57-58). As Jesus approaches Jerusalem, this command to silence is revoked (cf. 19:38-40).

The leaders of the crowd rebuke the blind man, just as the disciples did those bringing infants (the same verb is used in 18:15

and 39), but the blind man is not deterred. He keeps shouting (the imperfect verb *ekrazen* implies repeated action) even more loudly. He refuses to be ignored. Jesus asks, "What do you want me to do for you?" The beggar might have just wanted alms, but he has something bigger in mind. Jesus grants it, with the added statement "Your faith has saved you." The blind beggar joins the ranks of those who have found salvation through a bold and persistent faith that demands attention and ignores social barriers (cf. 5:20; 7:50; 8:48; 17:19). Furthermore, this time the person commended for faith follows Jesus. After the references to following Jesus as a disciple in 18:22, 28, the beggar's action should be understood to indicate that, in his case, healing leads to discipleship.

◊ ◊ ◊ ◊

In this scene Jesus gives sight to the blind, which was especially cited as part of his mission in 4:18 and 7:22. Thus this last event of Jesus' healing ministry (the healing of the ear in 22:51 has a special purpose) can be connected with Jesus' announcement at the beginning of his public ministry.

Salvation for Zacchaeus (19:1-10)

From the story of a beggar we now pass to the story of a rich man. This rich man will respond to Jesus differently than the rich ruler responded in 18:18-23 and will show that a rich man can be saved, despite the difficulty emphasized in 18:24-26.

The tax collectors have been responsive to Jesus, and Jesus has defended his ministry to them against critics. This scene shares features of previous scenes of this type (cf. 5:29-32; 15:1-32). But Jesus has also spoken harsh words about the rich. Zacchaeus is rich; he is also a *chief* tax collector, not one of the underlings like Levi (5:27) who sit at toll booths helping to make people like Zacchaeus rich (cf. Malina and Rohrbaugh 1992, 387-88). These mixed signals prevent the audience from making a quick judgment about Zacchaeus based on the narrative so far. He may not fit the previous image of responsive tax collectors.

◊ ◊ ◊ ◊

Zacchaeus is more individualized than most of the characters that appear in a single scene. We are told his name, a detail of his appearance (he is short), and an unusual action on his part (he climbs a tree). These details help to create interest in him as an individual who stands out somewhat from any group. The audience may also become involved with him because they must guess his purpose. The narrator indicates that he was seeking "to see who Jesus was." This could be mere curiosity, but he goes to great lengths to get a look at Jesus, even climbing a tree. The story of Zacchaeus is another quest story, a more elaborate type of pronouncement story that reports the success or failure of someone's quest (cf. Tannehill 1986, 111-12, 122-25). There are some subtleties in this story, for the true nature of the quest is unclear at the beginning. Only in verse 9 when Jesus declares what Zacchaeus has found does it become clear what he was seeking.

The crowd twice acts as a blocking force. First it prevents Zacchaeus from seeing Jesus. Then it grumbles when Jesus goes to the house of Zacchaeus, who is called a "sinner." The attitude expressed in the second case suggests that social rejection may have contributed to the tax collector's problem in the first case. Respect for persons of status and wealth would cause the crowd to make way for an honored member of the community. It did not treat Zacchaeus this way. Zacchaeus has been ostracized, and the story must respond to the harsh attitude expressed in verse 7. The scribes and Pharisees have been the grumblers in the similar scenes in 5:29-32 and 15:1-32. It is remarkable that "all" observers join the grumbling on this occasion. The narrative is concerned with the hostility between Zacchaeus and his community. He has been excluded from the Jewish community, but Jesus is going to declare that he must be reinstated as a "son of Abraham" (v. 9).

The narrative tries to persuade the audience that Zacchaeus, even though he is a chief tax collector, rightly belongs both to the children of Abraham, to whom the promises were given, and to the outcasts whom Jesus came to save. It presents Zacchaeus as remarkably interested in Jesus and remarkably responsive when Jesus sees him in the tree. He does just as Jesus says and welcomes him to his house "rejoicing" (the NRSV paraphrases in v. 6b). Jesus is still on his journey and is seeking a place to spend the night (compare the stop with Martha and Mary in 10:38-42). The reference to rejoicing should remind us of the joy that accompanies repentance in 15:4-24. Zacchaeus demonstrates that repentance in verse 8 by announcing a radical change in his handling of wealth.

To be sure, some interpreters argue that in verse 8 Zacchaeus is defending himself by stating what he regularly does rather than by resolving to act differently in the future (cf. Fitzmyer 1985, 1220-21, 1225). (The verbs translated "I will give" and "I will pay back" in the NRSV are actually in the present tense and could refer to his regular practice in the past and the present. However, they could also announce a new policy that begins at this time.) The context indicates that Zacchaeus is announcing a change in verse 8, a change that will demonstrate the "fruits worthy of repentance" (3:8). If Zacchaeus had previously been such a generous and honest person, it is hard to understand the antagonism of the crowd, nor why Jesus should respond by saying, "Today salvation has come to this house," since no change would have taken place in Zacchaeus "today," nor why Jesus should speak of saving "the lost." In 15:4-10 the lost are identified with sinners who repent.

It may seem surprising that Jesus approves of Zacchaeus's plan to give half of his goods to the poor, while he told the rich ruler to sell all and distribute it to the poor (18:22). Although some interpreters understand verse 8 as Luke's effort to arrive at a more reasonable (but still quite demanding) standard for rich people in the Lukan communities, I take the total statement in verse 8 as an indication that Zacchaeus recognizes two requirements for his money—care for the poor and fourfold compensation of those defrauded in his previous dealings—and simply divides his wealth between these two requirements. There is, of course, no accounting of how much Zacchaeus owes to those defrauded. Such details would not fit a pronouncement story. Nevertheless, the supposition is that such compensation will take all or most of the wealth not given away, leaving Zacchaeus pretty much in the same position as the rich ruler, had he chosen to follow Jesus (cf. Tannehill 1986, 123-24).

In verse 9 Jesus speaks "to him," that is, to Zacchaeus, yet he also speaks of Zacchaeus in the third person. This confusion arises because verse 9 has a double function in the story. It affirms for Zacchaeus that his quest has succeeded. It is also a part of Jesus' response to the crowd's objection in verse 7. Zacchaeus and Jesus are speaking to each other, but their dialogue presents an argument in response to the crowd, which is also being addressed, as verse 11 indicates. The argument has several components: In verse 8 Zacchaeus shows that he is no longer the man that the crowd has labeled a "sinner." In verse 9 Jesus reminds the crowd that Zacchaeus "too is a son of Abraham" (cf. 13:16). This statement presupposes that promises of salvation were given to the children of Abraham (i.e., the Jewish people; cf. 1:54-55, 72-75; Acts 3:25-26; 13:26) and that these promises include Zacchaeus, even though previously he has been excluded by other Jews. Jesus is reinstating Zacchaeus as a Jew and is bringing him the salvation promised by God to the Jews. Finally, in verse 10 Jesus describes his own mission, emphasizing that this consists of doing what he has just done, seeking and saving the lost. This provides a retrospective summary of Jesus' ministry to this point. It reminds the audience of the parables of finding the lost in Luke 15. It also fits nicely with another summary of Jesus' mission in 5:32. Together 5:32 and 19:10, placed early and late in the story of Jesus' mission, summarize and interpret Jesus' ministry to those excluded as sinners. Salvation for Zacchaeus is appropriate, for it fits Jesus' God-given mission.

In verse 3 Zacchaeus was "trying [or "seeking," *ezētei*] to see who Jesus was," the first indication of his quest, but in verse 10 Jesus states that he "came to seek" *(zētēsai)* people like Zacchaeus. Zacchaeus's quest is encompassed by a larger quest, which is the mission of Jesus.

◊ ◊ ◊ ◊

Different members of the Lukan audience could have heard different messages from this story. For outcasts like Zacchaeus, it could have been an affirmation of their right to belong to the people of God. For a community inclined to exclude, it could have been a challenging reminder of the meaning of Jesus' mission. For people with wealth, it could have provided a model—perhaps an ideal model that was seldom completely copied—of what conversion meant.

A Nobleman, His Slaves, and His Citizens (19:11-28)

This parable resembles Matthew's parable of the talents (Matt 25:14-30) except that another narrative thread has been added: The man goes away to receive royal power and his citizens oppose him. The story of the slaves entrusted with money is more fully developed in Matthew, and there are a number of differences in detail between the two versions.

19:11-14: Although the parable has broader significance, verse 11 makes clear that the narrator is using it to make a special point. The parable corrects the false expectation that the kingdom will appear when Jesus arrives in Jerusalem. (For an argument that this expectation is not false, see L. T. Johnson 1982, 139-59). The verse is not very clear about who is expecting the kingdom to appear immediately, but it is more likely to be the crowd that is following Jesus, including the disciples, than the people of Jericho. Only those who associate the coming of the kingdom with Jesus would expect it when Jesus arrives in Jerusalem. The narrative has also prepared for a false response by Jesus' followers by emphasizing that the disciples did not understand Jesus' announcements concerning his coming rejection and death (9:43-45; 18:31-34). When Jesus approaches Jerusalem, the disciples proclaim him king (19:37-38). Failing to understand Jesus' passion announcements, the disciples expect that he will be accepted as messianic king, and the kingdom of God will come.

The issue addressed in verse 11 is not the early church's concern with the delay of the parousia. The Lukan audience could hardly share the expectation that the kingdom would appear upon Jesus' arrival in Jerusalem. They knew what happened in Jerusalem. The narrator is developing a literary portrait of Jesus' followers as blind to God's way of working in the world, in which rejection and suffering become the means by which God's purpose advances. They expected triumph without suffering, even though Jesus had told them the opposite. This portrait would have continuing relevance for the Lukan audience, which would still prefer to triumph without suffering. In 24:21 we have further indication of what Jesus' followers expected in Jerusalem, and when the risen Jesus appears, hopes revive for the messianic kingdom immediately (Acts 1:6). These hopes are again corrected as Jesus directs the disciples toward a mission that will involve them in rejection and suffering similar to his own.

That the approach to Jerusalem would excite hopes for God's and the Messiah's reign can be explained from the conception of Zion found in Hebrew scripture. Mount Zion is "the place in which the human king, who is the viceroy of the divine king, sits enthroned" (Levenson in Freedman 1992, 6.1102). Texts used in Luke–Acts associate God's and the Messiah's rule with Zion or Jerusalem (cf. Pss 2:1-7; 110:1-2; Isa 52:7-10). Luke–Acts itself supports the hope for a messianic kingdom for Israel (Luke 1:32-33, 68-71; Acts 2:30-36; 3:20-21; 13:22-23, 32-34), but it did not come "immediately" because Jerusalem rejected her king.

Within the Roman Empire, a nobleman might indeed need to go "to a distant country to get royal power." Aspiring kings would travel to Rome to have their positions as client kings confirmed, and in the case of Archelaus, Herod's son, we also know of a delegation sent to oppose him (cf. Josephus *Ant.* 17 §299-314). In the Lukan narrative Jesus must travel to heaven, there to be enthroned at the right hand of God (Acts 2:30-36). The citizens who hate and oppose the nobleman anticipate Jesus' rejection in Jerusalem.

As in 12:35-38, 42-48, the departure of the master sets up a test for the slaves, who are left with certain responsibilities. In this case it involves money, and the slaves are explicitly told to "do business" or "trade" with it. The mina (translated "pound" in the NRSV) was a hundred drachmas. It was a moderate sum of money, not nearly as much as the talent that figures in Matthew's parable (a talent = sixty minas).

19:15-28: When the nobleman returns as king, there is a reckoning with his slaves. This involves a series of three slaves, even though ten were mentioned in verse 13. Ten would unnecessarily burden the narrative, while three allows a pattern to be established by the first two, who both make a profit, leading to a contrast with the third. The first two slaves are generously rewarded. Their success with a fairly small responsibility causes the king to appoint them governors over sections of his land. The third slave gets the most attention in the narrative. He returns the money to his master. If he had lost the money while trading, there would be a different sort of contrast (successful/unsuccessful traders), and a different issue would be raised. But the man simply kept the money wrapped up and returned it. He did not obey his master, but how serious is his offense? The reaction of the king will tell. The slave is allowed to explain his behavior in a short speech (vv. 20-21). He acted as he did because he was afraid of the master, whom he describes as a "harsh man" who is greedy for gain. He might lose the money, and surely he would then be punished. The king does react harshly. By his own reasoning the servant should have known that the king did want some profit from his money. The servant is punished by having the money taken from him and by loss of the possibility of sharing in the king's rule. However, there is no indication of further punishment comparable to Matt 25:30.

The slave calls his master a "harsh man." The master does not deny this but rejects it as an excuse. This view of the master is at least one-sided. The master is harsh with the slave who disobeyed, but he is generous with the others. They are given important positions, and in verses 24-25 the master adds even more. He does not take back the mina for himself but adds it to the resources of the most successful slave. The third slave says, "I was afraid of you." This fear paralyzed him. He was unable to risk trading with his master's money. The parable suggests that Jesus' followers must be willing to take risky responsibility. Preserving what they received is not enough. It must be put to work in the world so that the king's wealth and power grows. The risky moves into the Gentile world in Acts 10:1–11:18 and 17:16-34 might be examples of what the king requires.

After the king's reckoning with his slaves there is also a reckoning with the citizens who opposed his kingship (v. 27). The brutal slaughter commanded here is quite realistic in the setting of ancient politics. Such was the fate of the enemies of Herod (Josephus *Ant.* 15 §5-6). Since the return of the king probably refers to the future parousia of the Messiah, the destruction of enemies depicted in the parable does not refer to the destruction of Jerusalem in the Roman war. The parable omits an element that will be very important in Acts. The people who reject Jesus in Jerusalem are not immediately consigned to judgment but are called to repentance and forgiveness, and many respond (Acts 2:36-41, 47; 3:13-21).

◊ ◊ ◊ ◊

In close succession there will be additional anticipations of Jerusalem's rejection of its Messiah. In 19:41-44 Jesus will weep over the city that does not recognize the time of its visitation, and in 20:9-19 Jesus will add a parable about vineyard tenants who kill the owner's son.

Approach to Jerusalem: Acclamation and Lament (19:29-44)

The journey to Jerusalem is not over until 19:45 (cf. Denaux 1993, 385). The narrator carefully marks the final stages of the journey by threefold use of the verb *engizō*, "come near" (NRSV: "had come near," v. 29; "was . . . approaching," v. 37; "came near," v. 41). In verse 29 Jesus approaches Bethphage and Bethany. Bethany was on the eastern slope of the Mount of Olives, which Jesus must cross to reach Jerusalem. In verse 37 he is at the summit. In verse 41 he has begun the descent and can see Jerusalem.

19:29-40: Jesus has walked all the way from Galilee, but it is important that he have a mount for the last segment. The need, obviously, is not physical but symbolic. The animal must be borrowed, and Jesus gives careful instructions to two disciples on how to do this. It is remarkable that almost seven verses (vv. 29-35) are devoted to this arrangement. The animal is called a "colt" *(pōlos)*, which could be either a young horse or a young donkey. The chosen animal is one that has never been ridden. According to Num 19:2 and Deut 21:3, an animal to be used for certain sacred purposes must be chosen from those that have never been used for ordinary labor, and according to *m. Sanh.* 2.5, no one else may ride the king's horse. Jesus' word carries authority in this scene. The statement "The Lord needs it" is sufficient to obtain the colt.

There is no explicit reference to Zech 9:9 in Luke, but the best explanation for the attention given to obtaining a "colt" is the desire to fulfill this prophecy, which is cited as part of the parallel scenes in Matt 21:1-9 and John 12:12-16. Zechariah 9:9-10 proclaims the coming of Jerusalem's "king," mounted on a "colt" (the LXX specifies a "new colt," which could mean one not previously ridden). The king will destroy instruments of war, leading to peace (cf. Luke 19:42). Jesus, on the colt, approaches Jerusalem as its king, as verse 38 makes clear (the word "king" is absent from the parallels in Matt 21:9 and Mark 11:10, but is present in John 12:13). The spreading of cloaks on the road in verse 36 repeats what was done when a new king was proclaimed in 2 Kgs 9:13.

According to this account, Jesus deliberately presents himself as Jerusalem's promised king. A new king should be greeted by his subjects with shouts of acclamation, such as the words of verse 38. Yet the narrator carefully indicates in verse 37 that this acclamation comes from the "multitude of the disciples" traveling with Jesus, who had previously observed his deeds of power, and not from the people of Jerusalem. Jerusalem will not accept Jesus as its king. In verse 39 some Pharisees immediately object to addressing Jesus as king. When Peter confessed Jesus as the Messiah, Jesus "ordered" *(epitimaō)* the disciples to tell no one (9:20-21). In 19:39 the Pharisees want Jesus to "order" *(epitimaō)* the disciples to stop proclaiming him king. Jesus refuses. The time for secrecy is past. Now is the time of confrontation between Jerusalem's king and its present rulers. The opposition voiced by some of the Pharisees in verse 39 will be taken up in verse 47 by "the chief priests, the scribes, and the leaders of the people," who will seek Jesus' death.

Jesus' healings regularly lead to the praise of God (most recently in 18:43). This praise reechoes in verse 37, where the disciples recall "all the deeds of power" performed by Jesus, which are complete at this point. (The healing of an ear in 22:51 has the special purpose of undoing damage caused by a disciple.)

The first sentence of the acclamation in verse 38 is taken from Ps 118:26, with the addition of "the king." This text was used as a greeting for pilgrims coming to Jerusalem for a festival. James Sanders believes that Psalm 118 was originally a royal psalm, and verse 26 was a greeting of the king (cf. Sanders in Evans and Sanders 1993, 143-48). If so, the original use reappears in Luke. The second half of the acclamation is unique to Luke and closely resembles the words of the angels announcing the birth of the Messiah (2:14). (There is also a similarity between 2:13 and 19:37, with the disciples taking the place of the angels.) This reminder of the infancy narrative is important because Jesus is about to make a prophetic disclosure about the hopes for Israel raised in the infancy narrative (cf. 19:42-44). One difference between 2:14 and 19:38 may be significant. In the former the angels say, "on earth peace," but the disciples say, "in heaven peace" (according to the Greek word order). The disciples are rejoicing and are oblivious to Jesus' prophecies of the passion (cf. 18:31-34). They may be unaware that their words anticipate a tragic shift: the earthly Jerusalem will not find peace. The reference to Jerusalem's loss of peace in verse 42 supports this view.

19:41-44: The remarkable scene in verses 41-44 is found only in Luke. At this point there is a sharp shift in mood from rejoicing to lament. In spite of the general Lukan tendency to remove Jesus' expressions of emotion in Mark (cf. Fitzmyer 1981, 95), Jesus is depicted as weeping over Jerusalem. In this way the narrator suggests to the Lukan audience the attitude that they should take toward the destruction of Jerusalem by the Romans in AD 70. It is a tragedy and, like dramatic tragedies, the result of tragic blindness (on the tragic aspect, see Tannehill 1985, 69-85). Great expectations were raised in the infancy narrative. The Messiah would "reign over the house of Jacob" (1:33), "guide our feet into the way of peace" (1:79), and bring "the redemption of Jerusalem" (2:38). Now, however, Jesus mourns over Jerusalem's failure to recognize its opportunity. The theme of not recognizing (or not knowing; the verb is *ginōskō*) begins and ends Jesus' prophetic oracle in verses

42 and 44. This critical "ignorance" will be mentioned again in the Acts mission speeches (Acts 3:17; 13:27).

The tragic turn in the narrative is clearest when we compare 19:42-44 with the Benedictus, with which it shares a number of key terms. What was joyfully celebrated as the fulfillment of hope in the Benedictus is mourned as tragic loss in Jesus' words over Jerusalem. The Benedictus twice uses the rare term "visit" *(episkeptomai)* of God's saving action (translated "has looked favorably on" in 1:68 and "will break upon" in 1:78). Compare the unrecognized "time of your visitation" in 19:44. Compare also the reference to "the way of peace" in 1:79 with 19:42, and the expectation of being saved or rescued from "our enemies" in 1:71, 74 with destruction by "your enemies" in 19:43. The failure to "know" or recognize in 19:42, 44 also contrasts with the "knowledge of salvation" in 1:77. The national salvation proclaimed in the Benedictus is being lost, at least for the foreseeable future, not because it was an inappropriate hope but because Jerusalem, at the crucial time of "visitation," will reject its Messiah.

The language of 19:42-44 is full of pathos. Jesus' emotional bond with the city is expressed as he addresses it directly in the second person singular. He emphasizes this address in verse 42 ("even you"), and verses 42-44 are full of the pronouns "you" and "your" (often at the end of sentences in the Greek). The first statement in verse 42 is an incomplete sentence in the Greek, expressing a yearning that will find no fulfillment. The destruction of the city is depicted vividly in short, choppy sentences.

The destruction will take place "because you did not recognize the time of your visitation" (the NRSV has added "from God" as explanation). The destruction of the city is viewed as the consequence of its rejection of Jesus (cf. "because"). In historical terms, this is, at least, a great oversimplification. Yet, for the narrator, Jesus represents the alternative to the path taken by the Jewish rebels. He offered to Jerusalem the messianic peace (v. 42), and he would rule as he taught: by promoting the love of enemies (6:27-36).

◊ ◊ ◊ ◊

The phrase "time of visitation" is found in Jer 6:15; 10:15 LXX. This connection with Jeremiah should remind us that those trained in scripture would see history repeating itself, for Jerusalem was conquered and the temple destroyed in the time of Jeremiah, who wept over his people as Jesus weeps over Jerusalem (Jer 9:1; 14:17). The biblical themes of the people's guilt, divine punishment, and hope of restoration would burn painfully in the consciousness of many after the Roman conquest of Jerusalem. The Gospel of Luke shares the pain of Jews at this event (cf. Tiede 1980, 1-7, 65-86). Luke 19:41-44 fits with three other passages in Luke that present Jerusalem, the religious center of Israel, as the center of resistance to God's messengers and as the object of God's judgment. These passages contain other signs of sorrow that this is so (cf. 13:33-35; 21:20-24; 23:28-31).

JESUS IN THE TEMPLE (19:45–21:38)

Jesus Drives Out the Merchants; A Death Plot (19:45-48)

Jesus' destination is the temple. Entering it, he immediately begins to purge it of one of its abuses. Those selling in the outer court of the temple precincts (the court of the Gentiles) were providing a service to the worshipers who needed animals for the sacrifices. The Lukan account is quite short (Matt 21:12-13 and Mark 11:15-17 are somewhat longer; John 2:13-22 is the longest). The only indication of why the sellers are being driven out comes in verse 46: They have made the temple "a den of robbers." This seems to imply that the sellers are exploiting the people. (The Qumran Commentary on Habakkuk accuses the Jerusalem priests of amassing "money and wealth by plundering the peoples"; cf. Vermes 1987, 287.) The short Lukan version removes all violent details from the scene and centers attention on Jesus' statement in verse 46. This statement contains two scripture references. Isaiah 56:7 speaks of the temple as "a house of prayer for all peoples" or "nations." Mark 11:17 includes "for all the nations" in the quotation. However, the Lukan narrator recognizes that the temple, which will be destroyed, is not destined to be a house of prayer for

Gentiles. The reference to a "den of robbers" comes from Jer 7:11, part of a temple speech in which Jeremiah attacks the false sense of safety that the temple inspires, even though the worshipers are guilty of many crimes. The speech includes a threat that the temple will be destroyed. Knowledge of the Jeremiah context would reinforce Jesus' words in verses 43-44.

From the time of his cleansing of the temple until Passover, Jesus makes the temple his site of daily teaching. We do not know how long a period is envisioned, only that this is a period of intense teaching. Two types of response are clearly distinguished. On the one hand, "all the people were spellbound by what they heard" (literally, they "hung on him listening"). On the other hand, the powerful people of Jerusalem are now trying to kill him. This threatening group is made up of the chief priests, scribes, and leaders of the people. (Compare 9:22 and 20:1, which refer to chief priests, scribes, and elders.) They now take over the role of Jesus' opponents from the Pharisees and scribes in the earlier narrative, and they are more deadly. It is not clear why they want to eliminate Jesus. The entry to Jerusalem, the cleansing of the temple, and Jesus' temple teaching may all contribute. The authorities are temporarily unable to act because of the support Jesus is receiving from the people. This division between the people and the authorities in Jerusalem will continue through much of the following chapters.

The summary statement in verses 47-48 will be matched by a similar summary in 21:37-38, forming a frame around Jesus' temple teaching.

The Question About Authority and the Parable of the Tenants (20:1-19)

There is a longer section of temple teaching in Luke than in Mark, for Mark has Jesus leave the temple and go to the Mount of Olives for the eschatological discourse (Mark 13:1, 3). In Luke this discourse is presented in the temple (21:7-36). The first part of Jesus' temple teaching (20:1-44) is directed to the Jewish leaders in Jerusalem. The conflict between them and Jesus is portrayed in a series of controversy scenes. In three of the scenes (20:1-8, 20-26, 27-40) Jewish leaders present Jesus with testing questions designed to challenge and embarrass him. These are a subtype of pronouncement story that I call "testing inquiries" (cf. Tannehill 1981, 10, 115-16, and 1995, 60). In these scenes Jesus is being pressed hard by the chief priests, scribes, and elders. Not only Jesus' reputation but also his life is at stake in these discussions, for if the authorities can reduce Jesus' support among the people, they will be able to move against him. Jesus skillfully escapes their traps with responses that are impressive but provide no basis for an accusation.

20:1-8: Although 20:1-44 presents controversies with the Jerusalem authorities, verse 1 tells us first that Jesus "was teaching the people . . . and telling the good news." The controversies are interruptions in Jesus' main activity, which is described in verse 1. The teaching and preaching that Jesus has been doing since his ministry began continues in Jerusalem. The phrase "telling the good news" (using the verb *euangelizomai*) should remind us of the descriptions of Jesus' mission in 4:18, 43; 8:1. The rest of 20:1-8 unfolds very much as in Matt 21:23-27 and Mark 11:27-33.

The chief priests, scribes, and elders operate as a group. It is the same group that will reject Jesus, leading to his death, according to Jesus' prophecy in 9:22. The question about authority is dangerous, for it could expose Jesus' lack of authority or lead him to make dangerous claims (as he eventually does in 22:69-71). The question concerns Jesus' authority to do "these things." "These things" probably include his teaching in the temple (see the accusation in 23:5) but also the dramatic actions in 19:29-46.

As in other testing inquiries (cf. 10:26; 20:24), Jesus responds to a question with a counterquestion designed to move the discussion in a favorable direction. Jesus exploits the division between the leaders and the people mentioned in 19:47-48. It is assumed here that this division includes two different attitudes toward John the Baptist. The people accept John's message and baptism, while the religious leaders do not (cf. 7:29-30). Jesus' question in verse 4 poses two alternatives, but the leaders face a dilemma. They are not willing to answer either way and must shamefully admit that they, the religious leaders, do not know. Their failure to respond permits

Jesus also to refuse an answer and thus escape danger for the moment.

The reference to John the Baptist suggests that there is a parallel between him and Jesus. The leaders will be able to recognize Jesus' authority if they can recognize and accept the authority of a prophet like John. But Jerusalem has a bad record; it is the "city that kills the prophets" (13:34). The reference to John may also remind the Lukan audience of earlier scenes that show the source of Jesus' authority, for after Jesus' baptism the Spirit descended and the divine voice addressed Jesus as "Son," authorizing his mission (cf. 3:22; 4:18). The rest of Luke's Jerusalem narrative will also speak to the issue of Jesus' authority, which will be supported by scripture, by fulfilled prophecies, and by resurrection.

20:9-19: The scene does not end with Jesus' refusal to answer, for Jesus adds a parable that interprets his own role and that of his opponents. The parable, when understood allegorically, does say something about the source of Jesus' authority. It also speaks to one of the reasons for denying Jesus' authority. The fact that the recognized authorities of Judaism rejected him would, in the eyes of many, count heavily against the claims made for Jesus. The parable deals with this rejection in a way that incorporates it into a story of Jesus' authority.

The parable is told to the people (v. 9), but they are being told about their leaders, for in verse 19 the scribes and chief priests recognize that this parable was told "against them" (or "with reference to them"). The parable provides a preview of what will happen in Jerusalem and suggests some of the consequences.

Jesus has told other parables about a man going on a journey and leaving subordinates in charge (cf. 12:36-38, 42-48; 19:12-27). In none of these parables do the subordinates act as badly as here. The parallels to verse 9 in Matt 21:33 and Mark 12:1 contain clear references to Isa 5:1-7, in which Israel is identified as God's unfruitful vineyard. This reference is muted or absent in Luke. The story does not focus on the vineyard but on the behavior of the "tenants" (literally, "farmers," but they are evidently tenant farmers, with a contract to share the produce with the owner). When the time comes to share the harvest, the tenants refuse to deliver and badly mistreat the owner's representatives. Then the owner considers his options in a soliloquy, a device repeatedly used in Lukan parables so that the audience can listen while a crucial decision is being made (cf. 12:19; 15:17-19; 16:3-4). The owner decides to make one last attempt to settle the problem peacefully, by sending his son as his representative.

Reflecting on this decision, some may see the owner as weak and foolish; some may be impressed with his patience and commitment to settle the matter peacefully. The owner clearly hopes that the son will be accepted and the produce delivered. This hope is not completely irrational, for the tenants may not have accepted the claim of the slaves to represent their master. The slaves may not have been persons of sufficient authority in the master's household to command respect. Furthermore, the tenants did not show that they were capable of murder before the sending of the son (contrast Matt 21:35 and Mark 12:5). However, the master's decision proves costly. Instead of showing greater respect, the tenants kill the son as part of a plot to take over the vineyard. The tenants may have interpreted the owner's response to their behavior as a sign of weakness. He was not able to do anything except send defenseless emissaries. There is irony in the development: because he was the owner's son, the owner hoped the son would be respected; because he was the owner's son and heir, the son was killed.

The description of the son in verse 13 (literally, "my son, the beloved") reproduces the words of God to Jesus following his baptism (cf. 3:22). This provides a clear correlation between Jesus and the son in the story; it also reminds the audience of the source of Jesus' authority in response to the question in 20:2. The death in verse 14, then, also correlates with Jesus' prophecy in 9:22, where Jesus announced that the elders, chief priests, and scribes would reject him, leading to his death. Thus the story presents Jesus as the Son authorized by God to speak to Jerusalem and call its leaders to account, and it also anticipates Jesus' death.

The question in verse 15 ("What then will the owner of the vineyard do?") picks up the owner's question in verse 13 ("What shall I do?"). The last peaceful option has been tried. If the owner is to keep his vineyard, new tenants must be found and the old ones destroyed. Are the "others" to whom the vineyard will be given an identifiable group? There are several options. It would be possible to identify them with the leaders of the early Christian movement, but then the reaction of the people, "Heaven forbid" (literally, "May it not be"), is inappropriate, for (in the opinion of the narrator) this change of leadership is good and necessary. The people would be showing their blind opposition to this necessary development. It is possible, however, to understand the "others" to be the Roman troops that occupied Jerusalem (cf. 21:24). The people's horrified reaction to this possibility would be justified.

In spite of the allegorical elements in the present story, the owner in the parable cannot be simply equated with God. The owner miscalculates the degree of evil that he faces, resulting in the purposeless death of his son. As the text moves away from the parable imagery in verse 17, it declares that God has resources not available to the vineyard owner and that the Gospel story does not end with the son's death and the destruction of the tenants. A quotation from Ps 118:22 (the same psalm quoted in 19:38) hints at this possibility. The rejection of the stone by the builders corresponds to the killing of the son by the tenants, but a quote from the psalm adds that this stone "has become the cornerstone." There is movement here from rejection to vindication, from dishonor to high honor. The word "reject" *(apodokimazō)* was also used in 9:22 in Jesus' first announcement of his passion. The theme of God's vindication of the one who was rejected in Jerusalem will be central to the preaching of the death and resurrection of Jesus in the Acts mission speeches to Jews (cf. Acts 2:23-24, 32-36; 3:13-15; 4:10-11; 5:30-31), and Ps 118:22 will again be quoted in Acts 4:11 in connection with this theme. Along with Ps 110:1 (cf. Luke 20:42-43; 22:69; Acts 2:34-35), this verse is regarded by the narrator as a major scriptural testimony to God's plan of vindicating the rejected Jesus and enthroning him in heaven. We can assume that it is part of the discussion when the risen Messiah interprets "the things about himself in all the scriptures" (Luke 24:26-27).

In Acts the saving power of the exalted Messiah will be proclaimed, even for those who rejected him. In Luke 20:18, however, the destructive power of the stone is emphasized, in line with the reference to destruction in verse 16. It is possible that falling on the stone reflects Isa 8:14-15, and the stone falling and crushing reflects Dan 2:34, 44-45. In any case, the beloved son who seemed so vulnerable will prove to be invulnerable and enduring, while his enemies will not. In verse 19 the narrator makes clear that the parable applies to the Jerusalem scribes and chief priests. Their deadly purpose, noted in 19:47-48, is all the stronger now but is still frustrated by the people.

The Question About Taxes for the Emperor (20:20-26)

The scribes and chief priests keep Jesus under surveillance and hatch a plot. Even though Matthew and Mark report that Pharisees and Herodians address Jesus in this scene (cf. Matt 22:15-16; Mark 12:13), Luke speaks simply of spies sent by the scribes and chief priests. (In Luke, Pharisees are not mentioned after 19:39; they have no role in the plots against Jesus in Jerusalem.) Luke indicates the purpose of the plot: his enemies want incriminating evidence that can be used against Jesus before the Roman governor. Jesus does not give them the evidence they want, but at the trial before Pilate, Jesus is accused, in spite of his teaching in 20:25, of forbidding payment of taxes to the emperor (cf. 23:2).

◊ ◊ ◊ ◊

This scene is a pronouncement story of the testing inquiry subtype. The danger revealed in verse 20 heightens the tension in the scene. The question of the spies is preceded by an extended compliment (v. 21) that is part of the trap. To "show deference to no one" means, in context, that he does not show deference to the Roman power but teaches God's truth in spite of the Romans. The spies are prodding Jesus to say something seditious. The term translated "emperor" in the NRSV is actually "Caesar," the family name that became a title of the Roman dictators. In the question in verse 22, Luke uses a general term for tax or tribute in place of the term *kēnsos* (Latin "census"), used by Matthew and Mark. The latter term probably refers specifically to the tax imposed by the Romans on the basis of a census of the population. When the census was carried out in AD 6-7, it provoked a revolt led by Judas the Galilean (cf. Josephus *J. W.* 2 §118; 7 §253-55). Thus there was a history of Jewish resistance to Roman taxation for patriotic and religious reasons. The choice of a different term in Luke may simply reflect the author's desire to use a proper Greek word instead of a Latin loan word.

The compliment in verse 21 highlights a constraint upon Jesus' answer. He is committed to teaching the way of God in truth, which may get him in trouble. Yet he surprises the spies by both teaching God's truth and also escaping their trap. He first asks them to participate in answering the question themselves by supplying a coin and answering a question about it. Their participation will make it more difficult for them to escape the answer. The coin of the reigning emperor would show the emperor's head and bear the inscription "Tiberius Caesar, son of the divine Augustus, Augustus" (cf. Fitzmyer 1985, 1296). The coin, then, carried Caesar's claim to power, based on his divine origin. Jesus, however, treats the image and inscription as a claim to ownership of the coin. The coin is Caesar's; return it to him. The meaning of the first half of Jesus' answer in verse 25 is determined by the discussion about the coin, which bears the insignia of Caesar. The verb *apodidōmi* can mean simply give or pay, but it can also mean pay back or return, as when paying a debt (cf. Luke 7:42; 10:35; 12:59; 19:8). Thus, Jesus is saying, if you are going to use Caesar's denarius, you can't complain about returning it to him, since he is the real owner. This witty reply minimizes the importance of the issue being raised.

Jesus' remark about the coin is the first part of a brief, two-part aphorism. In the Greek there are only eleven words in Jesus' reply, four of which are articles and four of which are different forms of the two nouns Caesar and God. The aphorism repeats in the second part the construction of the first part, while substituting God for Caesar.

> Then give what is Caesar's to Caesar
> and what is God's to God.

The effect is to require the audience to think about the relation of these two parts. The aphorism does not provide a clear demarcation of duties to Caesar, on the one hand, and God, on the other; that cannot be done in an aphorism. The only specific thing that it authorizes (due to the context) is the payment of the Roman tax under discussion. It does not establish a doctrine of two realms in which the political realm is removed from the realm of God. Indeed, the emphasis falls on the claims of God. The first part of the aphorism has limited scope because it speaks directly to the question at hand: the payment of the tax. The second part is not limited by the context. Furthermore, it has climactic position at the end and catches attention as an artful reformulation of the first part. The effect of introducing the claims of God is to limit the claims of Caesar without attempting to specify where that limit should be drawn. The catchy aphorism thereby guards against accepting the claims of the earthly ruler without also considering the claims of God (cf. Tannehill 1975, 171-77).

In verse 26 the narrator indicates that the plan to trap Jesus has failed. The opponents are reduced to silence. They neither have grounds for an accusation with the governor nor have they weakened Jesus' support by the people.

◊ ◊ ◊ ◊

The issue of paying Roman taxes might not have been as acute for the Lukan communities, but they might have had to wrestle with the question of whether worship of God and proclamation of the kingship of Jesus were compatible with Caesar's claims to honor (cf. Acts 17:6-7). When Caesar's supporters claimed that he was divine, many Christians suffered for their conviction that this definition of the things of Caesar conflicted with the things of God.

The Question of the Resurrection (20:27-40)

The Sadducees were an aristocratic group made up of the families from which the chief priests were drawn and their allies. Their rejection of the oral tradition of the Pharisees included rejection of belief in a resurrection. Their appearance in 20:27 is not as sudden as it might seem, for the chief priests have been mentioned in 19:47; 20:1, 19. In Acts the temple officials, including the chief priests, are presented as leading opponents of the early Jerusalem church, and the Sadducees are associated with this group (cf. Acts 4:1, 5-6; 5:17).

This passage is again a pronouncement story that features a testing question. Since the Sadducees do not themselves accept the belief on which the question is based (that there will be a resurrection), it is obvious that they are not asking the question for their own information. The question is designed to make Jesus look foolish, thus shaming him and undermining the popular support that has prevented action against him. Jesus' answer is more elaborate than in most pronouncement stories and divides into two parts: a rejection of the question because it is based on a false assumption (vv. 34-36) and a statement about the underlying issue of resurrection (vv. 37-38).

20:27-33: The question refers to the practice of levirate marriage, the purpose of which was to perpetuate the name and family of a man who died childless. In such a case it was the duty of the man's brother to marry his widow, and the first child born to her is considered the offspring of the deceased (cf. Deut 25:5-10; Gen 38:8-9). The Sadducees present the case of seven brothers who had the same wife because of this practice, and they want to know whose wife she will be in the resurrection.

20:34-40: In his response, Jesus does not accept the assumption that marriage continues in the resurrection. "Those who belong to this age" in verse 34 is literally "the sons of this age," and "children" in verse 36 also translates "sons," but the NRSV is right to choose a gender-inclusive translation. Women are clearly included in these "sons," for those who "are given in marriage" (v. 34) are women. The resurrection of which verses 35-36 speak is a special privilege of the children of God who participate in the age to come, the consummated kingdom of God, as transformed beings, "like angels." The absence of marriage is linked to the absence of death. This need not imply that the sole purpose of marriage was to perpetuate the human race. It could imply that, in the transformed state, the deep relationships characteristic of good marriages no longer need to be guarded by the exclusive bond of marriage. The designation of the resurrected as "children of God" suggests that their resurrection life comes from their close relation to the eternal God, a view that will be supported by verses 37-38.

An argument in support of resurrection is presented in verses 37-38. This argument includes a reference to scripture, but fundamentally it is based on the nature of God. At the call of Moses, when God revealed the divine name to him, God also told Moses to use this authorizing definition of the God who sent him: "the LORD, the God of your ancestors, the God of Abraham, the God of Isaac, and the God of Jacob" (Exod 3:15; cf. 3:6). When God in scripture is spoken of as the "God of" someone, particularly the patriarchs, this often connotes that God is their faithful protector because they are bound by covenant relation, and this protection extends to their offspring (cf. Gen 24:27; 31:42; 46:3; 49:24-25). There is evidence that this sense of the phrase continued into New Testament times (cf. Dreyfus 1959, 216-20). By New Testament times, when a belief in resurrection was shared by many Jews, the understanding of God's faithful protection for Abraham, Isaac, and Jacob could be extended to include life after death (something assumed for the patriarchs in 13:28; 16:22-31). God is eternal, God gives life, God is the faithful protector of the patriarchs: This has come to mean that God gives them life after death. God is not God of the dead, as if God had no power, finally, to protect those chosen; rather, God is God of the living. The definition of God derived from God's revelation to Moses is taken in this strong sense in Luke. Although there are Lukan additions and variations in verses 34-38, this basic point is the same in the synoptic Gospels (cf. Matt 22:31-32; Mark 12:26-27).

The exact sense of "to him all of them are alive" is not clear. (This sentence is found only in Luke; the NRSV has added "of them," but the sentence could refer to people in general, not just the patriarchs.) In verses 35-36 the resurrection is for those "considered worthy," the "children of God," and it is part of the age to come. However, verse 38 seems to be talking about life after death that does not await a future resurrection (the patriarchs are already living) and that may apply to all. Belief in immediate afterlife could be combined with belief in a future resurrection, as in the views that Josephus attributes to the Pharisees and to himself: The soul is imperishable, but part of the reward of the good is that their souls will pass into new bodies; this change will take place at "the revolution of the ages" (cf. Josephus *J. W.* 2 §163; 3 §374). However, there is insufficient evidence to know how the Lukan narrator understood these details.

Some of the scribes approve Jesus' answer. They do not oppose him on all issues. "They" in verse 40 (those who no longer dared to ask questions) probably includes all of Jesus' opponents (the chief priests, scribes, and elders of vv. 1 and 19, and the Sadducees of v. 27), for from this point on Jesus takes the initiative in his temple teaching and is no longer responding to questions from skeptics. The attempt to catch Jesus by tough questions has failed.

Jesus' Question About David's Son (20:41-44)

In verse 41 Jesus is still addressing his opponents, but when he asks, "how can they say?" he is probably referring to the opinion of people in general, which the Jerusalem religious authorities may share. For the Lukan audience this passage functions as an anticipation of the key events of resurrection and exaltation that will follow Jesus' death. Jesus quotes Ps 110:1. This psalm, in which God pledges support to the king, is understood to refer to the Messiah. The author is understood to be David (this psalm is one of those traditionally ascribed to David), who speaks prophetically through the psalms (cf. Acts 2:30-31). Therefore, when the first line refers to "the Lord" (= God) speaking to "my Lord," David is acknowledging the Messiah as his Lord. "My Lord" is the address of an inferior to a superior. Yet the father normally has greater dignity than the son, and David was the most famous king of Israel. Jesus has been called "Lord" a number of times in Luke, both by persons in the narrative (e.g., 7:6) and by the narrator (e.g., 7:13), but this need not carry the same weight as David's phrase. If *King David* addresses someone as "my Lord," that one must be very great indeed.

The final question in verse 44 could be understood to imply that the Messiah is not David's son. That would not be the Lukan understanding of this passage, however. In Luke–Acts the Messiah is a descendant of David, and Jesus' Davidic ancestry is emphasized as part of his qualification for the messianic role (cf. Luke 1:32-33; 3:31; Acts 2:29-36; 13:22-23). Yet to call him "son of David" does not sufficiently acknowledge his rank once God says to him, "Sit at my right hand." This is the position of highest honor and includes God's pledge to subject all opponents so that the enthroned Messiah is universal ruler. Jesus is not yet sitting at God's right hand. That will begin with his heavenly enthronement following his resurrection (cf. Acts 2:32-36, where Ps 110:1 is quoted and interpreted). Jesus can be both "son of David"—ranking lower than him—and David's Lord because there are two stages to his career: his prophetic ministry and his rule as Messiah at God's right hand. In the second stage, the benefits of Jesus' ministry are multiplied and extended. Through his exaltation Jesus will become the royal benefactor who will "pour out" or "give" the Holy Spirit (Acts 2:33), repentance and forgiveness (5:31), and salvation through his name (4:11-12). This is a key aspect of Lukan soteriology (cf. Tannehill 1990, 38-40).

◊ ◊ ◊ ◊

Luke 20:41-44 only hints at the importance of Ps 110:1 for Luke's Christology and soteriology. In 22:69 we find a further hint, but Acts 2:29-36 first provides theological development. Psalm 110:1 stands alongside Ps 118:22, another important text connected with Jesus' exaltation as saving event (cf. Luke 20:17; Acts 4:11-12). We can understand, then, why the risen Jesus specifically includes the psalms when he refers to what has been "written about me" in scripture (Luke 24:44). These psalms make important contributions to the Lukan understanding of God's saving purpose being realized through Jesus.

Warning Against the Scribes (20:45-47)

In Luke 20 Jesus has been speaking primarily with the scribes, chief priests, and their representatives (including the Sadducees, who are allied with the chief priests). Now, however, he addresses his disciples, with the people listening. This will continue to be the situation throughout the eschatological discourse in Luke 21. Jesus is no longer talking to the scribes, but he is talking about them. That provides some continuity with the preceding material. In verse 46 the Greek does not make clear whether Jesus is talking about the scribes in general (in which case it is appropriate to put a comma after "scribes," as the NRSV does) or whether he is talking about those particular scribes who do the things listed in verses 46-47 (in which case, we should omit the comma).

◊ ◊ ◊ ◊

The disciples are being warned about these scribes because they are bad examples. Scribes and Pharisees are used in Luke to warn Jesus' followers against behavior that they, too, may share. The disciples in Luke show a desire for social prominence. In 9:46-48 they argued about who was the greatest, and this argument will reappear at the Last Supper (22:24-27). This makes them like the scribes in 20:45-47.

The long robes are evidently a distinctive way of dressing so that they will be recognized and given due respect. The signs of special respect that they crave are illustrated: greetings in the marketplaces and places of honor in the synagogues and at banquets. Jesus has already spoken negatively about these three practices in 11:43 and 14:7-10. The long prayers of these scribes may be motivated by the desire to be honored for their piety. They are also accused of devouring widow's houses. It is not clear why such an accusation would be made. One possibility is that, as persons trained in the law, they acted as guardians of some estates, and they are being accused of misusing this responsibility for their own gain (cf. Fitzmyer 1985, 1318). The warning is not only against self-inflation but also against rapacious greed (cf. the Pharisees in 11:39; 16:14). The introduction of widows in verse 47 prepares for the following story of the poor widow.

The Widow's Offering (21:1-4)

In the introduction to this pronouncement story, there is no indication of a change of time or place from the preceding scene. Jesus simply looks up and comments on what he sees. The minimal separation from 20:45-47 suggests that we should compare the behavior of the scribes who promote themselves with the selfless act of the widow.

◊ ◊ ◊ ◊

The story of the widow's offering is built around a contrast between rich people with their gifts and the poor widow with hers. This contrast is established by the narrative in verses 1-2 and interpreted by the comment in verses 3-4. The "two small copper coins" are two *lepta*. The word means "small," and the *lepton* was the smallest denomination of coin used in the area. Jesus states, however, that these two *lepta* are more than all the other donors contributed. This, of course, is not true according to the normal way of counting money. A different way of counting gifts has been introduced by Jesus' remark, and verse 4 provides an explanation. In verse 4 gifts contributed out of "abundance" are compared with the widow's gift contributed out of "poverty" (literally, "lack" or "need"). The others had plenty left, but the widow gave "all she had to live on." The widow's gift was more because it was all.

But was the widow foolish to give away her last two coins? According to Addison Wright, this story is told not in praise of the widow (the usual interpretation), but as a lament that she was led to use her money in this way (cf. Wright 1982, 256-65; Fitzmyer 1985, 1320-22). Wright notes indications in the Jesus tradition that Jesus placed human need higher than religious requirements and also notes the connection between this scene and 20:47. The story of the widow, then, shows how official religion devours widow's houses by promoting false values. The widow is led to give away money that she desperately needed to a temple that would later be destroyed (cf. 21:5-6).

Wright's interpretation is a helpful warning against a thoughtless use of this passage. However, it does not fit the structure of the scene. To make Wright's point, we would expect more emphasis on the bad consequences for the widow of giving away the money. Instead, we have a contrast between the gifts of the rich and the gift of the widow, with the widow's gift declared to be "more." This way of telling the story highlights the extraordinary value of the widow's gift. It promotes a way of evaluating gifts that is different from the act of simply counting the value of coins. Ignoring the question of whether this was a wise thing for the widow to do, the story defends the dignity of the poor. Their contributions, given in true sacrifice, are to be more highly honored than the contributions of the rich. This story would have something to say about the way the poor are treated within the Lukan communities.

An Eschatological Discourse (21:5-38)

The rest of Luke 21 is an eschatological discourse that has the same scope as the eschatological discourse in Mark 13 (cf. also Matt 24:1-36), yet is significantly different in details. One of the significant differences is that it is delivered not on the Mount of Olives to four leading disciples but as a public discourse in the temple. In Luke the eschatological discourse is the climax of Jesus' temple teaching. The audience is specified in 20:45: Jesus is talking to the disciples, but all the people are listening. Some of the discourse is directed especially to disciples (cf. vv. 12-19), but much of the discourse is as relevant to the people of Jerusalem as to the disciples. The people of Jerusalem are being warned about the future fate of Jerusalem (vv. 20-24), but the hope for a redemption beyond that destruction may also apply to them (v. 28). The few references to people in the scene (other than Jesus) are vague ("some," v. 5; "they," v. 7). Unlike earlier discourses, the narrator is not concerned to distinguish clearly who is being addressed at each stage.

The Destruction of the Temple (21:5-6)

The expansion of the temple area under Herod resulted in a huge temple precinct, encompassing some thirty-five acres. "In the Mediterranean world, one has to go to Egypt to find walled sacred areas larger than Herod's temple" (E. P. Sanders 1992, 58; cf. the description of the temple pp. 54-69). The decorations of the temple were correspondingly grand. The "gifts dedicated to God" were votive offerings. People could dedicate objects to God, and these became part of the decoration of the temple (cf. Judith 16:19). The temple and its decorations were impressive, but Jesus responds in verse 6 by declaring that all of this will be destroyed, repeating words used previously in 19:44.

Warnings About False Eschatological Signs (21:7-24)

Verses 5-6 form a brief pronouncement story, but they are also the beginning point for a longer discourse. Jesus' statement prompts the questions in verse 7, which lead to the eschatological discourse. The questioners are asking when the temple will be destroyed. The discourse deals with more than this question, but the destruction of Jerusalem has a prominent place in it. Jesus immediately issues a warning because in these matters people are very likely to be led astray by some who make false claims. Those who make these claims "will come in my name." This may mean that they are followers of Jesus who speak as prophets and announce the presence or imminent arrival of Jesus as returning Son of Man. Luke has added "The time is near" to what we find in Matt 24:5 and Mark 13:6, acknowledging that there have been false claims about the nearness of the final upheaval. These claims, too, should not be trusted.

This discourse gives warnings but also provides comfort and encouragement for difficult times. In doing so, it projects a picture of the way the future will unfold. Scripture could lead one to believe that the attack on Jerusalem by Gentiles will trigger the final intervention of God to rescue and exalt Jerusalem (cf. Zechariah 14). That did not happen in AD 70, when the Romans conquered Jerusalem. In verse 9 a clear space is set between the wars and insurrections and the time of God's redemption at the end (cf. v. 28). A new discourse tag ("then he said to them") sets off verses 10-11 somewhat from the preceding verses. Verses 10-11 briefly suggest a rising crescendo of turmoil. It is possible to understand these verses as a description of the time leading up to the Jewish-Roman war, for even the "great signs from heaven" correspond to signs in the sky recorded by Josephus (a star resembling a sword; a comet; cf. Josephus *J. W.* 6 §289). However, it is also possible to understand the disturbances in verses 10-11 as encompassing the whole time up to the end, connecting the "great signs from heaven" with the description in verses 25-27. That would explain why verse

12 begins "before all this." This strong temporal marker indicates that the persecutions about to be described are not signs of the imminent end.

In the eschatological material in 17:22-37, Jesus' instruction about the coming of the Son of Man is interrupted when he says, "But first he [the Son of Man] must endure much suffering and be rejected" (17:25). "Before all this" in 21:12 corresponds to "but first" in 17:25. Part of the point is that there is no easy road from here to the fulfillment; the only path leads through suffering—of Jesus in 17:25, and of the disciples in 21:12-19 (cf. also Acts 14:22). According to the Lukan portrait, the disciples have premature expectations of final salvation and are unprepared to suffer. The two failings go together, for if redemption is almost here, there is no time or need to suffer (cf. Tannehill 1986, 257-62).

In verse 12 "they will arrest you" is literally "they will lay on you their hands." The same expression is used of the desire to arrest Jesus in 20:19, and it will be used when Jesus' followers are seized in Acts 4:3; 5:18; 12:1; 21:27. It will also be the fate of both Jesus and his followers to be "handed over" (using the verb *paradidōmi*) to the authorities (Jesus in Luke 9:44; 18:32; 24:7; followers of Jesus in Luke 21:12, 16; Acts 21:11; 28:17). The reference to testimony before kings and governors in verses 12-13 anticipates scenes in Acts, for Paul will speak before governors and a king in Acts 24–26. The reference in verse 15 to wisdom that others cannot withstand is illustrated by Acts 6:10 (Stephen). Thus this section of Luke serves as a preview of the narrative of Acts and also hints at a theme that will be more broadly developed there, namely, that the sufferings of Jesus' witnesses correspond to those of Jesus (cf. Tannehill 1990, 68-72, 99-100, 264-66).

The reference to "synagogues," on the one hand, and "governors," on the other, shows that disciples will be at risk before both Jewish and Gentile authorities. The disciples are not to practice giving a polished defense speech beforehand, the way Greek and Roman orators did, for their speech and thought will be assisted by a power beyond themselves. In 12:11-12 this power was identified as the Holy Spirit; in 21:14-15 it is Jesus. Interrogation by officials is to be used as "an opportunity to testify," that is, to witness to

Jesus as Messiah and Lord. (In the Greek v. 13 is rather cryptic, but the NRSV offers the most likely interpretation.) Disciples who are arrested, even if they have no training as orators (cf. Acts 4:13), are encouraged to believe that their witness can be effective through Jesus' power. In verse 16 conflict with family because of loyalty to Jesus, a theme previously presented in Luke 8:19-21; 9:59-62; 12:51-53; 14:26, appears in sharp form. Disciples will actually be "betrayed" (or "handed over" for punishment) by close relatives and friends.

The statement, in verse 16, that some will be put to death does not fit easily with verses 18-19. It is possible that the saying in verse 18 is being stretched to include preservation after death. In verse 19 the term translated "souls" could refer to their "lives." (The word *psyche* is translated as "life" in 6:9; 9:24; 12:22-23; 14:26; 17:33 in the NRSV.) It is possible that both present and future life are encompassed by verse 19. That is, forthright witness and endurance of suffering may result in acquittal; if instead, death results, one's life is still preserved. In verse 19 there is strong manuscript evidence for an imperative instead of a future verb. ("By your endurance gain your souls" or "lives.")

In verse 8 the Lukan audience was warned against some people who claim that "the time is near." The same Greek verb *(engizo)* reappears in verse 20, but there it is the desolation of Jerusalem that "has come near." Only with the events of verses 25-27 are we told that "your redemption is drawing near" (v. 28, again using *engizo*). The eschatological discourse acknowledges that there have been premature expectations of final salvation. However, the author of Luke and its intended audience already knew about the destruction of Jerusalem, and the eschatological discourse leaves the relation between the destruction of Jerusalem and the coming of Jesus, Son of Man, unclear. (Verses 25-27 are connected to the preceding by a simple "and" in the Greek.) Thus the possibility is left open that now, after the destruction of Jerusalem, the Son of Man could appear at any time. Eschatological expectation has not died (cf. Carroll 1988, 103-19).

Evidence of prior knowledge of the destruction of Jerusalem by the author of Luke and its intended audience appears when we compare verses 20-24 with Mark 13:14-20 (and Matt 24:15-22, which remains close to Mark at this point). Some have argued that Luke's version is heavily influenced by scripture and describes things that are typical of the siege and conquest of an ancient city; Luke, therefore, need not be looking back on the actual conquest (cf. Dodd 1968, 69-83). However, one must ask why the author of Luke did not find the Marcan version satisfactory. Mark refers to "the desolating sacrilege" mentioned in Dan 9:27; 11:31; 12:11. Here the focus is on the desecration of the sanctuary. However, whatever desecration took place was incidental to the burning of the temple and city, and the later razing of the stone buildings (cf. Josephus *J.W.* 6 §232-7 §1). The author of Luke preferred an account that fit better what was widely known: that the Romans had laid siege to the city, conquered it, and destroyed it (see the details in 19:43-44). Describing known events with scriptural language was an effective way of declaring that prophecy has been fulfilled (cf. v. 22).

A fortified city is meant to be a refuge from enemy forces, but if it is finally conquered, it becomes a death trap. Hence the orders to flee in verse 21. The phrase "days of vengeance" in verse 22 probably comes from Hos 9:7, recalling this and other scriptural threats of divine punishment. The reference in verse 23 to pregnant women and women with nursing infants, who would find it difficult to flee, adds pathos (cf. also the weeping women and their children in 23:27-31). The narrator is aware that historical judgment, which often involves communal catastrophe, falls on the innocent as well as the guilty. The NRSV says, "distress on the earth," but it would be better to translate "distress on the land." This distress, in contrast to verses 25-26, is limited to a particular land and a particular people. The first half of verse 24 resembles Jer 20:4-6; 21:7. Reminders of Jeremiah would be natural, for the destruction of Jerusalem in his time provided a biblical precedent for the later destruction. (Josephus drew a parallel between the two destructions, claiming that the temple was burned on the very day of the year that the Babylonians had done the same; cf. *J.W.* 6 §250, 268).

That Jerusalem or the sanctuary has been or will be "trampled on" is a repeated theme in ancient Jewish writings, with Zech 12:3 LXX and *Pss. Sol.* 17:22 being, perhaps, the closest to Luke 21:24

(cf. also Isa 63:18; Dan 8:13; 1 Macc 3:45, 51; 2 *Baruch* 67:2). This trampling of Jerusalem will last only "until the times of the Gentiles are fulfilled." We are not told explicitly what will happen then, but if we return to the other texts that speak of this trampling, we find the expectation that Jerusalem will be restored. Zechariah 12:1-9 is an oracle of salvation for Jerusalem, and *Pss. Sol.* 17:21-25 is a prayer that the Messiah may come to rescue Jerusalem (cf. also Isa 65:17-25; Dan 8:14; 1 Macc 4:36-60; 2 *Baruch* 68:1-5; and cf. Chance 1988, 133-38). Furthermore, Acts 3:21 indicates that the "times of restoration of all that God spoke" through the prophets (my literal translation) can still come to the people of Jerusalem.

These observations also have a bearing on the interpretation of "your redemption" in verse 28. Although this is normally understood as a reference to the redemption of Jesus' followers, it is important to remember that Jesus in Luke is speaking both to the disciples and to the people of Jerusalem. The word "redemption" *(apolytrōsis)* is formed on a stem that elsewhere in Luke–Acts is consistently used of the redemption of the Jewish people or Jerusalem (cf. Luke 1:68; 2:38; 24:21; Acts 7:35). In Luke 2:38 the prophet Anna speaks specifically of the redemption of Jerusalem. Noting this thematic connection, there are two options for interpretation: (1) There is a twist in the narrative, for the redemption expected for Jerusalem is actually given to the community of Jesus. However, if the Lukan hope stops there, it is difficult to understand why the narrator portrayed Zechariah and Anna as inspired prophets in 1:67-68 and 2:36-38, since they turn out to be mistaken. (2) The redemption in 21:28 is not only for the disciples but also for the Jewish people and their sacred city Jerusalem. In this case, the statement "your redemption is drawing near" balances the statement "its [Jerusalem's] desolation has come near" (v. 20). I favor the second option.

The Coming of the Son of Man (21:25-28)

In verses 25-28 the Lukan Jesus moves on from the upheaval of a war that will primarily affect the Jewish homeland to an upheaval that will affect all people and the cosmos. As noted above, verse 25 is connected with the preceding discourse by a simple "and" in the Greek, leaving the temporal relation to preceding events unclear (see, however, v. 32). The final events sketched in verses 25-27 have no necessary connection with the destruction of Jerusalem. This is true in spite of the fact that the reference to "signs" in verse 25 picks up the request in verse 7 for a sign indicating when the temple will be destroyed. The scope of the discourse expands beyond this initial request. The only things explicitly recognized as "signs" are "from heaven" (v. 11) or concern the heavenly bodies (v. 25). Luke 21:25 abbreviates Mark 13:24-25. The Marcan text probably shows what is assumed in Luke: The signs consist of the sun and moon losing their light and the stars falling from the sky, or similar indications of cosmic dissolution. Prophetic texts like Isa 13:10; 34:4; Ezek 32:7-8; and Joel 2:10, 30-31 provide the source of these expectations. Similar ideas are behind the statement that "the powers of the heavens will be shaken" in verse 26 (cf. Hag 2:6, 21 for cosmic shaking).

The signs of cosmic disruption in the sky and sea have an effect on the whole human world, causing distress and fear. ("People will faint from fear" may be a correct translation, but the verb *apopsychō* basically means "stop breathing" and sometimes refers to dying.) Most people will be terribly afraid, for their concerns and interests tie them to the world that is disintegrating. In contrast, Jesus in verse 28 tells his audience that they are to greet what is happening courageously and eagerly. Rather than cringing in fear they are to "stand up" (literally, "straighten up," as from a bent position) "and raise your heads." These events are not bad news but good, for they mean "your redemption is drawing near." Here we see that a main function of the eschatological discourse is to provide encouragement in difficult times through maintaining hope in the realization of God's saving purpose.

Redemption is associated with the coming of the Son of Man. The picture of "the Son of Man coming in a cloud" is drawn from Dan 7:13. There the Son of Man comes to God to receive royal power. As used in the synoptic Gospels, however, the coming is a coming to earth (cf. Acts 1:9-11) after receiving royal power from

God. In Luke the coming of the Son of Man with power and glory is equivalent to the final realization on earth of the Messiah's rule. The close connection with kingship, present in Daniel, is not forgotten in Luke, for the coming of the Son of Man will also mean the coming of the "kingdom of God" (v. 31), in which Jesus Messiah will rule in God's name.

The Parable of the Fig Tree (21:29-33)

The simile of the tree putting forth leaves in the spring shows that certain things are recognized as authentic signs of the imminent coming of the Son of Man. To this extent, the previous emphasis on a sudden and unexpected coming (as in 12:39-40) is being modified. However, "these things" in verse 31, the authentic signs, probably refer to the cosmic signs in verses 25-26, while verses 8, 9, and 12 indicate that events up through verse 24 are not to be reckoned as signs of the imminent end of the old world. Probably the true signs had not yet appeared, according to the author. Yet the retention of verse 32 from Mark 13:30 (cf. Matt 24:34) encourages the audience to expect the glorious Son of Man rather soon. Various attempts have been made to interpret "this generation" to mean something other than the people living at the same time as Jesus. It is true that *genea* can mean a clan (i.e., a group that comes from a common ancestor) as well as a chronological generation, but the former meaning does not yield good sense in the context. Since no one was asserting that either the Jews or humanity in general (possible identifications of "this clan" in v. 32) would pass away before the end, denying this (emphatically) is not a meaningful statement. Therefore, "this generation" must be the one living at the time of Jesus, some of whom, presumably, were still alive at the time of the writing of Luke.

Concluding Exhortation (21:34-38)

The eschatological discourse ends with exhortation, showing that its prime purpose is to instill a particular style of life before the end. Verses 34-35 warn of certain dangers, and verse 36 shows what is needed to avoid those dangers. "Dissipation" (or "carousing") and "drunkenness" go together. They can represent the life in which short-term pleasures control, dulling awareness of the call to the kingdom. The parable in 12:42-46 provides an example. "The worries" (or "cares") "of this life" weigh the heart down when the need for possessions and social approval controls one's thinking and acting (cf. 8:14). Such people are unprepared for "that day." To avoid disaster, one must "be alert" (or "keep awake") "at all times" (cf. 12:35-46). This alertness requires constant awareness of the gifts and demands of the Lord so that these will guide one's life, making one ready for the Lord's coming. Such alertness results, in part, from prayer, which is here given a specific focus: "strength to escape all these things that will take place." (The last phrase recalls v. 7; thus the section is rounded off by returning to the beginning.) The persecutions and upheavals are potentially dangerous, but not for those who remain alert. *Standing* before the Son of Man is the opposite of cringing or bowing down in shame (cf. *1 Enoch* 62:7-10). Compare the upright posture in verse 28. Standing shows the confidence of the faithful servant who trusts and obeys the Lord.

◊ ◊ ◊ ◊ ◊

The eschatological discourse reflects experiences of disappointment and loss. Some people have said, "The time is near," when it was not. The mission had encountered persecution rather than joyful acceptance, and the worship center of the covenant people had been destroyed. This discourse also reflects the resilience of the early church's hope in spite of these experiences of disappointment and loss. Their hopes and desires were focused on the coming of Jesus as Son of Man in power and glory (v. 27) to fully establish the kingdom of God (v. 31). This hope separated them from the surrounding culture and helped them to live a different style of life (vv. 34-36).

The summary of Jesus' activity in verses 37-38 brings Jesus' temple teaching to an end by reminding hearers of the introduction to this teaching in 19:47-48. The threat from the religious leaders is not repeated because that is reserved for 22:2, where it helps to introduce the narrative's climactic stage.

The Rejection and Death of the Messiah (22:1–23:56)

Judas and the Plot Against Jesus (22:1-6)

The festivals of Unleavened Bread and Passover overlap. They begin with the removal of all leaven from houses and the slaughter of the Passover lambs in the temple on Nisan 14, followed by the feast of Passover in family groups that evening (Nisan 15). The festival of Unleavened Bread continues for a week (cf. Exod 12:1-28; Deut 16:1-8). Time indicators show the importance of this Passover feast, for the narrator carefully notes that it is "near" (v. 1), then that "the day" of Passover sacrifice had come (v. 7), followed by "the hour" for the meal (v. 14).

Since 19:47-48 the chief priests and scribes have wanted to get rid of Jesus but have been unable to act because of support for Jesus from the people. Judas now provides the opportunity for these powerful opponents to locate Jesus apart from the crowd so that he can be arrested without protest. Judas is "one of the twelve" (v. 3), we are reminded. The betrayer is someone very close to Jesus who breaks their relationship of friendship and trust. This will be emphasized further in verses 21-22 and 48; it is a cause of bitterness. There is no explanation of Judas's motive, but money is involved. The narrator will complete the story of Judas in Acts 1:16-20 by telling of his sudden and gory death after purchasing a field with the money. The word translated "betray" in verses 4 and 6 is *paradidōmi*, which basically means to give over or deliver, in this case, into the power of Jesus' enemies, resulting in his death. It is an important theme word in the passion prophecies and passion story (cf. 9:44; 18:32; 22:21-22, 48). Not only Judas but also Pilate and the Jerusalem religious leaders have a role in giving over Jesus to death, for the same word is applied to them in 23:25 and 24:20.

Satan, as well as Judas, is active in these events, according to verse 3. After being empowered for his mission, Jesus encountered the devil (4:1-13). Having defeated him on that occasion, Jesus could demonstrate his power over Satan (cf. 10:17-18; 11:20-22; 13:16; Acts 10:38). In the passion story, however, Satan mounts a full-scale counterattack. It will be felt both by the disciples (22:31-32) and by Jesus (22:53). The devil is the enemy of faith (8:12). One of the questions in the passion story is whether faith can endure Satan's worst attack (cf. Neyrey 1985, 31).

Preparation for the Passover Meal (22:7-13)

A surprising amount of attention is given here (and in Matt 26:17-19; Mark 14:12-16) to arrangements for the Passover meal. The story line may imply secrecy; only two disciples are involved, and they are not told directly where to go. They must meet a guide. The purpose, presumably, would be to prevent Judas and the authorities from knowing in advance where Jesus will be. The story does not make clear whether Jesus' statement that someone with a water jar would guide them is the result of prophetic foreknowledge or whether Jesus had made prior arrangements.

There is a significant change in verse 8, compared to the other synoptic Gospels. Rather than being asked by the disciples about arrangements, Jesus takes the initiative. Furthermore, the two disciples sent by Jesus are named: Peter and John. There is no indication that other disciples are present. The choice of Peter and John for this task is probably significant. Peter, John, and James have been privileged witnesses to certain events (cf. 8:51; 9:28). After Pentecost, Peter and John will appear together as leaders of the early mission (cf. Acts 3:1, 3, 4, 11; 4:13, 19; 8:14). Peter is the leading spokesman, and John is his principal supporting witness. Thus, in Luke, the two apostles who will be the principal leaders in the early church are selected to prepare the Passover meal. This choice fits nicely with the instructions to the apostles at the meal. According to 22:24-27, the apostles, who will be the church's first leaders, must act like table servants (cf. Schürmann 1970, 275-76). Jesus gives Peter and John practice by asking them to prepare the Passover meal.

The Farewell Meal (22:14-23)

22:14-20: The reference in verse 14 to "the hour" highlights this Passover meal as a time of special significance. In Luke the Last

Supper scene is expanded (compared to Matt 26:20-29 and Mark 14:17-25) with additional discourse by Jesus. It becomes the setting for a farewell discourse that extends to verse 38. "He took his place at the table" is literally "he reclined," that is, stretched out on a couch, the position at a formal banquet. "The apostles," that is, the twelve, were "with him." It is not clear whether this implies that only Jesus and the apostles were present. (For argument to the contrary, see Quesnell 1983, 59-79.) Attention focuses on the apostles at this point because they will take over as leaders of the mission and fellowship when Jesus departs. In receiving the cup and bread, they represent the whole community that they will guide.

Jesus' statement in verse 15 emphasizes the importance of Passover to Jesus. The Passover setting of the meal should not be ignored. Passover—a solemn act of remembrance of God's liberation of an oppressed people, leading to thanksgiving in the present and hope for the future (cf. *m. Pesah.* 10:5)—contributes to the meaning of the Lord's Supper. However, it is not certain that Jesus, according to Luke, did eat this last Passover with the apostles, for verse 16 can be understood as a statement that he will not eat (cf. also v. 18). The best manuscript witnesses to verse 16 do not include the word "again." Therefore, Jesus' remark can be understood to exclude his eating of the present meal.

Although this is a minority view, there is more evidence to support it than is usually recognized. In Matt 26:29 and Mark 14:25 we find an assertion similar to Luke 22:16, 18, but it is placed after the sharing of the bread and cup. In Luke the declarations of abstinence are placed before the actual eating and as Jesus passes the first cup. Furthermore, the words about the betrayer, which come before the bread and cup in Matthew and Mark, are placed after it in Luke, and the Lukan version avoids the references in Matthew and Luke to Jesus eating with the betrayer, substituting instead the statement that the betrayer's "hand" is "with me on the table" (v. 21, translating literally). The view that Jesus, according to Luke, abstained from the meal and the wine explains two more points: (1) "For" at the beginning of verse 18 makes little sense on the usual understanding. However, if "among yourselves" in verse 17 means "among you and not me," then "for" makes sense. Verse

18 explains that Jesus is not sharing in the cup that he is distributing to the rest. (2) We can also explain why Jesus emphasizes his eager desire to eat the Passover in verse 15. His desire is so strong because it is a frustrated desire; he cannot eat. Yet he wants the apostles to know that he would gladly share the meal with them if his actions now were not controlled by an overriding need.

If we follow this line of interpretation, verses 16 and 18 are avowals of abstinence from the meal. Why would Jesus do this? Such avowals or vows could be made both as a sign of strong determination to complete a task, which must be completed before food is again eaten (cf. the oath in Acts 23:12-14), or as part of an urgent petition to God. In the former case, the renunciation would be a sign of strong determination to carry through with the harsh destiny of suffering and death before him; in the latter case, the object of prayer is best taken from verses 16 and 18 themselves. It would be prayer for the coming of the kingdom, or, as verse 16 suggests, for the fulfillment of the Passover in the messianic meal of the kingdom of God (cf. further Jeremias 1966, 207-18).

In verse 18 Jesus declares that the renunciation will last "until the kingdom of God comes." Were the author of Luke and the Lukan communities still waiting for this, or had the kingdom already come? The answer in Luke–Acts is not very clear. Jesus' resurrection and enthronement at God's right hand (cf. Acts 2:29-36) could be understood as the next phase in the coming of the kingdom, and Luke 22:29-30 and Acts 10:41, taken together, might support the view that the risen Jesus is eating and drinking in the kingdom. But it is doubtful that Luke 22:29-30 refers to the time of Acts (see below), and Acts 10:41 does not clearly establish that Jesus has been released from his promises (which were, specifically, to abstain from the Passover and wine until God's kingdom comes).

There is another unusual feature to the Lukan Last Supper. The text as translated in the NRSV refers to sharing a cup, then bread, then another cup. Four cups of wine were used in the Passover meal, but it is not clear that this explains the sequence in Luke. The matter is complicated by textual variations, including a shorter text that many earlier scholars preferred, which, after "This is my body" omits the rest of verse 19 and all of verse 20. The earlier editions of the RSV followed this short reading, which eliminates the second cup and also the suggestions of vicarious benefits through Jesus' death (cf. "for you" in vv. 19 and 20). The number and general quality of the manuscripts with the long reading give it much stronger support than the short reading. This is seldom the only factor in decisions about text, but it is probably decisive in this case. Therefore, I will follow the text translated in the NRSV. (For further discussion see Metzger 1971, 173-77.)

The words with the bread and cup in verses 19-20 resemble most closely those in the Lord's Supper ritual in 1 Cor 11:23-25, while there are significant differences from Matt 26:26-28 and Mark 14:22-24. The first cup (v. 17) could be understood as simply one of the cups of the Passover meal, not part of the Christian Eucharist, but that may dismiss it too easily. So far as we know, drinking from a single cup was not the normal practice (cf. Nolland 1993, 1048). Sharing a single cup may be intended to strengthen the fellowship. Furthermore, the giving of thanks and the command "take" match language used in Mark with the eucharistic bread and cup (cf. Nolland 1993, 1051). The first cup already has a eucharistic aspect even though the word of interpretation is reserved for the second cup.

The four actions in verse 19—taking bread, giving thanks, breaking it, and giving it—parallel Jesus' actions in feeding the five thousand (9:16) and at the Emmaus meal (24:30), except that those verses substitute "blessed" for giving thanks. Jesus shared other meals with his followers, and the Last Supper continues those fellowship meals. On this occasion, however, the bread distributed is identified as "my body, which is given for you." The giving of Jesus' body refers forward to Jesus' death and assigns the benefits of that death to Jesus' assembled followers. Jesus' action is to be repeated (the Greek present imperative means "keep doing this"), which will enable others to share in these benefits. Sharing the bread that is Jesus' body is an act of remembrance, just as the Passover is "a day of remembrance" (Exod 12:14; cf. Deut 16:3; *m. Pesah.* 10:5). Since the bread "is my body," a vivid form of remembrance is intended—a kind of presence of the crucified and risen Lord.

The bread and second cup are separated by the eating of the meal ("after supper"), as in 1 Cor 11:25. Instead of saying "This is my blood of the covenant," as in Matt 26:28 and Mark 14:24, in Luke Jesus says, "This cup . . . is the new covenant in my blood." This puts the emphasis on "covenant"; blood is the subsidiary means by which the covenant is established. The hope for a new covenant was encouraged by Jer 31:31-34. The reference to blood, however, indicates that the memory of the Mosaic covenant is still alive, for that covenant was ratified by sprinkling blood on the altar and on the people (Exod 24:6-8). In the context of Luke–Acts, the new covenant established by Jesus' death would mean Israel renewed through its Messiah and open to the Gentiles, so that God's promise of "salvation" for "all flesh" (Luke 3:6) may be fulfilled.

The phrase "that is poured out for you" comes at the end of the sentence in the Greek, but the grammatical case shows that it describes the cup rather than the blood, as the NRSV indicates. This reference to a cup poured out raises the possibility that the second cup is a libation, or drink offering, similar to what the priests would give to God, pouring it out at the temple altar (cf. Sir 50:15; on drink offerings see also Num 28:7-9, 14, 24), just as basins of sacrificial blood were poured out there (Lev 4:18, 25, 30, 34). Perhaps we are to assume that a portion of the wine was poured out as an offering to God and the rest was drunk by the apostles. Or the second cup may not have been drunk at all. ("He did the same with the cup" may mean taking and giving thanks only. Presumably Jesus did not break the cup as he broke the bread, and he may not have given it to be drunk.)

The pouring out of the cup is, again, "for you." Sacrificial ideas are in play here, but the relevant background may be less an atoning sacrifice than a covenant-founding sacrifice, as in Exod 24:6-8. That Jesus' death, resurrection, and enthronement are saving events is clear in Luke–Acts, but there is a remarkable absence of the proclamation that Jesus' death in particular—because it is atonement—is a saving event. This is never claimed in the Acts mission speeches, and Mark 10:45 is omitted in Luke. Only Acts 20:28 (not in a mission speech) may add to Luke 22:20 a reference to the benefits of Jesus' blood. The peculiarly Lukan understanding of

Jesus' death should not be drawn from Luke 22:19-20, but the inclusion of the words over the bread and cup (assuming the longer text) shows that the author was not opposed to the rich imagery attached to Jesus' death through the Lord's Supper.

22:21-23: A strong "but" *(plēn)* introduces the words about the betrayer in verses 21-22. In spite of the covenant relation represented by the bread and cup, the bond of loyalty is being broken by one who is about to "hand over" Jesus *(paradidōmi;* NRSV: "betray"). The fact that he is a trusted companion and shares this meal makes it all the worse. In 18:31 Jesus said that everything "written about the Son of Man by the prophets will be accomplished." The statement in Luke 22:22*a* is basically the same. There Jesus speaks of what "has been determined" by God, and scripture is the fundamental witness to God's plan. The verb *horizō* ("determine") reappears in Acts with reference to divine determination and the divine plan (cf. Acts 2:23; 10:42; 17:26, 31). Jesus is following a divine destiny that includes his death in Jerusalem, but the woe pronounced in verse 22 shows that the one through whom he is arrested is not excused. In Mark 14:18-19 the announcement that one of the twelve will betray Jesus leads them to search their own hearts, asking, "Surely, not I?" According to Luke they simply ask who it could be. This permits us to think that, rather than examining themselves, they are searching for the villain among the other members of the group. Then the conversation of the apostles moves from suspicion of others to claims of greatness for oneself (v. 24), including the claim of outstanding loyalty to Jesus.

The Farewell Discourse (22:24-38)

The Lukan Last Supper scene continues with a discourse that lasts through verse 38. The additional discourse material, not found in this location in Matthew or Mark, develops the scene in the direction of a farewell or testamentary discourse. In a farewell discourse, an honored person who is near death speaks to family or associates about his past life and about the future, with warnings and exhortations to his successors concerning the problems and responsibilities they will face. (For comparison of Luke 22:14-38 with Jewish and Greco-Roman farewell discourses, see Kurz 1985, 251-68, and Nelson 1994, 97-119.) Succession in leadership is an issue that arises in such a context, and verses 25-30 relate to this issue. In the Markan parallel to verses 25-27, found not at the Last Supper but at Mark 10:42-45, Jesus' instructions are addressed to the one who "wishes to become great among you"; in Luke they are addressed to "the greatest among you" and "the leader." That is, in Luke, Jesus is not regulating ambitious striving for advancement but the behavior of people who already are, or soon will be, in the positions of leadership. The apostles' future authority is clearly indicated in verses 29-30. The question, then, is: How should the apostles, and the leaders of the church who will succeed them, behave?

Future Leaders Dispute About Greatness (22:24-27)

A dispute about greatness (v. 24) arose previously in 9:46-48. Its reappearance at the Last Supper shows that it is a continuing problem with the apostles and an important issue for the church, an issue that can be handled most effectively in light of Jesus' death.

Reputation and honor are highlighted in verse 25 by referring to what Gentile rulers "are called." "Benefactor" is a title that could be formally conferred on a ruler or an outstanding citizen by a city council or other body in recognition for some outstanding service to the community. In the ancient Mediterranean world, in which honor was very important (on honor as a cultural value, see Malina and Neyrey in Neyrey 1991, 25-65), power and wealth could be used to gain honor by giving benefits to those groups in a position to grant public honors. This sort of exchange was also a major feature of the patron-client system. A wealthy patron would give benefits to a group of clients. They, in turn, were expected to praise the patron and generally contribute to his public honor (on patron-client relations, see Moxnes in Neyrey 1991, 241-68).

In verse 26 this status system is rejected. There the greatest is asked to "become like the youngest, and the leader like one who serves." In a society that honors elders, the youngest are those who lack honor (recall the child introduced by Jesus in 9:46-48). Likewise, "one who serves" means someone who has the role and status of a servant, that is, very low status. Serving here does not have the general sense of contributing to the communal good. The "benefactors" were doing that and gained honor thereby; servants did not. The status distinction is made quite clear in verse 27a, where the dinner guest is contrasted with the servant who waits on the table. (Here the message is adapted to the meal setting.) When Jesus in Luke says that the leader should become like the servant, he is not just saying that the leader should act for the communal good. Nor is he advocating weak leadership. The point, rather, is that the necessary function of leadership is not to be regarded as a source of honor. The leader is to have no more honor in the community than the youngest or the servant. This would be a radical departure from prevailing expectations (cf. Nelson 1994, 49). Yet failure of leaders to adopt this new attitude would allow rivalry to divide the community, as demonstrated in verse 24. No doubt these instructions were as relevant to the leaders of Lukan communities as to the apostles in the Lukan narrative.

At the end of verse 27 Jesus points to the model of his own serving in order to convince his hearers. He could be referring to his life and mission in general. He could be referring to something done in the Last Supper scene, although there is no indication that he prepared and served the meal. Probably the most convincing proof that he is among them as a servant is his coming death. His words over the bread and cup (vv. 19-20) represent his death as a death "for you." Jesus' death not only benefits the community, it also degrades Jesus to the lowest of the low. The accusation scenes and crucifixion are social instruments for degrading Jesus in the eyes of others (cf. Malina and Rohrbaugh 1992, 406-8). Jesus "serves" in that he suffers dishonor in order that others might share in the kingdom. Such service without regard to status will continue to mark Jesus' character even in the time of fulfillment (cf. 12:37).

The Apostles' Role in the Messiah's Kingdom (22:28-30)

The shortcomings of the apostles are apparent in verse 24, and they will be revealed further as the passion story develops. But those failings are not the apostles' whole story. In verses 28-30 Jesus commends them for their loyalty during the trials of his ministry and speaks of their future. The future that he promises them indicates that humbly refusing to be honored will lead to being exalted in Jesus' kingdom, which follows the rule that Jesus established in 14:11 and 18:14.

In verse 29 Jesus announces a solemn decision. The word *basileia,* translated "kingdom" in the NRSV, can also be translated "royal power." Jesus is promising the apostles a share in his royal power. The verb translated "confer" *(diatithemai)* is related to the noun for "covenant" or "testament" *(diathēkē)* and can mean "make a covenant" or "assign by a will." Against the latter sense it has been objected that it cannot apply when the same verb is used with God as subject in verse 29. However, "assign by a will" is a common, specialized application of the basic meaning of "decree" or "assign," an application that will come into play when the context is appropriate. In the case of Jesus, the context here is appropriate. As part of his farewell discourse, he assigns to his apostles a share in the royal rule promised him by God, and Jesus' death will be instrumental in realizing that royal rule. One can also understand this as a covenant with the apostles that is a special aspect of the new covenant established by Jesus' death (cf. v. 20).

Sharing Jesus' royal power is divided in verse 30 into two privileges: dining at the king's table and sitting on thrones as the king's governors. (The word "judging" *[krinontes]* can have the broad sense of "governing," as in the Greek texts of Ps 2:10; 2 Kgs 15:5; 1 Macc 9:73; *Pss. Sol.* 17:29; this function is the result of the grant of royal power in v. 29.) There is some uncertainty about the time to which these promises refer. On the one hand, Acts 10:41 claims that the apostles ate and drank with the risen Messiah, and the apostles are recognized as authorities in the early church. Thus there may be a partial realization of these promises at that time. However, the expectation that the apostles will be "judging the twelve tribes of Israel" exceeds anything achieved in Acts. In Luke–Acts, "Israel" refers to the Jewish people, and "the twelve tribes of Israel" are the Jewish people in their restored wholeness. The twelve tribes have not been restored, and Jewish resistance in Acts prevents the apostles from functioning as governors of the whole Jewish people. The meals mentioned in Acts 10:41 do not eliminate the future messianic meal, and the role of governors of all Israel requires a future, eschatological fulfillment.

◊ ◊ ◊ ◊

The special honor denied the apostles in verses 26-27 appears to be reinstated in verses 29-30. However, according to 12:32 the kingdom *(basileia)* will be given to all of Jesus' flock, and elsewhere the faithful are promised that they will share in the eschatological reign (cf. Dan 7:18, 27; 1 Cor 6:2-3; 2 Tim 2:12; Rev 1:9; 3:21, and Nelson 1994, 241). These promises balance the prominence given the apostles in verses 29-30.

Satan's Attack on the Weak Apostles (22:31-38)

Although the apostles will sit on thrones, the immediate prospect is quite different. They were unable to understand Jesus' passion prophecy in 18:31-34, and they are unprepared for what lies ahead. Satan begins to work through Judas in 22:3. The other apostles must endure Satan's sifting; that is, they will be shaken up so as to reveal the chaff that is still mixed with the good grain. They will miss their last chance to escape Satan's testing when they fail to pray in 22:39-46.

22:31-34: "All of you" in verse 31 is the NRSV translation for "you" (plural) in the Greek, to distinguish it from "you" (singular), which is used consistently in verse 32. Jesus counters Satan's move against the apostles by focusing on Simon Peter. Jesus has prayed that Simon's faith will not give out, in spite of the sifting, and this prayer will be effective. As a result, Peter will be able to turn back and then strengthen his brothers. The "brothers" are the other apostles (perhaps other disciples as well), who will badly need strengthening. When Jesus speaks of Peter turning back, a word *(epistrephō)* is used that refers in Acts to conversion and repentance (Acts 3:19; 9:35; 11:21; 14:15; 15:19; 26:18, 20). Peter will need to repent because he will deny Jesus (cf. v. 34). Although Peter most clearly fails to be faithful, he will have the leading role in strengthening the others. That role will be performed in Acts 1–5, where

Peter will take the initiative in renewing the twelve and will become the chief spokesman and leading interpreter of scripture and of God's acts through Jesus.

The dialogue in verses 33-34 calls attention in advance to Peter's denial (vv. 54-62). Jesus' authoritative prophecy in verse 34 would tell members of the Lukan audience (even those who may not have heard the story before) that Peter speaks falsely in verse 33. He claims to be ready to suffer, but he is not. Later, he will be. In verse 33 we find a reference to going to prison that differs from Matt 26:33-35 and Mark 14:29-31. Peter will go to prison in Acts 5:18 and 12:3-4. Through cowardly denial, Peter will escape arrest and interrogation by the Sanhedrin in Luke 22, but in Acts 4–5 Peter will speak courageously when arrested and interrogated by the same group. Jesus' warnings in Luke 12:4-5, 9 show that Peter's denial is no petty weakness, but Jesus' prayer is more powerful than Satan's plot or Peter's sin.

22:35-38: The dialogue in verses 35-38, which concludes the farewell discourse, cannot be understood as an isolated unit, for verse 35 refers to the earlier mission instructions, and one of the swords that appear in verse 38 will be used in verses 49-50. The lack of purse, bag, and sandals, recalled in verse 35, fits the mission instructions to the seventy(-two) in 10:4, but only the bag is explicitly mentioned in the mission instructions to the twelve (9:1-5). Perhaps the two sets of instructions have merged in the mind of the narrator (and assumed audience) by now.

The apostles confirm that, despite the lack of normal necessities for travel, their needs were met through the hospitality of those who welcomed them. Their response also confirms the teaching of Jesus in 12:22-31 that disciples need not worry about food and clothing, for God would care for them. For some reason, however, Jesus announces in verse 36 that the situation has changed ("But now . . . "). It is unlikely that verse 36 is meant as a permanent change in Jesus' mission instructions. It is hard to understand why the narrator would give so much attention to the earlier mission instructions (doubling them in instructions to the twelve and the seventy) if they do not have at least some general relevance to the continuing mission of the church. Although verse 36 reflects a situation of danger and persecution, Jesus' previous instructions on how to respond to persecution (cf. 12:4-7; 21:12-19) fit poorly with the statements here. Here Jesus says that the apostles must prepare either for flight or fighting.

There is an ambiguity in the instruction about the sword. The Greek begins, "And the one who does not have," then an object must be supplied. The NRSV supplies "sword" from the end of the sentence, but one could just as well supply "a purse and bag" from the previous sentence. Then those without resources for flight are being told to buy a sword, even if it requires selling one's cloak. There is a strong tendency for interpreters to say that Jesus did not mean this literally. However, even if we take "sword" as a metaphor, the implications are disturbing. Jesus is not just saying that there is danger; he is telling the apostles how to respond to the danger. Even when taken metaphorically, the instruction about the sword says that the apostles must defend themselves at any cost to themselves and others.

Why would Jesus (as presented in Luke) say this? He is not preparing to resist the arresting party. When one of the swords is actually used at the arrest, Jesus steps in and heals the injury (vv. 49-50); then he submits without resistance. In order to understand Jesus' strange instruction, we must take account of the setting provided by verses 31-34 and the explanation given in verse 37. The difference between the previous mission instructions and Jesus' instructions now is due to the fact that the apostles are now under Satan's influence, and this will show itself in their failure to carry through with promises of loyalty to Jesus. Promises of divine protection no longer apply, for the apostles are no longer able to trust in them. Thus they are left to their own devices, and the alternatives are fleeing or fighting. Jesus' words highlight the failure of the apostles' faith at this point in the story. They also prepare for the fulfillment of scripture, as verse 37 explains. The quotation comes from Isa 53:12 and is part of the description of the vicarious suffering of God's servant. The narrator probably knew the emphasis on vicarious suffering in this passage, but the few words chosen from it make a different point. Jesus will be executed as a criminal.

That is central to the dishonoring that he must endure. And the prophecy anticipating this event places God's servant among lawless people. The near context suggests that these are the apostles, who, because they are scared, must violently resist the authorities, as happens in verses 49-50 (cf. Minear 1964, 128-34, and Tannehill 1986, 265-68).

The view that the apostles, in their present state, are "the lawless" is a minority opinion. More common is the identification of the lawless with the two criminals crucified with Jesus. But this does not explain why Jesus would counsel the apostles to buy swords. The explanation that Jesus is speaking figuratively and the apostles misunderstand is not sufficient, for even as a metaphor the command to sell one's cloak and buy a sword makes self-defense a priority that overrides all restraint.

As it turns out, the apostles already have two swords. The effect of Jesus' command is to expose what they have already done. Jesus' final remark, "It is enough," could be an expression of disgust (Enough of this conversation!), but it may simply mean that two swords, although insufficient for resistance at Jesus' arrest, are enough to fulfill the prophecy.

Jesus' Prayer on the Mount of Olives (22:39-46)

The NRSV encloses verses 43-44 in double brackets because there is substantial doubt that they are an original part of Luke. Early manuscript witnesses lack these verses. However, there is also early support for inclusion, and it is possible to explain either addition or deletion of these verses by copyists. Thus a decision is difficult. It may be best to recognize that we have two early versions of this Lukan prayer scene. In both cases the structure of the scene is rather simple in comparison with Matt 26:36-46 and Mark 14:32-42, where Jesus prays three times and three times finds the disciples sleeping. These accounts place greater emphasis on the disciples' failure. The shorter of the two Lukan versions is frugal in detail but has a clear structure. Jesus commands the disciples to pray, gives his own prayer (which is presented without emotional embellishment), and, when he discovers the disciples sleeping, repeats his command to pray. There is a simple contrast here between Jesus' prayer and the disciples' failure to pray at the time of crisis. The addition of verses 43-44 puts dramatic emphasis on the struggle of Jesus in prayer, a feature that is largely lacking in the short version.

◊ ◊ ◊ ◊

Jesus' "custom," mentioned in verse 39, was explained in 21:37. He used to "spend the night on the Mount of Olives." Judas would know where he stayed, which explains his arrival in verse 47. Luke does not call the place of prayer "Gethsemane." As the crisis approaches, the disciples should pray that they "not come into the time of trial" (or "into temptation"; *peirasmos*). It is not entirely clear why escape from the time of trial should be the object of the disciples' prayer. Jesus himself had to endure *peirasmos* (4:13; 22:28) and is about to face his greatest time of trial. The activity of Satan in the passion story (cf. 22:3, 31, 53) may suggest that the passion is a renewal of the intense testing of Jesus by the devil reported in 4:1-13. Yet the disciples are told to pray to escape their time of trial. Perhaps Jesus urges the disciples to pray to escape this testing because he knows that they are not strong enough to face it. The desire to escape the time of trial is not wrong. Jesus already taught the disciples to pray for this in 11:4.

Jesus' prayer in verse 42 shows that he also desires to escape testing, and this prayer provides a model that the disciples should follow. God is addressed as "Father" in prayer, as in 11:2 and when Jesus prays from the cross. He prays that God might remove "this cup," which represents his lot or destiny. No one is expected to desire suffering and death, and people are to bring their desire for life and health to God. But Jesus' request is preceded and followed by acknowledgment that God's will must prevail. In some situations the divine will must be realized through suffering and death. Jesus is now in such a situation.

In the longer version there is a response to the prayer in the form of an angel, who strengthens Jesus. He is being strengthened for a prayer-struggle that continues. The word translated "anguish" (*agōnia*) can also be translated "struggle," as in an athletic contest, and the profuse sweat fits this image. This description, too, could serve as a model for prayer in time of crisis. There is need to pray intensely, but divine help is available in this struggle.

When Jesus returns, he finds that the disciples have not been praying as he commanded. Instead, they are "sleeping because of grief." Grief *(lypē)* was viewed by some ancient moralists as one of four evil passions and a sign of weakness (cf. Neyrey 1985, 50-53, 65-68). Jesus is grieved, according to Mark 14:34, but in Luke grief is attributed only to the disciples. Their sleep is a sign of moral, as well as physical, exhaustion. Their behavior clashes with Jesus' instruction in 21:36 to "be alert [or "keep awake"] at all times, praying" so that they may have "strength." Jesus repeats his command to pray, but now it is too late.

The Arrest of Jesus (22:47-53)

Jesus is interrupted by the crowd come to arrest him. The arrest scene divides into three parts: (1) Jesus and Judas (vv. 47-48); (2) Jesus and the incident with the sword (vv. 49-51); (3) Jesus' response to the arresting party (vv. 52-53).

◊ ◊ ◊ ◊

The first part highlights the contrast between what Judas has been and still pretends to be and what he is doing. In Matt 26:48 and Mark 14:44 Judas's kiss serves as a sign by which Jesus can be identified in the dark. That part of the plot is omitted in Luke. Here the kiss simply calls to mind the close relation that existed between Jesus and Judas, who as "one of the twelve" was a trusted friend, a relation that is mocked by his present act of "handing over" Jesus to his enemies. (On the kiss as a warm greeting, see 7:45; 15:20; Rom 16:16, and Brown 1994, 255.)

One of the two swords revealed in verse 38 (see the previous discussion of vv. 35-38) comes into play in verses 49-51. A group of Jesus' followers asks permission to give armed resistance. Then one of the apostles with swords strikes without waiting for an answer, severing an ear from the slave of the high priest. He had no doubt intended to do more than that. Jesus' words in verse 51 are cryptic and can be understood in more than one way, but his act of healing and his submission to arrest in verses 53-54 show his opposition to such violent resistance. The words translated "No more of this!" in the NRSV can be translated, "Let them [the arresting party] go this far," that is, as far as arresting me (cf. Marshall 1978, 837). Healing a member of the arresting party is a specific example of the love of enemies that Jesus taught in 6:27-36 and fits with the prayer of forgiveness from the cross in 23:34 (if that is an authentic part of Luke).

Jesus' words in verses 52-53 are a protest. They lead, however, not to resistance but to submission. One of Jesus' followers may act like a "bandit," but Jesus does not. The first sentence of verse 53 recalls the public teaching of Jesus, when the support of the crowd prevented the authorities from taking action against him (cf. 19:47-48; 20:19). This reminder emphasizes the fact that the authorities can only act by stealth and at night. This night is "your hour, and the power of darkness." The reference to the "power" or "authority" of darkness recalls the role of Satan behind these events (cf. 22:3, 31; cf. Acts 26:18). From this point on, Satan as well as Jesus' enemies appear to hold Jesus in their power. The deeper truth is that another power is in control and will lead these events to a surprising result (cf. Acts 2:23-24).

According to Matt 26:47 and Mark 14:43 the arresting crowd comes *from* the Jerusalem religious authorities. Luke, however, assumes in verse 52 that the authorities are themselves present. Luke omits the flight of the disciples at the end of the scene. According to 23:49 they are still around to watch the crucifixion, though only "at a distance."

Peter's Denials (22:54-62)

Peter follows Jesus "at a distance," an indication of caution and fear. After Peter is settled in the high priest's courtyard, Luke moves directly into the story of Peter's denials, while Matt 26:57-66 and Mark 14:53-64 report first Jesus' witness before the Jewish council, which will contrast with Peter's denials that follow. The last of Peter's denials is not as forceful in Luke as in Matt 26:74 and Mark 14:71, since Peter does not swear an oath in Luke. Yet Luke retains the threefold denial, which makes it so emphatic, and adds a dramatic touch at the beginning of verse 61. It is clear in Luke, as well as the other Gospels, that Peter has not only lied and broken a specific promise (cf. 22:33) but has also fundamentally broken faith with his Lord. Peter fails, but not because he was weaker than the other apostles. Peter was the one who dared to follow Jesus into the courtyard of the high priest.

The light from the fire enables the servant-girl to get a look at Peter. She addresses her accusation to the surrounding group. Before reporting his words, the narrator summarizes Peter's response with the word "deny" *(arneomai),* and in verse 61 each of Peter's three statements are labeled denials. Thus denial becomes the dominant description of Peter's actions. The seriousness of Peter's failure is underscored by the use of the same root elsewhere. In 12:9 Jesus said that the one who denies him before people will be denied before God (but see 12:10). In Acts 3:13-14 Peter will accuse the people of Jerusalem of having denied Jesus before Pilate (NRSV: "rejected"). Peter's own behavior aligns him with this larger denial, and he must "turn back" (Luke 22:32), just as he will call on the people of Jerusalem to turn in repentance.

The statement in verse 57, "I do not know him," is a clear denial of relationship. It is a clearer denial than in Matt 26:70 and Mark 14:68. The second accusation is made directly to Peter and is phrased a little differently. It leads Peter to deny being part of the group of disciples. There is a respite of an hour between the second and third accusations, enough time for hope to rise that the danger had passed. Although Peter's responses do not necessarily grow in intensity, the accusations do. The third accuser picks up the first accusation and insists upon it. The accusations are piling up as new people are won over to the servant-girl's opinion. Furthermore, the third accusation adds supporting evidence: Peter is a Galilean. Peter again denies association with Jesus, but the threat of discovery is mounting.

Then comes the dramatic moment when Peter recognizes what he has done. It is not the cock crow alone that causes the change. Luke adds, "The Lord turned and looked at Peter." Then recognition and remembrance come. What Peter remembered was "the word of the Lord," a common phrase for divine messages delivered by prophets (cf. L. T. Johnson 1991, 358). Through fulfillment of his prophetic word in verse 34, Jesus' prophetic credentials are presented just before he is mocked as a helpless prophet in verses 63-65. Peter goes out to escape danger, but he also weeps bitterly. His turn back to Jesus, anticipated in verse 32, begins with this painful recognition of failure. Peter's faith does not fail so long as there is a desire and hope for return. Further details of Peter's return are not recorded, except for brief references at 24:12, 34. Peter's transformation is part of the transformation of all the disciples through the events of Easter and Pentecost.

◊ ◊ ◊ ◊

The Lukan audience might recognize in Peter's experience a situation they might face. There are reports of authorities trying, under threat of punishment, to force believers to deny Christ, indeed, to revile him (cf. Acts 26:11; Pliny, *Letters* 10.96-97; Justin, *Apology* 1.31.6; *Martyrdom of Polycarp* 9.2-3, and Brown 1994, 625-26). This tactic was a method of social control designed to force believers to break faith with their Lord in order to escape severe punishment.

Interrogation by the Council (22:63-71)

Although Matt 26:59-66 and Mark 14:55-64 report a formal trial before the Sanhedrin with witnesses and a verdict, there are neither witnesses nor a verdict in Luke's scene, which appears to be an interrogation rather than a trial. (The Gospel of John also lacks a formal trial before Jewish authorities.) The council is gathering evidence to be used in accusing Jesus before Pilate. This interrogation is preceded by the mocking and beating of Jesus (in Matthew and Mark this follows the trial).

22:63-65: Jesus predicted in 18:32 that he would be mocked and insulted. The mocking begins in 22:63-65 and will continue through the passion story (cf. 23:11, 35-39). The process ending in execution is a progressive act of degradation of Jesus as he is excluded from society as a criminal. The mocking scenes highlight this aspect of the passion. In 22:63-65 he is mocked as a false prophet. Ironically, he had prophesied this mocking (18:32), and his prophecy of Peter's denial had just come true. Furthermore, he is now suffering the violent rejection experienced by prophets, which he mentioned repeatedly (6:22-23; 11:47-51; 13:33-34).

22:66-71: In verse 66 "they brought him to their council" may refer to the council chamber. The interrogation takes place after dawn, not at night, as in Matthew and Mark (cf. Matt 27:1; Mark 15:1). Also, the interrogating is done by the assembly as a whole, and the high priest is given no special role, contrary to Matthew and Mark. In Luke the sole focus is on whether Jesus claims to be the Messiah, the Son of God. Evidence that he does make this claim will be used against Jesus before Pilate (cf. 23:2). When an answer is first demanded in verse 67, Jesus responds with a protest against his hostile hearers. He knows that they are not willing to believe his claims or respond if he, in turn, questions them. Note the reference to Jesus as questioner in verse 68. Jesus previously used probing questions as a way of opening the possibility of new understanding on matters of controversy (cf., e.g., 5:34; 6:9). In Jerusalem Jesus has posed questions that his opponents were unwilling or unable to answer (20:3-7, 17, 41-44). Dialogue on essential matters seems to have stopped. Yet in verse 69 Jesus points to something that could change the situation: Jesus' enthronement at God's right hand. Following Jesus' resurrection and ascension, and Peter's announcement of Jesus as the Messiah and Lord installed at God's right hand (Acts 2:29-36), there will be renewed effort to persuade even the Sanhedrin that the risen Jesus is God's Messiah (cf. Acts 4:8-12; 5:27-32).

In verse 69 Jesus makes a bold affirmation, that the one who is suffering as Son of Man will be given messianic power through the events now unfolding. Although the parallel statements in Matt 26:64 and Mark 14:62 combine reference to the Son of Man in Dan 7:13 with Ps 110:1, Mark's "coming with the clouds of heaven" disappears from Luke and with it any reference to Jesus' glorious return. The focus is solely on his heavenly exaltation. As a result, it is doubtful that we can speak of an allusion to Dan 7:13 in Luke 22:69. The use of "Son of Man" is best understood from Jesus' passion prophecies, which repeatedly use this phrase in connection with his suffering and rejection (cf. 9:22, 44; 17:24-25; 18:31-32; 22:22; 24:7). Thus verse 69 speaks of the transformation of Jesus' status from suffering Son of Man to enthroned Messiah. Psalm 110:1 continues to be influential in this statement, and its importance in Luke–Acts is shown by the climactic position that it is given in the Pentecost speech (cf. Acts 2:34-35). The Lukan audience has also been prepared to understand the importance of Jesus' coming exaltation by Luke 20:17, 41-44. Thus Jesus answers the question of whether he is the Messiah by declaring that he is about to be installed as Messiah in power. (Acts 2:29-36 shows the connection between enthronement as Davidic Messiah and exaltation to God's right hand.)

In the rest of the passage, there are some obscurities in the train of thought. Lukan usage indicates that "Son of God" in verse 70 is a further title for the messianic king, emphasizing the king's special relation to God, as in 2 Sam 7:12-14 and Ps 2:7 (contrary to the view of Fitzmyer 1981, 206-8, and 1985, 1467-68). The themes of Jesus as "Son" and as royal Messiah are combined in 1:32-33; 4:41; Acts 9:20-22; 13:22-23, 32-34. The two titles are also combined in Mark 14:61, a parallel to Luke 22:67*a*. Thus, in verse 70, the assembly is not raising a second issue but is commenting on the issue raised in verse 67*a*. Although the NRSV and most translations take the words quoted in verse 70*a* as a question, this is not required by the Greek and makes the train of thought unnecessarily difficult. It is better to take them as an exclamation: "Then you are the Son of God!" (i.e., this is what you claim about yourself). Otherwise, verses 70*b* and 71 do not make good sense. If verse 70*a* is a question, the assembly has asserted nothing about Jesus. Yet Jesus comments, "*You* ["you" is emphatic in the Greek] say that I am." In its exclamation, the assembly has ironically confirmed the truth about Jesus. In verse 71 the assembly takes Jesus' comment as a clear claim to be the Messiah, giving them the testimony that they need. This only makes sense if Jesus has confirmed what the assembly itself stated about him in verse 70*a*.

Jesus warned earlier that his followers will be handed over to the authorities for interrogation and punishment, and urged them to use this as an opportunity "to testify" (21:13). If Jesus' statement in verse 70*b* is only "half-affirmative at best" (Fitzmyer 1985, 1461), he would be a poor model for disciples who are supposed to be forthright and courageous in a similar situation.

The opponents now have evidence that can be used to accuse Jesus before Pilate. Since 11:54 some have sought to catch Jesus "in something he might say" (literally, "something from his mouth"), but Jesus repeatedly escaped danger. In 22:71 the Sanhedrin finally declares that they have heard the incriminating evidence "from his own lips" (literally, "from his mouth"), and they take Jesus to Pilate.

Interrogation by Pilate (23:1-5)

In Luke the trial before Pilate goes through several steps, and a final decision is not reached until verses 24-25. In spite of his initial decision that Jesus is innocent, Pilate is persuaded to hand Jesus over for crucifixion.

◊ ◊ ◊ ◊

In verse 1 the narrator gives the impression that the council is acting in concert because all of them want to get rid of Jesus. In 23:50-51, however, we will discover that there was at least one councillor who did not agree. The accusations against Jesus are more detailed in Luke than in Matthew or Mark. They are presented in such a way as to make Jesus seem dangerous to the Roman government. He is accused of "perverting" (or "misleading") the Jewish people, and this accusation is supported by two examples that affect Roman rule. The first is patently false, for Jesus in 20:20-26 did not forbid paying taxes to the emperor. The second specific charge is more plausible, since Jesus did provide evidence in 22:66-71 that he claims to be the Messiah, and he did not rebuke his disciples when they proclaimed him king in 19:37-40. Pilate responds to this charge by asking Jesus whether he is the king of the Jews.

Jesus' response, "You say so," has caused considerable debate among scholars (cf. Brown 1994, 489-93, 733, 741). The safest route to understanding, I think, is to note that the "you" is emphatic in the Greek and the reader should seek a reason for such emphasis in the context. The similar statement in 22:70 is taken as a positive answer by Jesus' hearers in 22:71. That is not the case in 23:3-4. Therefore, a different explanation of the emphasis may be necessary. "You say so" cannot be understood as a denial, for Jesus is regarded as the prophesied king of Israel in Luke (cf. 1:32-33; 19:12, 38). It can, however, be understood as a qualified response here. Then "You say so" means "That is your way of putting it." The Messiah is a king, but the narrative distinguishes between "Messiah," a term used by Jews, and "king of the Jews," which is Gentile language (cf. 23:2-3, 35-38). The latter shows a point of view that is ignorant of scriptural prophecy and the perspective of Luke's Gospel, a point of view that lacks understanding of the kind of king Jesus is and how his rule will be conducted (cf. Tannehill 1992a, 17-22). The Messiah, even though he does make political claims, must not be equated with the king-claimants who lead armed rebellions in order to establish their thrones.

There is a narrative gap between verses 3 and 4. The narrative does not explain how Pilate could conclude so quickly that Jesus is innocent. Jesus' brief response—which is not a clear denial—is hardly an adequate basis. It is possible to read Pilate's question as sarcastic: "Are *you* the king of the Jews—you a poor peasant?" (The "you" is again emphatic.) In that case, Pilate may have regarded the charge as ridiculous from the start. But the narrative does not clarify Pilate's thinking.

The gap may have been created by the narrator's desire to emphasize that Jesus is innocent of any offense that should concern Rome. Pilate will repeatedly indicate that Jesus is innocent (cf. vv. 14-15, 20, 22). A declaration of innocence is inserted already in verse 4 where it seems premature—an indication of the narrator's concern to emphasize this point. Yet Jesus' accusers do not give up. In verse 5 they cite Jesus' teaching. The statement that it "stirs up" the people is meant to suggest that it is politically dangerous. In both Galilee and Jerusalem there has been controversy over Jesus' teaching. The authorities' objections to Jesus' teaching reappear in the accusation in verse 5. The geographical scope of Jesus' teaching is emphasized. "All Judea" may mean the whole Jewish homeland, inclusive of Galilee (cf. 4:44).

Interrogation by Herod (23:6-12)

Pilate's motive for sending Jesus to Herod Antipas, tetrarch of Galilee, is not clear. Various explanations have been proposed: (1) Pilate is trying to get rid of a sensitive case. But then Herod's sending Jesus back would not be likely to produce friendship (cf. v. 12). (2) Herod is not being asked to try the case but to be an adviser to Pilate, who must still make the final decision. But in verse 15 Pilate regards Herod's return of Jesus as indication that Herod did not find him guilty. If he believed him to be guilty, Herod would not have sent him back but would have sentenced him to punishment. (3) Sending Jesus to Herod is a favor, a gesture of trust and respect, and Herod recognizes this. This explanation fits the note, in verse 12, about Pilate and Herod becoming friends.

◊ ◊ ◊ ◊

In verse 8 the narrator picks up a narrative thread from 9:7-9. According to that passage, Herod had heard what Jesus was doing, was perplexed about who he was, and wanted to see him. Herod finally gets his wish in Luke 23, and he is "very glad." But he is interested in Jesus for the wrong reasons. He wants to see if he can perform a miraculous sign. Curiosity and a desire to test Jesus in this way are not indications of openness to Jesus and his message (cf. 11:16, 29). Furthermore, Herod has previously been presented as a threat to God's prophets (cf. 3:19-20; 9:9; 13:31).

Both the interrogation by Herod and the accusations of the chief priests and scribes are vigorous, but Jesus does not answer. Although Jesus spoke briefly before the Jewish council and before Pilate, his silence here is not a shift in tactics. In his first statement to the council, Jesus protested that they would not believe him or respond to him (22:67-68). Then he responded only to the question about his identity and did so very briefly. He did not mount a defense, and by the time he reaches Herod, he has said all that he wants to say. Although the narrator sees a parallel between Jesus' trial and situations that his followers will face, Jesus' silence is not an example for others. When Jesus' witnesses are brought before authorities, they are to speak what the Spirit or the Lord gives them to speak (cf. 12:11-12; 21:14-15), and Paul makes a series of defense speeches in Acts 22–26. This is not wrong; indeed, it is an important opportunity for witness. But Jesus knows that his destiny is already set (cf. 22:22), and he does not struggle to escape it. (Some find an allusion to Isa 53:7 in Jesus' silence.)

Disappointed in his hope for a miracle, Herod and his soldiers show their contempt for Jesus by mocking him. "Even Herod" (v. 11) should, perhaps, be translated "Herod also," for this is the second mocking scene in Luke's passion story (cf. 22:63-65). This mocking is reminiscent of Matt 27:27-31 and Mark 15:16-20, a scene where Jesus is mocked by *Roman* soldiers, which is missing in Luke. The "elegant [or "shining"] robe" is also similar. It is not clear in Luke that it is meant to be a royal robe, but it is probably part of the mockery. The mockery by Herod and his soldiers is another step in the public dishonoring of Jesus. It will continue as he hangs on the cross (cf. vv. 35-39).

Although verse 12 is enigmatic, the best explanation is probably that Pilate had done Herod an honor by sending the case to him, and Herod recognized this. The resulting friendship is not necessarily a positive thing. In Acts Herod and Pilate are viewed as part of an alliance who "gathered together against the Lord and against his Messiah" (Acts 4:26-27). Even though they are used as witnesses to Jesus' innocence, they are numbered among the opponents who have a role in the blind rejection of God's Messiah.

◊ ◊ ◊ ◊

In verse 15 Herod's return of Jesus will be cited as evidence that he did not find him guilty. That is not the principal purpose of verses 8-12, however, for the scene is not narrated so as to make that point well. We would expect a declaration from Herod similar to Pilate's in verse 4, or at least signs of respect from Herod instead of the mocking in verse 11. The scene moves toward this mocking by a disappointed Herod. Its function, then, is to develop the theme of the public dishonoring of Jesus that permeates the passion story and to spread the responsibility among the rulers of that time and place. Acts 4:25-27 declares that both Jews and Gentiles, following their rulers, opposed God's Messiah. Herod is the Jewish ruler who is paired with Pilate, the Gentile. At the climax of Paul's defense scenes in Acts 26, another Roman governor and another Herodian ruler will be confronted with Paul's testimony to the risen Messiah as he reargues the case of Jesus before these authorities.

Jesus Is Sentenced to Death (23:13-25)

The trial comes to its climax in this scene. For the crucial decision, Pilate assembles not only the chief priests and leaders, who have been the accusers of Jesus, but also the "people" *(laos)*. This term, which sometimes alternates with "crowd" in Lukan usage, becomes especially frequent from 19:47 on and has a special connotation. It designates the Jewish people in their distinctiveness, that is, in light of their scriptural heritage, including the promises that give them a special place in God's purpose (cf. Tannehill 1986, 143-44). At this point a group that represents the "people" becomes involved in Jesus' death. They hear Pilate's declarations of Jesus' innocence yet call for his condemnation.

The scene is structured as a threefold interaction between Pilate, who repeatedly proposes to release Jesus, and the people with their chief priests and leaders, who repeatedly call for his death. (In v. 20 "wanting to release Jesus" should be understood as the content of Pilate's address. Thus he is basically repeating what he said in vv. 14-16.) The desire of the assembled people for Jesus' death, a position previously represented only by the chief priests and the rest of the Sanhedrin, is surprising. The eager support of Jesus by the people previously protected Jesus (19:47-48; 20:19; 21:38; 22:2). Now the people are suddenly supporters of the Sanhedrin's plot. If we were discussing the historical event, we could speculate about various reasons for this (e.g., this particular group was packed with Barabbas supporters who did not like Jesus). Within Luke's dramatic narrative there is no explanation, but there is an interesting plot line in which the people, who have been strong supporters of Jesus, somehow are persuaded to call for his death and then at his crucifixion realize their tragic mistake. First the women mourn for Jesus (v. 27). Then the crowd as a whole demonstrates its grief at Jesus' death and its regret for sharing in his condemnation (v. 48). In Acts, Peter will remind the people that they "denied" (NRSV: "rejected") Jesus, will note that they "acted in ignorance," and will call them to "repent" (Acts 3:13-19). There is an interesting parallel between the threefold denial of Jesus by Peter, after which he "wept bitterly" (Luke 22:54-62), and the threefold denial of Jesus before Pilate by the people and their leaders, after which the people beat their breasts. For the people, the passion narrative is a tragic story in which they blindly act against justice and their own good, then belatedly recognize what they have done (cf. Tiede 1980, 103-18; Tannehill 1985, 69-85). Nevertheless, the opportunity for repentance and forgiveness will be offered to the people of Jerusalem in Acts (cf. 2:22-40; 3:12-26).

◊ ◊ ◊ ◊

Before the people and their leaders, Pilate makes a solemn declaration of his findings in the trial and announces his intention to release Jesus. His statement in verse 14 that Jesus is not guilty of any of the charges presupposes a more thorough examination than was actually reported in verses 2-5. In verse 15 Herod is cited as support for Pilate's declaration of innocence. The fact that he sent Jesus back to Pilate rather than condemning him shows that he, too, recognized that Jesus "has done nothing to deserve death." (The last sentence in v. 15 may seem repetitious. In the Greek it begins in the same way as v. 14*b* and may be intended to summarize Herod's decision as a parallel to Pilate's decision about Jesus in v. 14*b*.) In verses 14-22 Pilate is given the function of officially proclaiming the innocence of Jesus. A concern to maintain the innocence of Jesus, rather than a need to avoid criticism of Roman officials, explains the relatively favorable portrait of Pilate at this point. When in the end Pilate does not stand up for justice, the favorable portrait disappears. There are further witnesses to Jesus' innocence in verses 41 and 47.

Pilate declares that he will release Jesus after he has been "flogged." The verb translated "flogged" in the NRSV *(paideuō)* means to administer disciplinary punishment. This should be distinguished from the flogging that accompanies crucifixion, which helps to cause death (cf. Mark 15:15). Even so, the preceding declaration of innocence does not explain why there should be punishment. Here Pilate seems to be trying to strike a bargain with

Jesus' accusers. This is immediately rejected with the first—and least specific—of the calls for Jesus' death. The statement that they shouted "all . . . together" indicates the temporary support of "the people" for Jesus' condemnation.

In verse 18 Barabbas is mentioned. Mark 15:6-11 gives a relatively full explanation about Barabbas's role in the negotiations between Pilate and Jesus' opponents. Luke's omission of most of this material leaves unclear why the release of Barabbas has anything to do with the release of Jesus. (In v. 17 the necessity of releasing a prisoner at the feast is explained, but this verse is lacking in a strong group of ancient manuscripts.) The narrator does make clear, however, that Barabbas had been imprisoned for insurrection and murder (v. 19; repeated v. 25), for this information suggests that the choice of Barabbas instead of Jesus is a choice between two political policies. Barabbas is a precursor of the rebels who will ignite the Jewish-Roman war in AD 66. According to 19:41-44 Jesus offers Jerusalem "the things that make for peace," but Jerusalem will miss this opportunity, leading to its destruction. That destruction is also anticipated in the context of the Pilate scene (cf. 23:28-31). The choice of Barabbas shows a preference for his violent policy, which will have terrible consequences. In rejecting Jesus, Jerusalem is also repudiating his way of peace.

Pilate tries a second and third time to get the crowd to agree to Jesus' release. Their second response is more specific than the first: they want him crucified. The crowd's urgent insistence is emphasized in the third response (v. 23). Pilate, in spite of his declarations about Jesus, is not willing to risk a riot for Jesus. He, like governors Felix and Festus after him, subordinates individual justice to the demands of pressure groups (cf. Acts 24:27; 25:9). So he finally gives in and thereby joins the chain of those who "hand" Jesus "over" (using *paradidōmi*) to death (see Judas in 22:4; Pilate in 23:25; the chief priests and rulers in 24:20; cf. Brown 1994, 854).

◊ ◊ ◊ ◊

In verse 25 there is emphasis on the responsibility of the chief priests, leaders, and people for what was happening. Barabbas was "the man they asked for," and Jesus was handed over "as they wished" (literally, "to their will"). What are the possible effects of this emphasis on the Lukan audience? When the scene is taken in isolation, Gentiles in the Lukan audience could easily understand it to mean that the Jews had rejected Jesus and would, in turn, be rejected by God. This response, however, would truncate the Lukan story in a dangerous way. It would ignore the promises to Israel expressed in Luke 1–2 and the drama of blind rejection, repentance, and forgiveness that is being played out in the larger narrative. This drama includes an ironic twist: human rejection becomes the means by which God's saving purpose for both Jews and Gentiles is realized (see below on 24:26-27).

The Lament for Jesus (23:26-31)

The opinion of some that the narrator wishes to spare Pilate and increase the responsibility of the Jews is sometimes thought to gain support from verse 26. Who is meant by "they" in this verse? In verse 25 "they" refers to the Jewish leaders and people, so the natural reading seems to be that this group, not the Romans, led Jesus away and crucified him (cf. J. T. Sanders 1987, 9-15). Closer consideration, however, indicates that a change of reference is assumed in verse 26. In 18:32 Jesus said that he would be handed over to the Gentiles for execution. The seemingly contrary statement in 24:20 probably abbreviates a more complicated process. The soldiers at the cross address Jesus with "outsider" language ("King of the Jews" rather than "Messiah"), indicating that they are Roman troops (23:36-37). Then verse 47 refers to a centurion (who would be the commander of the Roman troops), and Joseph of Arimathea must ask for the body of Jesus from Pilate, not from the chief priests (v. 52). Unclear pronouns (and subjects of Greek verbs) are difficult to avoid, and there are other examples in Luke. Thus in Luke, as in Mark 15:20, we should assume that Roman troops led Jesus away (cf. further Brown 1994, 857-59).

We are not told why someone other than Jesus is forced to carry the cross. In contrast to Matt 27:26 and Mark 15:15 there is no report of Jesus being flogged, weakening him, but a flogging may be assumed (cf. 18:33). The statement that Simon carried the cross "behind" or "after" Jesus might remind the Lukan audience of familiar words about disciples coming "after" Jesus and carrying their crosses (9:23; 14:27 [translated freely in NRSV]). At this point in the story the disciples are too frightened to follow Jesus in this way, and Simon of Cyrene becomes their stand-in.

The "people" *(laos)*, who entered the action in verse 13, follow Jesus from the scene of the trial. Although they appeared to be solidly opposed to Jesus in the trial scene, that is no longer the case, for in verse 27 women begin the mourning ritual, thus demonstrating their sorrow at Jesus' coming death. Jesus addresses the women as "daughters of Jerusalem." This is the plural form of an important phrase in the prophetic writings, where Jerusalem, or the people as a whole, is personified as "daughter (of) Jerusalem" or "daughter (of) Zion" (Isa 37:22; 52:2; 62:11; Zeph 3:14; Zech 9:9). Because of Jerusalem's future fate, Jesus redirects the women's mourning from himself to the women and their children. Jesus has already wept over Jerusalem (19:41) and previously warned of the dire fate of women and their children when Jerusalem is destroyed (21:23). This scene in the passion narrative caps the series of statements about Jerusalem's resistance to the things that make for peace and its coming destruction (13:33-35; 19:41-44; 21:20-24). It develops themes from these passages and adds to the mood of pathos by focusing on the plight of women and children who will be caught in the city. The Lukan audience is being asked to show compassion and sympathy for the Jewish women and children who died in Jerusalem. The sense of tragedy is also heightened when we consider Jesus' words to the "daughters of Jerusalem" as a reversal of the oracles of salvation in Isa 49:19-21 and 54:1. There Jerusalem, who was bereaved and barren, is promised many children. But Jesus, in a beatitude of bitter irony, declares that the barren are the blessed ones, since children will only bring pain.

In verse 30 the despair of that time is expressed in language borrowed from Hos 10:8, followed by an enigmatic saying in verse 31. Perhaps verse 31 can be explained in this way: Apparently, the time of Jesus' crucifixion is compared with green (or moist) wood and the time of Jerusalem's destruction with dry wood. Green wood makes poor firewood; it will burn much better when it has had time to dry. Already Jesus is suffering violence, but when the prophesied time of "great distress" (21:23) comes (i.e., when the wood is dry), the destructive fire will burn fiercely and consume many.

The Crucifixion (23:32-49)

The crucifixion of Jesus is the climax of a "status degradation ritual" that has been proceeding since 22:63 (cf. Malina and Rohrbaugh 1992, 406-9). Societies have various ways of publicly removing the honor of certain persons and labeling them as social deviants who can be abused. This dishonoring process, anticipated by the emphasis on rejection and mocking in the passion prophecies (cf. 9:22; 18:32), is dramatized in the mocking scenes of the passion narrative (22:63-65; 23:11, 35-39). Execution by crucifixion is part of this process, for it involves the public display of a person under torture. It is the final act of social rejection of one who is so dishonored that all kinds of verbal and physical abuse are permitted.

23:32-38: Jesus' prayer from the cross in verse 34a is enclosed in double brackets in the NRSV because there is a serious textual problem at this point. A group of early manuscripts lacks the bracketed words, causing some leading textual scholars to doubt that they were originally a part of Luke (cf. Metzger 1971, 180). Such doubt persists despite support for inclusion of these words from Codex Sinaiticus, in the original hand, a broad range of other manuscripts, and a number of early church fathers.

When there is strong manuscript support for two different readings, scholars must attempt to provide arguments for and against the variant readings. Relevant factors are: (1) Which reading best fits the tendencies of the document? (2) Is it easiest to explain the long reading as a secondary insertion or the short reading as a secondary omission by copyists?

In my opinion, the bracketed words fit Luke–Acts unusually well. If we assume that these words belong, this prayer balances Jesus' final prayer in verse 46. The one shows Jesus' attitude toward his opponents; the other his attitude toward God. The one is placed right after the crucifixion; the other at the point of death, thus bracketing the death scene. In both cases Jesus addresses God as

"Father" (as also in 22:42, the prayer on the Mount of Olives). In these words Jesus is doing what he told his disciples to do: praying for those who abuse them (6:28). He also prayed for Peter who was about to deny him (22:31-34). The statement that they do not know what they are doing fits the Lukan perspective. Previously Jesus wept over the city that did not recognize the things that make for peace, which were hidden from it (19:41, 44). In Acts, Peter will say to the people of Jerusalem that they acted in ignorance when they rejected Jesus (Acts 3:17; cf. 13:27). He will call them to repentance and offer them forgiveness. (These passages in Acts show that the prayer from the cross applies not only to Roman soldiers but also to the Jews who had a part in Jesus' death.) In Acts the suffering of Jesus' witnesses follows the pattern of Jesus' suffering. The death scene of Stephen, the first martyr, recalls Jesus' statement about Jesus being at the right hand of God (Luke 22:69; Acts 7:55-56), and there is a parallel to Jesus' prayer in Luke 23:46 (cf. Acts 7:59). It is appropriate, then, that Stephen's prayer of forgiveness (Acts 7:60) parallels a similar prayer by Jesus (Luke 23:34). While a later copyist might create a prayer for Jesus by copying what Stephen said, that has not been done. The wording is quite distinct (the author of Luke likes to vary expression), but the function and setting are parallel. Jesus provides a model for Stephen and later martyrs, showing how to die with forgiveness and faith (cf. Talbert 1982, 212-18).

It is possible to explain the short reading as a secondary omission by later copyists. Forgiveness might seem to conflict with the destruction of Jerusalem, for some in the early church might not be able to understand God's forgiveness working in spite of that and after that. Some might perceive a conflict with Matt 27:25. The hardening of Christian attitudes toward Jews as lines of positive communication were cut could lead to the belief that Jews cannot be forgiven for the crucifixion of Jesus, making this prayer for forgiveness seem inappropriate (cf. further Brown 1994, 979-80). Thus it seems easier to explain the omission of this sentence than to believe that a later copyist inserted a sentence that fits the perspective of Luke–Acts so well.

Mention of the two criminals crucified with Jesus reminds the audience that Jesus himself is being treated as a criminal. Casting lots for Jesus' clothing is mentioned because it seems to fulfill Ps 22:18, and the wording of verse 35 appears to be influenced by Ps 22:6-7 (Ps 21:7-8 LXX). In this psalm a righteous sufferer reports his abuse by people as he calls out to God. The early church understood the death of Jesus in light of this psalm. The soldiers offer Jesus sour wine in verse 36. Sour wine is the ordinary drink of Roman soldiers, but this detail may be included as a fulfillment of Ps 69:21, another psalm of the abused. However, the reference to mocking suggests that it could be part of a burlesque performance in which the soldiers pretend to be servants bringing the king his cup (cf. Brown 1994, 997).

Matthew 27:39-44 and Mark 15:29-32 also have three groups mocking Jesus on the cross, but the first is a group of passersby. In Luke this has become the people, standing and watching. They may have been attracted by the spectacle, and, apart from the mourning women, they do not yet show sympathy or remorse. Yet it is noteworthy that the people do not participate in the mocking. In Luke the three groups of mockers are the (Jewish) "leaders," the (Roman) soldiers, and one of the criminals. Inclusion of the soldiers among the mockers helps to make up for Luke's omission of the scene of Jesus being mocked by soldiers in Mark 15:16-20 (cf. Matt 27:27-31). It also develops the roles of Jews and Gentiles in the passion story: just as both had a part in condemning Jesus, so they both mock Jesus on the cross (cf. Acts 4:25-27).

The expressions of mockery are consistent in Luke's three cases. The mockery consists of treating Jesus' claim to be royal Messiah with derision. The Messiah was supposed to bring salvation (cf. 1:69; 2:11, 26, 30), so in each of the three cases Jesus' royal pretensions are mocked by the challenge to save himself. Jesus cannot save himself by escaping death, but, unknown to the mockers, this helplessness will have a place in God's saving purpose. The challenges to save himself can be understood as the return of the devil's final temptation in 4:9-12, where Jesus was challenged to show that he is invulnerable (cf. Neyrey 1985, 180). But Jesus told his disciples that "those who want to save their life will lose it, and those who lose their life . . . will save it" (9:24; cf. 17:33). This aphorism applies to Jesus as well, which means salvation for Jesus must come by God's action after Jesus' death.

23:39-43: Like the preceding mocking, the criminal's request "Save yourself and us!" is derisive and cynical, yet Jesus does accept the challenge, for he saves the other criminal. In a development unique to Luke, the second criminal takes a position contrasting with the first. He rebukes the mocker, noting that this mocking of the Messiah shows disrespect for God, whom the mocker must face as final judge. The second criminal also takes responsibility for his own deeds (an aspect of repentance), admitting that his condemnation is just. He distinguishes himself from Jesus, who has been condemned unjustly. Thus, another person witnesses to Jesus' innocence, as Pilate had previously. Then he turns to Jesus and requests his favor "when you come into your kingdom." His request is based on the belief that the one who is being mocked as Messiah and king, who is dying as a condemned criminal, really is the royal Messiah, and that his shameful death does not end his claim to royal power but is the means by which he will achieve it.

The criminal who makes this little speech is an important figure in the Lukan passion story, for this is a recognition scene in which the truth hidden from other humans, including the disciples, is disclosed. The disciples were unable to understand Jesus' words about rejection and death (cf. 9:44-45; 18:31-34), for a Messiah who was rejected and killed did not fit their assumptions. Neither does it fit the assumptions of the mockers. But the second criminal responds to all the mockers in a speech that pulls together important threads of the passion story. He declares Jesus' innocence. By his request he demonstrates faith that Jesus does have power to save, and he connects that power to Jesus' future kingdom, which means that he confesses Jesus as Messiah in spite of his shameful death on a cross. It is one of the outcasts, to whom Jesus previously ministered, who is capable of this unique insight.

Thus the theme of Jesus as God's Messiah, which has dominated the trial and mocking, continues here. In his request in verse 42 the second criminal is, in effect, asking for royal clemency (cf. Nolland

1993, 1151). There is a textual variant in verse 42, with some important manuscripts reading "come into your kingdom," while the majority of manuscripts read "come in your kingdom." The latter reading could be understood as a reference to Jesus' return in glory, for which the Lukan audience was still waiting. Beginning in Luke 19, however, there is a concentration of references to the exaltation of Jesus to the right hand of God and royal power (cf. Luke 19:12; 20:17, 42-43; 22:29-30, 69; 24:26; Acts 2:29-36). The reading "come into your kingdom" points to the same event, and its fit with the Lukan emphasis in this part of the narrative makes it the preferable reading (cf. Metzger 1971, 181).

Jesus' positive response to the man's request implies his approval of what he said. Jesus promises that the criminal "will be with me in Paradise." Here Jesus exercises his authority to forgive (cf. 5:24), which will become part of his royal power. The phrase "be with me" not only declares forgiveness but promises friendship. Paradise was originally a name for a pleasant garden or park, then was associated with the Garden of Eden, and became an image for the abode of the righteous dead (cf. Rev 2:7; *1 Enoch* 60:8; *2 Enoch* 8–9; 2 Esdr 7:36, 123; 8:52). In verse 43 it is understood to exist already, so that Jesus and his companion may enter it "today." Entering paradise is not necessarily the same as Jesus entering his kingdom, which may await his ascension to the right hand of God (Acts 2:29-36). "Today" tells the petitioner that he need not wait for the favor he seeks. Thus, in the midst of blind rejection and derisive mocking, this dialogue provides a sign that Jesus is indeed the Messiah who brings salvation.

23:44-49: The death of Jesus is accompanied by two portents in verses 44-45. People of the time were accustomed to think that signs accompanied the death of great men, and the darkening of the sun was repeatedly mentioned (cf. Brown 1994, 1043). Elsewhere Luke–Acts uses light and darkness symbolically, with light representing God's presence and the availability of God's salvation (Luke 1:78-79; 2:32; Acts 13:47; 26:18, 23) and darkness representing human lostness and the power of evil (Luke 1:79; Acts 26:18). In particular, Luke 22:53 has already designated the passion as the time of the power of darkness. As Jesus' death approaches, the darkness at midday suggests that Satan is fully in control. Yet immediately before and after the portents in verses 44-45 there are signs that God's saving purpose continues.

The tearing of the temple curtain has been moved from a position following Jesus' last words and death (Matt 27:51; Mark 15:38) to a position before. The significance of this event in Luke is uncertain, and a number of interpretations have been advocated (cf. Nolland 1993, 1157, for a list). Punctuation may affect interpretation in a case like this. In verse 45 the NRSV places a semicolon after "failed" and a period after "two," thus associating the tearing of the curtain more closely with the darkness than with Jesus' final cry. But the Greek does not make the relationship of the clauses clear. If related closely to the darkness, the tearing of the temple curtain can be understood as a threatening sign, perhaps an anticipation of the temple's destruction. Or it may anticipate not the physical destruction of the temple, but the end of its function of imposing social boundaries through segregating people by degrees of holiness. The tearing of the curtain would then anticipate the mission to all nations (cf. Green 1994b, 502-15). However, the tearing of the curtain can also be associated with Jesus' act of commending his spirit into God's hands (v. 46). Then it would represent God's readiness to receive Jesus' spirit (cf. Sylva 1986, 239-50). It is also possible that these and other interpretations simply show the scholar's tendency to try to squeeze too much out of a few words. It may be that in Luke the tearing of the temple curtain is simply an additional sign that the approaching death is the death of someone very great.

In all three synoptic Gospels, the dying Jesus' last words are a quotation from the Psalms, but the words from Ps 31:5 in Luke make quite a different impression than the cry of forsakenness in Matt 27:46 and Mark 15:34. In this, the third prayer addressed to God as Father in the passion story (cf. 22:42; 23:34), Jesus entrusts himself to God. The context indicates that he is expressing faith in God as the one who can rescue from death. Such rescue was anticipated in 22:69 and 23:43, and Jesus spoke of his resurrection in his passion announcements (9:22; 18:33; cf. 24:6-7). In Acts another psalm text, Ps 16:8-11, will be used to express Jesus' faith in God as the God of resurrection (cf. Acts 2:24-31; 13:35-37). According to it, the Messiah is aware of God's constant presence and therefore is not shaken in the face of death, for he knows that God will not let God's "Holy One experience corruption." The same faith stands behind the expression of trust in God's care with which Jesus dies on the cross in Luke. More is at stake than Jesus' personal destiny. From this point on, others cannot be saved through Jesus unless Jesus himself is saved (cf. Neyrey 1985, 146-55).

Nevertheless, Jesus' death has an immediate effect on others. The narrative focuses again on the major groups involved in the passion story, groups that have rejected or failed Jesus, but who now provide isolated or tentative examples of appropriate response to him. The Roman soldiers mocked Jesus in verses 36-37, but now a centurion affirms him. The people participated in the call for Jesus' death in verses 13-25, but now the crowds (equivalent to "the people" in vv. 27 and 35) beat their breasts. This is a sign of mourning (see the women in v. 27), but sorrow at Jesus' death entails remorse at their own part in this event. This is the beginning of repentance that should be completed by the people's response to Peter's preaching in Acts 2–3. The Jerusalem council had a leading role in Jesus' death, but in verses 50-53 we are introduced to a council member who opposed their action, who will now care for Jesus' body. In verse 49 Jesus' "acquaintances" are also mentioned, that is, his followers. (They are not now called disciples perhaps because they have not been acting like disciples.) They stand at a distance, a sign of their continuing weakness as followers. Their response is not clear at this point because that part of the story is reserved for Luke 24. In any case, signs of a different awareness are beginning to appear within the very groups who opposed or failed Jesus.

Both the centurion and the crowds are moved when they see "what had taken place." Their responses immediately follow Jesus' expression of trust in God, so this expression is probably part of the cause for their reaction. But more may be involved in their response: Jesus' prayer of forgiveness (v. 34), his attention to the criminal who appeals to him (vv. 42-43), and the accompanying signs (vv. 44-45). The manner of Jesus' death is impressive. The narrator permits the centurion to voice his response, which in the NRSV is translated "Certainly this man was innocent." There has been repeated stress on Jesus' innocence since verse 4. That is probably part of the meaning of the word *dikaios* here, but it can mean more. It would normally be translated "just" or "righteous." "Righteous One" is a significant title for Jesus, as is shown by its application in Acts 3:13-14 and 7:52 to Jesus as God's servant, the one foretold by the prophets. Although a number of scriptural references to the righteous may contribute to this usage, Wis 2:12–3:1 is striking because the situation parallels the passion story so closely. The ungodly lie in wait for the righteous one. They want to test his claim to be God's son, so they decide to condemn him to a shameful death. But they do not take account of the fact that death is not the end for humans nor that "the souls of the righteous are in the hand of God" (3:1). For the narrator, a description of this kind is fulfilled by the Davidic Messiah, who is called righteous in Jer 23:5; Zech 9:9 LXX; *Pss. Sol.* 17:32 (cf. Brown 1994, 1165). It may seem strange that the centurion's confession of Jesus as Son of God in Matt 27:54 and Mark 15:39 is changed to "righteous" in Luke, but this declaration probably has more theological weight than may at first appear.

The women who followed Jesus from Galilee receive special attention in verse 49 because they will play a special role in the following narrative. They were mentioned already in 8:2-3 as part of Jesus' company. The presence of Jesus' followers at the cross is important, even though they stand "at a distance," for Jesus' witnesses must be able to tell about his life and death, as well as his resurrection (cf. Acts 1:21-22).

The Burial (23:50-56)

In 22:70–23:1 it appeared that the Sanhedrin's opposition to Jesus was unanimous; now we are told that there was at least one exception. Joseph of Arimathea is given a clearly positive description, although he is not made a disciple of Jesus, as in Matt 27:57. He fits a character type that appeared in the Lukan infancy narrative (see the descriptions of Zechariah, Elizabeth, Simeon, and Anna in

1:5-6; 2:25, 36-38). These people are devout Jews who live according to the law. They are also "waiting expectantly" for the fulfillment of God's promises. (The same term *prosdechomai* is used in 2:25, 38 and 23:51.) Their expectancy is part of the Lukan picture of a true Jew. The appearance of such people in the narrative adds to the credibility of the Christian message, since Jews of outstanding piety can be sympathetic to it (see also Gamaliel in Acts 5:34-39). Their presence also speaks against Christian prejudice that non-Christian Jews must be hardened opponents and evil.

A decent burial is not something that the families of executed criminals could count on. The bodies could be left for carrion birds and scavenger animals to eat or could be thrown into a common grave (cf. Brown 1994, 1207-9). To bury the exposed dead was considered an act of charity and piety (cf. Tob 1:16-18). Joseph's action fits the statement that he "was a good and righteous man."

Although Jesus' body is laid in a rock-hewn tomb (there are a number of ancient tombs of this type in the vicinity of Jerusalem), proper preparation of the body was not completed because of the approach of the sabbath. This leaves something for the women to do. Again the Lukan audience is told that these women had come with Jesus from Galilee (cf. vv. 49, 55). Their past relation to Jesus is important. According to 8:3, these women "were serving" (NRSV: "provided for") Jesus and his apostles in Galilee. Now these women prepare to perform a final service. They are the only members of Jesus' company who "followed" (v. 55) in this, the last stage of Jesus' passion journey.

THE RISEN LORD'S REVELATION TO HIS FOLLOWERS (24:1-53)

All the resurrection appearances in Luke are set in or near Jerusalem. The events of Luke 24 take place in one momentous day, and Jesus' instructions end in verse 49 with the command that his followers stay in Jerusalem. Acts 1:3 allows for other resurrection appearances, but Jesus' command to stay in Jerusalem leaves no room for appearances to the disciples in Galilee, which are anticipated in Mark 16:7 and reported in Matt 28:16-20 and John 21:1-23. Jerusalem, the religious center of Judaism and the city that rejected Jesus, will be the focus of the earliest mission, and the Lukan Jesus does not allow the apostles and their companions to travel between Easter and Pentecost.

Like the infancy narrative, Luke 24 must be understood as a continuous series of interrelated events, not as separate pericopes that can be adequately understood in isolation. The resurrection narrative tells how disciples who previously could not understand Jesus' prophecies of death and resurrection (cf. 9:44-45; 18:31-34) not only encounter the risen Messiah but also finally come to understand, when instructed by Jesus, the ironic way that God's purpose is being achieved through the rejection and death of the Messiah. This understanding is crucial to the new mission that Jesus' followers must assume. Thus Luke's resurrection chapter is basically the story of the risen Messiah's revelation of God's redemptive plan to his followers, in preparation for their mission.

The Women at the Tomb (24:1-12)

Although the NRSV in verse 3 simply says, "They did not find the body," there is strong manuscript evidence for the reading "the body of the Lord Jesus," which anticipates use of the title "the Lord Jesus" in Acts 1:21; 4:33; 8:16. The "two men in dazzling clothes" are called angels in verse 23. Nevertheless, they are introduced in the same way (literally, "behold two men") as Moses and Elijah in the transfiguration scene (9:30). These two scenes, as well as Acts 1:10, show the tendency to introduce two heavenly messengers to interpret events at crucial points in Jesus' story. The preference for two may result from the conviction that two provide a more reliable witness than one (see the demand for at least two witnesses in Deut 19:15). In verse 5 the passive verb translated "has risen" *(ēgerthē)* can be so translated, but in light of the strong Lukan emphasis on God as the one who raises Jesus from the dead (cf. Acts 3:15; 4:10; 5:30; 10:40; 13:30, 37), it is probably better to translate "has been raised" (by God).

The messengers begin with a rebuke. The women should have known that Jesus would not be among the dead because Jesus had told them that he would rise on the third day. In verses 6-7 the messengers go on to remind the women of what Jesus had said. At this point Luke differs significantly from the accounts of the empty tomb in Matthew and Mark. There the women are told about a future meeting of Jesus and the disciples in Galilee (cf. Matt 28:7; Mark 16:7). In Luke, however, the messengers remind the women of what Jesus previously said in Galilee. This change not only fits Luke's concentration of resurrection appearances in Jerusalem, it also shows that Luke's agenda at this point is different. The angels' reminder of Jesus' words about his death and resurrection opens a discussion that will continue in the next two scenes (cf. vv. 19-27, 44-49). A key element of this discussion will be an understanding of the necessity of Jesus' destined path from rejection to glory. In verse 7 the word "must" is a translation of the Greek verb *dei* ("it is necessary"), and this verb will reappear in related expressions in verses 26 and 44, where the necessity is explained by reference to scripture (vv. 27, 44).

The discussion begins with the angels' reminder of what Jesus had said and the disciples had not understood. The statement in verse 7 is largely a composite of phrases from the major passion and resurrection prophecies of Jesus in 9:22, 44; 18:32-33. (The word "crucified," however, is different and reflects the passion story itself.) For the sake of continuity, the designation "Son of Man" is retained, but from this point on it will be obsolete (see, however, Acts 7:56), being replaced by "Messiah" in verses 26 and 46. There are repeated restatements of the death and resurrection prophecies in verses 26, 44, 46 because the disciples must come to understand the divine necessity of these events for the sake of the mission ahead. According to verse 8, the women remembered Jesus' words. Thus they had been informed about Jesus' prophecies.

The women's report is interrupted in verse 10 by the names of some of the women. Mary Magdalene and Joanna were also listed when the women were first introduced in 8:2-3, but Mary the mother of James has been added from Mark 16:1. These three are leading figures in a larger group of women who now speak to "the eleven" and "all the rest." (The eleven remaining apostles are important, but others share in the resurrection events; cf. vv. 18,

33.) The women's report, however, is rejected. The apostles and their companions are still where they were in 9:45 and 18:34, unable to understand or accept these events. Progress will require not only a personal encounter with the risen Messiah but also instruction from him about how God has been working in the world.

The fact that the report comes from women may be a factor in the negative response. The failure to believe the women hints at a cultural reality that helps to explain a further observation about Luke–Acts. It may seem surprising that, in spite of the importance of women in Luke, all of the missionaries who constitute the central figures in Acts are men. As others have noted (cf. D'Angelo 1990, 449-50; Seim 1994a, 162, 254-55), this reflects cultural resistance to women as witnesses (cf. Josephus *Ant.* 4 §219) and in public roles, such as speakers. Witnesses who were not credible in the public eye would not be effective. It is easy to see how this could lead to the assumption that women could not fulfill certain functions. Thus the statement in Acts 1:21-22 assumes that only men are qualified to be apostolic witnesses. The strong focus on the mission in Acts and the neglect of the internal life of the church contributes to the diminished role of women in the Acts narrative. In Luke 24, however, the witness of the women will be proved right.

Certain manuscripts omit verse 12. Earlier it was thought to be secondary, partly because it seems to borrow from the story in John 20:1-10. Recent scholarship, however, is inclined to credit the strong manuscript support for inclusion. According to verse 12, Peter does respond to the women's message by checking the tomb. He finds "the linen cloths by themselves" or "only the linen cloths" (i.e., without the body). Peter is "amazed," but this is not yet a believing comprehension. The women were "perplexed" when they did not find the body (v. 4), and a later summary indicates that the women's message "astounded" those who heard it (v. 22). Peter is in the same state of perplexity and astonishment. The special attention given to Peter here helps to bridge the gap between Jesus' prayer that Peter will turn back and strengthen his brothers (22:32) and his actual appearance in Acts 1:15–2:40 as leader of the church and Jesus' witness to the people of Jerusalem. In Luke 24 (cf. vv.

12, 34-53) the audience is given some sense of the steps in Peter's turning.

The Road to Emmaus (24:13-35)

The rest of the resurrection stories in Luke 24 have only a distant relation to anything in the other Gospels (see, however, John 20:19-20 and the addition to Mark in Mark 16:12-15). The most developed narrative concerns two disciples who are not apostles. Even though this narrative concerns subordinate characters, it is important because it enables the narrator to define the disciples' level of understanding and show the change that must take place for them to come to faith. It enables the narrator to present this change as a revelatory process. The narrator is not content with a resurrection appearance, which could have been told more briefly. The space given to the conversation on the road shows how necessary it is that believers have a new understanding of how Jesus' death and resurrection fit God's purpose.

Instruction on the Road (24:13-27)

The two disciples are already talking about what had happened to Jesus before Jesus joins them. The narrator identifies Jesus, but the eyes of the two disciples "were kept from recognizing him" (v. 16). We are not told who or what kept them from recognizing him. It is best to take this blindness as an inability to recognize the crucified and resurrected one, an inability that continues the earlier failure to understand Jesus' passion announcements. Here, as there, something crucial "was concealed" (9:45) or "was hidden from them" (18:34), but this concealment reflects their unreadiness to deal with Jesus' death. This is a culpable failure (see Tannehill 1986, 227) that must now be overcome.

The Lukan audience knows what the two disciples do not know: that Jesus is present. This results in an ironic perspective on these disciples. We observe them stumbling in their blindness, for Cleopas rebukes Jesus for not knowing what has taken place, although Jesus is the only one who really knows what has taken place. An ironic perspective can be used to denigrate people. That is not the case here, for by verses 26-27 the two disciples on the road are given crucial information that the Lukan audience must struggle to understand, turning the tables, so to speak. At the beginning of this narrative, irony allows the Lukan audience to experience events from a double perspective. They can experience the encounter with Jesus both from the perspective of the two disciples and from a superior perspective that reveals how human blindness looks when viewed from beyond. Since Luke–Acts witnesses to a God who works by irony, leaving humans in the position of the Emmaus disciples, the audience is thereby enabled to appreciate a basic human situation. The God who works by irony is especially revealed in the events of Jesus' death and resurrection (see below on vv. 26-27).

Jesus' probing questions lead the disciples to give a brief summary of Luke's story, which shows what the disciples understand and what they do not. The summary accurately reflects the perspective of Luke, and so is to be taken as true as far as it goes, but Jesus will add a crucial theological insight. In verse 19 Jesus is described as "a prophet mighty in deed and word." Jesus spoke of himself as a prophet in 4:24 and 13:33, and the preachers in Acts will present Jesus as the prophesied prophet like Moses in Acts 3:22 and 7:37. Furthermore, in Acts 7:22 Moses is described in almost the same way as Jesus in Luke 24:19. The resemblance to Moses does not mean that the disciples have a shallow Christology, for the Lukan narrator finds illumination in the fact that Jesus and his work follow a scriptural pattern (see below on v. 27). In verse 20 the disciples go on to speak of Jesus' death in language that resembles verse 7. They do not make a connection between Jesus' role as prophet and his violent death. When Jesus spoke of himself as a prophet in 4:24 and 13:33, it was in connection with his rejection and death, and elsewhere there are general statements indicating that prophets are regularly rejected and persecuted (6:23; 11:47-51; 13:34; Acts 7:52). This regular pattern of prophetic action and rejection may be important for understanding verses 26-27.

The dejected statement of lost hope in verse 21a is a summary of the hopes expressed in the Lukan infancy narrative. The verb "redeem" *(lytroomai)* and the noun "redemption" *(lytrōsis)* occur in Luke–Acts only in Luke 1:68; 2:38; and 24:21. The joyful expectations for the redemption of Israel in the infancy narrative have been passed on and are expressed again by the disciples on the Emmaus road. But now they speak of a past hope that has been disappointed. Reliable interpreters of God's purpose in Luke 1–2 (angels and inspired prophets) spoke of Jesus as the Messiah who would redeem Israel from oppression. The disciples on the road to Emmaus were right to share this hope, but they, like the other disciples, did not reckon with Jesus' rejection in Jerusalem. Because of this development, their hope can only be realized in a surprising way. The resurrection appearances will cause a rebirth of this hope for Israel (cf. Acts 1:6). In Acts 1:7 Jesus corrects the disciples' assumption that this hope will be fulfilled immediately (Jewish resistance will make that impossible), but he does not reject the hope itself (cf. Tannehill 1990, 14-17).

The disciples' report about Jesus is completed with a fairly detailed summary of the most recent events, those that took place "early this morning." (In vv. 21b-24 there is one variation from the account in vv. 1-12; according to v. 24 Peter was not the only one who went to the tomb to check the women's report.) The report of the women produced astonishment but not faith. The disciples' statement ends by noting that the women did not actually see Jesus. Jesus does not respond by immediately revealing himself. It is important first to give instruction so that the disciples will understand the theological appropriateness of Jesus' death and resurrection.

Jesus' reply begins with a rebuke, and it is more sharply worded than the rebuke of the angels to the women in verse 5. The disciples on the road, like the other disciples, have failed to show the needed insight and have not believed "all that the prophets have declared." This phrase may suggest that they believed some things but had missed other crucial things in the prophets' witness. In verse 26 Jesus focuses on a crucial deficiency in understanding and faith. In a pointed question that anticipates a positive answer, he asks, "Was it not necessary that the Messiah should suffer these things and then enter into his glory?" The necessity is theological; it derives from God's purpose as it seeks fulfillment in the world. Indeed, Acts 2:23

will declare that Jesus' death took place by "the definite plan and foreknowledge of God." Earlier in Luke 24 the women were reminded that Jesus had previously talked about this same necessity (expressed by forms of the word *dei* in both vv. 7 and 26). When previously told about Jesus' death, the disciples could not understand and accept it (9:44-45; 18:31-34). Now Jesus must insist that it was necessary that the Messiah enter his glory through suffering what he did. All of this emphasis suggests a mystery that is inherently difficult to understand. At this point the thoughtful reader may feel as much in the dark as the disciples were. Supposedly, Jesus' interpretation of scripture in verse 27 is meant to explain the divine necessity of the Messiah's suffering as the path to glory, but the narrator shares none of the details of Jesus' instruction with us.

For the Messiah to enter into his glory is the same as for him to enter into his kingdom (cf. 23:42). According to the Pentecost speech, this involves the enthronement of Jesus at the right hand of God (cf. Acts 2:29-36). The separation between resurrection and ascension to heaven in Luke–Acts makes it doubtful that Jesus has already entered into his glory as he speaks on the Emmaus road.

The references to the prophets in verse 25 and to Moses and the prophets in verse 27 make clear that the disciples should have been able to recognize from scripture the necessity of the Messiah passing through suffering to glory. The absence of references to a suffering Messiah in scripture (as distinct from the suffering servant of Isa 52:13–53:12) makes the train of thought puzzling at this point. Yet first-century Jews, whether they believed in Jesus or not, did not approach scripture as a document whose meaning was limited by the original historical context of the words. Secrets about God's work at later times were to be found there, secrets that come to light only as new events are illuminated by scripture. Thus the early church was able to find references to the suffering Messiah where modern historical critics do not. The narrative has already cited or alluded to some of the relevant texts in 20:17 (Ps 118:22), 42-43 (Ps 110:1); 22:37 (Isa 53:12); and 23:34*b*-35 (Ps 22:7, 18). These and other texts will appear in the preaching of the crucified Messiah in Acts (cf. Acts 2:25-28, 34-35; 4:11, 25-26; 8:32-33). (The presumption that David is the author of biblical psalms contributes to the ease with which psalm texts are applied to David's descendant, the Messiah; cf. Acts 2:29-31.)

Yet the global way in which the scriptures are mentioned (v. 27: "in all the scriptures"; v. 44: "everything written . . . in the law of Moses, the prophets, and the psalms") suggests that more is in mind than a few selected texts. A previous observation may be relevant here: The Messiah in his earthly ministry lived the life of a prophet, and prophets are regularly rejected, persecuted, and even killed (cf. 4:24; 6:22-23; 11:47-51; 13:33-34; Acts 7:52). Scripture and the story of Jesus are being read in light of a presumed pattern of prophetic destiny that includes suffering (cf. Dillon 1978, 139). The importance of this pattern within Luke–Acts is shown by Stephen's speech in Acts 7, where a parallel is drawn between the calling and rejection of Moses, the prophets, Jesus (the prophet like Moses), and Stephen (cf. Acts 7:30-60; on the significance of scriptural patterns for Luke–Acts, see Bock 1987, 49-50, 274-75). The importance of the story of Moses in Acts 7 suggests that "beginning with Moses" in Luke 24:27 may refer not just to the books of Moses—the beginning of scripture—but to the career of Moses, which provides the pattern of the rejected prophet. Thus we may guess that Jesus in verse 27 is interpreting scripture by pointing to a pattern of prophetic destiny revealed in the lives of Moses and the prophets, as well as to the words of the prophets and psalmists (cf. further Tannehill 1986, 284-88).

◊ ◊ ◊ ◊

It is ironic that rejection and shameful death are the means by which Jesus enters his glory. Dramatic irony is the result of people acting blindly and thereby producing something contrary to their intention. The rulers in Jerusalem sought to eliminate Jesus by dishonoring and killing him. Instead, the result is Jesus' exaltation to highest honor. This irony will be emphasized in the Acts speeches by a repeated contrast between what the Jerusalemites, acting in ignorance, did and what God did in raising Jesus and enthroning him as Messiah (cf. Acts 2:23-24, 36; 3:13-15, 17; 4:10-11; 5:30-31; 13:27-33). Behind the human purpose to eliminate Jesus there was a stronger divine purpose that could use blind opposition to thwart human plans. Thus God can leave the prophet-Messiah exposed to human resistance, like the prophets before him, yet in this way achieve an ultimate saving purpose (a purpose defined in 2:30-32 and 3:6). Recognition of the ironic quality of the death and resurrection of Jesus in Luke–Acts does not remove the mystery and the struggle of faith that the disciples faced. A God who works by irony is a God who continually surprises, a God who chooses to win by allowing blind opponents to win, and then reverses the results. This God requires the disciple to trust in God's power and goodness when all the evidence points to the triumph of evil (cf. further Tannehill 1986, 282-84, 288-89).

Recognition at the Meal (24:28-35)

The next step in the unfolding revelation depends on an invitation made to a stranger. Jesus does not presume that he will be invited to stay with the disciples. He acts as if he would go farther. But the invitation comes, which permits the following meal scene. At the meal Jesus does what he had done at previous meals: "He took bread, blessed and broke it, and gave it to them." The four actions listed here are most closely paralleled at the feeding of the five thousand (cf. 9:16), with the Last Supper being a close second. (There giving thanks substitutes for blessing; cf. 22:19.) The listing of these actions would not be necessary if they did not have special significance. Their special significance also appears from the result. These actions finally trigger recognition of the risen Lord. Recognition may come because Jesus is doing what he did in previous meals with his disciples, but the meal fellowship of the early church may also influence the narrative at this point. In verse 35 the meal is called "the breaking of the bread." In Acts the breaking of the bread is a special feature of the early church's life (cf. Acts 2:42, 46; 20:7, 11; 27:35). There is no explanation of the practice or its religious significance. The Emmaus meal may be our best clue as to the significance of these meals in Acts. It would suggest that breaking the bread in Acts is a continuation of the meal fellowship of the time of Jesus, with the expectation that the risen Lord will be present. Thus the early church's expectation of the Lord's presence in its meal fellowship may have influenced the account of the

Emmaus meal. In any case, the Emmaus meal provides a connecting link between the meal fellowship of Jesus' ministry and the breaking of bread in the early church.

There was important preparation for recognition at the meal. As soon as Jesus vanishes, the disciples recall the conversation on the road. Already then there were signs of awareness, for the disciples' hearts were "burning." The connection between the two phases of the Emmaus story is strengthened by reuse of the word "open" *(dianoigô)*. Before their eyes "were opened," Jesus "was opening" the scriptures to them (vv. 31-32; cf. also v. 45). The whole Emmaus narrative is a revelatory process, for the disciples needed to understand how death and resurrection befits the Messiah before they could recognize the risen Lord. So when the disciples report to Jerusalem, they tell about "what had happened on the road" (the conversation) as well as the recognition of Jesus "in the breaking of the bread" (v. 35).

The return to Jerusalem immediately results in a double witness mutually shared by two groups. On the one hand, "the eleven and their companions" report that the Lord has appeared to Simon. On the other hand, the two disciples report their encounter with Jesus on the road and at the meal. For some reason nothing further is made of the appearance to Simon Peter, which Paul lists first among the resurrection appearances (cf. 1 Cor 15:5). The name "Simon" is used in both 24:34 and 22:31-32. This connection may suggest that the appearance to Simon is a step in fulfilling the special role that Jesus gave to him at the Last Supper. The statement "The Lord has risen indeed" means in context: he has really risen (or "has been raised"), as the women were told but the disciples failed to believe.

Appearance at Jerusalem and Concluding Commission (24:36-49)

The revelatory process is not complete. The narrative continues with a further appearance and further instruction that will move beyond Jesus' death and resurrection to the coming mission (vv. 47-49).

24:36-43: Jesus' appearance in Jerusalem (vv. 36-49) has the basic elements of a "promise and commission epiphany" (a type of scene that describes the appearance of a divine messenger who transmits a promise and/or commission; cf. Tannehill 1995, 64-65). A reaction of fear to the appearance, followed by reassurance, is a common feature of these scenes. In this case the fear arises because the disciples "thought that they were seeing a ghost" (or a "spirit" *[pneuma]*), and the reassurance is expanded with various efforts by Jesus to show that he is not a ghost. First there is a rebuke (v. 38), similar to the rebukes in previous resurrection scenes (vv. 5, 25). Then the disciples are invited both to look at his hands and feet (with the marks of crucifixion) and feel him. Finally, he eats a piece of fish, which is probably further demonstration of his bodily reality. The emphasis here on the risen Jesus as a person of flesh and bones serves to refute the notion that he is a ghost. The appearance of a ghost would mean something very different than the resurrection of Jesus as Messiah. Some people claimed to be able to consult with the dead by calling up their ghosts (cf. Deut 18:11; 1 Sam 28:3-19). This, however, would be the ephemeral appearance of a dead person whose state remains basically unchanged. Jesus' resurrection means victory over rejection and death and entrance "into his glory" (v. 26) with new ruling power. The emphasis on bodily presence serves to distinguish Jesus' resurrection from the appearance of a ghost.

When Jesus appears, he first says, "Peace be with you." (This is missing in some manuscripts.) This peace greeting, followed by display of wounds, leading to joy and a new mission, makes this scene similar to John 20:19-21. The peace greeting takes on a special nuance in Luke in light of previous usage of peace as a term for messianic salvation (1:79; 2:14; 10:5-6; 19:42; cf. Acts 10:36). Joy is mentioned in verse 41, but in a strange way. While John 20:20 speaks clearly of joyful recognition, Luke speaks of a peculiar combination of disbelieving and joy. The term for disbelieving is the same as in verse 11, indicating that some of that initial disbelief still persists, competing with their joy. Thus the transformation of Jesus' followers into believing witnesses is not yet complete. Nor is there any indication of a change following verse 43. Just as with the

Emmaus disciples, Jesus must open their minds to understand the scripture in order for the transformation to be complete (v. 45), for only this new understanding enables the disciples to perceive the recent events as part of God's surprising, but prophesied, plan.

In Acts 10:41 Peter will report that the chosen witnesses "ate and drank with" the risen Lord. Acts 1:3-8 is a variant version of Luke 24:36-49 that probably also refers to a shared meal (Acts 1:4; cf. the NRSV footnote and Tannehill 1986, 291-92). These passages in Acts suggest that in eating the fish, Jesus is not only demonstrating his physical reality but also sharing food with the disciples. The phrase "ate in their presence" (literally, "before [enōpion] them") uses language that elsewhere implies a shared meal (cf. 13:26 and in the LXX, 2 Kgdms 11:13; 3 Kgdms 1:25). Thus the scene in Jerusalem probably parallels the Emmaus narrative by reporting a process of coming to faith and insight that includes both instruction in the scripture and a shared meal.

24:44-49: Jesus' address to the eleven and their companions in verses 44-49 begins with the third reminder in Luke 24 of Jesus' passion prophecies (cf. vv. 6-7, 26), the prophecies that the disciples could not understand (cf. 9:45; 18:34). Again Jesus opens minds to understand the scripture (cf. vv. 27, 32, 45). This repeated emphasis on understanding Jesus' death and resurrection as part of God's scriptural plan shows the importance of this point to the narrator. In verse 44 three divisions of scripture are mentioned: the law of Moses, the prophets, and the psalms. The unusual reference to the psalms reflects the importance of psalm texts in the Lukan interpretation of Jesus' death and exaltation.

This final address to the disciples is the climax of Jesus' instruction in Luke 24 and also anticipates the continuing story in Acts. In verses 47-49 Jesus goes beyond his previous comments on his death and resurrection to speak of future events in which the eleven and their companions will have a central role. In these verses Jesus commissions his hearers as his witnesses, giving them a task and a promise. Jesus' statement in verses 44-49 also provides a brief summary of central themes, including a preview of the early chapters of Acts as well as a review of themes in Luke.

In making the disciples responsible for the proclamation of repentance and forgiveness of sins, Jesus is handing over a task that was central to the missions of both John the Baptist and himself. The word *aphesis,* translated "forgiveness" in verse 47, describes John's mission in 3:3 and Jesus' mission in 4:18 (there translated "release"). Jesus has carried out his mission by proclaiming release of sins to the outcasts. (The noun *aphesis* occurs in Luke only at 1:77; 3:3; 4:18; and 24:47. The phrase is always "release [or "forgiveness"] of sins" except in 4:18, which agrees, however, with 3:3 and 24:47 in associating release with the task of proclamation.) In the early chapters of Acts, Jesus' witnesses will carry out their task of proclaiming repentance and release of sins (cf. Acts 2:38; 3:19; 5:31). The risen Messiah indicates that, from this point on, repentance and release of sins is to be proclaimed "in his name" (v. 47). The "name" of Jesus Messiah represents his royal power and authority, and there are repeated references to his "name" in the early chapters of Acts (2:21, 38; 3:6, 16; 4:7, 10, 12; cf. Tannehill 1990, 39-40, 49). In this way the mission of Jesus continues. It is also broadened, for this proclamation is to be carried "to all nations" (cf. Acts 1:8).

The phrase "beginning from Jerusalem" probably goes with the following sentence ("Beginning from Jerusalem, you are witnesses of these things"), for the participle "beginning" agrees in gender, number, and case with "you." Nevertheless, the reference to Jerusalem as the beginning point of mission balances the preceding reference to all nations. Jerusalem is the sacred center of the Jewish people. Making it the beginning point emphasizes the importance of the proclamation for Jews as well as Gentiles. Inclusion of Jews is required by God's purpose of bringing salvation to "all flesh" (3:6). The mission does begin in Jerusalem on Pentecost, and Jews continue to be the beginning point of mission even when the word has moved into predominantly Gentile territory. There is continued recognition that, because of scriptural promises, the good news of fulfillment must be addressed first of all to Jews (cf. Acts 3:26; 13:46).

The role of the apostles as "witnesses" is also prominent in the early chapters of Acts (1:8, 22; 2:32; 3:15; 4:33; 5:32). The apostles and their companions are now able to be Jesus' witnesses, for they have not only been taught by him and have worked with him, they have had their minds opened by him to understand the scripture. Their new perspective enables them to interpret Jesus' death and resurrection as key events in God's unfolding plan to bring salvation to the world. The proclamation to all nations is part of what is "written" in scripture, according to verses 46-47. Passages such as those quoted in Acts 13:47 (= Isa 49:6; cf. Luke 2:30-32) and Acts 15:16-18 (= Amos 9:11-12 LXX) may account for this belief.

Jesus concludes with a promise that his witnesses will receive the Holy Spirit, here called "what my Father promised" and "power from on high." This is a clear reference to the Pentecost event in Acts 2. The Spirit will again be called "the promise of the Father" in Acts 1:4; then God's scriptural promise will be cited in 2:17-18 (= Joel 2:28-29). Previously Jesus had said that the Spirit is one of the good gifts God the Father would gladly give his children (Luke 11:13). In Acts the Spirit continues to be called both "gift" and "power" (cf. 1:8; 2:38; 8:19-20; 10:38, 45; 11:17). The Spirit is power for the mission, and it is a gift of grace that creates a new relationship with God (cf. Tannehill 1990, 12-13). This new relationship is suggested by the repeated designation of God the *Father* as the source of the gift of the Spirit (Luke 11:13; 24:49; Acts 1:4-5; 2:33). The disciples must remain in Jerusalem in order to receive this gift and begin their mission. There is no return to Galilee to meet the risen Lord there.

Jesus' Departure (24:50-53)

In Acts 1:4-8 there is a good deal of repetition (with variation) of Jesus' final words in Luke 24:44-49. The anticipation of Acts in Luke 24:47-49 and the repetition of Luke in Acts 1:4-8 help to secure the continuity of the narrative in the transition from book one to book two. It may be that Jesus' final words in Luke and their counterpart in Acts are both followed by an account of Jesus' ascension. If that is the case, however, there is one detail that disturbs the continuity: in Acts the ascension takes place after forty days of resurrection appearances (1:3), but in Luke it apparently takes place during the night following Easter day. In Luke 24, compactness of time contributes to dramatic intensity. In Acts other interests have taken over, leaving an anomaly in the narrative.

This is the case, provided we follow the majority of manuscripts, which include the words "and was carried up into heaven" in verse 51. The minority reading that omits these words has, in the past, been given considerable weight by scholars, but more recent opinion has shifted against omission. (However, for a recent defense of the short reading, see Parsons 1987, 29-52.) In Luke–Acts the ascension is not only Jesus' departure from the earth but also his exaltation to the right hand of God, where he is enthroned as ruling Messiah. From there he can confer messianic benefits on his subjects (cf. Acts 2:30-36 and Tannehill 1990, 37-40). Soon after the first announcements of Jesus' passion, there were indications of the importance of Jesus' coming "departure," when he would be "taken up" (9:31, 51). Later, Jesus indicated that he would be "seated at the right hand of the power of God" (22:69). The time has now come for him to assume that seat and the authority that goes with it. The idea of a person being carried up to heaven was not strange in the ancient world (cf. 2 Kgs 2:11; Sir 44:16; 48:9; cf. also Fitzmyer 1985, 1587-88). Acts 1:9-11 adds some details (a cloud; two men in white clothing) to the cryptic statement in verse 51.

◊ ◊ ◊ ◊

Jesus' departure is preceded by a formal blessing. Genesis 49 and Deuteronomy 33 present extensive blessings by Jacob and Moses before their final departure through death. Lifting up the hands, however, suggests a priestly blessing, as in Lev 9:22 and Sir 50:20-21. In verse 52 the statement that they "worshiped him" is omitted in some of the same manuscripts that omit the ascension in verse 51. The Greek word *proskyneō* means prostrating oneself as a sign of homage. It is a gesture expressing deep respect or reverence, usually for a superior authority. Jesus is rather frequently approached in this way in Matthew, but this would be the first time that Jesus is so treated in Luke. Although the NRSV translates "worshiped," the action is directed not only toward God but also toward highly honored humans in the Greek Bible (e.g., Gen 42:6; 1 Kgdms 24:9). Nevertheless, the one time that an apostle is "worshiped" in Acts, the action is rejected as inappropriate (10:25-26).

The "great joy" of the disciples in verse 52 is an important step beyond the mixture of joy and disbelief in verse 41. Finally, the blindness and disbelief of the disciples have been overcome. They express their joy and thanksgiving by blessing God in the temple. Action in the Lukan narrative began in the temple (cf. 1:8-23), and "joy" was important in the infancy narrative (cf. 1:14; 2:10). Furthermore, the theme of blessing, whether of humans as in 24:50, or of God as in 24:53, is prominent in the infancy narrative (cf. 1:42, 64, 68; 2:28, 34). In particular, the final words about blessing God are related to the joyful hymns of Zechariah and Simeon, for what these prophets celebrated in advance has now reached a stage of fulfillment. The narrative achieves a sense of closure by returning to themes at the beginning.

◊ ◊ ◊ ◊

However, the closure is not permanent and the fulfillment not complete. Insofar as the Gospel of Luke is the story of Jesus, it is now complete. But the story of Jesus as an earthly figure is only part of a larger story, the story of how God's saving purpose for Jews and Gentiles is realized through Jesus Messiah (cf. 2:30-32; 3:6), a story that is incomplete. The narrator will reopen the narrative at the beginning of Acts in order to tell in detail the events anticipated in 24:47-49. Not only is it important to tell how the Spirit came and how the mission turned to the Gentiles, it is important to consider further an unresolved issue. Jerusalem and its leaders have rejected their Messiah. In the mission speeches in Acts 2–5 they will be confronted with this rejection and called to repentance, yet the leaders will continue their opposition. Jewish opposition remains a prominent part of the narrative as the mission moves into other territory, and the final scene of Acts highlights Jewish rejection. Even at the end of Acts, the story of God's saving purpose for Jews and Gentiles is incomplete, and continuing Jewish opposition makes it unclear how the story can reach its goal (cf. Tannehill 1985, 69-85; 1990, 346-57).

SELECT BIBLIOGRAPHY

WORKS CITED IN THE TEXT
(EXCLUDING COMMENTARIES ON LUKE)

Aland, Kurt. 1964. *Synopsis Quattuor Evangeliorum.* Stuttgart: Württembergische Bibelanstalt.

Alexander, Loveday. 1993. *The Preface to Luke's Gospel: Literary Convention and Social Context in Luke 1.1-4 and Acts 1.1.* SNTSMS 78. Cambridge: Cambridge University Press.

Allison, Dale C., Jr. 1983. "Matt. 23:39 = Luke 13:35b as a Conditional Prophecy." *JSNT* 18:75-84.

Apostolic Fathers. 1950, 1959. *The Apostolic Fathers.* With an English translation by Kirsopp Lake. LCL. 2 vols. Cambridge, MA: Harvard University Press.

Bailey, Kenneth E. 1976. *Poet & Peasant: A Literary-Cultural Approach to the Parables of Luke.* Grand Rapids, MI: Eerdmans.

———. 1980. *Through Peasant Eyes.* Grand Rapids, MI: Eerdmans.

Balz, Horst, and Gerhard Schneider, eds. 1990. *Exegetical Dictionary of the New Testament.* 3 vols. Grand Rapids, MI: Eerdmans.

Betz, Hans Dieter. 1995. *The Sermon on the Mount.* Hermeneia. Minneapolis: Fortress.

Bock, Darrell L. 1987. *Proclamation from Prophecy and Pattern: Lucan Old Testament Christology.* JSNTSup 12. Sheffield: JSOT.

———. 1994a. "Framing the Account: Alleviating Confusion on the Lukan Portrait of Jesus." In *Society of Biblical Literature 1994 Seminar Papers,* edited by Eugene Lovering, Jr., 612-26. Atlanta: Scholars Press.

Braun, Willi. 1995. *Feasting and Social Rhetoric in Luke 14.* SNTSMS 85. Cambridge: Cambridge University Press.

Brawley, Robert L. 1990. *Centering on God: Method and Message in Luke–Acts.* Literary Currents in Biblical Interpretation. Louisville: Westminster/John Knox.

Brodie, Thomas L. 1989. "The Departure for Jerusalem (Luke 9,51-56) as a Rhetorical Imitation of Elijah's Departure for the Jordan (2 Kgs 1,1-2,6)." *Bib* 70:96-109.

Brown, Raymond E. 1993. *The Birth of the Messiah: A Commentary on the Infancy Narratives in Matthew and Luke.* New edition with supplement. Anchor Bible Reference Library. New York: Doubleday.

_____. 1994. *The Death of the Messiah: A Commentary on the Passion Narratives in the Four Gospels.* 2 vols. Anchor Bible Reference Library. New York: Doubleday.

Busse, Ulrich. 1979. *Die Wunder des Propheten Jesus: Die Rezeption, Komposition und Interpretation der Wundertradition im Evangelium des Lukas.* Forschung zur Bibel 24. 2. Aufl. Stuttgart: Verlag Katholisches Bibelwerk.

Carroll, John T. 1988. *Response to the End of History: Eschatology and Situation in Luke–Acts.* SBLDS 92. Atlanta: Scholars Press.

Chance, J. Bradley. 1988. *Jerusalem, the Temple, and the New Age in Luke–Acts.* Macon, GA: Mercer University Press.

Charlesworth, James H., ed. 1983, 1985. *OTP.* 2 vols. Garden City, NY: Doubleday.

Coleridge, Mark. 1993. *The Birth of the Lukan Narrative: Narrative as Christology in Luke 1–2.* JSNTSup 88. Sheffield: JSOT.

Conzelmann, Hans. 1960. *The Theology of St. Luke.* Translated by Geoffrey Buswell. London: Faber & Faber.

Crossan, John Dominic. 1991. *The Historical Jesus: The Life of a Mediterranean Jewish Peasant.* San Francisco: HarperSanFrancisco.

D'Angelo, Mary Rose. 1990. "Women in Luke–Acts: A Redactional View." *JBL* 109:441-61.

_____. 1992. "*Abba* and 'Father': Imperial Theology and the Jesus Traditions." *JBL* 111:611-30.

Darr, John A. 1992. *On Character Building: The Reader and the Rhetoric of Characterization in Luke–Acts.* Literary Currents in Biblical Interpretation. Louisville: Westminster/John Knox.

de Jonge, Henk J. 1977-78. "Sonship, Wisdom, Infancy: Luke II.41-51a." *NTS* 24:317-54.

de Meeûs, X. 1961. "Composition de Lc., XIV et genre symposiaque." *ETL* 37:847-70.

Denaux, Adelbert. 1993. "The Delineation of the Lukan Travel Narrative Within the Overall Structure of the Gospel of Luke." In *The Synoptic Gospels: Source Criticism and the New Literary Criticism,* edited by Camille Focant, 357-92. BETL 110. Leuven: Leuven University Press.

Dillon, Richard J. 1978. *From Eye-Witnesses to Ministers of the Word: Tradition and Composition in Luke 24.* AnBib 82. Rome: Biblical Institute Press.

Dodd, C. H. 1968. "The Fall of Jerusalem and the 'Abomination of Desolation.'" In *More New Testament Studies,* 69-83. Grand Rapids, MI: Eerdmans.

Donahue, John R. 1988. *The Gospel in Parable: Metaphor, Narrative, and Theology in the Synoptic Gospels.* Philadelphia: Fortress.

Dreyfus, F. 1959. "L'argument scripturaire de Jésus en faveur de la résurrection des morts (Marc, XII, 26-27)." *RB* 66:213-24.

Esler, Philip Francis. 1987. *Community and Gospel in Luke–Acts: The Social and Political Motivations of Lukan Theology.* SNTSMS 57. Cambridge: Cambridge University Press.

Evans, Craig A., and James A. Sanders. 1993. *Luke and Scripture.* Minneapolis: Fortress.

Freedman, David Noel, ed. 1992. *ABD.* 6 vols. New York: Doubleday.

Garnsey, Peter. 1970. *Social Status and Legal Privilege in the Roman Empire.* Oxford: Clarendon.

Garrett, Susan R. 1989. *The Demise of the Devil: Magic and the Demonic in Luke's Writings.* Minneapolis: Fortress.

———. 1990. "Exodus from Bondage: Luke 9:31 and Acts 12:1-24." *CBQ* 52:656-80.

———. 1991. " 'Lest the Light in You Be Darkness': Luke 11:33-36 and the Question of Commitment." *JBL* 110:93-105.

Gowler, David B. 1993. "Hospitality and Characterization in Luke 11:37-54: A Socio-Narratological Approach." *Semeia* 64:213-51.

Green, Joel B. 1994a. "Good News to Whom? Jesus and the 'Poor' in the Gospel of Luke." In *Jesus of Nazareth: Lord and Christ. Essays on the Historical Jesus and New Testament Christology,* edited by Joel B. Green and Max Turner, 59-74. Grand Rapids, MI: Eerdmans.

———. 1994b. "The Demise of the Temple as 'Culture Center' in Luke–Acts: An Exploration of the Rending of the Temple Veil (Luke 23.44-49)." *RB* 101:495-515.

———. 1995. *The Theology of the Gospel of Luke.* New Testament Theology. Cambridge: Cambridge University Press.

Hamm, M. Dennis. 1987. "The Freeing of the Bent Woman and the Restoration of Israel: Luke 13.10-17 as Narrative Theology." *JSNT* 31:23-44.

Hengel, Martin. 1981. *The Charismatic Leader and His Followers.* Translated by James Greig. New York: Crossroad.

Hubbard, Benjamin J. 1977. "Commissioning Stories in Luke–Acts: A Study of Their Antecedents, Form and Content." *Semeia* 8:103-26.

Jeremias, Joachim. 1966. *The Eucharistic Words of Jesus*. Translated from the 3rd German edition by Norman Perrin. London: SCM.

Johnson, Luke Timothy. 1982. "The Lukan Kingship Parable (Lk. 19.11-27)." *NovT* 24:139-59.

Johnson, Marshall D. 1969. *The Purpose of the Biblical Genealogies*. SNTSMS 8. Cambridge: Cambridge University Press.

Josephus. 1927, 1928. *The Jewish War*. With an English translation by H. St. J. Thackeray. LCL. 2 vols. London: William Heinemann Ltd.

_____. 1957-69. *Jewish Antiquities*. With an English translation by H. St. J. Thackeray, Ralph Marcus, and I. H. Feldman. LCL. 6 vols. Cambridge, MA: Harvard University Press.

Justin. 1948. *Writings of Saint Justin Martyr*. The Fathers of the Church. New York: Christian Heritage.

Kilgallen, John J. 1985. "Luke 2,41-50: Foreshadowing of Jesus, Teacher." *Bib* 66:553-59.

Kingsbury, Jack Dean. 1991. *Conflict in Luke: Jesus, Authorities, Disciples*. Minneapolis: Fortress.

Kittel, Gerhard, and Gerhard Friedrich, eds. 1964-74. *TDNT*. 9 vols. Translated by Geoffrey W. Bromiley. Grand Rapids, MI: Eerdmans.

Kloppenborg, John S. 1989. "The Dishonoured Master (Luke 16,1-8a)." *Bib* 70:479-95.

Koet, Bart J. 1992. "Simeons Worte (Lk 2,29-32.34c-35) und Israels Geschick." In *The Four Gospels 1992: Festschrift Frans Neirynck*, edited by F. Van Segbroeck et al., 1549-69. BETL 100. Leuven: Leuven University Press.

Kurz, William S. 1984. "Luke 3:23-38 and Greco-Roman and Biblical Genealogies." In *Luke–Acts: New Perspectives from the Society of Biblical Literature Seminar*, edited by Charles Talbert, 169-87. New York: Crossroad.

_____. 1985. "Luke 22:14-38 and Greco-Roman and Biblical Farewell Addresses." *JBL* 104:251-68.

Linton, Olof. 1976. "The Parable of the Children's Game." *NTS* 22:159-79.

Malina, Bruce J. 1993. *Windows on the World of Jesus: Time Travel to Ancient Judea*. Louisville: Westminster/John Knox.

Metzger, Bruce M. 1971. *A Textual Commentary on the Greek New Testament*. London/New York: United Bible Societies.

Minear, Paul S. 1964. "A Note on Luke xxii 36." *NovT* 7:128-34.

_____. 1974. "A Note on Luke 17:7-10." *JBL* 93:82-87.

Moxnes, Halvor. 1988. *The Economy of the Kingdom: Social Conflict and Economic Relations in Luke's Gospel.* OBT. Philadelphia: Fortress.

———. 1994. "The Social Context of Luke's Community." *Int* 48:379-89.

Nelson, Peter K. 1994. *Leadership and Discipleship: A Study of Luke 22:24-30.* SBLDS 138. Atlanta: Scholars Press.

Neyrey, Jerome. 1985. *The Passion According to Luke: A Redaction Study of Luke's Soteriology.* Mahwah, NJ: Paulist.

———, ed. 1991. *The Social World of Luke–Acts: Models for Interpretation.* Peabody, MA: Hendrickson.

Noorda, S. J. 1982. " 'Cure Yourself, Doctor!' (Luke 4,23): Classical Parallels to an Alleged Saying of Jesus." In *Logia: Les paroles de Jésus—The Sayings of Jesus,* edited by Joël Delobel, 459-67. BETL 59. Leuven: Leuven University Press.

Osiek, Carolyn. 1992. "Slavery in the Second Testament World." *BTB* 22:174-79.

Parsons, Mikeal C. 1987. *The Departure of Jesus in Luke–Acts: The Ascension Narratives in Context.* JSNTSup 21. Sheffield: JSOT.

Petersen, Norman R. 1978. *Literary Criticism for New Testament Critics.* Guides to Biblical Scholarship. Philadelphia: Fortress.

Philo. *Philo.* 1935. With an English translation by F. H. Colson. Vol. 6. LCL. Cambridge, MA: Harvard University Press.

Philostratus. 1912. *The Life of Apollonius of Tyana.* With an English translation by F. C. Conybeare. Vol. 1. LCL. London: William Heinemann.

Piper, Ronald A. 1992. "Social Background and Thematic Structure in Luke 16." In *The Four Gospels 1992: Festschrift Frans Neirynck,* edited by F. Van Segbroeck et al., 1637-62. BETL 100. Leuven: Leuven University Press.

Pliny. 1950. *Natural History.* With an English translation by H. Rackham. Vol. 5. LCL. Cambridge, MA: Harvard University Press.

Pliny (the Younger). 1961. *Letters.* With an English translation by William Melmoth. Revised by W. M. L. Hutchinson. Vol. 2. LCL. Cambridge, MA: Harvard University Press.

Plutarch. *Plutarch's Lives.* 1919. With an English translation by Bernadotte Perrin. Vol. 7. LCL. London: William Heinemann.

Praeder, Susan Marie. 1987. "The Problem of First Person Narration in Acts." *NovT* 29:193-218.

Quesnell, Quentin. 1983. "The Women at Luke's Supper." In *Political Issues in Luke–Acts,* edited by Richard J. Cassidy and Philip J. Scharper, 59-79. Maryknoll, NY: Orbis.

Ramsey, George W. 1989. "Plots, Gaps, Repetitions, and Ambiguity in Luke 15." *Perspectives in Religious Studies* 17:33-42.

Ravens, D. A. S. 1988. "The Setting of Luke's Account of the Anointing: Luke 7.2–8.3." *NTS* 34:282-92.

Ringe, Sharon H. 1983. "Luke 9:28-36: The Beginning of an Exodus." *Semeia* 28:83-99.

_____. 1985. *Jesus, Liberation, and the Biblical Jubilee.* OBT 19. Philadelphia: Fortress.

Robbins, Vernon K. 1978. "By Land and by Sea: The We-Passages and Ancient Sea Voyages." In *Perspectives on Luke–Acts,* edited by Charles H. Talbert, 215-42. Perspectives in Religious Studies Special Studies Series 5. Danville, VA: Association of Baptist Professors of Religion.

_____, comp. and ed. 1989. *Ancient Quotes and Anecdotes: From Crib to Crypt.* Foundations and Facets. Sonoma, CA: Polebridge.

Sahlin, Harald. 1964. "Die Perikope vom gerasenischen Besessenen und der Plan des Markusevangeliums." *ST* 18:159-72.

Sanders, E. P. 1985. *Jesus and Judaism.* Philadelphia: Fortress.

_____. 1990. *Jewish Law from Jesus to the Mishnah: Five Studies.* London: SCM; Philadelphia: Trinity Press International.

_____. 1992. *Judaism: Practice and Belief 63 BCE–66 CE.* London: SCM; Philadelphia: Trinity Press International.

Sanders, Jack T. 1987. *The Jews in Luke–Acts.* Philadelphia: Fortress.

Schürmann, Heinz. 1970. "Der Dienst des Petrus und Johannes: Lk 22,8." In *Ursprung und Gestalt: Erörterungen und Besinnungen zum Neuen Testament,* 274-76. Düsseldorf: Patmos-Verlag.

Schüssler Fiorenza, Elisabeth. 1987. "Theological Criteria and Historical Reconstruction: Martha and Mary, Luke 10:38-42." *Center for Hermeneutical Studies Protocol* 53:1-12.

_____. 1992. *But She Said: Feminist Practices of Biblical Interpretation.* Boston: Beacon.

Scott, Bernard Brandon. 1989. *Hear Then the Parable: A Commentary on the Parables of Jesus.* Minneapolis: Fortress.

Seim, Turid Karlsen. 1994a. *The Double Message: Patterns of Gender in Luke–Acts.* Nashville: Abingdon.

Smith, Dennis E. 1987. "Table Fellowship as a Literary Motif in the Gospel of Luke." *JBL* 106:613-38.

Steele, E. Springs. 1984. "Luke 11:37-54—A Modified Hellenistic Symposium?" *JBL* 103:379-94.

Stegemann, Wolfgang. 1991. *Zwischen Synagoge und Obrigkeit: Zur historischen Situation der lukanischen Christen.* FRLANT 152. Göttingen: Vandenhoeck & Ruprecht.

Sterling, Gregory E. 1992. *Historiography and Self-Definition: Josephos, Luke–Acts and Apologetic Historiography.* NovTSup 64. Leiden: E. J. Brill.

Suetonius. *Suetonius.* 1979. With an English translation by J. C. Rolfe. Vol. 1. LCL. Cambridge, MA: Harvard University Press.

Swartley, Willard M. 1992. "Luke's Transforming of Tradition: Eirênê and Love of Enemy." In *The Love of Enemy and Nonretaliation in the New Testament,* edited by Willard M. Swartley, 157-76. Louisville: Westminster/John Knox.

Sylva, Dennis D. 1986. "The Temple Curtain and Jesus' Death in the Gospel of Luke." *JBL* 105:239-50.

Talbert, Charles. 1980. "Prophecies of Future Greatness: The Contribution of Greco-Roman Biographies to an Understanding of Luke 1:5–4:15." In *The Divine Helmsman: Studies on God's Control of Human Events, Presented to Lou H. Silberman,* edited by James L. Crenshaw and Samuel Sandmel, 129-41. New York: KTAV.

Tannehill, Robert C. 1974. "The Magnificat as Poem." *JBL* 93:263-75.

_____. 1975. *The Sword of His Mouth: Forceful and Imaginative Language in Synoptic Sayings.* Philadelphia: Fortress; Missoula: Scholars Press.

_____, ed. 1981. *Pronouncement Stories. Semeia* 20:1-141.

_____. 1983. "Response to John Dominic Crossan and Vernon K. Robbins." *Semeia* 29:103-7.

_____. 1985. "Israel in Luke–Acts: A Tragic Story." *JBL* 104:69-85.

_____. 1986, 1990. *The Narrative Unity of Luke–Acts: A Literary Interpretation.* Vol. 1: The Gospel According to Luke. Vol. 2: The Acts of the Apostles. Philadelphia and Minneapolis: Fortress.

_____. 1992a. "What Kind of King? What Kind of Kingdom? A Study of Luke." *WW* 12:17-22.

_____. 1992b. "The Lukan Discourse on Invitations (Luke 14,7-24)." In *The Four Gospels 1992: Festschrift Frans Neirynck,* edited by F. Van Segbroeck et al., 1603-16. BETL 100. Leuven: Leuven University Press.

_____. 1994. "Should We Love Simon the Pharisee? Hermeneutical Reflections on the Pharisees in Luke." *CurTM* 21:424-33.

_____. 1995. "The Gospels and Narrative Literature." In *The New Interpreter's Bible,* edited by Leander E. Keck et al., 56-70. Vol. 8. Nashville: Abingdon.

Theissen, Gerd. 1991. *The Gospels in Context: Social and Political History in the Synoptic Tradition.* Translated by Linda M. Maloney. Minneapolis: Fortress.

Tiede, David L. 1980. *Prophecy and History in Luke–Acts.* Philadelphia: Fortress.

Torjesen, Karen Jo. 1993. *When Women Were Priests.* San Francisco: HarperSanFrancisco.

Twelftree, Graham H. 1993. *Jesus the Exorcist: A Contribution to the Study of the Historical Jesus.* Peabody, MA: Hendrickson.

Tyson, Joseph B. 1992. *Images of Judaism in Luke–Acts.* Columbia, SC: University of South Carolina Press.

van Unnik, W. C. 1966. "Die Motivierung der Feindesliebe in Lukas VI 32-35." *NovT* 8:284-300.

Vermes, Geza. 1987. *The Dead Sea Scrolls in English.* 3rd ed. Sheffield: JSOT.

Wright, Addison G. 1982. "The Widow's Mites: Praise or Lament?—A Matter of Context." *CBQ* 44:256-65.

COMMENTARIES ON LUKE (BOTH CITED AND NOT CITED)

Bock, Darrell L. 1994b, 1995. *Luke.* Baker Exegetical Commentary on the New Testament. 2 vols. Grand Rapids, MI: Baker Book House. — A large commentary by an evangelical scholar who is conversant with the spectrum of Lukan scholarship. Often reviews the variety of opinions on debated points.

Bovon, François. 1989. *Das Evangelium nach Lukas (Lk 1,1—9,50).* Evangelisch-Katholischer Kommentar zum Neuen Testament. Zürich: Benziger Verlag & Neukirchen-Vluyn: Neukirchener Verlag. — A technical commentary by a scholar who has a thorough knowledge of Lukan scholarship. Provides sectional bibliographies and extensive comments on scholarly literature in footnotes.

Craddock, Fred B. 1990. *Luke.* Interpretation. Louisville: John Knox. — A nontechnical commentary for preachers and church school teachers.

Culpepper, R. Alan. 1995. "The Gospel of Luke: Introduction, Commentary, and Reflections." In *The New Interpreter's Bible,* edited by Leander E. Keck et al., 1-490. Vol. 9. Nashville: Abingdon Press. — The "commentary" on each passage is followed by "reflections" that suggest applications of the passage to the modern church and world.

Danker, Frederick W. 1988. *Jesus and the New Age: A Commentary on St. Luke's Gospel.* Rev. ed. Philadelphia: Fortress. — Helpful in understanding how Luke might have been understood in a Greco-Roman context. Frequently cites Greek terms, which are explained. Useful for sophisticated but nonspecialist readers.

Ellis, E. Earle. 1974. *The Gospel of Luke*. New Century Bible Commentary. Rev. ed. Grand Rapids, MI: Eerdmans. — A short commentary with a fairly extensive introduction. The comments are quite short and selective.

Evans, C. F. *Saint Luke*. 1990. TPI New Testament Commentaries. Philadelphia: Trinity Press International. — A rather extensive commentary in one volume, with a correspondingly extensive introduction. Fairly technical, although Greek words are translated. Frequently notes obscurities and other difficulties in the Lukan text.

Evans, Craig A. 1990. *Luke*. New International Biblical Commentary. Peabody, MA: Hendrickson. — Brief summary discussion of a passage is followed by "additional notes" on verses that are usually brief but occasionally stretch into an excursus. Considerable attention is given to the background of the story in Israel's scripture.

Fitzmyer, Joseph A. 1981, 1985. *The Gospel According to Luke*. AB. 2 vols. Garden City, NY: Doubleday. — A thorough commentary with extensive introductory essays. For each pericope, a section of comment is followed by technical notes and a bibliography. Concerned both with tradition history and Lukan theology.

Johnson, Luke Timothy. 1991. *The Gospel of Luke*. Sacra Pagina. Collegeville, MN: Liturgical Press. — Specific "notes" followed by broader "interpretation" of each passage. The author is sensitive to Luke as literature and independent in his interpretive decisions.

Malina, Bruce J., and Richard L. Rohrbaugh. 1992. *Social-Science Commentary on the Synoptic Gospels*. Minneapolis: Fortress. — The authors seek to illuminate passages by commenting on social relationships in Mediterranean culture. The comments frequently direct readers to brief essays on particular topics.

Marshall, I. Howard. 1978. *The Gospel of Luke: A Commentary on the Greek Text*. NIGTC. Grand Rapids, MI: Eerdmans. — Helpful comments on Greek words and syntax. Concerned with the historicity of the Lukan stories.

Nolland, John. 1989, 1993. *Luke 1–9:20; Luke 9:21–18:34; Luke 18:35–24:53*. WBC. 3 vols. Dallas: Word. — A major commentary. For each section of Luke there is bibliography, discussion of "Form/Structure/Setting," detailed comment, and a concluding summary of the discussion. Although this is a technical commentary, Greek words are translated and the concluding summaries make Nolland's main ideas accessible to nonspecialists.

SELECT BIBLIOGRAPHY

Plummer, Alfred. 1922. *A Critical and Exegetical Commentary on the Gospel According to S. Luke.* ICC. 5th ed. Edinburgh: T. & T. Clark. — An older commentary that is still useful in interpreting details of the Greek text.

Ringe, Sharon H. 1995. *Luke.* Westminster Bible Companion. Louisville: Westminster/John Knox. — Written for use in local churches by laypeople. Pays special attention to the place of the poor and women in Luke.

Schürmann, Heinz. 1969, 1994. *Das Lukasevangelium.* HTKNT. Freiburg: Herder. — Completion of this detailed commentary by a leading German Catholic scholar has been long delayed by the author's commitment to service of the church under Communism. After publication of the volume on Luke 1:1–9:50 in 1969, the section on Luke 9:51–11:54 appeared in 1994.

Schweizer, Eduard. 1984. *The Good News According to Luke.* Translated by David E. Green. Atlanta: John Knox. — The brief comments, which are compressed and disjointed, are balanced by general discussion in which the author shares his theological perspective. Frequently notes the relations among Luke and the other Gospels.

Seim, Turid Karlsen. 1994b. "The Gospel of Luke." In *Searching the Scriptures. Volume Two: A Feminist Commentary,* edited by Elisabeth Schüssler Fiorenza, 728-62. New York: Crossroad. — Not a full commentary but a reliable and useful discussion of those passages most important for feminist issues.

Stein, Robert H. 1992. *Luke.* New American Commentary. Nashville: Broadman — A fairly full commentary in one volume that focuses on the Lukan message (rather than Lukan tradition), using the method of "composition criticism." Detailed commentary on each section concludes with a summary of theological emphases in that section.

Talbert, Charles H. 1982. *Reading Luke: A Literary and Theological Commentary on the Third Gospel.* New York: Crossroad. — A short commentary that concentrates on the structure of Luke, its major themes, and its relation to literature of the Greco-Roman world.

Tiede, David L. 1988. *Luke.* Augsburg Commentary on the New Testament. Minneapolis: Augsburg. — Places Luke in the context of Jewish hopes for the fulfillment of God's promises, in spite of the people's failures. Regards the scripture of Israel as essential background. Useful to nonspecialists.

INDEX